Benjamin Kennicott

Remarks on Select Passages in the Old Testament

To Which are Added Eight Sermons

Benjamin Kennicott

Remarks on Select Passages in the Old Testament
To Which are Added Eight Sermons

ISBN/EAN: 9783337160647

Printed in Europe, USA, Canada, Australia, Japan

Cover: Foto ©Lupo / pixelio.de

More available books at **www.hansebooks.com**

REMARKS

ON

SELECT PASSAGES

IN THE

OLD TESTAMENT.

REMARKS

ON

SELECT PASSAGES

IN THE

OLD TESTAMENT:

TO WHICH ARE ADDED

EIGHT SERMONS.

BY THE LATE
BENJAMIN KENNICOTT, D.D.

OXFORD:
Sold by PRINCE AND COOKE, AND J. FLETCHER IN
OXFORD; AND MESS. RIVINGTON, PAYNE,
CADELL, AND ROBSON, IN LONDON.
M DCC LXXX VII.

ADVERTISEMENT.

THE Author, at the time of his death, had proceeded to print as far as the 194th. Page. What is now added, though in a more imperfect state, is faithfully given to the world from his papers, in compliance with the following clause of his Will.

"*Having often been grieved that the wri-*
"*tings of other men on Scripture difficulties*
"*have been lost, because not finished for the*
"*Publick, and having myself made many re-*
"*marks on different parts of the Sacred Book,*
"*which, however imperfect, may furnish some*
"*useful hints to others; I do hereby earnestly*
"*desire, that the Honourable and Right Rev^d.*
"*Dr. Barrington, the Rev^d. Mr. Cyril*
"*Jackson, and the Rev^d. Mr. Cracherode,*
"*whose Friendship I have happily enjoyed for*
"*many years, will examine my Sermons and*
"*Papers*

" *Papers of Criticism; and whatever they
" may think at all likely to illustrate any parts
" of Holy Scripture, though such observations
" be very imperfect, they will cause to be pub-
" lished at the expence of my Executrix; par-
" ticularly my Remarks on Scripture Chrono-
" logy, on the Prophecies descriptive of the
" Messiah, and a few passages of the book of
" Job, with my Sermons on* Matt. I. 1. Heb.
" X. 5, 6, 7. Isai. IX. 5, 6. Psal. LXXXV.
" 9, 10. Psal. VIII. 4, 5. 1 Cor. XI. 1.
" 2 Pet. III. 10, 11. &c. *with the plainest and
" perhaps the most useful on* Deut. XXXII.
" 46, 47."

THE Editors apprehend, that the *Remarks on Scripture Chronology* mentioned in this clause, were only those which Dr. KENNICOTT hath himself inserted in the former part of this Volume. At least nothing further on that subject was found among his papers.

IT is certain also, not only from the expression of his Will, but from many circumstances

stances which occurred in the perusal of his Papers, that Dr. KENNICOTT had intended to reduce the *Prophecies descriptive of the Messiah* into a connected and regular arrangement, and to illustrate them with notes. But he had not proceeded in the design, so as to leave any thing in a state which would admit its publication.

IT hath been thought right however to publish those translations of certain Psalms (*Page* 194 *to* 219) which appeared to have been transcribed fairly for the press. And for the same reason (*Page* 281 *to* 297) the translation of the song of Moses in Deut. XXXII: and Observations on two passages of the Prophet *Hosea* are likewise published.

The Notes upon the Psalms, from *Page* 222 *to* 280, are printed exactly as they stood in Dr. KENNICOTT's papers. It is conceived that they were written many years ago, and that they must be considered as his *Adversaria* for this part of the Old Testament. No alterations have been made, unless where by reference

reference to the paſſages cited, it was manifeſt that an error had been committed in tranſcribing. And wherever Dr. KENNICOTT had ſubjoined to a note any of thoſe marks which he uſed to expreſs either doubt, or an intention to reconſider the ſubject, theſe alſo have been faithfully expreſſed.

THE Volume is concluded by the Sermons enumerated in his Will.

Extract

Extract from The *Dedication* of
The prefent Englifh Bible to
HIS MAJESTY KING JAMES.

────── *AMONG all our joys, there was no one that more filled our hearts, than the bleffed continuance of the preaching of God's Sacred Word; that ineftimable treafure, which excelleth all the riches of the earth. Becaufe the fruit thereof extendeth itfelf, not only to the time fpent in this tranfitory world, but directeth and difpofeth men unto that eternal Happinefs, which is above in Heaven. Then, not to fuffer this to fall to the ground, but rather to take it up, and to continue it — nay, to go forward in maintaining the Truth of Chrift, and propagating it far and near — hath bound the hearts of all Your Majefty's religious people unto You. — When Your Highnefs had once apprehended, how convenient it was, that, out of the Original facred Tongues, together with comparing the labours (both in our own and other languages) of many worthy men who went before us, there fhould be one more exact Tranflation of the Holy Scriptures into the Englifh Tongue: Your Majefty did never defift to urge and excite thofe, to whom it was commended, that the Work might be haftened; and that the bufinefs might be expedited in fo decent a manner, as a matter of fuch importance might juftly require.* ──────

A

Extract from The *Preface*

to

The present English Bible.

ZEAL to promote the common good, whether it be by devising any thing ourselves, or revising that which hath been laboured by others, deserveth certainly much respect and esteem. — Now, what piety, without truth? What truth, what saving truth, without the Word of God? What Word of God, whereof we may be sure, without the Scripture? The Scriptures we are commanded to search. They are commended, that searched and studied them. They are reproved, that were unskilful in them, or slow to believe them. They can make us wise unto salvation. — We (translators) are so far from condemning any of their labours, who travelled before us in this kind, either in this land or beyond sea, either in King Henry's time, or King Edward's, or Queen Elizabeth's, that we acknowledge them to have been raised up of God, for the building and furnishing of his Church; and that they deserve to be had in everlasting remembrance. — Yet, as nothing is begun, and perfected, at the same time; so if we, building upon their foundation who went before us, do endeavour to make that better which they left so good; no man hath cause to mislike us: and they, if they were alive, would thank us. — Let us bless God, from the ground

ground of our heart; for working this religious care in His Majesty, to have the Translations of the Bible maturely considered and examined. For by this means it cometh to pass, that whatsoever is found already, will shine as gold more brightly: also, if any thing be halting or superfluous, or not so agreeable to the Original; the same may be corrected, and the truth set in place. —If we will be sons of the truth, we must consider what it speaketh; and trample upon our own credit, yea and upon other men's too, if either be any way an hindrance to it.—Christian Reader! we never thought to make a New Translation, nor to make a bad one a good one; but, to make a good one better.

If you ask, What we had before us; truly, it was the Hebrew Text of the Old Testament, and the Greek of the New. Neither did we think much to consult the translators or commentators Chaldee, Hebrew, Syrian, Greek, or Latin; no, nor the Spanish, French, Italian, or Dutch. Neither did we disdain to revise that, which we had done; and to bring back to the anvil that, which we had hammered: but, having and using as great helps as were needful, we have brought the Work to that pass which you see. — The eyes of the world are now open, God be thanked; and have been a great while. We desire, that the Scripture may speak like itself; and that it may be understood, even of the very vulgar.

It remaineth, gentle Reader! that we commend thee to God, and to the Spirit of his grace; which is able to build further than we can aſk, or think.—Others have laboured; and you may enter into their labours. Receive not ſo great things in vain! Deſpiſe not ſo great Salvation!

ENGLISH TRANSLATIONS.

Wickliffe's *Bible*, from Latin: in 1345—1382.

Tyndal's *Pentateuch*, from Hebrew: 1530.

Coverdale's *Bible*: 1535, 1550, 1553.

Matthewe's *Bible*: 1537.

Cranmer's (or Great) *Bible*: 1539, 1540, 1566 &c.

Taverner's *Bible*: 1539, 1549.

Parker's (or Biſhops) *Bible*: 1568, 1569, 1572 &c.

Geneva *Bible*: 1568, 1570, 1576, 1589, 1599.

Broughton's *Dan. Ecc. Lam. Job*: 1596, 1605, 1606.

Doway *Bible*, from Latin: 1609, 1610.

King James's *Bible*: 1611——to——178-.

INTRODUCTION
by
The Author of the following Remarks.

IN the reign of King James the first, about 180 years ago, though several different Translations of the Bible into English had been made within 70 years before; it was thought by the learned highly expedient, that there should be *one more exact* than that which had been in common use for the preceding 30 years. And the *Dedication* sets forth, that, as soon as HIS MAJESTY *apprehended, how convenient* such a Work would be, He was pleased to command it to be undertaken; and *expedited in so decent a manner, as a matter of such importance might justly require.* We learn also from the Dedication, that the plan was — to make a more exact Translation out of the *Original* sacred Tongues. And that this might be done with the greater perfection; the Translators were to consult the labours of many other worthy men, both in their own country and abroad. An excellent Plan this, most certainly! And it was executed far better than might have been expected; if we consider, how imperfect at that time was the state of *Literature* in general, and of *Sacred Literature* in particular.

In about 50 years afterwards, a Committee was appointed; for considering the *Translations*, and *Impressions*, of the Bible. And they met, at Chelsea; attended by the celebrated *Walton, Castell, Cudworth* &c. But it does not appear, what improvements were agreed upon, or even recommended, by these very learned men. (See *Lewis, Eng. Tranflat. Bible.*) And no Committee, of the fame nature, has been appointed from that time down to the prefent.

During the long extent of Years (almoft 2 whole Centuries) fince this laſt Tranſlation was made, many *imperfections* and *errors* in it have been difcovered by learned men. And feveral paffages have been lately pointed out, in which the *older* Englifh Tranſlations had *better* expreffed the fenfe of the Originals, both in the Old and in the New Teſtament. But, notwithſtanding thefe blemiſhes, and even miſtakes; and though it is certain, that great improvements might be now made in tranſlating the whole Bible, becauſe the Hebrew and Greek languages have been much cultivated, and far better underſtood, fince the year 1600: yet we ſhall then only fee the great *Expediency*, or rather the *Neceſſity*, of a more exact Engliſh Bible; when we reflect, that the *Heb. Text* itſelf is now found to be wrong in many inſtances, ſome of which are of confiderable confequence. Indeed the laſt Engliſh Tranſlators muſt have feen, and they do tacitly allow, that the printed Hebrew Text is *not always right*; becauſe they have fometimes inferted words *different* from thoſe in the Hebrew Text, and fometimes words which are *not* in the Hebrew Text at all. Thefe fentiments of theirs, with regard to fome miſtakes in the printed Hebrew Text, are now confirmed; and in a much greater degree, than they were at all aware of.

This difcovery of Errors in the prefent Text, together with the means of correcting them, will certainly promote the honour of *Revelation*, and therefore cannot be favourable to the caufe of *Deifm*: as the Text of the Old Teſtament has always been able to answer the great purposes intended by it; namely, to deliver down a true account of the *Creation* and *Descent* of Mankind — *a rule of Duty for the Jews*, till the commencement of Christianity — and sufficient evidence from Prophecy, to prove *Jesus Christ* to be *the true Messiah*. On the contrary: as the most formidable objections of Unbelievers have been grounded on these very *Corruptions* of the Original, and on the *Inconsistences* thence arising between the Old and New Testaments; so it is from a just correction of these mistakes, now discovered, that Infidelity will receive its deepest wound. For the reasoning of Unbelievers hath been this — *Some of the Citations in the New Testament, made from the Old, do not agree with the Old either in words or sense — but the Old Testament is allowed to be right — therefore the New Testament must be wrong.* Whereas the truth now appears to stand thus — *Some passages of the Old Testament, cited in the New, have been, since the days of the Apostles, corrupted in the Old — the most antient of those Manuscripts of the Old Testament, which are even now extant, prove its greater agreement formerly with the New Testament — and the original agreement of the two proves the truth of both.*

But the advantages of a Revisal of our English Translation, though assisted by a correction of many corrupted passages, are by no means confined to a more effectual vindication of the *New* Testament. For *the Hebrew Manuscripts* have brought to light very many *Various Readings*, which give a new and powerful sanction to the *Antient Versions*; and the *MSS* themselves contain many Various Readings of consequence, which are certainly genuine. And by this joint assistance of the *Hebrew MSS* themselves, and of the *Antient Verſions* thus confirmed, ſeveral parts of the Old Teſtament will be *reconciled* to others, with which they are now at variance; and *good ſenſe* will be clearly reſtored to many other parts, which are now exceedingly obſcure, if not abſolutely unintelligible.

Theſe general principles are here aſſumed, and at preſent taken for granted, becauſe they have been already proved. It is neither proper in itſelf, nor conſiſtent with the plan of this volume, to repeat now what I have already ſubmitted to the Learned: and it may be decently preſumed, that the Proofs thus offered have (in the main) been ſatisfactory; becauſe of the ſingular ſupport and favour, with which I have been honoured by the Public. My 1ſt Diſſertation, on *The State of the Printed Heb. Text of the Old Teſtament*, was publiſhed in 1753; and my 2d, on the ſame ſubject, in 1760. In conſequence of theſe Diſſertations, I was prevailed on to *collate* the Hebrew MSS, and *to publiſh their Various Readings*: which alſo has been now performed, and *a General Diſſertation* given concerning the whole Work. To theſe 3 Diſſertations I ſhall therefore refer, in the following pages; when I ſhall briefly mention here any ſuch points, as are there treated at large, and which are neceſſarily encumbered there with learned quotations.

It muſt alſo be carefully obſerved; that one great ſource of Correction, as to the 5 books of Moſes, could not be made uſe of by our laſt Tranſlators. For *the Samaritan Pentateuch* was not then known in Europe; but it was, ſoon after, brought hither from the Eaſt, and printed. I muſt add; that not only

INTRODUCTION. 9

the Variations *from the printed Hebrew Text* are numerous and important in the *printed Samaritan Pentateuch and its MSS*; but alſo, that the *older* even the *Hebrew* MSS are, the more they are found to agree with and to confirm the *Samaritan:* and many errors in the Samaritan copies, as *printed*, are correct̃ed by the Samaritan *MSS*. Nor ſhould it be omitted, that the Paris Polyglott, which firſt publiſhed the *Samaritan* Pentateuch in 1645, firſt alſo publiſhed the *Syriac* and *Arabic* Verſions. And it was the additional misfortune of our laſt Tranſlators, to want theſe very valuable Verſions; from which the learned have ſince derived many and eminent advantages, for *correcting* as well as illuſtrating the Old Teſtament.

But beſides the great advantages, which may be now derived from the ſeveral *Antient* Verſions; other Verſions have been made, in different countries, during the laſt and preſent centuries: and *theſe* likewiſe will furniſh conſiderable aſſiſtances. And it is probable, that ſtill greater advantages will follow, from a careful examination of the very many excellent Critics, both at home and abroad; who, ſince the year 1611, have publiſhed *Commentaries* on different books of the Bible, or *Diſſertations* on particular Paſſages, or *Remarks* on the Various Readings in the ſacred MSS themſelves, as well as on the Antient Verſions: all which circumſtances, now happily combined, call for the moſt ſerious attention of our Superiors to *a Reviſal of our preſent Tranſlation.*

That more Various Readings may be ſtill collect̃ed from *the Hebrew MSS*, is certain: and that greater aſſiſtance will be derived from *the Antient Verſions*, when their printed copies ſhall be correct̃ed by *their oldeſt MSS*, is certain alſo. But, does it at all follow, that, becauſe *more* may be done for illuſtrating the Old Teſtament an *hundred* years hence, therefore *nothing* ſhould be done *at preſent?* Important conſequences depend upon this queſtion, *in our own times.* Many corruptions in that ſacred Volume are now proved: and why muſt Unbelievers, even in theſe days, be permitted to avail themſelves of theſe corruptions, remaining any longer uncorrected? Many parts are now expreſſed *without ſenſe,* whilſt ſome are *inconſiſtent* with other parts both of the *Old* Teſtament and the *New:* and muſt not every ſerious *Chriſtian* wiſh, that the former were made intelligible, and alſo that the latter were fairly reconciled? This cannot but be the wiſh of every *good* man. And indeed every *learned* man will concur in deſiring, that *juſtice* may be done to the Old Teſtament; in repreſenting that very curious and moſt antient of all books, with the greateſt poſſible conformity to the *Originals* of Moſes and the Prophets.

That theſe wiſhes may appear well-grounded; a juſt repreſentation ſhould be made by thoſe, who are ſkilled in *Languages,* to thoſe, who are veſted with *Power.* And that I may not, at laſt, appear to withdraw my own endeavours, however inadequate, in a Cauſe of all others the moſt intereſting to the Public; I think it my duty to communicate, as plainly as I can, my remarks on *many Parts of our preſent Engliſh Tranſlation.* And I cannot but wiſh, and pray, that many other remarks on the ſame ſubject may be ſoon publiſhed by thoſe, who, with equal Zeal for THE GLORY OF GOD, have greater Abilities for promoting it.

INTRODUCTION. 11

To men of *Learning*, and alſo to men of *Power*, an appeal has lately been made, in the *New Tranſlation* of the whole book of ISAIAH; by an Author ſingularly qualified both to taſte the ſublime Poetry of this Evangelical Prophet, and alſo to expreſs in Engliſh the Form and Spirit of the Original. As this learned Prelate led the way to the correction of the Hebrew Text, by having convinced me of its being much corrupted; ſo he has, in this great Work of his, eſtabliſhed the importance of the Hebrew MSS, now fortunately brought to light: correcting the Text, in many places, from theſe *MSS themſelves*; and in many others, from the *Antient Verſions*, which the Hebrew MSS abundantly confirm. And indeed his Lordſhip's *Preliminary Diſſertation* is full of ſuch Critical Illuſtrations, as will be of the greateſt uſe—*whenever* (to uſe his own words there, pag. 69) *that neceſſary Work, a New Tranſlation, or a Reviſion of the preſent Tranſlation, of the Holy Scriptures, for the uſe of our Church, ſhall be undertaken.*

This Introduction of mine cannot be concluded ſo properly, as in the words of the ſame Author; from his juſtly celebrated *Viſitation-Sermon*, at *Durham*, in 1758 : *pag.* 23 &c. " The light, that aroſe
" upon the Chriſtian world at the Reformation, hath
" ſtill continued to increaſe, and we truſt will *ſhine*
" *more and more unto the perfect day*. The labours of
" the learned have from that time, by the bleſſing of
" God upon the free exerciſe of reaſon and private
" judgement, been greatly ſucceſsful in promoting
" religious knowledge; and particularly, in laying
" open the hidden treaſures of divine wiſdom con-
" tained in the Holy Scriptures. Much hath been

"done in this important work; and much still remains to be done. Those heavenly stores are inexhaustible: every new acquisition still leads on to further discoveries; and the most careful search will still leave enough to invite, and to reward, the repeated searches of the pious and industrious, to the latest ages. This is a work, that demands our first and most earnest regard; the studies and assistance, the favour and encouragement, of all. To confirm and illustrate these holy writings, to evince their truth, to shew their consistency, to explain their meaning, to make them more generally known and studied, more easily and perfectly understood, by all; to remove the difficulties, that discourage the honest endeavours of the unlearned, and provoke the malicious cavils of the half-learned: this is the most worthy object, that can engage our attention; the most important end, to which our labours in the search of truth can be directed. And here I cannot but mention, that nothing would more effectually conduce to this end, than the exhibiting of the Holy Scriptures themselves to the people in a more advantageous and just light, by an accurate REVISAL of our vulgar Translation by public Authority. This hath often been represented; AND, I HOPE, WILL NOT ALWAYS BE REPRESENTED IN VAIN."

Remarks

on select Passages in

THE OLD TESTAMENT.

GENESIS 1; 8—10.

THE Divine Approbation being expressed *once*, as to the parts of the Creation upon the first, fourth, fifth, and sixth days; *not at all* on the second day, and *twice* on the third: there can scarce be a doubt, but that here is now some mistake. The regular order will be restored, by admitting a *transposition*; and by allowing — either, that the latter part of verse 8 (*and the evening and the morning were the second day*) originally closed the 10th verse — or, that the latter part of ver. 10 (*and God saw that it was good*) originally belonged to ver. 8. And there (in ver. 8) the words are found in the *Greek* version; though they are also, in the present Greek copies, at ver. 10: and probably, in one of the 2 places, the Greek has been assimilated to the corrupted Hebrew. See my *General Dissertation*, pag. 35. The preceding observation is founded on a remark, inserted by the late learned Arch-Bp SECKER in the margin of his Hebrew Bible.

Gen. 2, 2.

And on the SEVENTH *day God ended his work*. This is not consistent with the Creation having been finished, *and ended*, on the 6th day. The 7th day was certainly *the day of rest:* and it was made so for an

example

example — that *men might ceafe from their works, as God did from his*; working on 6 days, and refting on every 7th, even unto the end of the world, as GOD Himfelf did at the beginning of it. As the cafe is therefore of confequence, and there are great authorities for confidering the *Numeral* here as corrupted; inftead of tranflating the verb *had ended*, it feems much more eligible to read *God ended his work on the fixth day* — agreeably to the Samar. Text, with the Greek and Syriac verfions. See Hallett's Notes; vol. 3, p. 109. And as to ז for ו, 7 for 6; fee my 1ft *Differt.* p. 96, 529; *Differt.* 2, p. 212; and *Gen. Differt.* p. 12, 13.

Gen. 2, 24.

— *and they shall be one flesh.* This verfe is evidently corrupted, by the omiffion of the word fignifying *two*; which word is preferved in the Samar. Text, with all the Antient Verfions. The learned *Cudworth* thought this word *neceffary*; and highly extolled the *Samar.* Pent. for preferving it. And the importance of this word will be more generally acknowledged; in confequence of its weight in the controverfy, concerning *a Plurality of Wives.* But there is one argument in favour of this word, which fhould determine every Chriftian; and that is *the exprefs authority of the New Teftament.* Where a Variation in the Old Teftament is furnifhed by Heb. MSS, or by the Samar. Text and Antient Verfions; and that Variation is clearly confirmed by a Citation in the *New* Teftament: there can fcarce remain any doubt, as to the authenticity of fuch Various Reading. But this general Canon of Scripture cannot, in any

any inftance, be more ftrongly confirmed from the *New* Teftament, than in the cafe before us. For St *Paul* hath twice quoted this text, with the word *two:* in 1 *Corinth.* 6, 16 and *Ephef.* 5, 31. And CHRIST, who is affirmed by St *Mark* (10, 8) to have quoted the word *two,* is affirmed by St *Matthew* (19, 5) to have quoted this fame word, as originally made ufe of here by GOD Himfelf — HE, *which made them,* SAID: *They* TWAIN *shall be one flesh.* See *Gen. Diff.* p. 8, 28, 33, 34.

Gen. 4, 8.

And Cain talked with Abel his brother: and it came to pafs, when they were in the field &c. The verb, here rendered *talked with,* is fo rendered no where elfe: and, by this rendering, our laft Tranflators endeavoured to conceal what is here omitted. Some of the Jews have acknowledged an *hiatus* in this verfe. And the 2 words, fignifying *let us go into the field,* which are omitted in the Heb. text and in our prefent verfion (but which Bp *Beveridge* thought neceffary) are ftill preferved in the Samar. Text; with the Greek verfion, reading now as formerly: fo *Philo,* and *Clemens Romanus.* The omiffion is further proved by the Targums of *Jerufalem* and *Jonathan*; and alfo by the Syr. and Vulg. verfions. And though different copies of the Vulgat read differently in many places; here, it is prefumed, they all agree. *Cranmer's* verfion is — and Cain fpake unto Abell his brother, (let us go forth.) And it fortuned, when they were in the felde &c. And fo *Wickliffe* — and Cain feide to Abel his brother, go wee out: when they weren in the feld &c. See, on this Text, my *Differt.* 1; p. 347: and *Gen. Differt.* p. 35, 52.

Gen. 4; 23, 24.

It is very difficult, if not impossible, to understand this speech of Lamech, in our present translation — *I have slain a man to my wounding, and a young man to my hurt : if Cain shall be avenged seven fold, truly Lamech seventy and seven fold.* But this passage is happily illustrated, and (which is entirely new) the true sense of it is confirmed, in the 3d edition of Bp Lowth's *Prelections*, pag. 52 — that, whereas Cain had been guilty of *wilful murder*, Lamech had only slain a man *in his own defence.* The present Hebrew words are there properly rendered, to this purpose —

I have slain a man, for having wounded me;
and a young man, for having bruised me.
If Cain shall be avenged seven fold;
truly Lamech seventy and seven fold.

Gen. 5, 3.

Whenever a Revisal of our English Translation takes place; if it is the opinion of the learned, that *the Heb. Chronology*, from the Creation to the Call of Abraham, has been *contracted:* it will be right to restore, in this and the following verses, *the larger* Numbers, according to the Greek version. Thus: *And Adam lived 230 years, and begat Seth.* See *Diss.* 1, p. 544; and *Gen. Diss.* p. 32, 33, 36, 37, 43, 45, 46. If this great point should still be thought doubtful; it may be right in this, as in many other cases, to retain (in our next Translation) the present reading here in *the Text*, and to add the different reading in the margin, or at bottom of the page. But this article of the Ante-diluvian Chronology must not be rested,

rested, entirely, on the pages just before referred to: though it has been there proved from *Eusebius*, that some *Heb.* copies, having the *larger* numbers, existed in the 4th century; and others, on the authority of *Jacobus Edessenus*, as late as the year 700; whilst others, much later, are mentioned in the Chronicle of *Ecchellensis*. And though such MSS are all, perhaps, now lost; yet are these testimonies confirmed by the traditions, still preserved amongst the JEWS themselves — as to *Seth being born* 130 *years after Abel's death*. (See *Gen. Dissert.* p. 33.) If therefore Adam, at the age of 130, begat *Seth*; and yet, if this was about 130 years *after the death of Abel:* then Abel was slain by Cain, when neither of them was 2 years old. But Abel, when slain, might be near 100 years old; and consequently, he might die 130 years before the birth of Seth: if Adam begat Seth at 230, agreeably to the *Greek* version. There yet remains one argument, of very considerable moment, to be drawn from the *Hebrew* Text, *against* itself. Though the ages of 6 Ante-diluvian Patriarchs (namely the 1st, 2d, 3d, 4th, 5th, and 7th) are regularly shorter; yet the remaining 3 (namely the 6th, 8th, and 9th) much exceed the ages of the other 6 — I speak of the age of each, before he begat his son. Whereas, in the Greek version, these 3 ages are regular, and consistent with the other 6. The truth seems clearly to be this — *The Jews had a mind to have left out a Century in the ages of all the Patriarchs before they begat children, and to have added it to the after-term of their lives: but they found, that, if they dropped the Centuries of the ages of* Jared, Methuselah, *and* Lamech, *before they begat children, (as*

B *they*

they had done of all the reſt) and added them to the remainder of their lives; they muſt by this reckoning have extended their 3 lives beyond the Flood. (Jackſon's Chronol. 1, p. 56.) Let it be added — that, though the age of *Jared*, who lived 962 years, could not be ſo altered; yet that of *Enoch*, his ſucceſſor, might be; becauſe he lived only 365 years. This proof will be more clear, from the following compariſon.

Lived years, before the Son's Birth.
Adam ——— Heb. 130 ——— 230 Greek.
Seth ——— Heb. 105 ——— 205 Greek.
Enos ——— Heb. 90 ——— 190 Greek.
Cainan ——— Heb. 70 ——— 170 Greek.
Mahalaleel — Heb. 65 ——— 165 Greek.
Jared ——— Heb. 162 ——— 162 Greek.
Enoch ——— Heb. 65 ——— 165 Greek.
Mathuſelah — Heb. 187 ———187* Greek.
Lamech ——— Heb. 182 ——— 182 Greek.

Gen. 11, 12.

And Arphaxad lived 35 years, and begat Salah. If the 2d CAINAN ſhall be here thought genuine, according to St Luke's Genealogy; *he* muſt be here inſerted, as *the ſon of Arphaxad*, and *father of Salah*: and the preceding number 35 will of courſe be corrected to 135. An objection, which may be drawn from *this Cainan* not being mentioned in 1 *Chron.* 1, 18, is anſwered in part by obſerving, that the name *Cainan* is preſerved there likewiſe in the Alex. MS and Complut. edition of the Greek verſion: the Vatic. MS is there defective, in ſeveral verſes.

In my *Gen. Diſſ.* (pag. 32 and 125) are many arguments to prove, that theſe 2 firſt Chronological

---
* See Jackſon's Chronology; vol. 1. p. 40.

Periods have been *contracted in the Heb. copies*, and not enlarged in the Greek. To the remarks already made I shall here add — that the Scripture represents the world as being well inhabited in the days of Abraham; " more people, more natives, more king-
" doms, than can easily be supposed to have been
" propagated from 3 men and 3 women, in 367
" years. Eastward, the Chaldeans; the 4 kings,
" who with their armies, in their way to Sodom,
" beat the Rephaims, the Amalekites &c. In Pa-
" lestine, the 7 nations seem to have been populous,
" beside the Philistines. Abraham himself had a fa-
" mily, or retinue, of 318 able to bear arms; be-
" side women, children &c. Westward, the king-
" dom of Egypt, populous and rich. Probably there
" were many more Nations in the East part of Asia,
" where the Ark had rested. So that, as Bp Stil-
" lingfleet observes — *Those Chronologers, who much*
" *streighten those times, are not the best friends to the*
" *Credibility of Scripture-history.* Another exception
" against the Heb. Chronology, which does not lie
" against the Greek, is — that the HEBREW copies,
" as well as *the Greek and Samaritan*, making *Shem*
" to live, after the birth of his son, 500 years (and
" his son Arphaxad, and many of the rest, above
" 400 years, after the birth of their children;) and
" yet (*contrary to the Samar. and Greek*) making the
" duration from the Flood to Abraham so short; do
" consequently make *Shem*, and many of those first
" Patriarchs, to have been living, not only at the
" time of the tower of Babel, not only at the birth
" of Abraham, but even to have *outlived Abraham*.
" But, if this were so; 'tis wonder, there is no men-
" tion

"tion of Shem, or the others, in all the hiſtory of
"Abraham, but only of his father *Terah*. The *Greek*
"has neither of theſe difficulties: becauſe that tranſ-
"lation, making the time of Abraham after the Flood
"to be above 1000 years, allows a time for peopling
"the world, as well as for the deaths of Shem, and
"of thoſe antient Patriarchs, before Abraham was
"born." See *Wall's Crit. Notes on the O. T.* pag. 3.
On this very important ſubject, I ſhall add — that as the Chronology, both *before and after* the Flood, hath been altered *wilfully*, and upon *one uniform plan*; it is not eaſy to ſuppoſe, that they who believe *the Greek* to be right *after* the Flood, can think the *Hebrew* to be right *before* the Flood: the nature of the caſe ſeeming to require, that either *the Greek*, or *the Hebrew*, be right in *both*. In ſhort: the Bible is univerſally allowed to be here corrupted; as to the ages of 6 Patriarchs *before* the Flood, and 7 *after* it: 1300 years being wilfully added here in the *Greek*, or taken away in the *Hebrew*. But at whatever time, and for whatever cauſe, this great corruption was thus *uniformly* made by *the Jews*, who in either caſe muſt have been the authors of it: can it be reaſonable to believe — that, if they *ſhortened* the Heb. by 700 years *after* the Flood, they did not alſo *take away* the 600 years *before* it? Or that the party, who *extended* the Greek by 700 years after the Flood, did not alſo lengthen before it? For, if not: then they, who ſhortened wilfully, did here alſo, and on the ſame plan, wilfully lengthen; and they, who lengthened wilfully, did here alſo, and on the ſame plan, wilfully ſhorten! Let it not be forgotten, what this plan really was — namely (according to many

antient Writers) to bring back the Birth of Jefus from the 6th Chiliad to the 4th — from about the year 5500 to 3760; in order to prove, that, at the Birth of Jefus, the time for *the Meffiah* was not then come. See *Gen. Diff.* p. 32, 36, 37, 46. *

Gen. 11, 32.

Among the many obligations we are under to *the Samar. Pent.* it is by no means one of the leaft, that, inftead of 205 years as *the age of Terah*, it reads 145. For this laft number removes the great difficulties, attending the other number, as to the O. Teftament; and (which is more important) it effectually vindicates the truth of *St Stephen's affertion*, in *Acts* 7, 4. † The cafe is this. St Stephen fays, that Terah died *before* his fon Abraham left Haran. Now, as Abraham, at leaving Haran, was 75 (*Gen.* 12, 4;) if he was born (as many of the Chronologers contend)

* BP WARBURTON, in his *View of L. Bolingbroke's Philofophy*, fays — " Tho' the *Hebrew* copy makes it no more than 300 " years from the Deluge to Abraham; yet the *Samaritan* Pen-" tateuch, the *Septuagint*, and *Jofephus*, reckon about 1000 — " And THE BEST Chronologers agree, in preferring the Sa-" maritan, the Septuagint, and Jofephus, to the Hebrew copy." Letter 3. And *Winder*, in his *Hiftory of Knowledge* (vol. 1, p. 133) tho' an advocate for the Heb. chronology, makes a conceffion, which muft not be here omitted — " A view of " thefe Difficulties, attending the *Difperfion* (of mankind) at " the time of Peleg's Birth (which was in the year 101 after " the Deluge, according to the *Heb.* Chronology) has been " manifeftly the chief reafon, which has induced feveral learned " men to embrace the Chronology of *the Greek Verfion*."

† This is one of thofe inftances, in which the Old and New Teftaments difagree; as they are collected in *Dr Doddridge's Lectures*, Propofition 121.

when Terah was only 70; the age of Terah could only be 145. That Terah was not 130 years old, at the birth of Abraham, is further deducible from the words of Abraham; who, if he himself had been born of so very old a father, would not have asked with so much wonder —*shall a child be born unto him, that is an hundred years old?* Gen. 17, 17 : see also *Rom.* 4, 19 with *Heb.* 11, 12. Lastly : if Abraham was not born, when Terah was 70, agreeably to *Gen.* 11, 26; it then follows, that the time of the birth of Abraham is *expressly recorded* no where — though Moses has recorded the times of the births of many others; who, in comparison of Abraham, were men of no note at all. See *Gen. Diss.* p. 8, 52, 53.

It must be added, that the supposition of Abraham's having many children *afterwards*, by Keturah, is well confuted by *Hallet's* Note on *Hebrews* 11, 12; in Peirce's Commentary, pag. 21—26.

Gen. 20, 16.

Great has been the confusion, in translating the words which are rendered in our version — *and with all other : thus she was reproved.* But this confusion would have been avoided; had it been known, that the letter *Vau*, prefixed to a verb, sometimes loses its conjunctive power, and serves only to change the Tense. This is a point of Heb. criticism, perhaps first observed by Bp *Lowth*; and yet it is of extensive use, and considerable consequence. See *Gen.* 44, 9 : *Exod.* 16; 6, 7 : *Lev.* 7, 25 : *Deut.* 5, 25; 18, 20 : *Jud.* 6, 17 : *Psal.* 25, 11 : *Isai.* 6, 1; 9, 4 : *Jer.* 44, 25 &c. If we judge here by this rule; and consider the verb as *future*, admitting of course an im-

perative fignification: we fhall foon difcover a juft fenfe, as well as a regular conftruction. For the Heb. Text is allowed to contain the adjective for *rectus*, and the fubftantive for *rectitudo*; which nouns are regularly deducible from the verb* in this place, as fignifying *recte dixit*. The verb being thus found; we muft highly efteem the Greek verfion, which reads here και παντα αληθευσεν. And of courfe the Heb. words are to be tranflated — *and in all things speak the truth*. See Clarke, on Coins; 4°. 1767: p. 217.

Gen. 25, 8.

In the Revifal of our Tranflation, it will be proper to print in the common character fuch words as are now printed in *Italics*; wherever a *conjecture* of our laft Tranflators has been fince confirmed. In this verfe, they fuppofed it impoffible that Mofes fhould fay — *Abraham died, an old Man and full* ; but that the word *years*, or *days*, muft originally have followed. They therefore inferted *of years*, in Italics. But the word *days* is certainly the true word; on the authorities of the *Samar*. Pentateuch, fome *Chald*. as well as *Heb*. MSS, and *the Antient Verfions* : agreeably to *Gen*. 35, 29; *Job* 42, 17 &c.

Gen. 25, 15.

Men, who have read their Bible with care, muft have remarked, that the Name of the fame perfon is often expreffed differently in different places. Indeed the Variation is fometimes fo great, that we can fcarce perfuade ourfelves, that *one and the fame* perfon is really meant. An uniform expreffion of Proper

---

* נכה — and the word ונבחת is here *vere dicet*, or *vere dicito*.

Names is diligently attended to, in other books; perhaps in every other book, except the Old Testament. But here we find strange variety in the expression, and consequently great confusion: and indeed there is scarce any one general source of error, which calls for more careful correction, than the same Proper Names now wrongly expressed. One remarkable instance occurs in this verse; where the person is wrongly called *Hadar*, who is rightly called *Hadad*, in 1 *Chron.* 1, 30. The word now *Hadar*, in the printed *Heb.* text of *Genesis*, is *Hadad* here in the *Samar.* Pent. and in the *Arab.* version, and also in 200 *Heb. MSS.* I shall add here, from the Pentateuch, some other Proper Names, which are strangely varied likewise: first, 23 Names expressed differently in the *Heb.* Text itself, and 17 of them in our *English* translation; and then, 31 Names expressed uniformly in the *Hebrew*, yet differently in the *English*.

Same Names, differing in the *Hebrew*.

1	*Gen.* 4,18	Mehujael	— Mehijael,	*in the same verse.*
2	——10, 3	Riphath	— Diphath	1 *Chro.* 1, 6.
3	—— 4	Tarshish	— Tarshishah	——— 7.
4	—— ——	Dodanim	— Rodanim	———
5	—— 23	Mash	— Meshech	———17.
6	—— 28	Obal	— Ebal	———22.
7	-32,30(31)	Peniel	— Penuel,	*in the next verse.*
8	——36,11	Zepho	— Zephi	1 *Chro.* 1, 36.
9	—— 23	Shepho	— Shephi	———40.
10	—— 39	Pau	— Pai	———50.
11	—— 40	Alvah	— Aliah	———51.
12	——46,10	Jemuel	— Nemuel	*Num.* 26, 12.
13	—— ——	Jachin	— Jarib	1 *Chro.* 4, 24.
14	—— ——	Zohar	— Zerah	*N.*26,13 & 1 *C.*4,24
15	——— 11	Gershon	— Gershom	1 *Chro.* 6, 1 (16)

THE OLD TESTAMENT. 25

16 *Gen.* 46, 13   Job   — Jashub   *Num.* 26, 24.
17 ——— 16   Ezbon   — Ozni   ———16.
18 ——— 21   Huppim — Huram   1 *Chro.* 8, 5.
19 ——— ——   Ard   — Addar   ——— 3.
20 ——— 23   Hushim — Shuham   *Num.* 26, 42.
21 *Exod.* 4, 18   Jether   — Jethro, *in the same verse.*
22 *Num.* 1, 14   Deuel   — Reuel   *Num.* 2, 14.
23 *Deut.* 32, 44   Hoshea   — Joshua   *Deut.* 34, 9.

Names, same in *Heb.* yet different in *Eng.*

1 *Gen.* 5, 3   Seth   — Sheth   1 *Chro.* 1, 1.
2 ——— 6   Enos   — Enosh
3 ——— 9   Cainan   — Kenan   ——— 2.
4 ——— 15   Jared   — Jered
5 ——— 18   Enoch   — Henoch   ——— 3.
6 ——— 21   Methuselah — Mathushelah
7 *Gen.* 10, 6   Phut   — Put   1 *Chro.* 1, 8.
8 ——— 14   Philistim — the Philistines ——— 12.
9 ——— ——   Caphtorim — Caphthorim
10 ——— 16   Emorite   — Amorites   *Gen.* 15; 16, 21.
11 ——— ——   Girgasite — Girgashites   ——— 21.
12 *Gen.* 10, 19   Gaza   — Azzah   *Deut.* 2, 23.
               Gaza *Jer.* 47, 5 — Azzah   *Jer.* 25, 20.
13 ——— 22   Ashur   — Ashur   1 *Chro.* 1, 17.
14 ——— 24   Salah   — Shelah   ———18.
15 —14; 2, 8   Zeboiim — Zeboim   *Deut.* 29, 23.
16 -14, 5; 15, 20 Rephaims — giants *Deut.* 2, 20 : 3; 11, 13.
17 ——— 25, 15   Naphish — Nephish   1 *Chro.* 5, 19.
18 ——— 29, 6   Rachel   — Rahel   *Jer.* 31, 15.
19 ——— 36, 34   Temani   — the Temanites 1 *Chro.* 1, 45.
20 ——— 37   Saul   — Shaul   ———48.
21 — 37; 25, 28   Ishmeelites — Ishmaelites   *Jud.* 8, 24.
22 *Exod.* 1, 11   Raamses — Ramescs   *Exod.* 12, 37.
23 ——— 6, 18   Izhar   — Izehar   *Num.* 3, 19.
24 ——— 19   Mahali   — Mahli   1 *Chro.* 6, 4 (19)
25 *Lev.* 18, 21   Molech   — Moloch   *Amos* 5, 26.
26 *Num.* 13; 8, 16 Oshea — Hoshea   *Deut.* 32, 44.

27	Num. 13,16	Jehoſhua	— Joſhua	Num. 14, 6.
28	——21,12	Zared	— Zered	Deut. 2, 13.
29	——32, 3	Jazer	— Jaazer	Num. 32, 35.
30	——33,31	Bene-jaakan	—children of Jaakan	D. 10,6.
31	Deut. 3,17	Aſhdoth-piſgah	—ſprings of Piſgah	D. 4,49.

Nothing can be more clear, than that theſe 54 Proper Names (at leaſt, the far greater part of them) ſhould be expreſſed with the very ſame Letters, in the places where they are now different. In the ſecond liſt, inſtances the 6th, 10th, and 13th have been corrected, and expreſſed uniformly; in the Engliſh Bible, printed at Oxford, in 1769. And ſurely the ſame juſtice in the tranſlation ſhould be done to the reſt of theſe Proper Names, and to all others through the Bible; at leaſt, where the Original words are now properly the ſame. Who would not wonder, at ſeeing the ſame perſons named both *Simon* and *Shimon*, *Richard* and *Ricard?* And can we then admit here both *Seth* and *Sheth*, *Rachel* and *Rahel?* Again: whoever can admit (as above) both *Gaza* and *Azzah*, with *Rameſes* and *Raamſes*, ſhould not object to *London* and *Ondon*, with *Amſterdam* and *Amſtradam*. In ſhort: in a hiſtory far more intereſting than any other, the names of *Perſons* and *Places* ſhould be diſtinguiſhed accurately, and defined with exact uniformity. And no true Critic will think lightly of this advice of Origen — *Contemnenda non eſt accurata circa* NOMINA *diligentia ei, qui voluerit probe intelligere Sanctas Literas.*

Gen. 31; 38 and 41.

If every reading, which introduces but a ſingle difficulty, demands our attention; much greater muſt that demand be, when several difficulties are caused by any one mistake, or any one mistranslation. Of this nature is the passage before us, which therefore shall be here considered more fully: especially, as I have not already submitted to the learned any remarks upon this subject. Jacob's age, at the time of his going to Laban, has (till very lately) been fixed, perhaps universally, at 77 years. But I think, it has been shewn by the learned *Mr Skinner*, in an excellent Dissertation (4°. 1765) that the number 77 cannot here be right.

Jacob was 130, when he went down (with 66 persons) into Egypt. Joseph had been then governor 10 years; and, when made governor, was 30: therefore Jacob could not be more than 90, at the birth of Joseph. Now, upon supposition that Jacob was 77, at going to Laban; and that he had no son till he was 85; and that he, with 11 sons, left Laban at 97: there will follow these, amongst other strange consequences, which are enumerated by Mr Skinner, p. 11 &c. 1. Though *Isaac* and *Esau* married at 40: *Jacob* goes, at 77, to look for a wife; and agrees to marry her 7 years after. 2. *Issachar* is born after the affair of the *mandrakes*; which *Reuben* finds, and brings home, when he (Reuben) was about 4 years old: that is, if Issachar was born *before* Joseph, agreeably to *Gen.* 30, 18 & 25. 3. *Judah* begets *Er*, at 13. For in the second of the following Tables, *Judah* is born in Jacob's year 88, and *Er* in 102. 4. *Er* marries at 9, and is destroyed for profligacy. *Er*, born in 102, marries in 111. See also *Gen.* 38, 7. 5. *Onan* marries at 8. For *Onan*, born in 103, marries in 111. 6. *Shelah*, being grown at 10, ought to be married. For *Shelah*, born in 104, is marriageable, but not married to Tamar, in 114. See *Gen.* 38, 14. 7. *Pharez* kept from marrying whilst young; yet has a son at 13. For *Pharez*, born in 115, had 2 sons, at going to Egypt, in 130. 8. *Esau goes to Ishmael*, and marries his daughter, after Jacob went to Laban at 77; though Ishmael died, when Jacob was 63 : see *Gen.* 16,16:. 25; 17 & 26: 28, 9. 9. If Jacob had no son, till he was 85; and if Joseph, the youngest except Benjamin, was born when his father was 90 : then the 11 sons, and Dinah, were born in 5 years. Lastly : if Jacob had no son till 85, and he went to Egypt at 130, with 66 persons; only 45 years are allowed for his family : whereas the larger sum of 65 years seems necessary, for the births of so many children and grandchildren. On this subject *Le Clerc* has pronounced —*Hisce in rebus occurrunt nodi, quos nemo hactenus solvit*; *neque porro, ut opinor, solvet*. But, upon the single principle of Mr Skinner, that Jacob went to Laban at 57 (instead of 77) these difficulties are solved. And it only remains to wish, that SOME AUTHORITY may be found to support this *Conjecture*, thus strongly founded on the *Exigentia loci*. The common opinion is formed, by reckoning back from the age of Joseph, when governor of Egypt, to the time of his birth ; and from *the* 20 *years*, which the Text says Jacob was with Laban. This number, Mr Skinner thinks, was originally 40. And I think, that the Heb. Text, *as it now stands*, confirms the Conjecture; and furnishes the very Authority, which is so much wanted.

After Jacob had served Laban 14 years, for his 2 wives; where was Jacob to reside? Esau was still living; and Jacob might well be afraid of returning to him, till more years of absence had disarmed his resentment: and had the death of Esau happened, Jacob would then have been secure. But let us also remember, that *Isaac* was still alive; and that Esau had determined to kill Jacob, whenever their father should die. It would therefore be no wonder, if Jacob should have desired to continue longer in Haran. And, to carry this point the more effectually, he might offer to take care of Laban's Cattle, and to live in his neighbourhood: upon such terms of advantage to Laban, as could not easily be withstood. Lastly: when the good effects to Laban from this connexion had been experienced, *without profit*, nay *with some losses*, to Jacob for 20 years; Jacob might naturally grow tired of thus assisting Laban, without providing for his own growing Family. Accordingly we find, that Jacob covenants with Laban, for 6 years of more close attendance, and service in Laban's own house; for which the wages were expressly settled. Agreeable to the preceding possibilities seems to have been the fact; Jacob living in Haran 40 years, and in this manner:

14 years, *in Laban's house*, a covenant-servant *for Rachel and Leah.*

20 —— in Laban's neighbourhood, as a Friend.

6 —— *in Laban's house*, a covenant-servant *for Cattle.*
—
40

Now the 20 concurrent years of *neighbourly assistance*, and the disjointed 20 of *covenant service*, seem both of them mentioned, and both of them distinguished guifhed, in the Hiftory itfelf. For, upon Laban's purfuit of Jacob, when Jacob is vindicating his paft behaviour, he mentions 20 *years* TWICE; which 2 fets of 20, if really different, make 40. Each mention of the 20 years is introduced with the word זה; which word, when repeated, is ufed in oppofition, or by way of diftinction: as when we fay *this and that, the one or the other.* Thus; *Exod.* 14, 20: *fo that the one came not near the other. Eccl.* 6, 5: *this hath more reft than the other.* And, with the 2 words at a great diftance; *Job* 21, 23: ONE *dieth —* — 25: *And* ANOTHER *dieth* &c. So here, in *Gen.* 31: at ver. 38 Jacob fays to Laban זה עשרים שנה אנכי עמך *During the* ONE *fet of* 20 *years, I was with thee* &c. meaning the time, in which he lived, not in Laban's houfe, but *in his neighbourhood;* not as a Servant, but *a Friend:* after he had ferved, in Laban's houfe, 14 years for his daughters, and before he ferved 6 years for his cattle. But then, as to the other 20; he tells Laban, at verfe 41, varying the phrafe very remarkably — זה לי עשרים שנה בביתך עבדתיך *During the other* 20 *years (* לי *)* FOR MYSELF (for my own benefit) IN THY HOUSE, *I ferved thee* 14 *years* — *and* 6 *years* &c. And, during this laft period, though only 6 years, he charges Laban with changing his *wages* 10 times. So that Jacob infifts upon having well earned his wages, through *the* 20 *years,* when he ferved for hire: but he makes a far greater merit of having, for *another* 20 *years,* affifted him without wages, and even with fome loffes; and therefore, with particular propriety, he reminds Laban of *that fet of* 20 *years* in the firft place.

The

THE OLD TESTAMENT. 31

The true *Chronology* of *Jacob* will be greatly elucidated, by the following Tables; taken, chiefly, from Mr Skinner. Table 1; on Jacob's being at Haran 40 years.

0	Jacob [and Esau] born.	
40	Esau marries 2 wives, Hittites. - - - -	*Gen.* 26, 34.
57	Jacob goes to Haran.	
58	Esau goes to Ishmael, and marries his daughter.	*Gen.* 28, 9.
63	Ishmael dies, aged 137. - - - - - -	*Gen.* 25, 17.
64	Jacob marries Leah and Rachel. -	*Gen* 29; 20, 21, 27, 28.
65	R E U B E N born, of Leah.	
66	S I M E O N ———	- - *Gen.* 29; 32—35.
67	L E V I ———	
68	J U D A H ———	
	Rachel, not bearing, gives Bilhah.	
69	*Dan* born, of Bilhah.	
71	*Naphtali* ———	
	Leah, not bearing, gives Zilpah.	
72	*Gad* born, of Zilpah.	*Gen.* 30; 6—24.
74	*Asher* ———	
78	Reuben, at 13, finds the Mandrakes.	
79	I S S A C H A R born, of Leah.	
81	Z E B U L U N ——— 82 Dinah.	
86	Judah, at 18, marries Shuah's daughter.	*
87	—— Er born —— 88 Onan —— 89 Shelah.	
91	J O S E P H born, of Rachel.	
6	- - - - - - - - - years service for cattle.	
97	Jacob comes, from Haran, to Succoth and Shalem.	
	Dinah defiled; and Shechemites destroyed.	
98	B E N J A M I N is born, and Rachel dies.	
103	Beriah, 4th son of Asher, born.	
105	Tamar married to Er —— 106 to Onan.	
108	Joseph, at 17, is carried to Egypt. - - - -	*Gen.* 37, 2.
109	Shelah, at 20, not given to Tamar.	
110	Pharez and Zarah born of Tamar, by Judah.	
110	Isaac dies, aged 180. - - - - - - - -	*Gen.* 35, 28.
121	Joseph, at 30, Governor of Egypt. - - -	*Gen.* 41, 46.
123	Beriah, at 20, marries.	
125	Heber —— 127 Malchiel —— born, to Beriah.	
128	Pharez, at 18, marries.	
129	Hezron —— 130 Hamul —— born, to Pharez.	
130	Benjamin, at 32, has 10 Sons.	
	Jacob goes to Egypt. - - - - - - - -	*Gen.* 47, 9.
147	—— and dies. - - - - - - - - - -	——— 28.

14 years service. 20 years assistance.

* Not recorded in order of time (*Gen.* 38) see Skinner, p. 23. See also his Note, p. 30, on *Keturah*; here mentioned already, in p. 22.

Table 2; on Jacob's being at Haran only 20 years.

0	Jacob [and Esau] born.	
40	Esau marries 2 wives, Hittites. - - - - - -	Gen. 26, 34.
63	Ishmael dies, aged 137. - - - - - - - -	Gen. 25, 17.
77	Jacob goes to Haran.	
84	—— marries Leah and Rachel. - - - -	Gen. 29; 20, 21, 27, 28.
85	REUBEN born, of Leah. ⎫	
86	SIMEON ——— ⎬	
87	LEVI ——— ⎬ - - - - Gen. 29; 32—35.
88	JUDAH ——— ⎭	
89	Dan born, of Bilhah. ⎫	
	Naphtali ——— ⎬	
	Gad born, of Zilpah. ⎬	
	Asher ——— ⎬ Gen. 30; 6—24.
	ISSACHAR, born of Leah. ⎬	
	ZEBULUN ——— and Dinah. ⎬	
91	JOSEPH born, of Rachel. ⎭	
97	Jacob returns from Haran.	
98	—— dwells in Succoth.	
99	—— comes to Shalem, and continues there 8 years.	
101	Judah marries Shuah's daughter.	
102	—— Er born —— 103 Onan —— 104 Shelah.	
106	Shechemites destroyed, by Simeon and Levi.	
107	BENJAMIN is born, and Rachel dies.	
108	Joseph sold, when 17. - - - - - - - - -	Gen. 37, 2.
111	Tamar married to Er, and immediately afterwards to Onan.	
114	Tamar's incest with Judah.	
115	Pharez and Zarah born, to Judah.	
120	Isaac dies, aged 180. - - - - - - - - -	Gen. 35, 28.
121	Joseph is made Governor of Egypt. - - - - -	Gen. 41, 46.
130	Jacob goes into Egypt. • - - - - - - -	Gen. 47, 9.
147	—— and dies. - - - - - - - - - -	28.

Our tranflation now is— 31, 38. THIS 20 YEARS HAVE I BEEN WITH THEE; *thy ewes and thy she-goats have not caft their young, and the rams of thy flock have I not eaten.* 39. *That which was torn of beafts I brought not unto thee; I bare the lofs of it: of my hand didft thou require it, whether ftolen by day or ftolen by night.* 40. *Thus I was: in the day the drought confumed me, and the frost by night; and my fleep departed from mine eyes.* 41. THUS HAVE I BEEN 20 YEARS, IN THY HOUSE: *I ferved thee 14 years for thy 2 daughters, and 6 years for thy cattle; and thou hast changed my wages ten times.*

The alteration, here recommended, is this. 31, 38. DURING THE ONE 20 YEARS, I WAS WITH THEE; *thy ewes and thy she-goats have not cast their young, and the rams* &c. &c. 41. DURING THE OTHER 20 YEARS, FOR MY SELF, IN THY HOUSE; *I served* &c. The same distinction is expressed, in 30, 29 — *Thou knowest how I have served thee, and how thy cattle was with me* i.e. how I behaved, during the time I was with thee, as thy servant; and how thy cattle fared, during the time they were with me, as thy friend.

It must not be omitted, that Arch-Bp *Usher* and Bp *Lloyd* ascribe sons to Jacob *very soon* after his coming to Laban; nay assert, that he was married almost as soon as he came to Haran: instead of waiting 7 years, as he most evidently did. And Mr *Jackson* allows, that *some* of the sons of Benjamin, who are expressly numbered, as going into Egypt with Jacob, might be born in Egypt! From such distresses, and such contradictions, does the distinction of *the 2 sets of* 20 *years* happily deliver us. *

Gen. 31, 51.

And Laban said to Jacob — behold this pillar, which I have cast betwixt me and thee. But, this pillar (not *cast,* but *set up*) was certainly set up by *Jacob*; for in ver. 45 we read — *And Jacob took a stone, and set it up for a pillar.* 'Tis therefore for the honour of 1 *Hebrew* and 1 *Samar.* MS, that they have preserved the true reading in ver. 51 — ירת *thou hast set up.*

* *Hoc temporis intervallo nemo concipere poterit tot res contingere potuisse.* Spinoza, Tractat. Theolog. Polit. 4°. Hamb. p. 116.

Gen. 31, 53.

The God of Abraham, and the God of Nahor [the God of their father] *judge betwixt us.* The words are here inverted; in the Heb. they stand thus: *The God of Abraham, and the God of Nahor, judge betwixt us,* [the God of their father.] Now the Heb. words אלהי אביהם *the God of their father* being still in the Samar. Text אלהי אברהם *the God of Abraham*; 'tis plain, they are an improper repetition, with the additional corruption of one letter afterwards: especially, as this repetition is not in the *Greek* version, and 2 *Heb. MSS* are without it. See *Diss.* 1; p. 368.

Gen. 36; 2 and 14.

In both these verses, the Heb. Text now tells us, that *Anah* was *Zibeon's* DAUGHTER: but, that *Anah* was his SON, is certain from ver. 24. *These are the children* (rather sons) *of Zibeon, Aiah and Anah:* (הוא *hic*) H E *was that Anah, who found* (מצא masculine) *the mules in the wilderness, as* HE *fed the asses of Zibeon* HIS *father.* In both the preceding verses, the *Sam.* Text reads *son*; as does the *Greek* version in both, and the *Syr.* in the first of them. See *Diss.* 1; p. 372.

Gen. 36, 16

The 2 first words in this verse, *duke Korah*, are interpolated. The verses 15 and 16 stand thus —— *These were dukes of the sons of Esau: the sons of Eliphaz, the first-born of Esau; duke Teman, duke Omar, duke Zepho, duke Kenaz:* Duke Korah, *duke Gatam, duke Amalek.* Now 'tis certain from ver. 4, that Eliphaz was Esau's son by *Adah*; and, from verses 11,12, that Eliphaz had but 6 sons: *Teman, Omar, Zepho,*

THE OLD TESTAMENT. 35

Gatam, Kenaz, and Amalek. 'Tis alſo certain, from ver. 5 and 14, that *Korah* was the ſon of *Eſau* (not of Eliphaz) by *Aholibamah*; and as ſuch, he is properly mentioned in ver. 18: *theſe are the ſons of Aholibamah, Eſau's wife*; *duke Jeuſh, duke Jaalam*, DUKE KORAH. 'Tis clear therefore, that ſome tranſcriber has improperly inſerted *duke Korah* in the 16th verſe; from which corruption both *the Samar. Text* and *its Verſion* are free. See *Diſſ.* 1; p. 376.

Gen. 36; 31—43.

In theſe 13 verſes are mentioned *the kings, which reigned in Edom*, BEFORE *any king reigned over Iſrael*: conſequently, this record was written *after* there had been *kings* in Iſrael. Not being therefore written by *Moſes*, theſe verſes ſeem evidently taken from 1 *Chron.* 1, 43—54: from whence, having been inſerted in the *Margin* of ſome very antient MS, here in *Geneſis*, they were afterwards taken into the *Text*. A fate, like this (as will be ſoon ſeen) has attended ſome other marginal inſertions, which now very improperly make parts of the Text. See *Gen. Diſſ.* p. 9.

Spinoza has quoted theſe verſes, as furniſhing one clear proof, that *the Pentateuch* was not written by MOSES — *Ex his luce meridianâ clarius apparet, Pentateuchon non a Moſe, ſed ab alio, et qui a Moſe multis poſt ſæculis vixit, ſcriptum fuiſſe.* See *Tractat. Theolog. Polit.* p. 108; 4º. Hamb. 1670.

Gen. 39, 9.

Bp *Kidder*, in his Commentary on this place, has the following excellent Note. Joſeph gives *two* reaſons for his refuſal: firſt, that, by conſenting to his Miſtreſs, he ſhould be *ungrateful to his Maſter*; and

C 2 ſecondly,

secondly, he should be *a great offender against God.* For (says he) the Heb. word (ואיך) which we render *how then*, is rather *and how*; which words usher in a distinct reason: whereas the present version is not so distinct, nor so agreeable to the original.

Gen. 41, 8.

We read in ver. 1; that *Pharaoh dreamed* — in 4; that *he awoke:* — in ver. 5; that *he dreamed the second time* — and in ver. 8; that *he told his* DREAM: *but none could interpret* THEM. In some places, much depends on the correction of a singular or plural number; which is not here pretended. But nothing can be more evident, than that the word חלמו *his dream* should be חלמיו *his* DREAMS: as it is in the Samar. Text, with the Syr. and Arab. versions.

Gen. 44, 5.

The speech, which Joseph commands his steward to make, is now very imperfect. *Wherefore have ye rewarded evil for good? Is not* THIS *it, in which my lord drinketh — ye have done evil in* so *doing.* In doing *what?* No crime is here specified; nor is any thing mentioned, by which the word *this* can properly be explained. The Greek version hath happily preserved the words, which are now wanting both in the Heb. and Sam. Texts — WHY HAVE YE STOLEN MY CUP, THE SILVER CUP? *Is it not* THAT, *in which my lord drinketh — ye have done evil in so doing.*

Let it be added: that there seems no authority in the original, for considering this cup as used by Joseph for *divination.* In ver. 5 the words * signify — *Is it not* THAT, *in which my lord drinketh? therefore he*

* והוא נחש ינחש בו

would certainly discover (or *find out*) *concerning it.* And in ver. 15 Joseph says: *What deed is this, that ye have done? Wot ye not, that such a man as I could certainly discover it?* † Taylor, in his Concordance, gives this verb as signifying — *to observe with great attention, in order to discover.* And Simonis, in his Lexicon, giving *fodit*, as the radical idea of this verb, says — *verba fodiendi etiam sensum habent explorandi.* And certainly *observing* in order to *discover*, and *digging* in order to *bring to light*, are the very ideas here necessary.

Gen. 47, 31.

And Israel bowed himself upon the bed's head. But, why is it rendered upon the head of the *bed?* The Epistle to the Hebrews says (11, 21) *upon the top of his* STAFF. It is also certain, that מטה signifies a *rod*, or *staff*, as well as a *bed*. And it should be here, and every where, matter of great care, to render the *Old* Testament like the *New*; provided that the Heb. words will bear it. See other remarks on this wrong version here, in *Hallet's* Note on *Heb.* 11, 21; in Peirce's Commentary.

Gen. 49; 5 — 8.

It would be attended with very many, and very great advantages; if all the *Poetical* parts of the Old T. were printed in short lines, *like Poetry:* as has been here done with the words of Lamech, in p. 16. Let the verses, now quoted, be compared with their *Prose-form*, as another specimen.

5. *Simeon and Levi are brethren; instruments of cruelty are* IN THEIR HABITATIONS. 6. *O my soul,*

† כי נחש ינחש איש אשר כמני †

come not thou into their secret; unto their assembly, mine honour, be not thou united: for in their anger they slew A MAN, *and in their self-will they* DIGGED DOWN A WALL. 7. *Cursed be their anger, for it was fierce; and their* WRATH, *for it was cruel: I will divide them in Jacob, and scatter them in Israel.* 8. *Judah, thou art he whom thy brethren shall praise;* &c.

5. *Simeon and Levi are brethren;*
 their very contracts *are instruments of violence.*
6. *O my soul, come not thou into their secret;*
 unto their assembly, mine honour, be not thou united.
 For in their anger they slew the men;
 and in their self-will they destroyed the princes.
7. *Cursed be their anger, for it was fierce;*
 and their confederacy, *for it was cruel.*
 I will divide them in Jacob;
 and I will scatter them in Israel.
8. *Judah!* thou! thee *shall thy brethren praise!*

[Note 1.]

Exod. 1, 21.

Great certainly was the increase of the Israelites, during their abode in Egypt; from 70 persons, to 600,000 men: during the term (as generally allowed) of 215 years. But, if any one should be disposed to pronounce this account incredible; let him well consider this chapter, which seems to describe

[Note.] As it is my wish, that the more learned Reader of these pages may not be interrupted unnecessarily, and that the less learned may not be discouraged by the sight of a multitude of words to him unknown; I have determined that the Notes, wherever *many* may be required, should be placed together at the end of this Volume: beginning in a series from this passage, marked [Note 1.]

the increase, not only as wonderful, but as arising from the particular favour of God. Ver. 7 says — *The children of Israel were fruitful, and increased abundantly, and multiplied, and waxed exceeding mighty; and the land was filled with them.* Ver. 12 — *The more they were afflicted, the more they multiplied and grew!* And here, in ver. 21, God is said to have multiplied them, and built them up, into *houses* and families — *And it came to pass (because, or for, the midwives feared God) that he made them houses.* For these words should be thus distinguished; agreeably to the remark of Bp Kidder, who says — *God made houses* (or families) *for* THEM i.e. for *the* ISRAELITES, and not for the *midwives*; the Heb. pronoun being here of the *masculine* gender. See *Ruth* 4, 11: and also *Gen.* 48, 4.

Exod. 2, 22.

And Zipporah bare Moses a son, and he called his name Gershom: for he said, I have been a stranger in a strange land. Then, in the Syr. Arab. and Vulg. versions, are these words, not now here in the Heb. text — *She also bare another son to Moses, and he called him Eliezer; saying: the God of my fathers hath been my helper, and delivered me from the hand of Pharaoh.* It is not probable, that this 2d chapter should originally mention the birth of *one son only*; when we read in 4, 20 — *And Moses took his wife, and his* SONS, *and returned to Egypt.* This 2d son is mentioned in 18, 4; but even there he is again preceded by the mention of *Gershom*, and also with the reason of that name.

Exod. 2, 25.

——— *and God had respect unto* . Our version adds *them*; but, if this were the true reading, a pronoun, so necessary here, could not have been omitted. The transposition of one letter removes the difficulty: and the word אליהם (instead of אלהים) after וידע makes a regular sense — *and God looked upon the children of Israel; and he was made known unto them.* So the Greek — και εγνωσθη αυτοις.*

Exod. 3, 18.

The Lord God of the Hebrews hath met with us. The words נקרה עלינו do not connect well, in this sense; nor is it likely, that God should command himself to be described to Pharaoh, by such a circumstance of *locality*. The presumption therefore is, that the verb was originally נקרא (*vocatur* super nos) as here in the Samar. text, supported by the Gr. and Vulg. versions, and by more than 20 Heb. MSS. And the truth of this reading is established by 5, 3; where the *Heb.* text itself has the verb with א, and yet our version there again is — *hath met with us*. The true sense is — *Say unto Pharaoh:* JEHOVAH, *the God of the Hebrews, is called upon us* i. e. is our God, *we are called by his name*, and are his servants; therefore *let us go, and sacrifice to* JEHOVAH *our God*.

Exod. 3, 22 and 11, 2.

The necessity of correcting our Translation is not more apparent from any single instance, than from the word *borrow*, in these places; because the reproach of *borrowing* what *was not repaid*, nor *intended to be repaid*, has been objected freely and frequently, not only to the *Israelites*, but also to GOD himself. As it will not be easy to answer this charge, thus stated; 'tis happy that the verb, here used, signifies to

---

* That the verb may be here in *Hophal*, see *Buxt. Thesaur.*

aſk, beg, and *pray for.* Certainly the Iſraelites might *aſk* and *beg* from their cruel oppreſſors ſome rewards for their ſufferings: and no doubt the Egyptians would be glad to *give* them the richeſt Preſents, in hopes of ſaving themſelves from the further vengeance of Heaven. Should any one ſtill contend for rendring the verb שאל *borrow*; let him try to render it ſo in *Pſal.* 122, 6 — *O borrow the peace of Jeruſalem:* and the verb is exactly the ſame in this, as in the former places. Lord Shaftesbury's reflection is this — *The wit of the beſt Poet is not ſufficient to reconcile us to the retreat of a Moſes, by the aſſiſtance of an Egyptian Loan.* Characteriſt. 1, 358. See alſo *Chriſtianity as old as the Creation:* p. 263, 349 &c. &c.

Exod. 4, 23.

Our tranſlators have greatly obſcured the ſenſe here, by inſerting the particle IF; which is not in the Text, and which perverts the whole meaning of this and the preceding verſes. Moſes is told here, in the beginning of his commiſſion, that he was to perform many wonders before Pharaoh, but without ſufficient effect; and that *at laſt,* after performing theſe wonders (doubtleſs at the time when he was to denounce *the deſtruction of the firſt-born*) THEN *thou ſhalt ſay unto Pharaoh, Thus ſaith the Lord: Iſrael is my ſon, my firſt-born. And* I SAID *unto thee, Let my ſon go, that he may ſerve me;* but THOU HAST REFUSED *to let him go: behold,* I SLAY *thy ſon, thy firſt-born.* Thus far all is now clear. But, if Moſes was to ſay this at laſt; *did* he ſay it? And if he ſaid it, when he denounced the deſtruction of the firſt-born; did he not ſo *record* it? Let the reader remember, that though such record is not now in the *Heb.* Text of *Exod.* 11, it is there preserved in the *Samar.* Pentateuch. See hereafter, at p. 46.

Exod. 5, 2.

Pharaoh said: *Who is the Lord — I know not the Lord.* It seems absolutely necessary here to express the word JEHOVAH. And, as these words of Pharaoh are in reply to Moses; 'tis plain, that Moses himself did not think it profane, to *pronounce* this sacred Name, even in the presence of a Heathen-King.

Exod. 6, 3.

I appeared unto Abraham, unto Isaac, and unto Jacob, by the name of GOD ALMIGHTY; *but by my name* JEHOVAH *was I not known to them.* The word *Jehovah* is found in *Gen.* 2, 4; and often in the same book afterwards. Moses affirms, that this name was used by *Eve:* 4, 1. He also affirms (12, 8) that *Abraham called upon the name of Jehovah:* and the first address to GOD, which Moses has recorded of Abraham, (15, 2) begins with this name. See, as to *Isaac* and *Jacob,* 27, 27 and 28, 13. Now, if we could suppose, that Moses in all these places wrote by a Prolepsis; and used a name known to himself, tho' not known to these earlier fathers: yet it must be granted, that *Abraham* was actually acquainted with this word; because (in 22, 14) he called the name of a place *Jehovah-jireh.* Observe also carefully, that the Heb. words here signify strictly thus: *and my name Jehovah was I not made known to them:* words, without sense. But if it be allowed, that the verb now *passive* is corrupted from the *active,* signifying *notum feci, manifestavi, probatum dedi* *— exactly

* הודעתי from נודעתי

expreffed by εδηλωσα in the *Greek* verfion, as well as in the *Syr.* and *Vulgat*; then there arifes this fenfe — that the Deity had often appeared to the Patriarchs as a GOD *of power, able to protect thofe who trufted in him*; but that he had not given to them any fignal proof, that he was JEHOVAH, *the one true* GOD, *the only felf-exiftent and eternal Being:* of which he was now about to make the moft illuftrious manifeftation, in his triumph over *all the Gods of Egypt. Exod.* 12, 12; 18, 11: *Num.* 33, 4. If thefe remarks are juft; the tranflation fhould be — *but my name* JEHOVAH *I did not make manifeft to them.* See *Exod.* 14, 18: 15; 3, 11: and 18, 11.

Exod. 6, 20.

And Amram took Jochebed to wife; and fhe bare him Aaron and Mofes. But, did fhe not alfo bare *Miriam?* So fays here the *Sam.* Pent. with the *Greek* and *Syr.* verfions: and fo, at leaft one *Heb. MS.* See *Gen. Diff.* p. 125.

Exod. chapters 7, 8, 9, 10, 11.

Within thefe 5 chapters are 7 very great differences between the *Heb.* and *Samar.* Pentateuchs; relating to the *Speeches*, which denounced 7 (out of the 10) judgments on the Egyptians: fc. *Waters into blood, frogs, flies, murrain, hail, locufts,* and *deftruction of the firft-born.* The *Heb.* Text gives the Speeches, concerning thefe judgments, *only once*, at each; but the *Samar.* gives each Speech TWICE. In the Heb. we have the Speeches concerning the 5 firft, as in command from GOD to Mofes, *without reading that Mofes delivered them*: and concerning the 2 last, as delivered by Moses to Pharaoh, *without reading that* GOD *had commanded them*. Whereas in the Samar. we find every Speech twice: GOD *commands Moses to go and speak thus, or thus, before Pharaoh — Moses goes, and denounces the judgment — Pharaoh disobeys*, and *the judgment takes place*. All this is perfectly regular; and exactly agreeable to the double Speeches of *Homer*, in very antient times. I have already (*Diss.* 1; p. 380—394) treated this subject at large; and have not the least doubt, but that the Heb. Text now wants many words, in each of the 7 following places: ch. 7, between verses 18 and 19 — end of ch. 7 — ch. 8, between 19 and 20 — ch. 9, between 5 and 6 — again, between 19 and 20 — ch. 10, between 2 and 3 — and ch. 11, at verses 3, 4.

The Reader will permit me to refer him (for all the words thus omitted) to *my own Edition of the Hebrew Bible*, where the whole differences are most clearly described. As this is a matter of very extensive consequence; I cannot but observe here, that the present *Heb.* Text of *Exod. ch.* 11 did formerly, and does still, appear to me to furnish a *demonstration* against itself; in proof of the *double* speech being formerly recorded there, as it is now in the *Samaritan*. And some very learned men have confessed the impossibility of explaining this Chapter, without the assistance of the *Samar.* Pentateuch. I shall now give this important chapter, as I presume it stood originally; distinguishing by *Italics* all such words, as are added to, or differ from, our present Translation. And before this chapter must be placed the 2 last verses of the chapter preceding.

Exod. 10, 28. And Pharaoh said unto him, Get thee from me, take heed to thyself, see my face no more; for in that day thou seest my face thou shalt die. 29. And Moses said, Thou hast spoken well; I will see thy face again no more.

EXOD. XI.

Heb. *and present Version.*

1. And the Lord said unto Moses, Yet will I bring one plague more upon Pharaoh, and upon Egypt, afterwards he will let you go hence: when he shall let you go, he shall surely thrust you out hence altogether.

2. Speak now in the ears of the people; and let every man BORROW of his neighbour, and every woman of her neighbour, *jewels* of silver, and *jewels* of gold.

3. *And* THE LORD GAVE *the* people favour in the sight of the Egyptians.

Samar. *and new Version.*

1. THEN Jehovah said unto Moses, Yet will I bring one plague more upon Pharaoh, and upon Egypt; *and* afterwards he will send you out hence: when he shall send you away, he will surely drive you hence altogether.

2. Speak now in the ears of the people; and let every man ASK of his neighbour, and every woman of her neighbour, *vessels* of silver, and *vessels* of gold, *and raiment.*

3. *And* I WILL GIVE *this* people favour in the sight of the Egyptians, *so that they shall give them what they ask.*

4. *For about midnight I will go forth into the midst of the land of Egypt.*

5. *And every first-born in the land of Egypt shall die; from the first-born of Pharaoh, who sitteth upon his throne, unto the first-born of the maid servant that is behind the mill: and even unto the first-born of every beast.*

6. *And there shall be a great cry thro' all the land of Egypt; such, as there was none like it, nor shall be like it any more.*

Hebr.

Moreover, THE MAN MOSES was very great, in the land of Egypt, in the fight of Pharaoh's fervants, and in the fight of the people.

4. And Mofes faid; thus faith the Lord: About midnight will I go out into the midft of Egypt.

5. And all the firft-born in the land of Egypt fhall die, from the firft-born of Pharaoh, that fitteth upon his throne, even unto the firft-born of the maid-fervant that is behind the mill: and all the firft-born of beafts.

6. And there fhall be a great cry thro' all the land of Egypt, fuch as there was none like it, nor fhall be like it any more.

Samar.

7. *But againſt any of the children of Iſrael ſhall not a dog move his tongue; againſt man, or even againſt beaſt: that thou mayeſt know, that Jehovah doth put a difference between the Egyptians and Iſrael.*

8. And THOU ALSO SHALT be greatly honoured, in the land of Egypt; in the fight of Pharaoh's fervants, and in the fight of the people.

9. THEN *Moſes ſaid unto Pharaoh; Thus ſaith Jehovah: Iſrael is my ſon, my firſt-born; and I ſaid unto thee, Let my ſon go, that he may ſerve me.*

10. *But, thou haſt refuſed to let him go; behold, Jehovah ſlayeth thy ſon, thy firſt-born.*

11. And Mofes faid; thus faith Jehovah: About midnight will I go forth into the midft *of the land* of Egypt.

12. And every firft-born in the land of Egypt fhall die; from the firft-born of Pharaoh, who fitteth upon his throne, unto the firft-born of the maid-fervant that is behind the mill; and even unto the firft-born of every beaft.

13. And there fhall be a great cry thro' all the land of Egypt; fuch, as there was none like it, nor fhall be like it any more.

Hebr.

7. But against any of the children of Israel shall not a dog move his tongue, against man or beast: that ye may know, how that the Lord doth put a difference, between the Egyptians and Israel.

8. And all these thy servants shall come down unto me, and bow down themselves unto me, saying, Get thee out, and all the people that follow thee; and after that I will go out.

And he went out from Pharaoh in great anger.

9. And the Lord said unto Moses, Pharaoh *shall* not hearken unto you: that my wonders may be multiplied in the land of Egypt.

10. And Moses and Aaron did all these wonders before Pharaoh: and the Lord hardened Pharaoh's heart, so that he would not let the children of Israel go out of his land.

Samar.

7. But against any of the children of Israel shall not a dog move his tongue; against man, or even against beast: that thou mayest know, that Jehovah doth put a difference, between the Egyptians and Israel.

15. And all these thy servants shall come down to me, and bow down themselves to me, saying; Go forth, thou and all the people that follow thee: and then I will go forth.

16. THEN went he forth from before Pharaoh, in great indignation.

17. And Jehovah said unto Moses; Pharaoh *doth* not hearken unto you, that my wonders may be multiplied in the land of Egypt.

18. And Moses and Aaron performed all these wonders before Pharaoh; but Jehovah hardened Pharaoh's heart, so that he would not let the children of Israel go out of his land.

The Reader has now the whole of this Chapter before him. When therefore he has first read the 28th and 29th verses of the preceding chapter; and has then observed, with due surprize, the confusion of the *Heb.* Text

48   *Remarks on select Passages in*

Text in chapter XI: he will be prepared to acknowledge, with due gratitude, the regularity and truth of the *Samar.* Text, thro' these many and very considerable differences.

Exod. 9, 15.

For now I WILL STRETCH OUT *my hand, that I may smite thee and thy people with* PESTILENCE. But, was a *Pestilence* one of the plagues upon Egypt? Only 10 are recorded: of which 7 have been already enumerated; and the other 3 are *Lice, Boils,* and *Darkness.* Was there then *no Pestilence,* which cut off *Pharaoh* &c? And, if not; how are we to conceive of the Divine Menace, thus positively denounced, yet not at all inflicted? This difficulty, and it is not a small one, can only (I presume) be solved properly, by observing — that the preter verb שלחתי, now rendered *I will stretch out,* ought to be rendered here I MIGHT HAVE *stretched out — Verily now I* MIGHT *have stretched out my hand, and smitten thee and thy people with Pestilence* (I *might* have cut you off, on a sudden, by pestilence) *but I have raised thee up* (made thee to stand) *in order to shew* (still more perfectly) *my Power; that my name may be declared thro' all the earth.* See ch. 11, 9.

That the circumstances of a verb, usually preter or future, may be thus qualified by *might, would, should* &c, appears from hence. In *Gen.* 12, 19 we read ואקח אתה *so I* MIGHT HAVE *taken her.* And *I said, I* WOULD *scatter — I* WOULD *make to cease — left their adversaries* SHOULD *behave — lest they* SHOULD *say:* see these 4 futures, in *Deut.* 32; 26, 27.

Exod.

Exod. 15; 1—21.

This triumphant Ode was sung by *Moses* and *the Sons of Israel*. And *the Women*, headed by *Miriam*, *answered* the men, by repeating the 2 first lines of the Song, altering only the first word: which 2 lines were probably sung more than once, as *A Chorus*.

The conclusion of this Ode seems very manifest. And yet, tho' the antient Jews had sense enough to write this Song differently from Prose; and tho' their authority has prevailed, even to this day, in *this*, and 3 other Poems in the Old T. [*Deut.* 32, *Jud.* 5, and 2 *Sam.* 22] still expressed by them as Poetry: yet have these Critics carried their ideas of the Song here to the end of ver. 19. The reason, why the same has been done by others, probably is — they thought, that the particle כִּי *For*, which begins verse 19, necessarily connected it with the preceding Poetry. But this difficulty is removed, by translating כִּי *When*: especially if we take verses 19, 20, 21 as being a *prose* explanation of *the manner*, in which this Song of triumph was performed. For these 3 verses say — that the *Men-singers* were *answered* in Chorus by *Miriam and the Women*, accompanying their words with musical instruments —— " *When* the horse of " Pharaoh *had gone* into the sea, and the Lord *had* " *brought* the sea upon them: *and* Israel *had passed*, " on dry land, in the midst of the sea: *Then* Mi- " riam took a timbrel, and all the women went out " after her with timbrels and dances; and Miriam " (with the women) *answered them* [לָהֶם the men] " (by way of Chorus) in the words *O sing ye* &c."
That this Chorus was sung *more than once*, is thus stated

stated by Bp Lowth — *Maria, cum mulieribus, virorum choro* IDENTIDEM *succinebat.* Prælect. 19.

I shall now give what appears to me to be an exact Translation of this whole Song.

MOSES. *Part* 1.

1. I will sing to JEHOVAH, for he hath triumphed gloriously;
the horse and his rider hath he thrown into the sea.

2. My strength, and my song, is JEHOVAH;
and he is become to me for salvation:
this is my God, and I will celebrate him;
the God of my father, and I will exalt him.

3. JEHOVAH is mighty in battle! } Perhaps a Chorus,
JEHOVAH is his name! } sung by *the Men*.

Chorus, by *Miriam and the Women*;
Perhaps sung first in this place.

O sing ye to JEHOVAH, *for he hath triumphed gloriously!*
the horse and his rider hath he thrown into the sea.

MOSES. *Part* 2.

4. Pharaoh's chariots, and his host, hath he cast into the sea;
and his chosen captains are drowned in the red sea.

5. The depths have covered them, they went down;
(they sank) to the bottom, as a stone.

6. Thy right hand, JEHOVAH, is become glorious in power;
thy right hand, JEHOVAH, dasheth in pieces the enemy.

7. And, in the greatness of thine excellence, thou overthrowest them that rise against thee;
thou sendest forth thy wrath, which consumeth them as stubble:

8. Even at the blast of thy displeasure, the waters are gathered together:
the floods stand upright, as an heap:
congealed are the depths, in the very heart of the sea.

O sing ye to JEHOVAH &c. Chorus, by *the Women*.

MOSES. *Part* 3.

9. The enemy faid : " *I will purfue, I fhall overtake;*
" *I fhall divide the fpoil, my foul fhall be fatiated with them:*
" *I will draw my fword, my hand fhall deftroy them.*"

10. Thou didft blow with thy wind, the fea covered them; they fank, as lead, in the mighty waters.

11. Who is like thee, among the gods, O JEHOVAH? who is like thee, glorious in holinefs!

12. Fearful in praifes! performing wonders! thou ftretcheft out thy right hand, the earth fwalloweth them!

13. Thou, in thy mercy, leadeft the people, whom thou haft redeemed;
thou, in thy ftrength, guideft to the habitation of thy holinefs!

O fing ye to JEHOVAH &c.   Chorus, by *the Women.*

MOSES. *Part* 4.

14. The nations have heard, and are afraid; forrow hath feized the inhabitants of Paleftine.

15. Already are the dukes of Edom in confternation; and the mighty men of Moab, trembling hath feized them: all the inhabitants of Canaan do faint.

16. Fear and dread fhall fall upon them; thro' the greatnefs of thine arm, they fhall be ftill as a ftone:

17. Till thy people, JEHOVAH, pafs over;   [Jordan] till the people pafs over, whom thou haft redeemed.

18. Thou fhalt bring them and plant them, in the mount of thine inheritance:
the place for thy reft, which thou, JEHOVAH, haft made; the fanctuary, JEHOVAH, which thy hands have eftablifhed.

Grand Chorus; by ALL.
JEHOVAH SHALL REIGN FOR EVER AND EVER!

[Note 2: fee pag. 38.]

Exod. 16, 15.

They said one to another, It is manna: for they wist not what it was. Very strange, and unintelligible! Let the words then be translated literally thus —— *They said one to another, What is this? for they wist not what it was.* From this question מן *Man* (which in Chaldee now signifies *what*) the Manna afterwards took its name. See the Greek version Τι εςι τȣτο. And Josephus says —— " *Man*, secundum nostram lo-
" cutionem, interrogationis particula est." L. 3, c. 1.

Exod. 18; 5—7.

*5. And Jethro came unto Moses into the wilderness —
6. And he said unto Moses, I thy father in law Jethro am come unto thee — 7. And Moses went out to meet his father in law* &c.

The great impropriety of Jethro speaking to Moses before he met him, and of Moses going out to meet Jethro after he had been spoken to by Jethro, will convince us, that the word אני *I* is corrupted from a word very similar in sound הנה *behold*; agreeably to the Greek and Syr. versions. And tho' the *Samar.* Text is *printed* with the same corruption here as the Hebrew; almost all the Samar. *MSS* read here הנה. As to the first verb, in ver. 6; see *Gen.* 10, 9 and 2 *Kings* 5, 4. The whole difficulty is therefore removed by rendering ver. 6 —*And it was told Moses; Behold, thy father in law Jethro is come* &c.

Exod. 19, 15.

Verse 12th strictly forbids the people, from coming near and touching mount Sinai; which mount then burnt with FIRE. The words therefore in ver. 15[*]

[*] אל תגשו אל אשה

seem rather to signify — *come not near unto the* FIRE: especially, as the phrase *ne appropinquetis ad* mulierem (sing.) is not at all probable. But *the fire* is on this occasion* spoken of so very emphatically; that we are naturally led, either to consider אשה here as האש transposed, or to say (with *Simonis Lexicon*) אשה *fæm. idem quod masc.* אש *ignis.* †

Exod. 26; 35   36.

Here are omitted 10 verses; which are improperly inserted at the beginning of ch. 30, in all the *Heb.* copies: but in all the *Samar.* copies they are found here, in their proper place. These 10 verses relate to *the Altar of Incense*; and the transposition of them will be soon evident. The chief articles of furniture for the Tabernacle were 6 — in *the Holy of Holies* was THE ARK, having on it *the Mercy Seat*; in *the Holy place* were THE TABLE FOR THE SHEW-BREAD, THE GOLDEN CANDLESTICK, and THE ALTAR OF IN-CENSE: and without, in the Court, were *the Altar for burnt-offerings,* and *the Laver for washing.* In this order are these 6 articles commanded, and described, in the *Samar.* Text; and, in the same order are they enumerated afterwards, no less than 6 times, in the *Heb.* Text itself: ch. 31, 7—11: 35, 12—16: 37, 1 to 38, 8: 39, 35—39: 40; 3—7: and 40, 21—30. Yet in the present Heb. Text, Moses here first describes *the Ark* — then *the Table* and *Candle-stick*, in the Holy place — then (without mentioning *the Altar of Incense*) goes out into the Court, de-

---

* See *Deut.* 5; 4, 5, 22—25.

† So, among many other instances — אבר & אברה *ala*, אור *ala*, & אורה *lux*, אמץ & אמצה *robur*, אמר & אמרה *sermo*. Buxt.

scribing *the Altar for burnt-offerings* — then returns into the Holy place, and describes *the Altar of Incense* — and then goes out again into the Court, to *the Laver for washing*. If Moses cannot be supposed so vague, and desultory, in his description; nor so inconsistent with himself, in the 6 other places: then the Transposition, which here certainly obtains, will be ascribed, not to the Samaritan, but to the Heb. Text. Consequently *the* 10 *verses* are to be brought back from chapter 30; and inserted in this chapter, as their true and original station.

This dislocated Passage, consisting of 10 Verses, which contain 126 words, might antiently fill 1 page or 1 side of a leaf of vellum. And this odd Leaf, when the parts of an old Roll (separated by time or accident) were to be again sewed together, might be fastened in improperly i.e. *after* 2, 3, 4 or any other pieces, which ought to have *followed* it. These verses now make 25 lines, in one of the oldest Samar. MSS. And 'tis remarkable, that 25 is the number of the lines also at *Job* 40; where the first 14 verses are a similar dislocation. Both these large Transpositions must have been made very early: and this in the Pentateuch happened before the Time of the Greek Version; unless that Version has been altered, *in conformity to the corrupted Hebrew*. As to other Transpositions: see, under *Heb. Text. transpos.* in the Index to my *Gen. Differtation*; and also *Hallet's Notes*, vol. 1, p. 98, 119: vol. 2, p. 91.

'Tis observable, that the Heb. Pentateuch is divided into 54 *Sections*; the 20th of which ends with these 10 verses, in the 30th chapter. So that these verses, being omitted at their proper place, were joined on at the end of the 20th section, in some very antient MS, from which one or more copies were taken. And one of these, happening to belong to some eminent *Synagogue*, or renowned *Rabbi*, has from thence derived sufficient authority to mislead (in this instance) all the modern copies of the Heb. Text, and likewise the Antient Versions.

Exod. 30, 6.

The progress of error in this place is remarkable. The great error has been noted already; which is, that the first 10 Verses, now here, belong to chapter 26. The 2d error is, that here, in the 6th of these 10 verses, 6 words have been carelesly expressed twice; tho' the 5th of them has been (in the repetition) since omitted, except in a few MSS. But the chief circumstance is, that the word הפרכת *the vail* is changed to a word very different in sense, though consisting of the same letters (with *one* transposed) הכפרת *the mercy-seat*: and yet here 4 MSS have the word rightly expressed, that is, the same as *the vail*. These words, here repeated, are not in the *Sam.* Text, nor in the Gr. and Ar. versions; and 18 Heb. MSS confirm these authorities. It must also be observed, that by this *corruption of a corruption* (the whole repetition, and the subsequent alteration of this one word) the *Heb.* Text is now made to contradict *itself*, as well as the *Epistle to the Hebrews*. For it places *the Altar of Incense* BEFORE (לפני *in the presence of*) *the Mercy-Seat*; and if so, it must have been *in the Holy of Holies*: whereas, the Altar of Incense was attended *every day*, and yet the Holy of Holies was entered but *once a year*.

Exod. 33, 7.

And Moses took the tabernacle, *and pitched it without the camp.* But, the Tabernacle was not yet made: the preparation for making it being set forth in chapters 35, 36 &c; and in ch. 39, 32 we read — *Thus was all the work of the Tabernacle finished.* And besides, the word for *a Tabernacle* (משכן) is very different from (אהל) the word here used, which signifies *a Tent:* consequently, this word is wrongly translated here, and in 8 other places which follow in this one chapter.

Num. 2, 14.

— *the captain of the sons of Gad shall be Eliasaph the son of* REUEL. 'Tis strange, that the Jewish Rabbies could permit so many of their antient copies to continue corrupted by so gross a blunder, as REUEL for *Deuel:* and it would be still more strange, if Christians did not all agree in correcting it. In 1, 14 it is *Eliasaph the son of* DEUEL. In 7, 42 and 10, 20 it is also *Eliasaph the son of* DEUEL. It is likewise DEUEL here (2, 14) in the Sam. Text, with the Ar. and Vulg. versions; to which is to be added the authority of 80 Heb. MSS: and in about 50 of these MSS the *D* seems altered to *R,* in conformity to the corrupted reading of the Masorets. If then no man of sense could bear to read *Remosthenes* for Demosthenes, or *Cicedo* for Cicero; let *Reuel* be here corrected to *Deuel.*

Num. 12, 3.

Now the man Moses was very MEEK, *above all the men which were upon the face of the earth.* This verse strikes almost every reader with surprize; partly on its own account, partly from its connection. That

Moses was *meek above all men,* if true, was not at all likely to have been recorded by *himself.* It is still less likely to have been said by one, who has recorded himself as a man of *great warmth.* See Exod. 2; 11—14: 5, 22: 11, 8: 32; 19, 22: Num. 11, 13 and 16, 15. And as to Num. 20; 10—12: see *Pf.* 106; 32, 33. But, if Moses had been in fact *the meekest of men;* the record of such a quality seems to have no connection with the Context here. The preceding verses set forth, that *Miriam and Aaron* exalted themselves as *rivals to Moses;* boasting, that *God had spoken* by *them* likewise. And in the verses following GOD declares, that he *revealed himself* to Moses *more* than to any other Prophet. It therefore seems necessary to consider this 3d verse, as connected with the Divine Communications; and to translate the words thus — *Now the man Moses gave forth more answers* (from GOD) or *was* HIGHLY FAVOURED WITH ANSWERS, above all the men which were upon the face of the earth —— *erat responsor eximius* (ענו מאד) *præ omni homine* &c. Such is the excellent version of this place, in a Thesis under the very learned *Albert Schultens,* in 1725.* This author refers to *Juchasin;* where *Ezra* is called ענוי כמשה *responsor similis Mosi.* And 'tis very remarkable, that 16 MSS read עניו here, agreeably to the word in *Juchasin.* Spinoza (cap. 8, p. 107) quotes this verse (*Num.* 12, 3) as one proof, that Moses did not write the Pentateuch.

Num. 14, 34.

— *and ye shall know my breach of promise.* 'Tis no wonder, that such an expression as *breach of promise,*

* Sylloge Dissert. 4°. Leid. 1772; pag. 145—153.

when spoken of GOD, should be objected to by the Deists. In anfwer to *Christianity as old as the Creation*, Dr Waterland has thefe excellent obfervations — "*My breach of promife* is a harfh tranflation, " and merely conjectural, not warranted by the Heb. " original. Some of our older Eng. tranflations had " a jufter rendering. Matthewes's Bible, of 1537, " has, 𝔓𝔢 𝔰𝔥𝔞𝔩𝔩 𝔣𝔢𝔩𝔢 𝔪𝔶 𝔳𝔢𝔫𝔤𝔢𝔞𝔲𝔫𝔠𝔢. And the Great " Bible, of 1539, 𝔓𝔢 𝔰𝔥𝔞𝔩𝔩 𝔨𝔫𝔬𝔴𝔢 𝔪𝔶 𝔡𝔦𝔰𝔭𝔩𝔢𝔞𝔰𝔲𝔯𝔢. — " The Seventy have here τον θυμον της οργης μȣ. " Jerom has *ultionem meam*. And Le Clerc acquief" ces in this rendering: *Ye shall know my vengeance.*" The proper verfion therefore will be — *and ye shall know my vengeance*, or *my indignation*. The above quotation from Dr Waterland is taken from his *Scripture Vindicated*; part 2, p. 30. And to this quotation I shall here add another; from his 3d part, pag. 64 — *This tranflation I offer, with fubmiffion, to better judgments; if ever a proper time should come for revifing, and correcting, our laft Eng. tranflation: which, tho' a very good one, and upon the whole fcarce inferior to any, yet is undoubtedly capable of very great improvements.*

Num 16, 1.

Now Korah, the fon of Izhar, the fon of Kohath, the fon of Levi, and Dathan and Abiram, the fons of Eliab, and On, the fon of Peleth, fons of Reuben, took

Our Eng. verfion adds *men*. But fo material a word cannot be underftood; and indeed, the whole turn of the verfe calls for a different conftruction. A short attention to the hiftory, and a few critical remarks, will clear up the difficulties attending this verfe at prefent. *Korah* was certainly at the head of

THE OLD TESTAMENT. 59

this rebellion: see verses 5, 12, 16, 22, 40, 49: 27, 4 &c. It is also certain, that the verb, which is singular and begins the verse, signifies to *take* (or *take in*) in the sense of *alluring, winning,* or *gaining by persuasion:* see *Prov.* 6, 25 and 11, 30. The beginning of the verse therefore should be: *Now Korah — won over both Dathan and Abiram.* One thing, which has kept this sense of the passage out of sight, has been the conjunction (*and*) before *Dathan*; which (agreeably to Bp Patrick) is here rendered *both:* as it is rendered now, in *Num.* 9, 14; *Neh.* 1, 6; & *Pf.* 76, 6. Note also, that *Eliab* being a *Reubenite* (*Deut.* 11, 6) as well as *Peleth*; the latter word *sons* is here rightly plural, because it refers to these two. And the whole verse may be rendered thus. *Now Korah, the son of Izhar, the son of Kohath, the son of Levi, won over both Dathan and Abiram, the sons of Eliab, and also On, the son of Peleth, sons of Reuben.*

Num. 20, 10.

And Moses said unto them: Hear now, ye rebels; must we fetch you water out of this rock? The crime of Moses, which was certainly great, in what he said at this time, does not appear clearly from this version. But, as GOD had told Moses, in ver. 8, that *he* (Moses) *should bring forth water out of the rock* ; and, as GOD says, in ver. 12, that *Moses believed him not, to sanctify him before the children of Israel:* it is necessary, that the words in this 10th verse do express Moses as *not believing,* that he could thus bring forth the water. And it is happy therefore, that the words may be rendered — CAN *we fetch you water out of this rock?* Other verbs, in the future tense, are now rendered alfo by *can*, in the following places; *Gen.* 39, 9 : 41, 38 : *Job* 6, 6 : 22, 2 and 13 : *Pf.* 89, 6 : *Jer.* 2, 32 : *Amos* 3, 3 and 5.

Numbers, chapter 21.

This one Chapter has feveral very confiderable difficulties; and fome Verfes, as now tranflated, are remarkably unintelligible. A true ftate of this Chapter is not however to be defpaired of; and it has in it fome circumftances, which merit more than common attention. It contains the hiftory of the laft part of the Travels of the Ifraelites, in their way to the promifed Land : beginning with them at *mount Hor*, the 34th encampment; and concluding with them, as in their 42d and laft encampment; near Jordan, in the country which they had acquired by conqueft over Sihon king of the Amorites.

It begins with faying — that *king Arad the Canaanite, who dwelt in the fouth* (in the land of Canaan — *Num.* 33, 40) attacked Ifrael, and was defeated; and that *Ifrael deftroyed their cities :* and that, after deftroying thefe *Canaanite cities*, and confequently after being in a Part of *Canaan*, a part of the very country they were going to, on the *weft* of the *Dead* Sea, they returned towards the *Red* Sea; and near the *Eaftern* tongue or gulph of the Red Sea, on the *South of Edom*, marched round *Edom* to the *Eaft* of the *Dead* Sea, in order to enter Canaan from the *Eaft* fide of *Jordan !*

This furprizing reprefentation of fo vaft and dangerous a March, quite unneceffarily performed, is owing to 2 circumftances. The firft is (21, 1) — the Canaanites heard, that Ifrael was coming by *the way of the spies* — meaning, by the way *the spies* went *from Kadesh-Barnea* into Canaan. But this being impossible, because Israel had now marched from *Meribah-Kadesh* to *mount Hor*, beyond *Ezion-geber*; and were turning round *Edom*, to the South-East: it is happy, that the word rendered *spies*, in our version, is in the Greek a proper name (*Atharim*) which removes that difficulty. And the other difficulty (verses 2, 3) is removed by the Greek version likewise: according to which, the vow made, with the fact subsequent, does not signify *destroying* the Canaanite cities, but *devoting them to destruction* at some future time. See Wall's Crit. Notes.

This chapter proceeds, with saying — that after defeating the Canaanites at *mount Hor*; they journeyed *from mount Hor, by the way of the red sea* (in the road from *Ammon*, *Midian* &c: to the *Eastern* gulph of the red sea) *to compass the land of Edom* — that, on their murmuring for want both of Bread and of Water, they were punished by fiery serpents — after which, they marched to *Oboth*, and thence to *Ije-abarim*, in the *wilderness east of Moab*. The encampments of the Israelites, amounting to 42, are recorded all together, in historical succession, in ch. 33: where *Ije-abarim* is the 38th — *Dibongad* 39 — *Almon-Diblathaim* 40 — *mountains of Abarim* 41 — and *the plains of Moab*, by Jordan, 42. This regular detail in ch. 33 has occasioned great perplexity, as to ch. 21: where, after the stations at *Oboth* and *Ije-abarim*, in verses 10 and 11, we have in ver. 19 and 20 the words *Mattanah*, *Nahaliel* and *Bamoth*; which are usually considered as the proper names of 3 places, but widely different from the 3 proper names after *Ije-abarim*, in the Catalogue at ch. 33.

But there is, in reality, no inconfiftence here. In the plain and hiftorical catalogue (ch. 33) the words are ftrictly *the proper names of the 3 places:* but here the words *Mattanah, Nahaliel* and *Bamoth* follow fome lines of Poetry, and feem to form a continuation of the Song. They evidently exprefs figurative and poetical ideas. The verbs *journeyed from*, and *pitched in*, are not found here; though neceffary to profe-narration: fee ver. 10 and 11 here, and ch. 33. Laftly: verfe the 20th (in this 21ft chapter) ufually fuppofed to exprefs *the laft encampment*, does not. *Pifgah* fignifies *a hill*; and the Ifraelites could not encamp on the top of any fingle hill, fuch as this is defcribed. Balak took Balaam to *the top of Peor*, which *looketh toward Jefhimon* (23, 28) which *Peor* undoubtedly was in *Moab*. He took him to another hill in *Moab*; when he took him (23, 14) to the top of *Pifgah*, in *the field of Zophim*. And if the Pifgah or hill, in 21,20, was in the country of *Balak*; it could not point out *the laft encampment*, which was not in Balak's country, but *North of Arnon*.

The word *Mattanah* probably alludes to a place diftinguifhed by fome *Gift* or bleffing from GOD. Fagius fays — *Nomen loci, ab eventu* AQUARUM *quas Dominus ibi dedit, fic appellati*; * *nam fignificat* DONUM. *Nahaliel* † is *torrentes Dei* i.e. Streams particularly feafonable or falutary. And *Bamoth* ‡ (ver. 28) may point out any high places, of fignal benefit, in the country of *Moab*; or it may anfwer to *the laft ftation but one*, which was *the mountains of Abarim*. If therefore thefe words were meant to exprefs poetically fome eminent bleffing; what bleffing

* מתנה ‎ † נחליאל ‎ ‡ במות

was so likely to be then celebrated, as *copious streams of Water?* And, after they had wandered, near 40 years, thro' many a barren desart; and after (comp. *Deut.* 8, 15) having passed thro' *that great and terrible* WILDERNESS, wherein were *fiery serpents* and DROUGHT, where there was *no water:* 'tis no wonder, they should shout for joy at finding *Water in plenty*; and finding it almost on the banks of *Arnon*, the last river they were to pass, in the way to their last station, east of Jordan. No wonder, they should sing, in poetic rapture — that, after *the wilderness* was (*Mattanah*) the GIFT of GOD; meaning *the great Well* in Moab, dug by public authority — and no wonder, that, after such a *Gift*, there were (*Nahaliel*) *blessed streams*; by which they passed, till they came to (*Bamoth*) the high places, from which perhaps these streams descended. And the Thanksgiving ends, where the Blessing was no longer wanted; on their coming down into *the Valley*, along the banks of Arnon, which was then the North-Boundary of Moab.

The Israelites had spent no less than 38 years, in coming from *Kadesh-Barnea*, to their encampment north of *Zared*. Here, at this 40th station, they were commanded to pass thro' Moab, by עָר *Ar*, the chief city; but were not to stop, till they came to *the valley* on the south of Arnon. At this last station but one they probably continued no longer, than was necessary for *sending Messengers to Sihon* king of the Amorites at Heshbon, and receiving his answer. They then crossed the Arnon; and, having vanquished *Sihon* and *Og*, took possession of the 42d and last encampment.

This one chapter has 3 pieces of Poetry; either fragments, or compleat. And Poetry, feldom found in an hiftorical narrative, may be here accounted for —from the exuberance of Joy, which muft have affected thefe wearied Travellers, when arriving thus happily near their Journey's End. What occurs firft is in ver. 14; and has often been called *the fragment of an old Amorite Song*. But it may have been *Amorite* or *Moabite*, or *either* or *neither*, for the fubject-matter of it; as it is generally underftood: if indeed it can be faid to be underftood at all. The words, ufually fuppofed to contain this fragment, * do not fignify, as in our Eng. verfion —*What he did in the red fea, and in the brooks of Arnon*. Without enumerating the many interpretations given by others, I fhall offer a new one; which feems to make good fenfe, and a fenfe very pertinent. Obferve firft, that there muft have been *a place* called *Suph*, near the conflux of the *Arnon* and *Jordan*; becaufe Mofes, whilft in that laft ftation, begins *Deuteronomy* with faying — he was on *this* fide (i.e. Eaft) of Jordan, over againft *Suph*. By this word is not here meant *the red fea*: partly, becaufe that has every where elfe the word for *fea* before it, and partly becaufe of the great diftance of the red fea now from Mofes. The fingle word therefore fignifies here fome *place*, in itfelf obfcure; becaufe no where mentioned but in thefe 2 paffages. And yet we cannot wonder, that Mofes fhould mention it twice; as the word *Suph*, introduced in fpeaking of the 2 laft encampments, recalled to mind the *Sea of Suph*, fo glorious to Ifrael, near the beginning of their march towards Canaan.

* את והב בסופה ואת הנהלים ארנון

THE OLD TESTAMENT. 65

Moses had now led Israel *from the red sea* to the river Arnon; thro' many dreadful dangers, partly from hostile nations, partly from themselves: such dangers, as no other people ever experienced; and such, as no people could have surmounted, without the signal favour of *The Almighty*. And here, just before the battles with *Sihon and Og*; he reminds them of *Pharaoh* &c. And he asserts, that *in the history of the wars it shall be recorded,* * that JEHO-VAH, who had triumphantly brought *Israel* thro' *the sea of Suph* near Egypt at first, had now conducted him to *Suph* near Arnon: that ——

> JEHOVAH *went with him to* SUPH;
> *and he came to the streams of Arnon.*
>
> [Note 3: see pag. 38.]

The general meaning of the next piece of Poetry seems to be this: that at some distance from the city of *Ar*, by which the Israelites were to pass (*Deut.* 2, 18) they came to A WELL, of uncommon size and magnificence; which seems to have been *sought out, built up,* and *adorned,* for the public, by *the rulers* of Moab. † And 'tis no wonder, that, on their arrival at *such a Well,* they should look upon it as *a Blessing from Heaven*; and speak of it, as a new miracle in their favour.

---

* This version removes the difficulties, urged by *Hobbs* pag. 266, fol. 1750: by *Spinoza*; pag. 108, 4°. 1670: and retailed in a Deistical pamphlet, called *The Doubts of the Infidels*; pag. 4: 8°. 1781. And, as to this version; see my *Gen. Dissert.* p. 113.

† See Vitringa; on *Isa.* 15, 8.

E

17. *Then Israel sang this Song.*
Spring up, O WELL! Sing ye thereto!
18. THE WELL! princes searched it out;
the nobles of the people have digged it:
by their decree, by their act of government.
So after the *wilderness*, was *Mattanah!*
19. and after *Mattanah*, were *Nahaliel!*
and after *Nahaliel*, were *Bamoth!*
20. And after *Bamoth*, was the *valley*;
where, in the country of *Moab*,
appeareth the top of *Pisgah*,
which is over against *Jeshimon*.

[Note 4: see pag. 38.]

The 3d piece of Poetry is an *Epinicion*; expressing the triumph of Israel, over *Sihon king of the Amorites*; who had conquered the Moabites in and around *Heshbon*, and driven them to the south of Arnon. The Ode, consisting of 15 lines, divides itself into 3 parts: part 1st is 6 lines, the 2d is 5, and the 3d is 4. The 1st part records, with bitter *irony*, the late insults of *Sihon* and his subjects, over the conquered *Moabites*. In part 2d is expressed the *compassion of Israel over Moab*; with a beautiful *Sarcasm* upon *Chemosh*, the Moabite idol. And in part 3d Israel sets forth the revenge now taken by *them*, upon the whole country of *Sihon*; from *Heshbon* to *Dibon*, and from *Nophah* even to *Medeba*. Isai. 15; 1, 2.

That this Ode was written by *Moses* seems highly probable. For the last part must (I apprehend) be understood, as spoken by THE ISRAELITES. The *Sarcasm* on *Chemosh*, in the 2d part, is much more likely to come from a worshipper of the true GOD, than from an *idolater*. And if Moses wrote *the 3d* part, he doubtless wrote *the 2d*, and consequently *the 1st:* for, the 1st difplays the late exultation of the *Amorites* over Moab; to which the Conclufion forms a very happy contraft.

27. Wherefore they fay, who utter fententious fpeeches—
   " Come ye to Hefhbon, let it be rebuilt;
   " and let the city of Sihon be eftablifhed.
28. " For fire went forth from Hefhbon;
   " and a flame from the city of Sihon:
   " it devoured, even unto Moab,
   " the lords of the heights of Arnon."

---

29. Woe was to thee, O Moab!
    thou didft perifh, O people of *Chemofh!*
    he gave up his fons, who fled,
    and his daughters, taken by the fword,
    to the king of the Amorites, even Sihon.

---

30. But we have caft upon them deftruction,
    from *Hefhbon* even to *Dibon:*
    and we have laid wafte unto *Nophah*;
    the fire was unto *Medeba.*
    [Note 5: fee pag. 38.]

Num. 22, 5.

The defcription now given of Balaam's refidence, inftead of being particular, agrees with any place in any country, where there is *a river* — for he lived at *Pethor,* which is *by the river of the land of the children of his people!* But, was Pethor then near the *Nile,* in *Egypt?* Or in *Canaan,* near *Jordan?* Or in *Mefopotamia,* on the *Euphrates,* and belonging to the *Ammonites?* This laft was in fact the cafe: and therefore it is well, that 12 *Heb. MSS* confirm the *Sam.* text here, in reading (inftead of עמו *his people*) עמון *Ammon:* with the Syr. and Vulg. verfions.

Num. 22, 22.

That the anger of GOD should be kindled against Balaam, merely *because he went*, if he had before given him leave to go, is not to be supposed. But leave seems to have been given him; and the context requires, that in ver. 20 the words should be rendered — *for as much as the men are come — go with them :* and we are therefore to assign the cause of this divine displeasure. With the leave to go, was given a caution as to behaviour; and reason enough there was, because *Balaam loved the wages of unrighteousness:** and, if he went with such a bias on his mind, 'tis no wonder, that GOD was angry for that wrong disposition. This wickedness of his intention, and *perverseness of his way*, seems to have been set before him by *the Vision* of an Angel reproving him : and he himself twice says, that *he saw the vision of the Almighty, falling into a trance, but having his eyes open*, or *opened*. See 22; 31, 34, 35 and 24; 4, 16.

Observe also, that the Angel still bids him go, but commands him to be cautious and obedient. On these repeated authorities from the context, we may safely adopt the reading preserved here in the *Arab.* version; in which there is a word expressing this very disposition — GOD *was angry with him, because he went (avarè)* WITH A COVETOUS INCLINATION. And the *Arab.* version will be the more easily admitted now; because of the proofs lately given, that it agrees with *Heb. MSS* in several places, where it does not agree with the versions either Greek or Syriac : consequently it has a right to be considered, as being sometimes a *primary* version likewise. See my *Gen.*

* *Deut,* 23, 5 : *Jos.* 24, 10 : 2 *Pet,* 2, 15.

Differt. p. 20. It muſt be added, in favour of *the Viſion* here; that this has been the opinion of many of the learned, both Jews and Chriſtians. It ſeems neceſſary to allow, that ſome other things, related as commanded by GOD, and executed by Prophets, are to be *ſo* conſidered. See the ſeveral paſſages mentioned by *Dr Waterland,* in *Scripture Vindicated:* part 3; pag. 45, 72, 85, 92, 96, 110, 122. On one of theſe caſes, p. 60, he remarks thus — *there is nothing in the Text, or Context, which directly intimates, that it was a mere Viſion, or Parable: a ſafe rule to go by, in ſuch caſes.* On another paſſage; p. 78 — *had the Text itſelf called it a Viſion, there could be no further doubt of it.* And this, I apprehend, will apply concluſively to the *Viſion* of Balaam; on the authorities of the 4th and 16th verſes of the 24th chapter. As to *Prophetic Parables,* related as plain matters of Fact; ſee *Stillingfleet's Letter to a Deiſt,* p. 145: Works, 2d Vol. fol. 8 edit. 1709.

Num. 23, 21.

HE (GOD) *hath not beheld iniquity in Jacob, neither hath he ſeen perverſeneſs in Iſrael.* This account is contrary to that given by Moſes, in many places; particularly *Deut.* 9; 6—24. 'Tis happy therefore, that the Samar. Pent. reads here אבים, in the 1ſt perſon; which makes a good and conſiſtent ſenſe. *Balaam,* from an high place viewing the Iſraelites, ſaw them regular and decent, not noiſy or tumultuous; without any diſorderly violence, or idolatrous outrage, on which he could at all fix, as a ground for cenſure or malediction. He therefore ſays, as the words ſhould be expreſſed — I *do not behold iniquity in Jacob, neither do I ſee perverſeneſs in Iſrael.*

The word ראה (if not originally אראה) is a participle, *videns*; and *videns fum* is *video*. The Syriac verſion is rendered here — *non video, nec aſpicio*; and in the Chald. par. the 1ſt verb is rendered *intueor*.

Num. 25, 4.

And the Lord ſaid unto Moſes: Take ALL THE HEADS OF THE PEOPLE, *and hang them up before the Lord, againſt the ſun.* If theſe words do not mean, that he was to hang up *all the people*; they muſt mean *all thoſe,* who were *heads* or *judges* of the people. But neither were theſe *judges* to be hanged up; becauſe, in the next verſe, Moſes commanded theſe very *judges* to ſlay (each in his proper diviſion) ſuch of the people, as had then been idolatrous. The truth is, that ſome words have been here omitted in the *Samar.* text, and ſome in the *Hebrew*; and both, taken together, will compleat the ſenſe, thus — *And the Lord ſaid unto Moſes:* SPEAK *unto all the heads of the people*; AND LET THEM SLAY THE MEN, THAT WERE JOINED UNTO BAAL-PEOR; *and hang them up before the Lord, againſt the ſun: that the fierce anger of the Lord may be turned away from Iſrael.*

Num. 26, 10.

This verſe is very remarkable: for, according to the *Heb.* text here, KORAH was ſwallowed up, with the *Reubenites*; but the *Samar.* text ſays, he was deſtroyed by fire, with his brethren the *Levites*. See alſo ch. 16; ver. 6, 7, 16, 17, 27, 38, 40. This difference is well ſtated by *Mr Whiſton*; in theſe words. *We have in the book of* Numbers *a very particular account of the deſtruction of the ſeditious Reubenites,* Dathan *and* Abiram, *and their partners*; *with* Korah, *and his* 250 *Levites. Of the Reubenites*, by the earth fwallowing them up: *and of the Levites*, by fire. *But, what death* Korah *himfelf died, is not directly told us in our prefent Heb. and Greek Bibles: it rather feems by them, that he was* fwallowed up, *than that he was* burnt — *contrary to the reafon of the thing itfelf, which would rather require, that* Korah, *the head of the Levites that burnt incenfe, fhould perifh* with thofe that burnt incenfe with him; *as* Dathan *and* Abiram, *the heads of the Reubenites, were fwallowed up* with the other Reubenites. *Now here we have both the* Samar. Pent. *and* Jofephus, *as authentic witneffes that the original Hebrew afferted, that* Korah was burnt with his Levites; *and in effect the Pfalmift's teftimony alfo* (Pf. 106, 17) *who mentions only Dathan and Abiram, as fwallowed up, and not burnt. Alfo we have the teftimony of the* Apoftolical Conftitutions, *and in effect of* Clement *of Rome, of* Ignatius, *and* Eufebius, *that the Septuagint verfion originally gave the fame account. So that here we have a clear inftance of the alteration of both the* Heb. *and* Gr. *copies of the Old Teftament, fince the firft century.* Effay on the true Text of the Old Teftament; p. 64, 65.

Deut. 1, 2.

(There are *eleven days* journey *from Horeb, by the way of mount Seir, unto Kadefh-barnea.*) When the learned fhall obferve, how clofely connected the 3d verfe is with the 1ft, how foreign this 2d verfe feems here (which our tranflators have therefore put in a parenthefis) and how natural a place there is for this 2d verfe between the verfes 19 and 20; they will probably applaud the following remark of *Dr Wall*, in his Critical Notes — *I cannot apprehend the coherence of this parenthesis with the matter spoken of. It would have fitted at ver. 19, where the Israelites travel between those two places is recited: to shew, that, how long soever they were in making it, it was in ordinary course of travelling but eleven days journey; or perhaps, that they went it in eleven days.*

Deut. 2; 9 — 13, and 17 — 25.

In this chapter are two very large interpolations: in the 1st of which are described the antient inhabitants of the country of the *Moabites*; and in the 2d, the antient inhabitants of the country of the *Ammonites*. If these 2 historical memoirs were not written by Moses; they must have been inserted, as glosses, in the *margin* of some very antient MS, and from thence taken afterwards into the *Text*. 'Tis by no means probable, that this Anecdote of the EMIMS and HORIMS (ver. 10 — 12) made part of the Speech of GOD himself; separating the beginning from the end of that Speech, in the strange manner we see at present: or that the history of the ZAMZUMMIMS and AVIMS (ver. 20 — 23) separated as strangely the 2d Speech. It will follow therefore that the 2d is an interpolation, as well as the 1st. And the 1st could not be written by Moses, because it records what was done after the time of Moses, *after Israel had got possession of Canaan:* for it says — that the *children of Esau dwelt in Seir, after driving out the Horims,* just as *Israel* DID *in the land of his possession,* that is, after driving out the Canaanites. Our last *translators* endeavoured to assist the first of these passages, by putting in the words *said I* very improperly, in the midſt of the words of GOD, not of Moſes: and the 2d paſſage appeared to *them* ſo unconnected with the divine Speech, that they have put the whole 4 verſes in a Parentheſis.

Deut. 6, 13,

Thou ſhalt fear the Lord thy God, AND SERVE HIM *and ſhalt ſwear by his name.* The Scripture tells us, that ſome men worſhipped falſe gods together with the true. And if this text commanded the worſhip of *the God of Iſrael,* and not of *him only*; it would not clearly condemn ſuch falſe communion: nor would it be concluſive, as CHRIST himſelf has quoted it. The Context, when clear, is a ſafe guide; and here it is quite *excluſive*. It therefore follows, that the Heb. Text, now ואתו תעבד *et ei ſervies,* was originally ואתו לבדו תעבד *et ei* SOLI *ſervies:* as in the Greek and Vulgat verſions. This reading, thus confirmed, juſtifies the citation of it made by *Chriſt*; when he put the tempter to ſilence and flight, by ſaying: IT IS WRITTEN — *and him* ONLY *ſhalt thou ſerve.* Matt. 4, 10; Luk. 4, 8. The Greek verſion has alſo in this verſe και προς αυτον κολληθηση — which words are confirmed by 6 Heb. MSS reading here ובו תדבק. And in the preceding verſe, where the Heb. Text has only יהוה, but the Greek has κυριω τω θεω σου; the Greek is confirmed by above 50 Heb. MSS.

Deut. 7, 1.

The Nations, to be driven out by Iſrael, are here enumerated thus; *Hittites, Girgaſites, Amorites, Canaanites, Perizzites, Hivites, Jebuſites:* and they are here expreſsly called SEVEN. They are alſo named in 6 other parts of the Pentateuch; but in the *Heb.*

text imperfectly in all thefe 6 places. Gen. 15; 20, 21 — omitted *Hivites*. Exod. 3, 8 — omitted *Girgafites*. Exod. 13, 5 — omitted *Girgafites* and *Perizzites*. And *Girgafites* are alfo omitted, in Exod. 33, 2; 34, 11: and in *Deut.* 20, 17. But, in all thefe places, the 7 nations are all expreffed in the *Samar.* Pentateuch.

Deut. 10; 6—9.

The book of *Deuteronomy* contains the feveral Speeches made to the Ifraelites by Mofes, juft before his death; recapitulating the chief circumftances of their hiftory, from their deliverance out of Egypt to their arrival on the banks of Jordan. What in this book he has recorded, as *fpoken*, will be beft underftood, by comparing it with what he has recorded, as *done*, in the previous hiftory; and this, which is very ufeful as to the other parts of this book, is abfolutely neceffary, as to the part of the 10th chapter here to be confidered.

The previous circumftances of the Hiftory, neceffary to be here attended to, are thefe. (*Exod.* ch. 20) GOD fpeaks the 10 Commandments — (24) Mofes, on mount Sinai, receives the 2 Tables; and is there 40 days and nights — (ch. 25, 26, 27) GOD commands the Tabernacle — (28) Separates Aaron and his fons, for the prieft's office; by a ftatute for ever, to him and his feed after him — (32) Mofes, incenfed at the golden Calf, breaks the Tables; yet he prays for the People, and GOD orders him to lead them towards Canaan — (34) Mofes carries up 2 other Tables, and ftays again 40 days and nights. (*Num.* ch. 3) Tribe of Levi felected — (8) confecrated — (10 and 11) Ifraelites march from Sinai, on 20th day of the 2d month in the 2d year — (13) Spies sent — (14) the men sentenced to die in the wilderness, during the 40 years — (18) Levites to have no lot, or large district, in Canaan; but to be the Lord's inheritance — (20) Aaron dies on mount Hor — Lastly; in the compleat Catalogue of the whole March (ch. 33) we are told, that they went from *Moseroth* to *Bene-jaakan* — thence to *Horhagidgad* — to *Jotbathah* — to *Ebronah* — to *Ezion-geber* — to *Zin*, (which is Kadesh) — and thence to *mount Hor*; where Aaron died, in the 40th and last year.

In *Deut.* 9 Moses tells the Israelites (ver. 7) that they had been rebels, from Egypt even to Jordan; particularly at Horeb (ver. 8—29) whilst he was with GOD, and received the Tables at the end of 40 days and nights — and that, after breaking the Tables, he fasted and interceded for his brethren, during a 2d period of 40 days and nights: and this 9th chapter ends with the Prayer which he then made. Chapter the 10th begins thus — *At that time the Lord said unto me, Hew thee 2 tables of stone, like unto the first, and come up* &c. And, from ver. 1 to the end of ver. 5, he describes the 2d copy of the Ten Commandments; as written also by GOD, and deposited by himself in the Ark.

After this, we have now 4 Verses (6 and 7, 8 and 9) which not only have no kind of connexion with the verses before and after them; but also, as they stand in the present Heb. Text, directly contradict that very Text: and the 2 first of these verses have not, in our Heb. Text, the least connexion with the 2 last of them. Our Heb. Text (ver. 6) says — that Israel journeyed *from Bene-jaakan to Mosera.*

Whereas, that very Text, in the compleat Catalogue (*Num.* 33, 31) fays — they journeyed *from Moferoth to Bene-jaakan*. Again: Aaron is here faid to have died at *Mofera*; whereas he died on *mount Hor*, the 7th ftation afterwards: fee *Num.* 33, 38. And again: they are here faid to go from *Bene-jaakan* to *Mofera* — thence to *Gudgodah* — and thence to *Jotbath*; whereas the compleat Catalogue fays — *Moferoth to Bene-jaakan* — thence to *Horhagidgad* — and thence to *Jotbathah*. But, if the marches could poffibly be true, as they now ftand in thefe 2 verfes; yet, what Connexion can there be, between JOTBATH and the SEPARATION OF THE TRIBE OF LEVI?

'Tis very happy, that thefe feveral difficulties, in the *Heb.* text, are removed by the SAMAR. Pentateuch. For *that* text tells us here rightly, that the march was from *Moferoth* to *Bene-jaakan* — to *Hagidgad* — to *Jotbathah* — to *Ebronah* — to *Ezion-geber* — to *Zin* (which is Kadefh) and thence to *mount Hor*, where Aaron died. Again: as the regular deduction of thefe Stations ends with *mount Hor* and *Aaron's Death*; we have then, what we had not before, a regular connexion with the 2 next verfes: and the connexion is this — that, when AARON (the fon of *Amram*, the fon of *Kohath*, the fon of LEVI) died; neither the *Tribe of Levi*, nor the *Prieflhood*, was deferted. But GOD ftill fupported the latter, by maintaining the former: and this, not by allotting that Tribe any one large part of Canaan, but feparate Cities among the other Tribes; and by allowing them to live upon thofe Offerings, which were made by the other Tribes to GOD Himfelf.

Thefe

These 4 verses therefore (6, 7, 8, 9) in the *Sam.* text stand thus. (6) WHEN *the children of Israel journeyed from Moseroth*, and encamped in *Bene-jaakan:* from thence they journeyed, and encamped at *Hagidgad:* from thence they journeyed, and encamped in *Jotbathah*, a land of rivers of water: (7) *from* thence they journeyed, and encamped in *Ebronah:* — in *Ezion-geber:* — in the wilderness of *Zin*, which is *Kadesh:* — and then, at *mount Hor*. *And* AARON DIED THERE, *and there he was buried; and Eleazar his son ministered as priest in his stead.* (8) *At that time the Lord* HAD *separated the tribe of Levi; to bear the ark of the covenant of the Lord, to stand before the Lord to minister unto him, and to bless in his name, unto this day.* (9) *Wherefore Levi hath no part, nor inheritance, with his brethren: the Lord is his inheritance, according as the Lord thy God promised him.*

But, however consistent these 4 verses are now with themselves; it will be still demanded, *What Connexion* have they with the 5*th* verse *before* them, and with the 10*th* verse, *after* them? I confess, I cannot discover their least pertinency here; because AARON'S DEATH and LEVI'S SEPARATION seem totally foreign to the Speech of Moses in this place. And this Speech, *without these 4 verses*, is a regularly-connected Admonition from Moses, to this purpose — that his brethren were for ever to consider themselves as indebted to *Him*, under GOD, for the Renewal of the 2 Tables; and also to *His* Intercession, for rescuing them from Destruction. The words are these. (10, 4.) *The Lord wrote again the ten commandments, and gave them unto me.* (5.) *And I came down from the mount, and put the tables in the ark,* *which I* HAD *made* — (10) *Thus I ſtayed in the mount according to the firſt time,* 40 *days and* 40 *nights: and the Lord hearkened unto me at that time alſo*; *the Lord would not deſtroy thee.* (11) *And the Lord ſaid unto me, Ariſe, take thy journey before the people, that they may go in, and poſſeſs the land &c.*

But then — if theſe 4 verſes were not at firſt a part of this chapter, but are evidently interpolated: there ariſes another enquiry, Whether *they are an Inſertion entirely ſpurious*; or *a genuine part of the ſacred Text, tho' removed hither out of ſome other chapter.* As they contain nothing ſingular, or peculiar — are of no particular importance — and relate to no ſubject of Diſputation; they are not likely to have ariſen from fraud or deſign: but, perfectly coinciding in ſenſe with other paſſages, they may ſafely be conſidered as another inſtance of a large Tranſpoſition [86 words] in the preſent Text, ariſing from accident and want of care. And the only remaining queſtion therefore is — *Whether we can diſcover*, tho' not to demonſtration, yet with any conſiderable degree of *Probability*, the Original Place of theſe 4 Verſes: that ſo they may be at laſt reſtored to that Neighbourhood and Connexion, from which they have been for ſo many Ages ſeparated.

It was natural for Moſes, in the courſe of theſe ſeveral Speeches to his brethren in *Deuteronomy*, to embrace the firſt proper opportunity of impreſſing on their memories a matter of ſuch particular importance, *as the Continuation of the Prieſthood among the Levites after Aaron's Death.* And the firſt proper place ſeems to be in the 2d chapter after the 1ſt verſe. At ch. 1, 19 he ſpeaks of their march from

Horeb to *Kadesh-barnea*, whence they sent the Spies into Canaan. He then sets forth their murmurings, and GOD's sentence that they should die in the wilderness: and he ends the 1st chapter with their being *defeated by the Amorites*, their *weeping before the Lord*, and *abiding many days* in KADESH — which is KADESH-BARNEA near Canaan.

Chapter 2d begins thus — *Then we turned, and took our journey into the wilderness, by the way of the Red sea, as the Lord spake unto me:* and WE COMPASSED MOUNT SEIR MANY DAYS. Now the many days, or long time, which they spent in *compassing mount Seir* i.e. going round on the *South-west* coasts of *Edom*,* in order to proceed *North-east*, from Edom thro' *Moab* to *Arnon*, must include *several* of their Stations; besides that eminent one at *mount Hor*, where *Aaron died*. And as part of their road, during this long compass, lay through *Ezion-geber* (which was on the *Eastern tongue* of the Red Sea, and the *South* Boundary of *Edom*; † — thence to *Zin* (which is KADESH i.e. MERIBAH-KADESH) — and thence to *mount Hor*, as they marched to the *North-East*: so, 'tis probable, that the 5 Stations, preceding that of *Ezion-geber*, were on the extremity of mount Seir to the *South-West*. And if their first Station, at entering the South-West borders of Edom, and beginning to *compass mount Seir*, was *Moseroth*; this gives the reason wanted — Why Moses begins this passage at *Moseroth*, and ends it with Aaron's death at *mount Hor*. And this will discover a proper Connexion between the 4 dislocated Verses and the Context here — *Deut.* 1, 46. *So ye abode in*

---

* See *Gen.* 32, 3; 36, 8.   † 1 *Kings* 9, 26.

Kadesh (barnea) *many days.* 2, 1. *Then we turned, and took our journey into the wilderness, by the way of the Red-Sea; as the Lord spake unto me: and* WE COMPASSED MOUNT SEIR MANY DAYS. [*For the children of Israel journeyed from Moseroth, and pitched in Bene-jaakan. From thence they journeyed, and pitched in Hagidgad. From thence they journeyed, and pitched in Jothbathah, a land of rivers of water. From thence they journeyed, and pitched in Ebronah. From thence they journeyed, and pitched in Ezion-geber. From thence they journeyed, and pitched in the wilderness of Zin, which is Kadesh. From thence they journeyed, and pitched in mount Hor. And Aaron died there, and there he was buried; and Eleazar, his son, ministred as priest in his stead. At that time the Lord had separated the tribe of Levi; to bear the ark of the covenant of the Lord, to stand before the Lord to minister unto him, and to bless in his name, unto this day. Wherefore Levi hath no part nor inheritance with his brethren: the Lord is his inheritance, according as the Lord thy God promised him.*] And this paragraph being thus finished, at the end of the 1st verse; the 2d verse begins a new paragraph, thus. *And the Lord spake unto me, saying. Ye have compassed this mountain long enough; turn you northward* — thro' the East side of Seir (or Edom) towards Moab on the North: see verses 4, 5, 6, 7, 8.

Deut. 23, 3.

If an *Ammonite* or *Moabite* were not to enter into the congregation of the Lord, *till* the 10th generation; then they were to enter *after* the 10th generation: and if so, then they were not excluded *for ever* — as the Text here now affirms. On the contrary: if they were not to enter *for ever*; the clause concerning the 10th generation cannot here be genuine. The folution feems to be this — that the 7 words, expreffing *the 10th generation*, are here taken in, and improperly repeated from the verfe preceding. And what is thus probable from the Context, is made certain from a MS of undoubted Authority; which was in ufe about 2200 years ago. For *Nehemiah* fays (13, 1) *On that day they read in the book of Mofes; and therein was found written, that the Ammonite and the Moabite fhould not come into the congregation of God for ever.* For the preceding remarks on this verfe, which are curious and decifive, the reader is indebted to a very learned and very worthy Prelate, my Friend, Bp BARRINGTON.

Deut. 27, 26.

The word *all*, which our tranflators have inferted as wanting before *the words of this law*, was thought by *Jerom* abfolutely neceffary to juftify St Paul's quotation, in *Gal.* 3, 10. See *Gen. Diff.* p. 38. And 'tis very remarkable, that this important word is now found here, not only in the Samar. Text and its Verfion, but alfo in 4 *Heb.* MSS. The Lat. verfion of the Chald. paraphrafe has *omnibus* here, in *Walton's Polyglott*; tho' the word is not in the adjoining column of the Ch. paraphrafe. And tho' it is not in the Syr. Arab. or Vulg. verfions, as there printed; I have no doubt, but it may be found in fome *very antient MSS* of thefe verfions. It has been found in 6 *Chaldee* MSS.

Deut. 32.

This very fublime Ode is diftinguifhed even by the Jews, both in their MSS and printed copies, as being *Poetry*. In our prefent tranflation, it would appear to much greater advantage, if it were printed hemiſtically: and the tranſlation of ſome parts of it may be much improved.

1. Let the heavens give ear, and I will ſpeak;
and let the earth hear the words of my mouth.

2. My doctrine ſhall drop, as the rain;
my ſpeech ſhall diſtill, as the dew;
as the ſmall rains upon the tender herb,
and as the ſhowers upon the graſs.

3. Verily the name of JEHOVAH will I proclaim;
aſcribe ye greatneſs unto our GOD.

4. He is the rock, perfect is his work;
for all his ways are judgment:
a GOD of truth, and without iniquity;
juſt and right is He.

5. [POLLUTION; THEY ARE CORRUPTED, NOT HIS, CHILDREN OF a generation, perverſe and crooked!

6. Is this the return, which ye make to JEHOVAH?
O people, fooliſh and unwiſe!
Is not He thy father, thy redeemer?
he, who made thee, and eſtabliſhed thee?

7. Remember thou the days of old;
conſider the years of many generations:
aſk thy father, and he will ſhew thee;
thy elders, and they will tell thee.

8. When the moſt High gave inheritance to the nations;
when he ſeparated the ſons of Adam:
he appointed the bounds of the peoples,
according to the number of the children of Iſrael.

9. For the portion of JEHOVAH was his people;
Jacob was the lot of his inheritance.

It muſt be here obſerved, that verſes 8 and 9 give us expreſs authority for believing, that the Earth was very early divided, in conſequence of *a Divine Command*; and probably by *lot*, of which *the whole difpofing* was *of the Lord.* See alfo St Paul; *Acts* 17, 26. And as Africa is called *the land of Ham* (Pf. 78, 51: 105; 23, 27: and 106, 22) probably that country fell to *him* and his defcendants, at the fame time that Europe fell to *Japhet*, and Afia to *Shem* — with a particular referve of *Palestine*, as to be *the Lord's portion*, for fome one peculiar people. And this Separation of Mankind into 3 bodies, called *the general Migration*, was commanded to Noah and by him to his Sons (Eufebius fays — 20 years before his death) as to take place about 200 years afterwards, foon after the death of *Shem*, and in the days of *Peleg*; which general Migration was prior to *the partial Difperfion* from Babel by about 500 years. See Winder's *Hift. Knowledge*; 1, 14: and the very excellent remarks, in Bryant's *Mythology*; 3, 14.

As to the preceding 5th verfe; it has been thought impoffible to give any regular conftruction to the firft part of it, as it now ftands in the Heb. Text. And it is therefore happy, that the Samar. Pentateuch, and the Greek and Syr. verfions, difcover 2 tranfpofitions in the prefent Hebrew; and agree to exprefs that fenfe, which has been given to it in the oppofite page. See alfo *Gen. Diff.* pag. 31.

To this *General Differtation* (pag. 39) I muft refer likewife for feveral authorities, which juftify our tranflators, for inferting the word *with* in ver. 43. For we muft affert, that this paffage predicted the *Adoption of the Gentiles under the Meffiah*; to which fenfe this prepofition is quite neceffary: unlefs we will chofe to allow, that St PAUL (*Rom.* 15, 9—12) was *ignorant* of the true reading and the true fenfe here, or was *difhoneft* enough wilfully to mif-quote it — in an argument of the greatest consequence. Besides; the preceding part of this Song has expresly foretold this same Event — that *the jealousy* of the Jews would be, in the latter days, excited, by the favour of God shewn to those, who had not been called *his people*: see ver. 21, and *Rom.* 10, 19.

Deut. 33; 1—5.

This *introduction* to the final benediction by Moses is generally considered as relating only to the *Israelites*. But the learned Father *Houbigant* seems justly to suppose, that it relates also to *the rest of Mankind*, as not excluded from the divine regard; but who were *all* to be favoured, in future times, with the revelation of God's will, as certainly as Israel had been already. If then these last words of Moses were intended to celebrate God's *universal* love to Men, in *Christ* and *his Gospel*; the true translation of the 3d and 5th verses may be this ——

2. JEHOVAH came from Sinai;
And he arose from Seir upon them:
he shone forth from mount Paran;
and he came with ten thousands of saints;
from his right hand (*went*) a fiery law for them.

3. *Truly he loveth* (עמים) *the* NATIONS,
and all that are holy he will bless:
for they shall sit down at his feet;
and they shall receive of his words.

4. A law hath he commanded unto us;
the inheritance of the congregation of Jacob.

5. But *there shall be a King* in Jeshurun;
when the heads of the NATIONS *shall* assemble themselves,
together with the tribes of Israel.

THE OLD TESTAMENT. 85

The prediction of *Meſſiah* by Moſes here does by no means end with him (in ver. 5) as an *univerſal King*; becauſe the ſame perſon ſeems clearly meant in ver. 7 *bring* HIM *unto his people* i.e. bring unto his people, in thy good time, *him*, the KING, the *Shiloh*, of the tribe of *Judah*.* And let what is here mentioned, in ver. 7, as to this deſcendant from *Judah* — and in ver. 11, as to this ſuperior of *Levi* — be compared with *Pſalm* 110. For this extraordinary perſon was alſo to be a *Prieſt*; to whom even *the High Prieſt*, in the tribe of *Levi*, was to ſurrender up his *Urim and Thummim*. For, this *Holy One of* GOD, who was tempted at *Maſſah* and *Meribah*, is affirmed

---

* *The following are ſome of Houbigant's pertinent remarks.* —— Tangit hìc Moyſes עמים *populos*, non ſolùm *Iſrael*; ſignificatque, omnes gentes verbum Dei ſuſcepturas, ad cujus pedes ſe olim abjicient *ſancti ejus*, qui de gentibus vocabuntur, ſeu de populis univerſis, quia Deus *diligit populos*. In ver. 7 — In CHRISTUM *unum* hæc aptari poſſunt, *Adduc eum ad populum ſuum*. In ver. 8 — Non fuit is ſtatus tribûs *Levi*, nec ea indoles, ut filii parentes ſuos non agnoſcerent &c. — Hæ, neque minimæ, difficultates attentum lectorem tanquam manu ducunt, et fere cogunt ſic ſentire, in hac de Levi benedictione opponi ſacerdotium *Levi* ſacerdotio *Meſſiæ* futuro; ſic dicere igitur Moſen: *Thumim tuum, et tuum Urim*, VIRI SANCTI *tui eſt*; *quem tu tentâſti*: i. e. perfectio illa et doctrina, quam præ ſe ferunt tui ſacerdotes, erit propria *Sancti ejus*; quem Dominus *non dabit videre corruptionem* — quem tu tentâſti, eundem de quo Paulus, *neque tentemus Chriſtum* — qui dicturus eſt *patri et matri, non novi*; idem qui ſic aiebat, *Quæ eſt mater mea, et qui fratres? qui facit voluntatem patris mei, hic meus eſt frater, et ſoror, et mater*. In eam ſententiam recte dicitur, *Filios ſuos non novit*, NISI *eos qui cuſtodient verbum tuum*. Poſt כי addimus אם, ſine quâ particulâ oratio pugnantia loquitur: loquitur enim de illis, quos *Sanctus* agnoſcet ut *ſuos*, qui Evangelii legem promulgaturi ſunt, et Sacrificium Deo acceptum oblaturi,

to be CHRIST: see 1 *Cor.* 10, 9. But verses 9 and 10 here still more clearly describe *The Messiah*, as acknowledging none to be either *his relations* or *his disciples*, but such only as *do the will of* GOD: for this seems the meaning of these 2 verses, which in our present version are unintelligible, and stand thus. 8. *And of Levi he said*, Let *thy Thummim and thy Urim be with thy holy one, whom thou didst prove at Massah*, and with *whom thou didst strive at the waters of Meribah*; 9. *Who said unto his father, and to his mother, I have not seen him, neither did he acknowledge his brethren, nor know his own children: for they have observed thy word, and kept thy covenant.* It must now be carefully observed, that *He*, who was *proved* at Massah, and was *tempted* at Meribah, is here called *Thy Holy One*; and that this *Holy One* (whom St Paul affirms to have been *Christ*) must be also *He*, who said unto, or spake of, *his Relations* what here follows. And what here follows is wonderfully confirmed by the event. For we read — *While Jesus talked to the people; behold his mother and his brethren stood without, desiring to speak with him. Then one said unto him, Behold, thy mother and thy brethren stand without, desiring to speak with thee. But he said, Who is my mother? and who are my brethren? And he stretched forth his hand toward his Disciples, and said, Behold my mother, and my brethren. For whosoever shall do the will of my Father, which is in heaven, the same is my brother, and sister, and mother.* Matt. 12, 46—50: add *Mar.* 3, 32; *Luk.* 2, 48; 8, 21: and also *Malachi* 1, 11 and 3, 3; with *Heb.* 13, 15. The following version is now submitted to the learned Reader.

8. And

8. And of LEVI he said: [One;
Thy Thummim and thy Urim *be* to the man, thy Holy
whom thou didſt prove at Maſſah,
and with whom thou didſt ſtrive at the waters of Meribah.

9. Who ſaid *of* his father and his mother, *I regard not:*
and who does not acknowledge, as his brethren;
and who does not own, as his children;
but thoſe, *who* obſerve thy word, and keep thy covenant:

10. Thoſe, who teach Jacob thy judgments;
and Iſrael thy laws:
thoſe, who put incenſe before thee,
and *a perfect oblation* upon thine altar.

[Note 6: ſee pag. 38.]

Joſ. 1, 4.

The extent of the Country, granted to the Iſraelites, is not deſcribed here very clearly. For, tho' the 4 boundaries are mentioned, the *Wilderneſs* on the South with *Lebanon* on the North, and the *Euphrates* on the Eaſt with the *Mediterranean Sea* on the Weſt: yet, as Joſhua was now at a great diſtance from Lebanon, it is not likely he ſhould ſay *this* Lebanon; and it is leſs likely, that he ſhould deſcribe the whole of this Country by the words *all the land of the Hittites*. The Vulgat verſion is free from the word *this*; and the Greek verſion is free from both difficulties. But, there is much greater authority; namely, that of *Moſes*, expreſsly referred to here, in ver. 3: and *Deut*. 11, 24 has neither the word *this*, nor the words *all the land of the Hittites* — either in the *Heb*. text or the *Samaritan*.

Joſ. 4, 9.

It is well known, that, when Joſhua led the Iſraelites over Jordan, he was commanded to take 12 *ſtones* out of the *midſt of Jordan*; to be a memorial, that the ground in the very *midſt* of that river had been made dry, and the river miraculouſly divided, on that occaſion. But, *where* was this memorial to be ſet up? The verſe here referred to ſays — *Joſhua ſet up theſe ſtones* IN *the midſt of Jordan.* But, is it likely, that the ſtones ſhould be placed, or ſet down, where they were taken up; and that the memorial ſhould be erected there, where (when the river was again united) it would be concealed, and of courſe could be no memorial at all? This, however, flatly contradicts the reſt of the chapter; which ſays — theſe ſtones were pitched in *Gilgal,* where Iſrael lodged in Canaan for the firſt time. The ſolution of this difficulty is — that בתוך *in medio* ſhould be here מתוך *e medio*; as in verſes 3, 8, 20: and as the word is here alſo in the Syr. verſion. The true rendering therefore is — *And Joſhua ſet up the* 12 *ſtones* (taken) FROM *the midſt of Jordan* &c. See verſe preceding.

Joſ. 5, 1.

When all the kings — heard, that the Lord had dried up the waters of Jordan from before the children of Iſrael, until WE *were paſſed over.* On theſe words Dr Wall remarks thus. "If the word (WE) be a right " reading; this muſt have been written by *Joſhua,* " or ſome one preſent at the paſſing. But as the wri-" ter never ſpeaks in the firſt perſon, but at this " place in Hebrew, and never at all in the *Greek* " or *Vulg.* the reading in *them* ſeems more probable " — *till* THEY *were paſſed over.* So, ver. 6; where " *Eng.* is *that he would give* US; Vulg. is *them,* and " the Greek reads *their fathers.*" It muſt be added, that the preceding correction of *we were paſſed* to *they were paſſed* is confirmed by 27 Heb. copies.

Jof. 7, 17.

In verſe 14 is an exact deſcription of the method commanded for diſcovering a tranſgreſſor; which method was undoubtedly followed. All Iſrael came near *by* TRIBES, and one *tribe* was fixed on: then, that tribe came by its FAMILIES, and one *family* was fixed on: then came that family by its HOUSEHOLDS, and one *houſehold* was fixed on: and then, that houſehold coming MAN BY MAN, one *man* was fixed on. Yet, according to the preſent text, in the execution of this command, *all Iſrael* came and *the tribe of Judah* was fixed on: 2dly, came *the families* of Judah, and *the family of the Zarhites* was fixed on: 3dly, came *the family of the Zarhites* MAN BY MAN, and Zabdi was fixed on: and 4thly, came *the houſehold of Zabdi*, MAN BY MAN, and *Achan* was fixed on. So that in the 3d article, the word for *by houſeholds* is moſt certainly left out, and the 4th article *man by man* is improperly expreſſed twice. Inſtead of לגברים *man by man*, in ver. 17, the true word לבתים *by houſeholds* is preſerved in 6 Heb. copies and the Syr. verſion. By this method was diſcovered *Achan*, as he is called here 5 times; tho' the valley, in which he was ſtoned, is called *Achor*: he is alſo called *Achar* (in the Text and all the Verſions) in 1 *Chron*. 2, 7. He is *Achar*, in the 5 places of *Joſhua*, in the Syr. verſion; alſo in all 5, in the Greek of the Vatican MS, and twice in the Alex. MS: and ſo Joſephus.

Jof. 9, 1.

— *all the kings, on this ſide Jordan, in the hills, and in the vallies, and in all the coaſts of the great ſea* over againſt *Lebanon*. Dr Wall, having remarked that the Greek and Vulg. verſions read here *and thoſe about*

Lebanon, gives this opinion — "There are, I think, *one hundred* Texts, where the adverb, which the *Gr.* and *Vulg.* verſions tranſlate *nigh to*, is in *Tremellius* and *Eng.* tranſlated *over againſt*; and that, many times, to the utter perverting of the ſenſe of the place."

Joſ. 10, 15.

And Joſhua returned, and all Iſrael with him, unto the camp to Gilgal. The ſame Critic has well obſerved — that this verſe is not in the *Vat.* or *Alexand.* Greek MSS. And he adds — "The Greek agrees with the *Heb.* at ver. 21; that, as ſoon as the battle was ended, all the people returned to Joſhua, to the camp at *Makkedah*. *Makkedah* was nigh the place of battle; *Gilgal* a great way off. And that Joſhua, who (in the next words, v. 17) hearing of the 5 kings hid in a cave, bad that they ſhould be ſhut in; yet the ſoldiers ſhould not ſtay, but purſue the enemies — that he (I ſay) ſhould in the mean time have led back the army to their camp at *Gilgal*, about 15 miles off, is very improbable. I think this one of the places, where the preſent Heb. may be amended by the old Greek, which has not this verſe; but goes on to ſpeak of the remainder of the action till evening."

Joſ. 14, 15.

One is much ſurprized here, at reading — *the name of Hebron before was* Kirjath-arba, (which Arba was) *a great man among the Anakims*. But, ſtrange as this verſion is; it is the more ſtrange, becauſe it is corrected in ver. 13 of the very next chapter — *the city of* Arba, *the father of Anak, which city is Hebron:* and again, in 21, 11 — *the city of* Arba, *the father of Anak.*

Jof. 15; 59 60.

Jerom, on *Mic.* 5, 1, fpeaks of the eleven towns, which are mentioned here in the Greek verfion, but not in the Heb. text; doubting, whether they were malitioufly erafed out of the Hebrew (becaufe of *Bethlehem - Ephrata* in the tribe of Judah) or added in the Greek. But, as they could not be invented and added by defign; fo neither do they feem defignedly left out by the Jews: becaufe there is in the Text itfelf an obvious caufe of the Omiffion, which is — the fame word, (וחצריהן *and their villages*) occurring immediately *before* this paffage, and at the *end* of it; fo that the tranfcriber's eye paffed from one to the other by miftake. It will be found, under the next article, that the fame accident hath caufed an omiffion of 2 whole verfes, in chapter 21 of this fame book. Thefe XI *cities* (rather towns) are recorded in both the Greek MSS, Vat. and Alexandrian; and they were in Jerom's Greek copies. And as there is fo evident a caufe of their omiffion, they fhould be carefully reftored —*Theco, and Ephratha (that is Bethlehem) and Phagor, and Etan, and Kulon, and Tatam, and Thobes, and Karam, and Galem, and Thether, and Manocho: eleven towns, and their villages.* See Gen. Diff. p. 88.

Jof. 21; 35 36.

Having thus mentioned a *probable* omiffion of many words; I come now to a large omiffion, that is *certain*, and (if any thing can be) *indifputable*. Verfes 41 and 42 of this chapter tell us, that the Levitical cities were XLVIII, and that they had been *all* as fuch defcribed: fo that they muft have been all previoufly fpecified in this chapter. Whereas now, in all the Heb. copies printed in full obedience to the Mafora (which excludes 2 verfes containing 4 of thefe cities) the number amounts only to XLIV. The cities are firft mentioned, in the general; as being 13 and 10, with 13 and 12; which are certainly 48. And yet, when they are particularly named; verfes 13 to 19 give 13 cities — verfes 20 to 26 give 10 cities — verfes 27 to 33 give 13 — verfes 34 and 35 give 4 cities — and then verfes 35, 36 give 4 more — all which can make but XLIV. And what ftill encreafes the wonder is, that verfe 40 infers from the verfes immediately preceding, that the cities allowed to the Merarites were 12; tho' they here make 8 only: unlefs we admit the 4 other cities, expreffed in thofe 2 verfes, which have been rejected by that blind guide *the Mafora*. In defiance of this authority, thefe 2 Verfes, thus abfolutely neceffary, were inferted in the moft early *Editions* of the Heb. Text; and are found in Walton's Polyglott, as well as in our Eng. Bible. But they have fcarce ever been, as yet, printed compleatly; thus —

And out of the tribe of Reuben, A CITY OF REFUGE FOR THE SLAYER, *Bezer* IN THE WILDERNESS, *with her fuburbs*; *and Jahazah, with her fuburbs*; *Kedemoth, with her fuburbs*; *and Mephaath, with her fuburbs*: 4 *cities*. See on this place my Edition of the Heb. Bible: where no lefs than CXLIX copies are defcribed; which happily preferve thefe verfes, moft clearly effential to the truth and confiftency of this chapter. See alfo *Gen. Diff.* p. 19, 26, 54.

Jof. 22, 34.

Nothing can be more clear, than that *the name* of the altar is here omitted—*And the children of Reuben*,

*and the children of Gad, called the altar   for it
shall be a witness between us, that the Lord is* GOD.
Our tranflators have inferted the neceffary word *Ed*;
which however, in an *English* tranflation, had been
better expreffed by *Witnefs*. The word, here omitted, has the authority of 17 Heb. copies; with the
Syr. and Ar. verfions. See *Gen. Diff.* pag. 24.

Jof. 24, 19.

Can we, without great furprize, obferve the affirmation, with the reafon for it, contained in the words
following? — Jofhua faid to the people: *Ye* CANNOT
ferve the Lord; FOR *he is an holy God*; *he will not
forgive your fins!* 'Tis very happy, that the omiffion of that letter, which the Collation of the Heb.
MSS proves to have been inferted or omitted in ten
thoufand words and almoft at pleafure, will reftore
to this important fentence its neceffary meaning.
Was it poffible, when Jofhua had been labouring to
perfuade, and fix Ifrael in the worfhip of *Jehovah*,
and which the people had juft promifed to do, that
he fhould immediately tell them, *Ye cannot ferve Jehovah!* This feems impoffible. Whereas, what he
was likely to have faid is now expreffed, only *that* 1
letter being omitted — *Ceafe not to ferve Jehovah*
(perfevere, keep the vow now made) *for he is an
holy God, he is a jealous God; he will not forgive your
defection, nor your fins. If ye fhall forfake Jehovah*
&c. This paffage has been well confidered, in *Mr
Hallet's Notes*; vol. 3, p. 2. Yet it will be neceffary
to add — that the verb תכלו is regularly *ceffabitis*
or *ceffetis*; and that the particles לא *non* and אל *ne*
are very often put for one another, or fignify the
fame thing: fee 1 *Kin.* 3; 26, 27.

Judg. 1, 19.

It has been one objection of the Deists, that Scripture gives here a deplorable account of the Divine *Omnipotence*: becaufe, *tho' the Lord was with Judah,* HE COULD NOT *drive out thofe who had chariots of iron.* But this, like many other objections to Revelation, is founded entirely on Miftranflation. For the Hebrew has here no verb for *could*; tho' that word is not diftinguifhed by *Italics*. The true verfion is this — JEHOVAH *was with Judah, fo that he drove out the inhabitants of the mountain*; but not TO DRIVE OUT *the inhabitants of the valley, becaufe they had chariots of iron*: i.e. he was with them, and gave them poffeffion of the former; but not, with them, *to give* them poffeffion of the latter: he was with them, for one conqueft, but not for the other. And the reafon is, becaufe thefe inhabitants of the valley were very ftrong; and therefore were fit to be one of the parties left, up and down in Canaan, to be the fcourges of Ifrael, when they might become rebellious. See chapter 2; 3,20—23 and 3; 1—4.

Judg. ch. 5.

This celebrated Song of triumph is moft defervedly admired; tho' fome Parts of it are at prefent very obfcure, and others unintelligible, in our Eng. tranflation. Befides particular difficulties; there is a general one, which pervades the whole: arifing (I humbly apprehend) from its being confidered as *entirely* the Song of *Deborah*. 'Tis certain, tho' very little attended to, that it is faid to have been fung *by Deborah* AND BY BARAK. 'Tis alfo certain, there are in it parts, which *Deborah* could not fing; as well as parts, which *Barak* could not sing. And therefore it seems necessary, in order to form a better judgment of this Song, that some probable *distribution* should be made of it; whilst those words, which seem most likely to have been sung by either party, should be assigned to their proper Name: either to that of *Deborah* the *Prophetess*, or that of *Barak* the *Captain-General*. For example: *Deborah* could not call upon *Deborah*, exhorting *herself* to *awake* &c; as in ver. 12. Neither could *Barak* exhort himself to *arise* &c; in the same verse. Again: *Barak* could not sing, *Till I Deborah arose, a mother in Israel*; in ver. 7. Nor could *Deborah* sing about *a damsel or two* for every soldier; in ver. 30: tho' indeed, as to this last article, the words are probably misunderstood. There are other parts also, which seem to require a different rendering. In ver. 2 — *for the avenging of Israel:* where the address probably is to those, who *took the lead* in Israel, on this great occasion; for the address in the next words is to those among *the people*, who were volunteers: as again, in ver. 9. Verses 11, 13, 14, and 15 have many great difficulties. It seems impossible, that (in ver. 23) any persons should be *cursed*, for not coming to *the help of* JEHOVAH, to *the help of* JEHOVAH, *against the mighty*. Nor does it seem more possible, that *Jael* should (in a sacred Song) be stiled *Blessed above women*, for the death of Sisera. Verse 25 mentions *Butter*; of which nothing is said in the history, in ch. 4, 19. Nor does the history say, that *Jael smote off* Sisera's head *with a hammer*; or indeed, that she *smote it off* at all: as here, in ver. 26. Lastly, as to ver. 30: there being no authority for rendering the words *a damsel* or 2 *damsels*; and the words in Hebrew being very much like to 2 other words in this same verse, which make excellent sense here: it seems highly probable, that they were originally the same. And at the end of this verse, which contains an exquisite compliment paid to *the Needlework* of the daughters of Israel, and which is here put with great art into the mouth of *Sisera's* MOTHER; the true sense (which has seldom, if ever, been expressed) seems to be — the hopes SHE had of some very *rich prize*, to adorn HER OWN NECK.

I shall now venture to give this whole Song, in the best Version I can make of it; assigning to *Deborah* and *Barak* separately, or together in Chorus, the Parts which to me appear most probable: and reserving (at present) my authorities, for the alterations here made in the common translation.

[Title] 1. *Then sang Deborah, and Barak the son of Abinoam, on that day; saying.*

2. Deb. For the *leaders*, who took the lead in Israel;
   Bar. For the *people*, who offered themselves willingly:
   Both —— BLESS YE JEHOVAH!

3. Deb. Hear, O ye kings!
   Bar. Give ear, O ye princes!
   Deb. I unto JEHOVAH will sing;
   Bar. I will answer in song to JEHOVAH,
   Both —— THE GOD OF ISRAEL.

4. D. O JEHOVAH! at thy going forth from Seir;
      at thy marching from the field of Edom:
   B. The earth trembled, even the heavens poured down;
      the thick clouds poured down the waters.

5. D. The mountains melted at JEHOVAH'S presence;
   B. Sinai itself, at the presence of JEHOVAH,
   Both —— THE GOD OF ISRAEL.

6. D. In the days of Shamgar, the son of Anath;
    in the days of Jael, the highways were deserted.
   B. For they, who had gone by straight paths,
    passed by ways that were very crooked:
7.   deserted were the villages in Israel.
   D. They were deserted, till I Deborah arose;
    till I arose a mother in Israel:
8.   they chose new gods!
   B. Then, when war was at the gates,
    was there a shield seen, or a spear,
    amongst forty thousand in Israel?
9. D. My heart is towards the rulers of Israel:
   B. Ye, who offered yourselves willingly among the people;
    Both —— BLESS YE JEHOVAH.

10. D. Ye, who ride upon white asses;
    ye, who sit upon the seat of judgment;
11. B. And ye, who travel upon the roads;
    talk of him with the voice of praise.
   D. Let them, who meet armed at the watering-places,
    there shew the righteous acts of JEHOVAH;
   B. And the righteousness of the villages in Israel:
    then shall they go down to the gates,
    Both —— THE PEOPLE OF JEHOVAH.

PART 2.

12. B. Awake, awake, *Deborah*!
    awake, awake, lead on the song.
   D. Arise, *Barak*, and lead thy captivity captive;
    Barak, thou son of Abinoam.   [chiefs,
13. B. Then, when the remainder descended after their
    JEHOVAH's people descended after me, against
    the mighty.   [*Amalek*;
14. D. Out of *Ephraim* was their beginning, at (mount)
    and after thee was *Benjamin*, against the nations.
   B. From *Machir* came masters in the art of war;
    and from *Zebulon* those, who threw the dart.

G

15. D. The princes in *Issachar* were numbered,
       together with Deborah and Barak.
    B. And *Issachar* was the guard of Barak,
       into the valley sent close at his feet.
    D. At the divisions of *Reuben*,
       great were the impressions of heart.
16. B. Why sattest thou among the rivulets?
       what, to hear the bleatings of the flocks?
    D. For the divisions of *Reuben*,
       great were the searchings of heart.
17. B. *Gad* dwelt quietly beyond Jordan;
       and *Dan*, why abode he in ships?
    D. *Asher* continued in the harbour of the seas;
       and remained among his craggy places.
18. B. *Zebulun* were the people, and *Naphtali*;
    D. Who exposed their lives unto death:
       Both — ON THE HEIGHTS OF THE FIELD.

19. D. The kings came, they fought;
       then fought the kings of Canaan:
    B. At Taanac, above the waters of Megiddo,
       the plunder of riches they did not receive.
20. D. From heaven did they fight;
       the stars, from their lofty stations,
       fought against *Sisera*.
21. B. The river Kishon swept them away;
       the river intercepting them, the river Kishon:
       it was there my soul trod down strength.
22. D. It was then the hoofs of the cavalry were battered
       by the scamperings, the scamperings of its strong [steeds.
23. B. Curse ye the land of Meroz,
       said the messenger of JEHOVAH:
    D. Curse ye heavily its inhabitants;
       because they came not for help.

       Both —— JEHOVAH WAS FOR HELP!
       JEHOVAH AGAINST THE MIGHTY!

PART 3.

24. D. *Praised among* women will be *Jael*,
  the wife of Heber the Kenite;
  among women in the tent she will be *praised*.
25. B. He asked water, she gave him milk;
  in a princely bowl she brought it.
26. D. Her *left* hand she put forth to the nail;
  and her right hand to the workmen's hammer.
  B. She struck *Sisera*, she smote his head;
  then she struck thro', and pierced his temples.
27. D.   At her feet, he bowed, he fell!
  B.   At her feet, he bowed, he fell!
  Both —— WHERE HE BOWED,
    THERE HE FELL DEAD!

28. D. Thro' the window she looked out, and called;
  even *the Mother of Sisera*, thro' the lattice:
  B. "Why is his chariot ashamed to return?
  "why so slow are the steps of his chariot?"
29. D. Her wise ladies answered her;
  nay, she returned answer to herself —
30. B. "Have they not found, divided the spoil?
  "*embroidery, double embroidery, for the captain's head!*
  "a prize of divers colours for SISERA!"
  D. "A prize of divers colours, of embroidery;
  "a coloured piece, of double embroidery, for
    [" MY NECK a prize!"

    Chorus,
   by Deborah and Barak.
31. SO PERISH ALL THINE ENEMIES, O JEHOVAH!

    Grand Chorus;
   by the whole Procession.
AND LET THOSE, WHO LOVE HIM,
BE AS THE SUN, GOING FORTH IN HIS MIGHT!

    [Note 7, see p. 38.]

Judg. 11, 31.

Whether Jephthah *did*, or *did not*, sacrifice his daughter — has been of late the subject of much controversy. But the chief difficulty seems happily removed by the learned Dr *Randolph*: who has shewn, that the latter clause in this verse does not necessarily refer to *any thing*, or *any person*, to be offered up; but that it may be translated — *and* (*or*) *I will offer up* TO HIM (to GOD) *a burnt-offering*. The pronoun, thus suffixed, is often *dative*; just as, in English — *offer* HIM *a present, do* HIM *honour*. The vow therefore was; that if what came forth to meet him was fit to be *devoted to the immediate service of God*, it should be so: if not, *he would offer unto God a burnt-offering*. The event corresponded. The daughter of Jephthah, coming forth, voluntarily consented to withdraw from the world, and devote the remainder of her life towards assisting in such sacred matters, as were in those days transacted near the Ark of the Lord, and in the services of Religion. See all that follows, in verses 35—39 of this chapter of *Judges*; and *Levit.* 27, 2—4. See also the whole of Dr *Randolph*'s excellent Sermon, on this subject, preached at Oxford, 1766; and Bp *Lowth*'s Note on *Isaiah*, pag. 199.

Judg. 15, 4.

The 300 *Foxes*, caught by Samson, have been so frequently the subject of banter and ridicule, that we should consider, whether the words may not admit a more rational interpretation. For, besides the improbability arising here from the *number* of these Foxes, the *use* made of them is also very strange.

If

If thefe animals were tied tail to tail; they would probably pull contrary ways, and confequently ftand ftill: whereas a firebrand, tied to the tail of each fox fingly, would have been far more likely to anfwer the purpofe here intended. To obviate thefe difficulties, it has been well remarked, that the word שועלים, here tranflated *foxes*, fignifies alfo *handfuls* (*Ezek.* 13, 19 *handfuls of barley*); if we leave out that one letter ו, which has been inferted or omitted elfewhere almoft at pleafure. No lefs than 7 Heb. MSS want that letter here; and read שעלים. Admitting this verfion, we fee—that Samfon took 300 *handfuls* (or fheaves) of corn, and 150 *firebrands*—that he turned the fheaves *end to end*, and put a firebrand *between the two ends, in the midft*—and then, fetting the brands on fire, *fent the fire into the ftanding corn* of the Philiftines. The fame word is now ufed twice in one chapter (*Ezek.* 13, 4 and 19) in the former verfe fignifying *foxes*, in the latter *handfuls*: and in 1 *Kin.* 20, 10, where we render it *handfuls*, it is αλωπεξι in the Greek verfion. See *Memoirs of Literature*, fol. 1712, p. 15.

Judg. 16; 2, 13 and 14.

'Tis no great wonder, that *one verb*, however plainly neceffary, has been omitted in the Heb. copies, in the beginning of this 2d verfe; when about 20 *Heb. words* have been omitted at the end of verfe 13. The verb (ויגד) omitted in the 2d verfe, is expreffed in the Greek verfion. And in ver. 13, after the Heb. text has begun the fentence thus—*And he faid unto her: If thou weaveft the 7 locks of my head with the web* [the Greek verfion goes on—*and fafteneft it with a pin unto the wall; then fhall I be weak,*

weak, and be as another man. And it came to pass, when he slept, that Delilah took the 7 locks of his head, and wove them with the web] *and she fastened it with a pin; and said unto him, The Philistines be upon thee.*

Judg. 18, 30.

This first idolatrous priest in Israel is called *Jonathan, the son of Gershom, the son of* MANASSEH (מנשה) which word was originally (משה) MOSES. Some Rabbies have confessed, that the *suspended* letter has been here added, *for the honour of Moses:* that He might not be recorded, as Grand-father of the *first* idolatrous *Priest.* The word is still *Moses* in some Greek *MSS,* as it is now in the printed Vulgat. See my *Gen. Diff.* p. 10 &c.

1 Sam. 5; 6, 7.

The Present, made to Israel by the Philistines, was *double*; consisting of 5 golden *Emerods,* and also of 5 golden *Mice* (ch. 6; 4, 11, 18): and the double Present proves, that there had been a double Calamity. This chapter now mentions historically the calamity of the *Emerods* only: but the Greek and Vulg. versions record here another calamity, arising from *a multitude of Mice*; which also is recorded by Josephus: p. 311. It is afterwards mentioned incidentally, in the present Heb. Text, at ch. 6, 5.

1 Sam. 6, 19.

On this very remarkable passage, I have already (in a Dissertation, 8°. 1768) published several arguments to prove, that the number 50,000 is a corrupt addition; and that the original number here of the men destroyed, for looking into the Ark, was

not

not 50070, but only 70: agreeably to 3 *Heb. MSS*, confirmed by the authority of *Jofephus*, p. 313.

1 Sam. 12, 11.

And the Lord fent Jerubbaal, and BEDAN, *and Jephthah, and* SAMUEL; *and delivered you out of the hand of your enemies on every fide.* That *Jerubbaal* (i.e. Gideon) and alfo *Jephthah* had been eminent Deliverers, is certain. But, that the Ifraelites were ever delivered by *Bedan*, is no where faid. And that *Samuel* fhould name himfelf, as having been one of their Deliverers, is by no means probable, if it had been really true. 'Tis happy therefore, that for *Bedan* the name is BARAK; in the Gr. Syr. and Arab. verfions, and alfo in fome old MSS of the Vulgat: and that *Samuel* is SAMSON in the Syr. and Ar. verfions; the word *Samfon* being now alfo in the Chald. paraphrafe, and in fome old MSS of the Vulgat. The heroes, here mentioned, are thus quoted in *Hebrews* 11, 32 — *the time would fail me to tell of Gideon, and of Barak, and of Samfon, and of Jephthah.*

1 Sam. 13, 8.

— *according to the fet time that Samuel* (had appointed): *but Samuel came not.* Tho' the verb, fo evidently neceffary, is omitted in the common Heb. Text: yet 4 Heb. MSS read here שם *had appointed*; whilft 2 others, with the 3 oldeft Editions, have here אמר *had faid*. The verb *fam* has been evidently left out, becaufe the next word *Samuel* begins with the fame letters.

1 Sam. 17; 12—31.

Thefe 20 Verfes feem to be an *Interpolation*. Various arguments in proof of it were offered in my 2*d*
Differtat.

Differtat. on the Heb. Text, p. 418—431; which arguments have appeared to many very satisfactory, and to others highly probable: see *Dr Chandler's Life of David*; vol. 1, p. 64, 69.

Next to the authority of the *Context*, was urged that of the *Vat.* Gr. MS, which has not these verses; and also that of the MS, from which the *Alex.* MS was copied: for the latter, tho' it has these verses, was copied from a MS which had them not. My *Gen. Differtat.* (p. 9) furnishes new arguments: namely, that several other Greek MSS have not these 20 verses; and that some old Greek MSS retain them, but marked with *asterisks*, because not found by Origen in his Gr. copies of the LXX. If then they were not in Origen's MSS of that old version, 'tis very probable, they were not in that version at first: if they were not in the LXX at first, 'tis very probable they were not in the Heb. Text 150 years before Christ: and if not then in the Heb. Text, 'tis very probable they were not in that Text originally. If conviction shall arise from the Context, supported by these arguments; in the next Revisal of our Translation, these 20 Verses will be omitted.

1 Sam. 18, 27.

David slew of the Philistines 200 *men* &c. Dr Wall has properly observed, that the Gr. version here has only 100: and that the number is only 100, in Saul's covenant, ver. 25; as well as in the words of David himself, 2 *Sam.* 3, 14.

1 Sam. 20, 12.

The following words must surprize all, who read them with attention — *And Jonathan said* UNTO *David:*

vid: O Lord God of Israel, *when I have founded my father* &c. But excellent sense is restored; if, by inserting the word חי (*vivit*) agreeably to 2 Heb. MSS, we read thus — As Jehovah the God of Israel LIVETH! *When I have founded my father; if there be good, and I then send not unto thee, and shew it thee* &c.

1 Sam. 23, 22.

The men of Ziph having informed Saul, that David hid himself in strong holds, in the wood, south of Jeshimon; Saul here says to them — *Go, I pray you,* PREPARE YET, *and know, and see his place, where his haunt is.* 'Tis evident, that הכינו עוד *prepare yet* should be הבינו עוד *understand further, learn more particularly:* and this reading has the authority of 2 MSS, with the first printed Edition. This is one of the many mistakes introduced, on account of the great likeness between the Heb. letters *Beth* and *Caph.*

1 Sam. 28; 16, 17.

— *the Lord is departed from thee, and is become thine enemy. And the Lord hath done to* HIM, *as he spake by me: for the Lord hath rent the kingdom out of thine hand* &c. Tho' David is mentioned afterwards; yet the order of the words seems evidently to require, that לו *to him* should be לך *to thee:* as in 3 Heb. MSS, with the Gr. and Vulg. versions.

2 Sam. 5; 6 and 8.

A correction of some very great corruptions in the Text of these 2 verses, and an alteration of our English version, make a considerable Part of my *First Dissertation* on the Heb. Text; from p. 27 to 47.

47. And I shall here give our present version; subjoining, in the *Italic* character, what seems to be a just emendation of this remarkable passage.

6. And the king and his men went to Jerusalem, unto the Jebusites, the inhabitants of the land; who spake unto David, saying: Except thou take away the blind and the lame, thou shalt not come in hither; thinking, David cannot come in hither. 8. And David said — Whosoever getteth up to the gutter, and smiteth the Jebusites, and the lame and the blind, that are hated of David's soul, wherefore they said, The blind and the lame shall not come into the house. * * * *

6. *And the king and his men went to Jerusalem, unto the Jebusites, the inhabitants of the land; who spake unto David, saying: Thou shalt not come in hither; for the blind and the lame shall drive thee away, by saying, David shall not come in hither.* 8. *And David said —Whosoever smiteth the Jebusites, and thro' the subterraneous passage reacheth the lame and the blind, who hate the life of David (because the blind and the lame said, He shall not come into the house) shall be chief and captain. So Joab the* * * * * * * *son of Zeruiah went up first, and was chief.*

2 Sam. 6, 5.

Amongst all the assistances for correcting the Heb. Text, one of the best certainly is *a comparison of parallel places*; not with a design of reducing both to a constant *agreement* in *words*, but to a *consistency* in *sense:* particularly, where one place is clearly corrupted, that we correct it by the other where it is clearly right. The utility of this method will be very evident from the following passage; which represents

prefents David and the Ifraelites, when bringing up the ark, as *playing on all manner of firwood, even on harps, and on pfalteries, and on timbrels, and on cornets, and on cymbals.* But the words are literally *on all the woods* (or *trees*) *of the firs, and on harps* &c. Here then it is fair to prefume a corruption; efpecially, as from this account the whole Mufic was *inſtrumental*, and nothing was *fung* at all. If now we confult and apply the parallel place (1 *Chro.* 13, 8) we ſhall find theſe matters perfectly right; while the true readings in *Chronicles* are confirmed by the Gr. verſion in *Samuel.*

S. משחקים בכל עצי ברושים ובכנרות ובנבלים ובתפים &c.
C. - - - - - עז ובשירים - - - - - - - &c.
— played on all manner of firwood, even on harps &c.
—played *with all their might, & with fongs,* & with harps &c.

2 Sam chap. 7.

This chapter is one of the moſt important in the Old Teſtament; and yet ſome of its moſt intereſting verſes are very improperly rendered in our Tranſlation: it therefore demands our moſt careful conſideration. And as, in the courſe of theſe *Remarks*, I propoſe to conſider, and hope to explain ſome of the Prophecies deſcriptive of THE MESSIAH, which were fulfilled in JESUS CHRIST; amongſt which Prophecies, *that* contained in this chapter is worthy of particular attention: I ſhall introduce it, with a general ſtate of this great Argument.

It having pleaſed GOD, that, between the time of *a Meſſiah* being firſt promiſed, and the time of his coming, there ſhould be delivered by the Prophets a variety of *Marks*, by which *the Meſſiah* was to be known, and diſtinguiſhed from every other man;

man; it was impossible for any one to prove himself *the Messiah*, whose *character* did not answer to these *Marks:* and of course it was necessary, that *all these Criteria*, thus divinely *foretold*, should be *fulfilled* in the Character of *Jesus Christ*. That these prophetic descriptions of the Messiah were *numerous*, appears from Christ and his Apostles (*Luk.* 24; 27, 44: *Acts* 17; 2, 3: 28, 23 &c) who referred the Jews to the Old Testament, as containing abundant evidence of *His* being THE MESSIAH, because *He fulfilled all the Prophecies* descriptive of that *singular* Character. The chief of these Prophecies related to

— his being *Miraculously born of a Virgin*;
— the *Time*, and *Place*, of his Birth;
— the *Tribe*, and *Family*, he was to descend from;
— the *Miracles*, he was to perform;
— the *Manner* of his preaching;
— his *Humility*, and *mean* Appearance;
— the perfect *Innocence* of his life;
— the Greatness of his *Sufferings*;
— the *Treachery* of his Betrayer;
— the Circumstances of his *Trial*;
— the Nature of his *Death*, and *Burial*;
— and, to his *Miraculous Resurrection*.

Now amongst all the circumstances, which form this Chain of Prophecy; the first reference, made in the New Testament, relates to his *Descent:* for the New Testament begins with asserting, that JESUS CHRIST *was the son of David, the son of Abraham*. As to the descent of Christ from ABRAHAM; every one knows, that Christ was born *a Jew*; and consequently descended from Jacob, the grandson of Abraham. And we all know, that the Promise given to Abraham

ham concerning the Messiah is *recorded* in the *history* of Abraham's life: in *Gen.* 22, 18. Christ being also to descend from DAVID; there can be no doubt, but that this promise, as made to David, was *recorded* likewise in the *history* of David. 'Tis remarkable, that David's life is given more at large, than that of any other person in the Old Testament; and it cannot be supposed, that the historian omitted to record *that promise*, which was more honourable to David than any other circumstance. The *record* of this Promise, if written at all, must have been written in this chapter; in the message *from* GOD *by Nathan to David*, which is here inserted. Here (I am fully persuaded) the promise was, and still is, recorded: and the chief reason, why our Divines have so frequently missed it, or been so much perplexed about it, is owing to our very improper translation of the 10th and 14th verses.

This wrong translation, in a part of Scripture so very interesting, has been artfully laid hold of, and expatiated upon splendidly, by the Deistical Author of *the Grounds and Reasons of the Christian Religion*; who pretends to demonstrate, that the promise of a Messiah could not be here recorded. His reasons (hitherto I believe unanswered) are 3 — 1st: because, in ver. 10, the prophet speaks of *the future* prosperity of the Jews, as to be afterwards *fixed*, and *no more afflicted*; which circumstances are totally repugnant to the fate of the Jews, as connected with the birth and death of Christ — 2dly: because the Son, here promised, was (ver. 13) to *build an house*; which house, it is pretended, must mean *the temple of Solomon*; and of course *Solomon* must be the

Son

Son here promised — and 3dly: because verse 14 supposes, that this Son *might commit iniquity*; which could not be supposed of *The Messiah*. The first of these objections is founded on our wrong translation of verse 10; where the words should be expressed as relating to the time *past* or *present*. For the prophet is there declaring what great things GOD *had already done* for David and his people — that he *had* raised David from the sheepfold to the throne — and that he *had* planted the Israelites in a place of safety; at rest from all those enemies, who had so often before afflicted them. That the verbs ושמתי and ונטעתי may be rendered in the time *past* or *present*, is allowed by our own translators; who here (ver. 11) render והניחתי *and have caused thee to rest*, and also render והגיד *and telleth:* which construction, made necessary here by the context, might be confirmed by other proofs almost innumerable. The translation therefore should run thus: *I took thee from the sheepcote — and have made thee a great name — and I* HAVE APPOINTED *a place for my people Israel; and* HAVE PLANTED *them, that they dwell in a place of their own, and move no more. Neither* DO *the children of wickedness afflict them any more; as before time, and as since the time that I commanded judges to be over Israel: and I* HAVE CAUSED *thee to rest from all thine enemies.*

Objection the 2d is founded on a mistake in the sense. David indeed had proposed to build an house to GOD; which GOD did not admit. Yet, approving the piety of David's intention, GOD was pleased to reward it by promising — that HE *would make an house for* DAVID; which house, to be thus erected

by

by GOD, was certainly *not material*, or made of stones; but *a spiritual house*, or *family*, to be raised up for the honour of GOD and the salvation of mankind. And this house, which GOD would make, was to be built by *David's* SEED; and this seed was to be raised up, AFTER *David slept with his fathers:* which words clearly exclude *Solomon*, who was set up, and placed upon the throne, BEFORE *David was dead*. This Building, promised by GOD, was to be erected by one of David's descendants, who was also to be *an everlasting King:* and indeed the *House*, and the *Kingdom*, were both of them to be *established for ever*. Now that this *House*, or spiritual building, was to be set up, together with a *Kingdom*, by the Messiah, is clear from *Zachariah*; who very emphatically says (6; 12, 13) *Behold the man, whose name is the* Branch — HE SHALL BUILD THE TEMPLE *of the Lord. Even* HE SHALL BUILD THE TEMPLE *of the Lord; and he shall bear the glory, and shall sit and rule upon his* THRONE. &c. Observe also the language of the *New* Testament. In 1 *Corinth*. 3, 9—17; St Paul says —*Ye are God's* BUILDING— *Know ye not, that* YE *are the Temple of God? — the Temple of God is holy, which Temple* YE *are*. And the author of the Epistle to the *Hebrews* seems to have his eye upon this very promise in *Samuel*, concerning *a Son* to David, and of the *House* which he should build; when he says (3, 6) — CHRIST, AS A SON, OVER HIS OWN HOUSE; WHOSE HOUSE ARE WE.

As to the 3d and greatest difficulty; *that* also may be removed, by a more just translation of verse 14: for the Heb. words do not properly signify what they are now made to speak. 'Tis certain, that the

principal

principal word בהעותו is not the active infinitive of *Kal*, which would be בעותו; but העות from עוה is in *Niphal*, as הגלות from גלה. 'Tis also certain, that a verb, which in the active voice signifies to *commit iniquity*, may in the passive signify to *suffer for iniquity:* and hence it is, that nouns from such verbs sometimes signify *iniquity*, sometimes *punishment*. See Lowth's *Isaiah*, p. 187; with many other authorities, which shall be produced hereafter. The way being thus made clear, we are now prepared for abolishing our translation — *if he commit iniquity*; and also for adopting the true one — *even in his suffering for iniquity*. The Messiah, who is thus the person possibly here spoken of, will be made still more manifest from the whole verse thus translated. *I will be his father, and he shall be my son:* EVEN IN HIS SUFFERING FOR INIQUITY, *I shall chasten him with the rod of men* (with the rod *due to men*) *and with the stripes* (due to) *the children of* ADAM. And this construction is well supported by *Isaiah* 53; 4 & 5 — *he hath carried* OUR SORROWS (i.e. the sorrows *due to* us, and which we must otherwise have suffered) — *he was wounded for our transgressions, he was bruised for our iniquities: the chastisement of our peace was upon him; and with his stripes we are healed.* See Note p. 479, in Hallet, on *Heb.* 11, 26. Thus then GOD declares himself the father of the Son here meant;[*] and promises, that, even amidst the *sufferings* of this Son (as they would be for the sins of others, not for his own) his mercy should still attend him: nor should his favour be ever removed from *this king*, as it had been from *Saul*. And

[*] See also *Heb.* 1, 5.

thus

thus (as it follows) *thine house* (O David) *and thy kingdom, shall* (in Messiah) *be established for ever, before* ME (before GOD): *thy throne shall be established for ever.* Thus the Angel, delivering his message to the Virgin-Mother (*Luk.* 1; 32, 33) speaks, as if he was quoting from this very prophecy — *The Lord God shall give unto him the throne of his father* DAVID; *and he shall reign over the house of Jacob* FOR EVER: *and of his kingdom there shall be no end.* In ver. 16 לפניך is here rendered as לפני; on the authority of 1 Heb. MS, with the Gr. and Syr. versions; and indeed nothing could be established *for ever,* in the presence of *David,* but in the presence of GOD only. So Dr S. Clarke.

Having thus shewn, that the words fairly admit here the promise made to David, that *from his seed* should arise *Messiah, the everlasting King*; it may be necessary to add — that, if the *Messiah* be the person here meant, as suffering innocently for the sins of others, *Solomon* cannot be; nor can this be a prophecy admitting such double sense, or be applied properly to two such opposite characters. *Of whom speaketh the prophet this? of* HIMSELF, *or of* SOME OTHER *man?* — This was a question properly put by the Ethiopian treasurer (*Acts* 8, 34) who never dreamt, that such a description as he was reading could relate to different persons: and Philip shews him, that the Person was *Jesus* only. So here, it may be asked — *Of whom* speaketh the prophet this? of *Solomon,* or of *Christ?* It must be answered — of *Christ:* one reason is, because the description does *not agree* to *Solomon*; and therefore *Solomon,* being necessarily excluded in a single sense, must also be

excluded

excluded in a double. Lastly: if it would be universally held absurd, to consider the promise of Messiah made to ABRAHAM, as relating to *any other* Person *besides* Messiah; why is there not an equal absurdity, in giving a *double* sense to the promise of Messiah thus made to DAVID?

Next to our present very improper translation, the cause of the common confusion here has been —— not distinguishing the promise here made, as to *Messiah* alone, from another made as to *Solomon* alone: the 1st brought by *Nathan*, the 2d by *Gad*; the 1st near the *beginning* of David's reign, the 2d near the *end* of it; the 1st, relating to Messiah's *Spiritual* kingdom, *everlasting without conditions*; the 2d, relating *to the fate* of the *Temporal* kingdom of Solomon, and his heirs, depending entirely on their *obedience* or *rebellion*. 1 *Chron.* 22; 8—13 & 28, 7. Let the first Message be compared with this second in 1 *Chron.* 22; 8—13: which the Syr. version (at ver. 8) tells us, was delivered by *a prophet*, and the Arab. says — by *the prophet* GAD. This 2d message was after David's *many wars*, when *he had shed much blood*; and it was this second message, that, out of all David's sons, appointed *Solomon* to be his successor. At the time of the *1st* message *Solomon* was *not born*; it being delivered soon after David became king at Jerusalem: but Solomon *was born*, at the time of this 2d message. For tho' our translation very wrongly says (1 *Chron.* 22, 9) — *a son* SHALL BE *born to thee — and his name shall be Solomon*; yet the Heb. text expresly speaks of him as *then born* — *Behold, a son* (נולד *natus est*) IS BORN *to thee*: and therefore the

words

words following muſt be rendered — *Solomon is his name, and I will give peace in his days: he ſhall build an houſe for my name* &c.

2 Sam. 7, 19.

From David's addreſs to GOD, after receiving the meſſage by Nathan, 'tis plain that David underſtood *the Son* promiſed to be THE MESSIAH; in whom *his houſe* was to be *eſtabliſhed for ever*. But the words, which ſeem moſt expreſſive of this, are in this verſe now rendered very unintelligibly — *and is this the manner of man?* Whereas the words וזאת תורת האדם literally ſignify — *and this is* (or *muſt be*) *the law of the man, or of the Adam* i.e. this promiſe muſt relate to *the law*, or ordinance, made by GOD to *Adam*, concerning *the Seed of the Woman; the Man, or the ſecond* ADAM: as the Meſſiah is expreſsly called by St Paul: 1 *Cor.* 15; 45, 47. This meaning will be yet more evident from the parallel place, 1 *Chron.* 17, 17: where the words of David are now miſerably rendered thus — *and thou haſt regarded me, according to the eſtate of a man of high degree*. Whereas the words וראיתני כתור האדם המעלה literally ſignify— *and thou haſt regarded me, according to the order of the* ADAM THAT IS FUTURE, or THE MAN THAT IS FROM ABOVE (for the word המעלה very remarkably ſignifies *hereafter* as to time, and *from above* as to place): and thus St Paul, including both ſenſes — THE SECOND MAN *is* THE LORD FROM HEAVEN — and, *Adam is the figure of him that was to come, or the future*: Rom. 5, 14. See the *Preface* of the late learned Mr *Peters*, on *Job*; referred to, and confirmed as to this intereſting point, in a Note ſubjoined to my Sermon on A VIRGIN

SHALL CONCEIVE &c. pag. 49—52; 8°. 1765: a part of that Note here follows — "The Speech of "David (2 *Sam.* 7, 18—29) is such, as one might "naturally expect from a person overwhelmed with "the greatness of the promised blessing: for it is "abrupt, full of wonder, and fraught with repeti- "tions. *And now, what can David say unto thee?* "What, indeed! *For thou,* LORD GOD, *knowest thy* "*servant:* thou knowest the hearts of all men, and "seest how full my own heart is. *For thy word's* "*sake,* for the sake of former prophecies; *and ac-* "*cording to thine own heart,* from the mere motive "of thy wisdom and goodness; *hast thou done all* "*these great things, to make thy servant know them.* "I now perceive the reason of those miraculous "providences, which have attended me from my "youth up; *taken from following the sheep,* and con- "ducted thro' all difficulties *to be ruler of thy people:* "and shall I distrust the promise now made me? "*Thy words be true.* If the preceding remarks on "this whole passage are just, and well-grounded; "then may we see clearly the chief foundation of "what St Peter tells us (*Act.* 2, 30) concerning "DAVID: that, *being a prophet, and* KNOWING *that* "*God had sworn with an oath to him, that of the fruit* "*of his loins, according to the flesh, he would raise up* "CHRIST, *to sit on his throne?*"

2 Sam. 7, 18.

And king David went in, and SAT *before the Lord; and he said: Who am I, O Lord God?* &c. It seems very strange, that David, when coming before the Ark, to express his solemn thanks, should SIT; and
not

not rather *stand*, as Solomon did: 1 *Kings* 3, 15.
The original word here has 2 significations, as derived from different verbs; in the 1st verse of this chapter it signifies *he sat*; but in the 20th verse of the preceding chapter it signifies, and is properly translated, *he returned*. David was come back from the Ark to his own house: there he passed the night: there he was visited the next day by Nathan: and then, he *returned* to the Ark, there to offer up to GOD his thanksgiving.

2 *Sam.* 8 & 10 compared with 1 *Chr.* 18 & 19.

The very great utility of comparing *Parallel* places may be further ascertained, by a comparison of some Parts of the chapters above specified.

S. 8, 1—David took Metheg-ammah   3. David smote
C. 18, 1—*David took Gath and her towns*   3. *David smote*

S. Hadadezer   4. And David took from him 1000
C. *Hadarezer*   4. *And David took from him* 1000 *chariots*,

S. and 700 horsemen, and 20000 foot.   6. Then Da-
C. *and* 7000 *horsemen, and* 20000 *foot.*   6. *Then Da-*

S. vid put garrisons in Syria   8. And from Betah and
C. *vid put   in Syria*   8. *And from Tibbath and*

S. Berothai cities of Hadadezer   9. When Toi heard, that
C. *Chun cities of Hadarezer*   9. *When Tou heard, that*

S. David had smitten Hadadezer   10. Then Toi sent Jo-
C. *David had smitten Hadarezer*   10.   *He sent Hado-*

S. ram his son   12—Syria and Moab   13—Syrians, in
C. *ram his son*   11—*Edom and Moab*   12—Edomites, in

S. the valley of salt, 18000   17—Ahimelech—& Seraiah
C. *the valley of salt,* 18000   16—*Abimelech — & Shavsha*

S. was the scribe.   10,16 Shobach the captain   17 David
C. *was   scribe.*   19,16 *Shophach the captain*   17 *David*

118   *Remarks on select Passages in*

S. passed over Jordan, and came חלאמה to Helam   18 David
C. *passed over Jordan, and came* אלהם *upon them*   18 *David*

S. slew   700 chariots of the Syrians, and
C. *slew of the Syrians* 7000 *chariots,*   and

S. 40000 horsemen; and smote Shobach &c.
C. 40000 *footmen;   and killed Shophach* &c.

2 Sam. 12, 31.

— *and put* them *under saws, and under harrows of iron, and under axes of iron, and made them pass thro' the brick-kiln.* If it is a duty of humanity to vindicate every man's character, when charged wrongfully; this is the more necessary, in proportion as the character is more exalted. DAVID was a prince truly eminent and illustrious. And tho' it is certain, that he was guilty of some great crimes; yet it is as certain, that he ought not to be charged with crimes, or cruelties, of which he was really innocent. One heavy charge has been urged against him, from this part of the Sacred History; as if it represented him *sawing,* and *harrowing,* and *chopping,* and *burning,* all the Ammonites: a savage representation! which has raised much clamour among the enemies of Revelation. But, a charge so severe as this, and so very unlikely to be true, should be examined into with great care: and if the Original Records are consulted accurately; they will, I humbly apprehend, set the matter in a different light. Here in *Samuel,* the 2 first words signify *et posuit in serra,* as in the interlinear Lat. version: which words are a true key to the following; and fairly shew, that David *put* them *to the saw,* and sentenced them to the other hard works of Slavery. The whole mistake

here

here seems to have arisen from an error in the Heb. text of the *parallel* place in *Chronicles*; by the omission of one small part of one letter: for the word, instead of וישׂם *et posuit*, is now וישׂר *et serravit*, in 1 *Chron*. 20, 3. This corruption was probably very antient, because expressed in the Greek version. But still, there can be little doubt, that the 2 words were at first the same: and if so, the Context requires the word in *Samuel*; especially, as that reading is confirmed by 5 Heb. MSS in *Chronicles*.

2 Sam. 13, 21.

But when king David heard all these things, he was very wroth ——— The Greek and Vulg. versions here add—*yet he would not grieve the soul of Amnon his son; for he loved him, because he was his firstborn.* 'Tis scarce possible to suppose, that this censure upon *David*, for his improper fondness for a wicked son, could be inserted in these Versions; unless found formerly in the Heb. Text: and 'tis still less credible, that *Josephus* also should pass the same censure on a favourite King, without sufficient authority. Why this censure may have been *omitted*, is not difficult to conjecture.

2 Sam. 13, 37.

Notice has been already taken of some genuine words now omitted: and another instance occurs here, where the name *David* is absolutely necessary, and as such is inserted in our present translation. This word is in all the Antient Versions; and it is also happily preserved in a curious Heb. MS, belonging to HIS MAJESTY's library: tho' (which is also very remarkable) it has been found in *that*

MS only. Another name quite neceſſary, yet omitted likewiſe, is that of *Iſhboſheth*, in 2 *Sam.* 3, 7: but this word is preſerved in 4 Heb. MSS, and in the 3 firſt Editions; as well as in all the Antient Verſions.

2 Sam. 15, 7.

— *after* 40 *years.* 'There being no Æra, from which theſe 40 years are to be computed; it can ſcarce be doubted, but the true number here is 4: for when Abſalom fled to Geſhur, *he was there* 3 *years* (13, 38;) and this event was ſoon after his return. In my 2d *Diſſert. on the Heb. Text,* pag. 357, I obſerved — that this number 4 is confirmed by the Syr. verſion, by Joſephus, Theodoret, the famous Vulgat of Sixtus, with the Gothic Lat. MS, and ſome others. To theſe may be now added 4 Lat. MSS, in my own poſſeſſion; all of which have 4, not 40: and, what is more important, the numeral here is alſo 4, in at leaſt 4 Greek MSS; namely, *Paris S. Germ.* 3, *Royal library* 2, *Carmelite,* and *Vatican* 330. One inſtance this, amongſt many, to prove the great advantages, which would reſult from a Collation of the *Greek* MSS, and the MSS of the other antient Verſions of the Old Teſtament.

2 Sam. 15, 8.

— *while I abode at Geſhur in Syria.* Inſtances have been already given, in which the ſimilar words ארם *Syria* and אדום (or אדם) *Edom* have been exchanged by miſtake: and another plain proof occurs here. For, that *Geſhur,* the country of Talmai, to whom Abſalom fled, lay on the ſouth of Canaan, and in or near *Edom,* is certain from *Jud.* 1, 10; 2 *Sam.* 13, 37; and 1 *Sam.* 27, 8.

2 Sam. 18, 3.

The adverb עתה *nunc* is frequently confounded with the pronoun אתה *tu*; becaufe fometimes pronounced, tho' very improperly, in the fame manner. The word here fhould evidently be the pronoun; for otherwife the fentence runs thus — *But the people anfwered David, Thou fhalt not go forth: for if* WE *flee away, they will not care for* US; *neither, if half of* US *die, will they care for* US: *but* NOW *art worth ten thoufand of* US. The word is the pronoun in the Gr. and Vulg. verfions, and 1 Heb. MS. We have a remarkable inftance of each of thefe 2 words being altered to the other; and the exchange takes place in 1 *Kin.* 1, 18 and 20 verfes. The Text of ver. 18 fays — *And now behold, Adonijah reigneth; and* NOW, *my lord the king, knoweft it not:* where the word is the pronoun *thou*, in all the antient Verfions and Chald. paraphrafe, confirmed by no lefs than 200 Heb. MSS. And the Text of ver. 20 fays — *And* THOU, *my lord O king, the eyes of all Ifrael are upon thee &c:* where the word is the adverb *now* in the Syr. Ar. and Vulg. verfions, with the Chald. paraphrafe, confirmed by near 100 Heb. MSS.

2 Sam. 21, 8.

The king took the 2 fons of Rizpah, the daughter of Aiah, whom fhe bore (ילדה) *unto Saul — and the 5 fons of* MICHAL *the daughter of Saul, whom fhe brought up* (ילדה) *for Adriel the fon of Barzillai.* Tho' our laft Eng. tranflators have fometimes expreffed, not what they found in the Heb. text, but what in their opinion ought to be there; yet at other times, rather than admit a corruption, they have offered violence to the fenfe of the plaineft words:

as in this instance — by rendering the same verb, in the very same connexion, very differently and without authority. But, the corruption is obvious. For, 'tis clear from 2 *Sam.* 6,23, that *Michal*, Saul's daughter, had no child. And, 'tis clear from 1 *Sam.* 18, 19, that Adriel's wife was *Merab*. It is therefore for the honour of 2 Heb. MSS, to have preserved here the name *Merab*, undoubtedly the true reading.

2 Sam. 21, 19.

My first Dissertation on the Heb. Text (8°. 1753, pag. 78) pointed out 3 great corruptions, in this one verse; all of them chiefly corrected by the parallel place 1 *Chron.* 20, 5. Without repeating here the whole proof, I shall observe, that one corruption is the insertion of a word signifying *weavers*, taken in carelessly from the line under it: the next is, that the proper name of *Lahmi* (את לחמי) is corrupted into (בית הלחמי) *a Bethlehemite:* and the last is, that the word for *brother* is become a particle signifying only *the*. It may be proper however to add here the Eng. passage of *Samuel*, compared with that in *Chronicles*.

Sam. Elhanan the son of Jaare (weavers) a Bethle-
Chro. *Elhanan the son of Jair   slew Lahmi*
Sam. hemite, slew Goliath the Gittite; the staff of whose
Chro. *the brother of Goliath the Gittite; whose spear —*
Sam. spear was like a beam of the weavers.
Chro. *staff was like a beam of the weavers.*

2 Sam. 22.

The very sublime Poetry, contained in this chapter, is universally admired: and yet it cannot be perfectly understood, till it is known, WHO is *the Speaker* — *Who* the Person, thus triumphant over mighty enemies — *Whose* sufferings occasioned such a dreadful convulsion of nature — and *Who*, upon his deliverance, inflicted such vengeance on his own People, and also became thus a King over the Heathen. Should we be told, that this person was *David*; it will be very difficult to shew, how this description can possibly agree with that character. But, if it did in fact agree; yet would it contradict *St Paul*, who quotes part of it, as predicting *the Conversion of the Gentiles, under Christ the Messiah.* Rom. 15, 9; and Heb. 2, 13: see *Peirce*'s Comment. p. 50. Now if the Person, represented as speaking thro' this divine Ode, be *David only*; the Messiah is excluded: and if it be the *Messiah only*, then David is excluded. In consequence of the difficulties, resulting from each of these suppositions; the general idea has been, that it relates *both to David and to Messiah*, as *a prophecy of a double sense:* first, as spoken by David of *himself*; and yet, to be understood, in a secondary sense, of the *Messiah*. But, it must be remarked here; that, if spoken only of David, it is not *a prediction* of any thing future, but a *thanksgiving* for favours past; and therefore is no *prophecy* at all. And further: it could not be a prophecy descriptive of David, unless the particulars agreed to David; which they evidently do not. If then David be here necessarily excluded from the *single* sense, he must be excluded also from the *double* sense: because nothing can be intended, by any sacred writer, to relate to *two* persons; unless it be TRUE of *Both*. But it not being the case here, as to David; we must conclude, that this Song relates only to *the Messiah:* and on this subject an excellent Dissertation by the late Mr *Peirce* is subjoined to his

Comment on the *Epiftle to the Hebrews*. It may be neceffary to add here two remarks. The 24th verfe now ends with — *I have kept myfelf from mine iniquity*; which words, it is objected, are not proper, if applied to the Meffiah. But this difficulty is removed in part by the Context, which reprefents the Speaker as *perfectly innocent and righteous*; and this exactly agrees with the proof arifing from the Syr. and Ar. verfions (and alfo the Chald. par.) that this word was antiently מעונים *ab iniquitatibus*: confequently this is one of the many inftances, where the final *Mem* is improperly omitted by the Jewifh tranfcribers. See my *Gen. Differt*. p. 12. Laftly: the difficulty arifing from the Title, which afcribes the Pfalm to *David*, and which feems to make *him* the Speaker in it, may be removed; either by fuppofing, that the Title here (like thofe now prefixed to feveral Pfalms) is of no fufficient authority; or *rather*, by confidering this Title as only meant to defcribe *the time*, when David compofed this prophetic Hymn — that, *when delivered from all his other enemies, as well as from the hand of Saul*, he *then* confecrated his leifure, by compofing this fublime Prophecy concerning MESSIAH, his Son: *whom* he reprefents here as *fpeaking* (juft as in *Pfal*. 22, *Pfal*. 40, and other places;) and as defcribing, firft, his triumph over Death and Hell — 2dly: the manifeftation of Omnipotence, in his favour; Earth and Heaven trembling at GOD's awful prefence — 3dly: the Speaker's Innocence, thus divinely attefted — 4thly: the vengeance, he was to take on *his own People* the Jews, in the deftruction of Jerufalem — and 5thly: the adoption of the *Heathen*, over whom he was to be the Head and Ruler.

Another instance of *a Title,* denoting only *the Time* of a Prophecy, occurs in the very next Chapter: where a Prophecy concerning the Messiah is entitled *The* LAST *words of David* i.e. an Hymn, which he composed a little before his Death, *after all his other Prophecies.* And perhaps this Ode in chap. 22, which immediately precedes that in chap. 23, was composed but a little while before; namely, *when all his wars were over.* Let it be added, that Josephus, immediately before he speaks of David's mighty men (which follow in this same chapter of *Samuel*) considers the 2 Hymns (in ch. 22 and 23) as both written after his Wars were over—*Jam Davides, bellis et periculis perfunctus, pacemque deinceps profundam agitans, Odas in Deum Hymnosque composuit.* Tom. I, p. 401.

2 Sam. 23; 1—7.

We are now arrived at a part of Holy Scripture, which is of more than common importance: a part, which promises something very magnificent, but sadly disappoints (at present) our reasonable expectations. It is not in the power of words, to form a more solemn and splendid *Introduction:* and yet, when we have perused the whole Song, whether the darkness be owing to errors in the present Text, or mistakes in our Version, or to Both; the general Subject, as well as most of the Particulars, want much illustration.

The great point is, to fix and ascertain the Subject: whether it be — the celebration of a good and righteous *Governor,* in general; or, in particular, that righteous and just one, *The Messiah.* In favour of this latter sense, new evidence has arisen from an investigation of the Heb. MSS; the oldest and best of which has preserved the word JEHOVAH, in one part of this hymn; where, if the word be genuine, it solves the chief difficulty. As this word appeared to me from the first, and does still, to be of very great consequence; I represented it in my *1st Dissert. on the Heb. Text*, pag. 468—471: adding, that the old Greek version proves the antient existence of the word in this place. With what success this discovery was made to the public, the reader will in part judge from the Review of that Dissertation by the learned Professor *Michaelis*; who says — *Ultima verba Davidis mendis laborare quibusdam, vix audemus dubitare: frustra in illis explicandis desudâsse totum interpretum tanquam collegium intelligentes; neque ipsi, sollicitâ verborum investigatione, adhibitâ etiam luce quam Arabia ac Syria præferre solet, aliquid satis tuti invenientes. Quicquid ex verbis eruas, hiat; nec apparet, ad quem finem pertineat. Legimus et sicut lux matutina orietur sol, sive, et circa tempus lucis matutinæ orietur sol; languente utrâque sententiâ. Quod igitur verum, felix, reique Christianæ faustum sit, codex Kennicotianus, omnium hucusque inspectorum antiquissimus, habet* atque ut lux matutina orietur JEHOVA sol — *quod Dei nomen, nunc deletum, in nostro commate legebat interpres Græcus. Vaticinium ergo de* MESSIA *deprehendisse se credit Kennicotus; dignum* ευρημα *quod ei gratulemur, cupiamusque magis confirmari.*

I therefore presume, that the Subject of this sacred Song, composed near the close of David's life, is *The Messiah:* and certainly no other subject was so worthy to employ the *last* poetry of *the man after God's own heart.* He labours to introduce it with an accumulation of all such expressions, as would command the greatest attention to what he was about to deliver, as he was *King*, and as he was *Prophet*. That a good *Ruler*, in the general, should be here treated of, seems impossible: not only from the introductory pomp and splendour, but also from the subsequent particulars being inapplicable to any King or Ruler, but *Messiah*. The *everlasting* Covenant, concerning this son of David, is expresly mentioned; as well as the *spiritual* nature of his Kingdom. All the particulars agree to the Messiah: and while some describe *the fate of his Enemies*, others are descriptive of his own *Crucifixion*; all very similar in sense to what is foretold elsewhere. We read in *Psal.* 22: *they pierced my hands and my feet; they parted my garments, and cast lots upon my vesture.* And if David was thus circumstantial, in *that* Psalm; why may he not have mentioned *here* the same or other circumstances, relative to the same Event? 'Tis no just objection, that this Song is not quoted in the New Testament; for the New Test. does not quote the other words, *they pierced my hands and my feet.* And should it be objected further, that nothing of this interesting nature appears, at present, in these *last words:* I reply, that nothing clear appears at all; not only no consistent plan, but not even common sense is to be made out of the words in our present version. If therefore, by the assistance of Heb. MSS, and a better Eng. Version, this passage shall be found to contain a consistent Prophecy of *The Messiah*; we cannot but be particularly struck with the mention made here of the *Iron* and the *Spear.* With spikes of *iron* was he to be *filled*; as he was fastened to the cross by these, at the opposite extremities

mities of his Body, his hands and his feet: and with the *spear* was his side pierced. So that if, with the Apostle, who at first doubted, we should at last see here the print of the *Nails*, and the wound made by the *Spear*; let us, like that Apostle, be no longer *faithless*, but *believing*.

In the present case I shall postpone, and reserve for a more Critical Appendix, the several Notes which may be necessary, in support of the Alterations here proposed: as I have before expressed my intention, in relation to other very difficult passages. And I shall now give our common translation of these verses; subjoining such a correction of it, as appears to me just and necessary.

1. *Now these be the last words of David. David the son of Jesse said, and the man who was raised up on high, the anointed of the God of Jacob, and the sweet psalmist of Israel, said,* 2. *The spirit of the Lord spake by me, and his word was in my tongue.* 3. *The God of Israel said, the rock of Israel spake to me, He that ruleth over men must be just, ruling in the fear of God.* 4. *And he shall be as the light of the morning, when the sun riseth, even a morning without clouds; as the tender grass springing out of the earth by clear shining after rain.* 5. *Although my house be not so with God, yet he hath made with me an everlasting covenant, ordered in all things, and sure: for this is all my salvation, and all my desire, although he make it not to grow.* 6. *But the sons of Belial shall be all of them as thorns thrust away, because they cannot be taken with hands:* 7. *But the man that shall touch them must be fenced with iron and the staff of a spear; and they shall be utterly burned with fire in the same place.*

New Tranflation of 2 *Sam.* 23, 1—7.

TITLE.
Now thefe are the laft words of David.

PROEM.

THE oracle of David, the fon of Jeffe;
Even the oracle of the man raifed up on high:
The anointed of the GOD of Jacob;
And the compofer of the pfalms of Ifrael.

The fpirit of JEHOVAH fpeaketh by me;
And his word is upon my tongue:
JEHOVAH, the GOD of Ifrael, fayeth;
To me fpeaketh the rock of Ifrael.

SONG.

THE JUST ONE ruleth among men!
He ruleth by the fear of GOD!

As the light of the morning, arifeth JEHOVAH;
A fun, without clouds, for brightnefs;
And as the grafs from the earth, after rain.

Verily thus is my houfe with GOD;
For an everlafting covenant hath he made with me,
Ordered in all things and fafely fecured:
For he is all my falvation, and all my defire.

But the fons of Belial fhall not flourifh;
As a thorn rooted up, fhall be all of them:
For they will not be taken kindly by the hand.

And the Man, who fhall reprove them,
Shall be filled with iron, and a wooden fpear:
But in the fire fhall they be utterly burnt, with igno-
miny.

2 Sam. 23; 8—39.

These 32 verses, recording David's mighty men, have been examined at large, and corrected, in my 1st Dissertation on the Hebrew Text. The first of these verses (which is too important to be here omitted) contains 3 great corruptions in the Hebrew; which, till they are corrected, must render the verse totally unintelligible in any just translation. The 1st corruption is — that the proper name of the Hero, *Jashobeam*, is turned into two common words, rendered *that sat in the seat*. The 2d is — that the common words signifying *he lift up his spear* (which words are here absolutely necessary) are turned into 2 *proper names* totally inadmissible; it being nearly as absurd to say, that *Jashobeam the Hachmonite was the same with Adino the Eznite*, as that *David the Bethlehemite was the same with Elijah the Tishbite*. And the 3d is — that the number 800 probably was at first 300; as it is now in the parallel place 1 *Chron.* 11, 11.

2 Sam. 24, 13.

We have here, delivered by the prophet Gad, a solemn message: David is commanded to choose 1 of the following Judgments — *7 years* Famine — *3 months* Flight — or *3 days* Pestilence. But, in 1 *Chron.* 21, 12, the same proposal is (not 7 years, but) 3 years, 3 months, or 3 days. If therefore, an error has been admitted any where; can it be doubted here? If this message was delivered once only; the prophet could not propose the years of famine both as 7, and as 3. Consequently, if he said 3; the number 7 is wrong — if 7; the number 3 is wrong: the appeal may be safely made here to common sense. This is one of the *Inconsistencies*, frequently held up to view by Unbelievers. But the whole difficulty is solved, and the true reading (3) is established by observing — that *all* the antient Versions agree in *Chronicles*, and that the *Greek* version has the same number 3 here also in *Samuel*.

1 Kings 2, 9.

David is here represented, in our Eng. version, as finishing his life with giving a command to Solomon, to kill Shimei; and to kill him on account of that very crime, for which, as David here says, he had sworn to him by the Lord, he would not put him to death. The behaviour thus imputed to the King and Prophet, and which would be justly censurable if true, should be examined very carefully, as to the ground it stands upon. And, when the passage is duly considered; I presume, it will appear highly probable, that an injury has been here done to this illustrious Character. The point, to which I now beg the reader's attention, is this — that it is not uncommon in the Heb. language to omit the Negative in a 2d part of the sentence, and to consider it as repeated; when it has been once expressed, and is followed by the connecting particle. And thus, on *Isai.* 43, 22, the late learned Annotator says — "The "Negative is repeated, or referred to, by the con-"junction *vau*; as in many other places." See also *Isai.* 23, 4. The necessity of so very considerable an alteration, as inserting the particle NOT, may be here confirmed by some other instances. Thus Psal. 1, 5: *The ungodly shall not stand in the judgment*, NOR (the Heb. is *and*, signifying *and not*) *sinners in the con-*

gregation of the righteous. Pf. 9, 18 : *The needy shall not alway be forgotten:* (and then the negative understood as repeated by the conjunction now dropped) *the expectation of the poor shall* (NOT) *perish for ever.* Pf. 38, 1 : *O Lord rebuke me not in thy wrath;* NEITHER (*and* for *and not*) *chasten me in thy hot displeasure.* Pf. 75, 5 : *Lift not up your horn on high:* (and then the negative understood as repeated by the conjunction now dropped) *speak* NOT *with a stiff neck.* Prov. 24, 12 : our version is this — *doth not he, that pondereth the heart, consider it? and he that keepeth the soul, doth* (NOT) *he know it? and shall* (NOT) *he render to every man according to his works?* And Prov. 30, 3 : *I neither learned wisdom,* NOR (*and* for *and not*) *have the knowledge of the holy.* If then there are in fact many such instances; the question is — Whether the Negative, here expressed in the former part of David's command, may not be understood as to be repeated in the latter part: and if this *may* be, a strong reason will be added why it *should* be, so interpreted. The passage will run thus. *Behold, thou hast with thee Shimei, who cursed me — but I swore to him by the Lord, saying, I will not put thee to death by the sword. Now therefore hold him* NOT *guiltless (for thou art a wise man, and knowest what thou oughtest to do unto him) but bring* NOT *down his hoary head to the grave with blood.* Now, if the language itself will admit this construction, the sense thus given to the sentence derives a very strong support from the Context. For, how did Solomon understand this charge? Did he kill Shimei, in consequence of it? Certainly, he did not. For, after he had immediately commanded Joab to be slain, in obedience to his Father; he sends for Shimei: and, knowing that Shimei ought to be well watched, confines him to a particular spot in Jerusalem for the remainder of his life. Ch. 2; 36—42. See also *Job* 23, 17: 30, 20: 31, 20.

1 Kings 2, 22.

Ask for him the kingdom also; (for he is mine elder brother) even for him, and for Abiathar the priest, and for Joab the son of Zeruiah. In these words of Solomon to Bathsheba, it is by no means easy to understand, how the Kingdom could be asked *for Abiathar* and *for Joab*; tho' it might for Adonijah. All the antient Versions agree, and are supported by the Targum, in a different sense; namely — *he* (Adonijah) *is my elder brother; and he has* FOR HIM (already declared on his side) *both Abiathar and Joab.* This sense arises from the present 2 words; omitting in each the preposition, which seems inserted in conformity to the word preceding. *Josephus* understands this passage in the same manner: that Solomon wondered at the request thus made for Adonijah, *amicos potentes habenti Joabum et Abiatharem.* Lastly: this construction (*nam ei* or *pro eo sunt* ET *Abiathar et Joabus*) has been supported already, pag. 59; to which may be added *Job* 34, 29: where the words ועל גוי ועל אדם are in the Greek version καὶ κατὰ ἔθνος καὶ κατα ανθρωπου; and in the Vulg. *et super gentes, et super homines.* Add also 1 *Sam.* 25, 6. Tho' the preceding correction has considerable merit: I can assume nothing more to myself here, than the pleasure of publickly expressing my Thanks for it; as it has been most obligingly communicated, with many other learned observations, by the Reverend Dr ROBERTS, Provost of Eton College.

1 Kings 8, 16.

Mention is here made of some one *Place*, and some one *Person*, preferred before all others; and the preference is that of *Jerusalem* to other places, and of *David* to other men. In consequence of this remark, we shall see the necessity of correcting this passage by its parallel, in 2 *Chron.* 6; 5, 6: where the 13 Heb. words, now lost in *Kings*, are happily preserved. Let us compare the passages.

K. Since the day that I brought forth my people Israel out
C. *Since the day that I brought forth my people*   *out*

K. of   Egypt, I chose no CITY out of all the tribes
C. *of the land of Egypt, I chose no* CITY *among all the tribes*

K. of Israel to build an house,   that my name might be
C. *of Israel to build an house in, that my name might be*

K. therein;   *   *   *   *   *   *
C. *there;*   *neither chose I any* MAN *to be a ruler over my people*

K.   *   *   *   *
C. *Israel: but I have chosen* JERUSALEM, *that my name*

K.   *   *   but I   chose DAVID to be over my
C. *might be there; and I have chosen* DAVID *to be over my*

K. people Israel.
C. *people Israel.*

1 Kings 13, 20.

A great clamour has been raised, against this part of the history; on account of GOD denouncing sentence upon the true Prophet by the mouth of the *false* Prophet. But, if we examine with attention the original words here; they will be found to signify either *who brought him back,* or *whom he had brought back.* For the very same words אשר השיבו occur again in ver. 23; where they are now translated *whom he had brought back,* and where they cannot be tranflated otherwife. This being the cafe, we are at liberty to confider the word of the Lord as delivered to the *true* Prophet, thus brought back; and then, the fentence is pronounced by *God* himfelf, *calling* to him out of heaven: as in *Gen.* 22, 11. And that this doom was thus pronounced by *God*, not by the falfe prophet, we are affured in ver. 26 — *the Lord hath delivered him unto the lion, according to the word of the* LORD, *which* HE *fpake unto him.* Note alfo — *Jofephus* exprefsly afferts, that the fentence was declared by GOD to the *true* Prophet.

1 Kings 14, 31.

Among the various corruptions, to which antient MSS have been liable, none have happened more eafily than the corruptions of *Numbers* and *Proper Names:* and yet, as no words are of greater confequence to the Senfe, proportionable care fhould be taken for the correction of fuch miftakes. The name of this king of Judah is now expreffed 3 ways. Here, and in 4 other places, it is *Abijam* or *Abim*; in 2 other places, it is *Abihu*; but in 11 other places it is *Abiah* — as it is expreffed by St *Matthew*, at 1, 7 — Ροβοαμ εγεννησε τον ΑΒΙΑ. 'Tis remarkable, that in this firft inftance, *Abijam* is *Abiah* in our oldeft Heb. MS, fupported by 10 other copies. Note alfo, that it is here *Abiah* in the Gr. and Syr. verfions; and, tho' the *printed* Vulgat has *Abiam*, yet it is *Abia* in the only Latin *MS* confulted on this occafion.

1 Kings 15, 6.

And there was war between Reboboam and Jeroboam all the days of his life. As the hiftory of *Reboboam* was ended in the former chapter, where the laft verfe but one had mentioned the continual war between HIM and Jeroboam: 'tis highly improbable, that the account of his succeſſor *Abiah* ſhould be interrupted by a repetition of the ſame notice concerning *Rehoboam.* And as there was a very memorable war between *Abiah* and Jeroboam; 'tis probable, that ſuch a war did not paſs entirely unnoticed here. It is therefore much to the honour of 8 Heb. MSS, to have preſerved here the true word *Abiah,* inſtead of the corrupted word *Rehoboam.* As to the words now in the next verſe, *and there was war between Abijam and Jeroboam*; they are entirely wanting in 1 Heb. MS.

1 Kings 17, 6.

—— THE RAVENS *brought him bread and fleſh.* In my 2d Diſſertat. on the Heb. Text (p. 581) I obſerved, that the words of *Jerom* are —' ORBIM, *accolæ villæ in finibus Arabum, Eliæ dederunt alimenta.* And as the authority of this learned Father is certainly great, with regard to Places *in* or *near* Paleſtine; the beſt interpretation of this paſſage ſeems to be, that this food was brought to Elijah by the *Orbim,* the inhabitants of *Oreb* or *Orbo,* a ſmall village near Arabia.

1 Kings 20, 30.

— A WALL *fell upon* 27000 *men.* If this paſſage will fairly admit any other conſtruction; ſuch conſtruction will be readily accepted. The alteration, which I ſhall here offer, is founded on this — that חומה *murus* becomes a word very different in ſenſe; when it is read without the *vau,* on the authority of 18 Heb. MSS, and the 3 firſt Editions. Now the Heb. noun חמה, from חמם, Caſtel explains by *calor* and *sol*: in Chaldee, by *fervor*, *æstus*, *calor solaris*: and in Arabic, by *æstus meridiei*, *vehementia caloris*, *nomen* VENTI. And the same noun, from חם׳, he explains by *excandescentia*, *furor*, *venenum*. These renderings all concurring to establish the sense of *a burning Wind*, eminently blasting and destructive; I shall now cite some other sacred passages, in which such a Wind is mentioned: and then subjoin a few remarks. We read in *Job* 27, 21 — *the east-wind carrieth him away*: where the word קדים is καυσων in the Greek version, and in the Vulgat *ventus urens*. In *Ezech*. 19, 12 — *she was plucked up* בחמה, *she was cast down to the ground, and the east-wind dried up her fruit, her strong rods were withered, the fire consumed them*. *Hosea* (13, 1-.) mentions the desolation brought on by *an east-wind, the wind of the Lord*. What in *Amos* (4, 9) is *I have smitten you with blasting*, is in the Vulg. *in vento vehemente*; in the Syr. Lat. *vento calido*. Let us now apply ourselves to the history, in 1 K. chap. 20. When Benhadad, king of Syria, was besieging Samaria the second time; the children of Israel slew of the Syrians 100,000 footmen in one day: and it follows, that, when the rest of the army fled to Aphek, 27000 of the men that were left were suddenly destroyed — *by a burning wind*. That such is the true interpretation, will appear more clearly; if we compare the destruction of Ben-hadad's army with that of the army of *Sennacherib*: whose sentence is, that *God would send upon him* A BLAST — רוח *a wind*, doubtless such a wind as would be suddenly destructive. The event is said to be, *that, in one night,* 185000 *Assyrians were smitten by the angel of the Lord*: 1 *Kings* 19; 7, 35. The connection of this sentence

with this execution of it is given by the Pfalmift;
who fays (104, 4) *God maketh his angels* WINDS,
or *maketh* רוחות THE WINDS *his angels* i.e. Mef-
fengers, for the performance of His Will. In a
Note on *Pfal.* 11, 6 Prof. Michaelis has thefe words
— *Ventus Zilgaphoth peftilens Eurus eft, Orientalibus
notiffimus, qui obvia quævis necat.* And Le Clerc fays
— *Vox* (kadim) *orientalem ventum fonat, et quafi
ventus adurens defcribitur — Thevenotius memorat, anno
1658 und noEte fuiffe occifa καυσωνι viginti millia ho-
minum.* — Again: *Ventus calidus et urens vocatur in
Oriente* Samiel: *anno* 1665 (*ait Thevenot.*) *interie-
runt* 4000 *homines, hoc vento adflati.* See on *Gen.* 41,
6 and *Job* 27, 21. Upon the whole I conclude, that,
as Thevenot has mentioned 2 great multitudes deftroyed by this burning Wind, fo has holy Scripture
recorded the deftruction of 2 much greater multitudes by a fimilar caufe: and therefore, that we
may tranflate the words in queftion thus — *But the
reft fled to Aphek, into the city; and* A (or THE)
BURNING WIND *fell upon twenty and feven thoufand
of the men that were left.*

2 Kings 7, 13.

Several inftances have been given of words improperly repeated by Jewifh tranfcribers; who have
been carelefs enough to make fuch miftakes, and
yet cautious not to alter or erafe, for fear of difco-
veries. This verfe furnifhes another inftance, in a
carelefs repetition of 7 Heb. words, thus:

הנישארים אשר נשארו בה הנם ככל ההמון ישראל אשר
נשארו בה הנם ככל המון ישראל אשר תמו

The exact Englifh of this verfe is — *And the fervant
faid, Let them take now five of the remaining horfes,*
which

which remain in it; behold, they are as all the multitude of Israel, which [remain in it; behold, they are as all the multitude of Israel, which] *are consumed: and let us send, and see.* Whoever considers, that the 2d set of these 7 words is neither in the Gr. nor Syr. versions; and that those translators, who suppose these words to be genuine, alter them, to make them look like sense; will probably allow them to have been at first an improper repetition — consequently, to be now an interpolation strangely continued in the sacred Text. The preceding remarks are strongly confirmed by our oldest Heb. MS, with 35 others, in which these 7 words are found but *once* only.

2 Kings 8, 16.

This verse, when exactly rendered, is — *And in the 5th year of Joram, the son of Ahab, king of Israel, and of Jehoshaphat king of Judah, Jehoram the son of Jehoshaphat king of Judah began to reign.* In my General Dissertation, p. 44, notice was taken of the confusion here introduced (as Vignoles, Jackson, and other chronologers have remarked) by the interpolation of 3 Heb. words, signifying *et Jehosaphati regis Judæ*. 'Tis certain, that Jehoshaphat reigned 25 years; and that Jehoram his son reigned but 8 years; (1 *Kin.* 22, 42 : 2 *Kin.* 8, 17 : 2 *Chro.* 20, 31 and 21, 5 :) so that he could not have reigned during his father's life, without being king 20 years and 8 years. I also specified several copies of the Vulgat, both written and printed, which are free from this interpolation. It was observed likewise, that these words are wanting in 2 Heb. MSS; and lastly, that the Hexaplar Syr. MS, above 1000 years

years old, made from the Greek, (now preserved at Paris) has not these words, tho' they are found in the Vat. and Alexand. MSS.

2 Kings 15, 1.

The confusion arising from a corruption of Proper Names has been already noted; and is a just cause both of surprize and complaint. The person here mentioned is no less than a King of Judah; and yet we can scarce tell, what his real name was: at least, it would be very difficult, if we consulted only the printed Heb. text; for there it is expressed 4 different ways in this same chapter — *Ozriah, Ozrihu, Oziah* and *Ozihu!* Our oldest Heb. MS happily relieves us here, by reading truly (in verses 1, 6 & 7) עזיהו *Ozihu* (*Uzziah*) where the printed text is differently corrupted. This reading is called *true*; because it is supported by the Syr. and Ar. versions, in these 3 verses — because the printed text itself has it so, in verses 32 and 34 of this very chapter — because it is so expressed in the parallel place, in *Chronicles* — and because it is (not Αζαριας, but) Οζιας, in St Matthew's Genealogy.

2 Kings 23, 16.

This verse is now remarkably defective, in the Heb. text; but is happily compleat in the Gr. version, supported by the old Hexaplar Syr. MS, in this manner — *And as Josiah turned himself, he spied the sepulchres that were there in the mount; and sent, and took the bones out of the sepulchres, and burnt them upon the altar, and polluted it: according to the word of the Lord, which the man of God proclaimed* [when Jeroboam stood by the altar, at the feast. And (king Josiah) turning about, cast his eyes on the sepulchre

of the man of God] *who proclaimed thefe words. Then
he faid* &c. See 1 *Kin.* 12, 32 — 13, 3: and *Hallet's Note*; 2, 5.

1 Chron. 1, 17.

It will foon appear, that there is an omiſſion here
of 2 Heb. words, preſerved in 1 Heb. MS; which
are neceſſary to ſhew, that *Uz, Hul* &c. were the
ſons, not of *Shem*, but of *Aram*. See *Gen.* 10, 23.
And by another omiſſion, in ver. 36, *Timna* is now
made a *ſon* of Eliphaz, tho' really his *concubine*. See
Gen. 36, 12.

1 Chron. 6, 13 (28.)

A ſtrange miſtake here has been pointed out by
the very learned JOSEPH MEDE: namely, that the
word ויאל *Joel* is here omitted, which was the name
of Samuel's firſt-born; and that והשני *et ſecundus* is
now turned into *Vaſhni*. See 1 *Sam.* 8, 2, and *Diſſert.
Gen.* p. 51.

1 Chron. 8, 28—38 and 9, 34—44.

The fame Genealogy is here unexpectedly repeated; but the repetition brings with it this advantage,
that it will correct ſeveral corruptions. An exact
view of theſe two paſſages will reſtore ſome whole
Words, in different verſes: particularly, *and Mik-
loth*, now wanting at the end of 8, 31; as well as
and Ahaz, now wanting at the end of 9, 41. See
the whole compariſon minutely ſtated, in my Edition
of the Heb. Bible; vol. 2, pag. 657.

1 Chron. 11, 13.

Amongſt the parallel places, a compariſon of
which may be of very conſiderable ſervice, ſcarce
any paſſages will more effectually correct each other
than *the Catalogue of David's mighty men*; as it now

stands in 2 *Sam.* 23, 8—40, and also in this chapter. This Catalogue was the chief subject of my 1st *Dissertation on the Heb. Text.* And I presume it was there proved, (p. 128—144) that about 34 Heb. words have been lost out of this part of the passage in *Chronicles*; which are happily preserved in *Samuel.* The chief point of proof is this — that the Catalogue divides these 37 Warriors into the Captain-General, a first Three, a second Three, and the remaining 30: and yet, that the 3d Captain of the first Ternary is now here omitted. The following juxta-position will shew the whole deficiency, and properly supply it. Note, that *Jashobeam*, the 1st Captain of the first Ternary had been already mentioned; and that the history is here speaking of the 2d Captain, namely *Eleazar*.

2 Sam. 23, 9. And after him was Eleazar, the son of Dodo,
1 Chro. 11, 12. *And after him was Eleazar, the son of Dodo,*

S. the Ahohite,　　　 one of the 3 mighty men
C. *the Ahohite, who was one of the 3 mighties.*　　13. *He*

S.　　with David when they defied　　　 the Philistines
C. *was with David at Pasdammim, and there the Philistines*

S. that were there gathered together to battle, and the men
C.　　were　　 *gathered together to battle,*

S. of Israel were gone away. 10. He arose, and smote the
C.

S. Philistines until his hand was weary, and his hand clave
C.

S. unto the sword; and the Lord wrought a great victory
C.

S. that day: and the people returned after him only to spoil.
C.

S. 11. And after him was SHAMMAH, the son of Agee
C.

S. the Hararite: and the Philiſtines were gathered together
C.

S. into a troop, where was a piece of ground full of lentiles:
C. *where was a parcel of ground full of barley,*

S. and the people fled from   the Philiſtines. 12. But
C. *and the people fled from before the Philiſtines.* 14. *And*

S. he   ſtood   in the midſt of the ground, and defended
C. *they ſet themſelves in the midſt of that parcel, and delivered*

S. it, and ſlew the Philiſtines: and the Lord   wrought
C. *it, and ſlew the Philiſtines: and the Lord ſaved them by*

S. a great victory.
C. *a great deliverance.*

2 Chron. 9, 12.

And Solomon gave to the queen of Sheba all her deſire, whatſoever ſhe aſked, beſides that which SHE HAD BROUGHT UNTO THE KING. It being not eaſy to believe, that Solomon gave back to this Queen her own Preſents; we are prepared to accept thankfully the fact as ſtated in the parallel place: 1 *Kin.* 10, 13. And there we read, that Solomon gave her all ſhe aſked, beſides that which *he gave her of his royal bounty.*

2 Chron. 13, 3.

Abijah ſet the battle in array, with an army of 400,000 *choſen men*; againſt Jeroboam, with 800,000 *choſen men*; *mighty men of valour.* And ver. 17 tells us, that there fell down ſlain of Iſrael 500,000 *choſen men.* Theſe prodigious numbers have been conſidered at large, in my 2d Diſſertat. on the Heb. Text, p. 196—219: where many authorities are produced, for believing, that the 3 numbers here

were

were originally 40000, 80000 and 50000: as stated in the excellent edition of the Vulgat by SIXTUS V, in 1590.

2 Chron. 19, 8.

— *and for controversies, when they returned to Jerusalem.* Mr Hallet (2, 76) has well observed here, that it is difficult to know, *who* they were that returned to Jerusalem. He also shews, that the word וישבו must have been antiently וישבי, agreeably to the Gr. version; thus — *and for the controversies of the inhabitants of Jerusalem.* He should have added, that, if the last word had meant TO *Jerusalem*, it would most probably have been לירושלם, as it is in verse 1 of this same chapter. 'Tis still more strange, that even the true word for *and the inhabitants of* is absurdly translated *and they returned to*, in ch. 34, 9.

2 Chron. 21, 2.

— *Jehoshaphat, king of* ISRAEL. It would be an affront to the scriptural reader, to endeavour to prove, that *Jehoshaphat* was king of *Judah*. And it will be unnecessary to point out the notoriety of this corruption; any further than by barely adding, that this correction is supported by about 30 Heb. MSS and all the antient Versions.

2 Chron. 21, 12.

And there came a writing to him, from ELIJAH *the prophet, saying* &c. This Letter to king Jehoram was written in the 6th year of his reign; because he reigned 8 years, and it was written 2 years before his death. See 2 *Chro.* 21; 15, 19, 20. But then, *Elijah* had been taken up to Heaven about 13 years before the time of this writing. For *the Ascension* is recorded in the 2d ch. of the 2d book of Kings; and the chapter following says, that Jehoram king of Israel began to reign in the 18th year of Jehoshaphat: consequently *the Ascension* took place about 7 years before the death of Jehoshaphat, who reigned 25 years. If therefore this Letter was written so long after Elijah's Ascension; it will readily be allowed that *the writer* of it was (not *Elijah*, but) ELISHA — a correction, which seems absolutely necessary; tho' not confirmed perhaps by any one MS or antient Version.

2 Chron. 22, 2.

If there ever was a corruption made, in any antient book; such a thing must be admitted here. 'Tis here affirmed at present, that *Ahaziah*, when he began to reign, was FORTY and *two* years old. 'Tis also said, that his father Jehoram was 40 years old, at his death: see 2 *Kin.* 8, 17 and 2 *Chro.* 21; 5 & 20. And, if both these circumstances could be true; it would then follow, tho' a very strange consequence, that Ahaziah was born 2 years before his father! 'Tis happy therefore, that this corruption is corrected by 2 *Kin.* 8, 26; where the number is still right TWENTY and *two*. As to the old Versions; they all agree with this reading in *Kings*; the *Vulgat* only agrees with the present reading in *Chronicles*. The Syr. and Arab. confirm *here* the num. 22. And, tho' the words και δυο are now wanting in the Vat. and Alex. copies, yet both these copies read εικοσι. And, as it is compleatly εικοσι και δυο in the Aldine edition; so is it, fully and compleatly, in at least 3 Gr. MSS — n°. 7, Royal library, and in a MS of the Carmelites, at Paris; also in the Vatic.

MS 330. 'Tis likewise remarkable, that this true number is found in the Margin of the very excellent Heb. MS at *Vienna*, n°. 590. See my *Differt*. 1, p. 97; and *Differt. Gen.* p. 51.

2 Chron. 28; 22, 23.

On this place is the following valuable observation of Mr Hallet; 2, p. 78. "This passage greatly "surprized me. For *the sacred Historian himself* is "here represented as saying, that *the Gods of Da-* "*mascus* had smitten Ahaz. But 'tis impossible to "suppose, that the inspired author could say this. "For the Scripture every where represents *the heathen* "*idols* as *nothing* and *vanity*; and as incapable of "doing either good or hurt. All difficulty is avoid- "ed, if we follow the old Heb. copies, from which "the Gr. translation was made; which is — *And* "AHAZ SAID, *I will seek to the gods of Damascus,* "*who smote* ME. And then it follows, both in "Hebrew and Greek — *He said moreover, Because* "*the gods of the kings of Syria help them; therefore* "*will I sacrifice to them, that they may help me.*"

2 Chron. 36; 22, 23.

This book of *Chronicles* gives us the history of the Jews, from David to *the Babylonish Captivity:* and at this period of the Jewish Monarchy, we might have expected to find this Extract from the public Registers to have been concluded. But there are now, at the end of the book, *Two Verses*, not chronologically connected with the preceding, which *begin* the Decree of Cyrus; and leave it quite *unfinished*, breaking off *in the very midst of a sentence.* Proofs have lately been given, that there are yet extant some Heb. MSS, in which the book of *Ezra* immediately follows that of *Chronicles:* see *Differt. Gener.* nº. 93, and 431. It therefore can scarce be doubted, but that some antient transcriber, having finished *Chronicles* at ver. 21, without leaving the distance usual between different books, wrote on from the beginning of *Ezra:* but that, on finding his mistake, he broke off abruptly; and so began *Ezra* again at the customary distance — without publishing his error, by erasing or blotting out what he had carelessly subjoined to *Chronicles.* The reader will see, how strangely this book now ends; when he compares the conclusion here with the beginning of the next book.

Chro. Now in the first year of Cyrus, Jehovah stirred up
Ezra. *Now in the first year of Cyrus, Jehovah stirred up*

C. the spirit of Cyrus; so that he made a proclamation,
E. *the spirit of Cyrus; so that he made a proclamation,*

C. saying. " Thus saith Cyrus: Jehovah, the God of
E. *saying.* " *Thus saith Cyrus: Jehovah, the God of*

C. " heaven, hath given me all the kingdoms of the earth;
E. " *heaven, hath given me all the kingdoms of the earth;*

C. " and he hath charged me to build him an house in Jeru-
E. " *and he hath charged me to build him an house in Jeru-*

C. " salem, which is in Judah. Who is there among you,
E. " *salem, which is in Judah. Who is there among you,*

C. " of all his people? Jehovah his GOD be with him; and
E. " *of all his people?   Let   his God be with him; and*

C. " let him go up
E. " *let him go up to Jerusalem, which is in Judah; and*

C.
E. *build the house of the Lord God of Israel (he is the God)*

C.
E. *which is in Jerusalem. And whosoever remaineth in any place*

C.
E. *where he sojourneth, let the men of his place help him* &c.

Ezra 1, 7—11.

In these verses is an account of the *number* and *quality* of the Sacred Vessels, restored to Jerusalem by Cyrus; but the account is now become exceedingly inaccurate. Nothing can prove this more clearly, than the great want of consistency between the *particulars* of the account and its own sum *total*; for the total is now 5400, tho' the particulars amount to no more than 2499. Had no account of these Vessels been preserved, but in this chapter only; the true solution of this difficulty might have been impossible. But another and more exact account is happily found in the 2d ch. of the 1st Apocryphal book of *Esdras*: and a short comparison will soon discover the truth; especially, as the total now in *Ezra* bears strong testimony in favour of *Esdras*. See Dissert. 2, on Heb. Text; p. 213, 508.

EZRA.					ESDRAS.
Chargers, gold	30	1000	Cups, gold.		
Chargers silver	1000	1000	Cups, silver.		
Knives	—	29	29	Censers, silver.	
Basons, gold	30	30	Vials, gold.		
Basons, 2d sort	410	2410	Vials, silver.		
Other Vessels	1000	1000	Other Vessels.		
called	5400	5469	called		
but only	2499		truly so called.		

Ezra 2, 1 &c.

The advantage, derived from a *second* copy of the sacred Vessels, leads us to be thankful for *two* other copies of the Catalogue, in which are recorded the *Names* and *Numbers* of those Jews, who returned from Babylon, in the first year of Cyrus; which copies are now preserved in *Ezra* 2, 1—67; in *Ne-*

hem. 7, 6—69; and in 1 *Esdras* 5, 7—43. These 3 copies have been already compared, in my 2d *Dissert.* on the Heb. Text, p. 508—514. From the triple comparison, there made, I shall here give only *the beginning*; tho' the whole of it affords still more ample conviction.

Ezra.	Nehemiah.	Esdras.
[THE CHIEF MEN]		
Zerubbabel	Zerubbabel	Zorobabel
Jeshua	Jeshua	Jesus
Nehemiah	Nehemiah	Nehemias
Seraiah	Azariah	Zacharias
Reelaiah	Raamiah	Reesaias
	Nahamani	Enenius
Mordecai	Mordecai	Mardocheus
Bilshan	Bilshan	Beelsarus
Mispar	Mispereth	Aspharasus
Bigvai	Bigvai	Reelius
Rehum	Nehum	Roimus
Baanah	Baanah	Baana
THE CHILDREN OF		
Parosh 2172	Parosh 2172	Phoros 2172
Shephatiah 372	Shephatiah 372	Saphat 472
Arah 775	Arah 652	Ares 756
Pahath-moab 2812	Pahath-moab 2818	Phaath-moab 2812
Elam 1254	Elam 1254	Elam 1254
Zattu 945	Zattu 845	Zathui 945
Zaccai 760	Zaccai 760	Corbe 705
Bani 642	Binnui 648	Bani 648
Bebai 623	Bebai 628	Bebai 623
Azgad 1222	Azgad 2322	Sadas 3222
&c.	&c.	&c.
WHOLE 42,360	WHOLE 42,360	WHOLE 42,360

Nehem. 9, 17.

— *and* [in their rebellion] *appointed a captain to return to their bondage.* The whole impropriety of this passage does not appear, till the words are reduced to their proper order; thus — *and appointed a captain to return to their bondage in their rebellion.* But here it must be added; that, if the word במרים could signify *in their rebellion*, yet the Gr. version shews clearly, that the reading was antiently במצרים *in Egypt.* This curious emendation is confirmed by the excellent *Vienna* MS, where the text has this word clearly; also by the very first printed Edition; and lastly, by *Numb.* 14, 4 — *let us make a captain, and let us return into* EGYPT.

Nehem. 9, 35.

For they have not served thee in THEIR *kingdom.* On this passage a late eminent Prelate has made this remark: *The sense, I think, requires that the Septuagint reading should be here preferred, which says* εν βασιλεια σȣ *in* THY *kingdom. And this the Syr. and Ar. versions follow.* To these authorities *Bp Warburton*, had he been now living, might have added another; namely, that of at least *one* of the *blind* Heb. MSS. See *Divine Legation*; book 4, sect. 6; book 5, sect. 3; and *Pref.* to *The Doctrine of Grace*: with a Note, subjoined to my Sermon on *Isai.* 7, 14; pag. 98.

Esther 3, 7.

In the first month, that is the month Nisan, in the twelfth year of king Ahasuerus, they cast Pur, that is the lot, before Haman, from day to day and from month to month [ωϛε απολεσαι εν μια ημερα το γενος Μαρδοχαιȣ·

χαις· και επεσεν ο κληρος εις την τεσαρεσκαιδεκατην τȣ μηνος, ες] *of month the twelfth, that is the month Adar*. We shall see the utility of the many words here preserved in the Gr. version, and the real omission of them in the Heb. text; if we observe, that this verse now sets forth the method used by Haman, in consulting *by Lot*, for several *Months* together, that so he might fix on *the most lucky Day*, for this destruction of the Jews. But the consequence of these frequent consultations, as to any one Day at last *fixed upon*, and what that *particular Day* in fact was, is only told us by the Gr. version. And the latter part of the words, above quoted from thence, is also necessary, to introduce with any sense the last words still in the Hebrew — [AND THE LOT FELL ON THE FOURTEENTH DAY OF MONTH] *the twelfth, that is the month Adar*. For the substance of this remark, I am indebted to my late very learned Friend Mr CHAPPLE, of *Exeter*.

The book of JOB.

This Book is universally and justly admired; tho' it appears at present inconsistent in some passages, and in many others is now very obscure. These inconsistences and obscurities we must, all of us, wish to see removed: and whilst it is the duty of the learned to contribute their observations, it is the duty of others to encourage and promote such truly-laudable undertakings. It is by no means intended here to offer *a perpetual Commentary*, but only detached remarks on some particular passages; and these I shall introduce with a few general matters, expressive of my own opinion.

1. My opinion is, that JOB was *a real perfon*, and not an imaginary or fictitious character: as appears to me certain, upon the authority of *Ezekiel*; who reckons *Job* with 2 other illustrious persons, both of them certainly real, *Noah* and *Daniel*: see ch. 14, verses 14 & 20.

2. WHEN Job lived, seems deducible from his being contemporary with *Eliphaz the Temanite*; thus:

		Abraham			
1		Isaac			1
2	Esau		Jacob		2
3	Eliphaz		Levi		3
4	Teman		Kohath		4
5	ELIPHAZ, TEMANITE		Amram	JOB	5
			Moses		*

3. WHERE Job lived, namely in *Idumea* (Edom) south of Judea, between the Dead Sea and the Eastern tongue of the Red Sea, seems proved by the learned Author of the *Lectures on the Heb. Poetry*: see *Prælect.* 32, Edit. 3; pag. 414—418.

4. As Job lived at the same time with *Eliphaz the Temanite*, and probably with *Amram*, the father of Moses; the story of Job's fortunes was very recent, and must have been much talked of, in the time of *Moses*. And when we reflect, that *Moses*, after living many years in *Midian*, spent near 40 years more on the very borders of *Idumea*; we shall be strongly inclined to suppose, that *Moses himself* was the Author of this Book. To *Him* it has been ascribed by very many of the learned, both Jews and Christians.

---

* Mr HEATH places Job's death *about 14 years before the Exodus*. Pref. p. 23.

On *His* authority it might well be admitted amongst the sacred Books, and would be received with due veneration. And, perhaps, the more frequent admission of *Words*, not commonly used in Hebrew elsewhere, may be best accounted for, by supposing the book written in the neighbourhood of *Chaldea* and *Arabia*, and as celebrating an *Idumean* history:* at least, this argument will have weight with all those, who consider this Poem as equal in antiquity to the age of Moses. See on this subject *Grey, Lib. Job.* præf. p. 12: *Observationes Miscell. in Job.* (Boullier) 8°. *Amstel.* p. 6; *Peters on Job*; p. 131: *Lowth, Prælect.* 32: and *Michaelis, Epimetron,* p. 185—195.

5. It is my opinion, that *the Speeches* of Job and his Friends, after being originally delivered in *Prose*, have been faithfully represented, as to the *substance* of them, in this beautiful *Poetry:* which seems to me to bear no small resemblance, in the construction of it, to the Song of MOSES, in *Deuteron.* ch. 32. As to any remarkable *Sameness* in the expression, between Moses and the author of this Poem, one proof, hitherto perhaps undescribed, may be here specified. 'Tis well known, that the sense of Heb. verbs is changed by the conversive particle, either prefixed to the verb itself, or to some previous word in the

---

* Note, that all the *Chaldaisms* &c, now in this book, may not have obtained there originally. For the author himself would scarce have given to the same word (for *verba*) the *Chaldee* from מלין 13 times, and yet the *Heb.* form מלים 10 times. And as to the 2 instances of ש used for אשר (15, 30 & 19, 25) these will not prove this book so late as the Captivity: unless the 5 similar instances, which are now in *Judges* (chapters 5, 6, 7 and 8) will prove the equally-late age of that book; and unless the instance of בשגנ (6, 3) will also overthrow the Antiquity of the book of *Genesis.*

same hemistic. And it has often been observed, that a *preter* verb is sometimes used by the prophets, to express the *certainty* of an event then *future*. But the circumstance, here to be noted, is — that a verb *future* is used to express a *past* action, not less than 9 times in one ch. of *Job*; and also 9 times in one ch. of *Moses*. See *Job* 29; 2, 3, 7, 12, 13, 22, 24, 24, 25: & *Deut.* 32; 10, 10, 10, 10, 12, 13, 16, 16, 17.*

6. Lastly; as to the *Argument* of this book: it teaches the great and important duty of *Submission to the Will of* GOD. And the Encouragement is, that every good man, suffering patiently, will be rewarded: since even *Job* was rewarded abundantly; tho' he sometimes heavily *lamented*; and tho' he even *accused God as unjust*, on account of the uncommon SUFFERINGS inflicted on a man of his uncommon INTEGRITY.

This *Integrity*, or *Righteousness*, of Job's character being resolutely maintained by *Job* himself; and the whole Poem turning on the *multiplied Miseries* of a man EMINENTLY GOOD: the grand difficulty thro'

---

* Other instances occur both in *Job* and the *Pentateuch*. See *Job* 1, 5: 3; 11, 16: 4. :6 — and *Exod.* 15; 7, 12: *Num.* 23, 7: 24; 7, 26. Not that this mode is confined to the books already quoted. For it occurs also in *Jud.* 5; 28, 29, 30; and in *Isai.* 1, 21 &c. But this idiom, being *seldom* found elsewhere, and yet being found *so often*, and within so few verses, both in the *Pentat.* and *Job*, certainly adds some weight to the opinion, that *these books came from the same Writer*. Add — that the argument here does not relate to *such futures*, as may signify in the *present* tense; of which the instances are numerous. Nor does it relate to such futures, as are probably corrupted; or where the conversive *Vau* is now omitted. See 2 *Sam.* 22; 5, 8, 14, 16; compared with *Psal.* 18, 5 &c: in pag. 596 of Vol. I, in my Edition of the Heb. Bible.

the Poem seems to be — how these positions can consist with the several passages, where Job is now made to own himself *a very grievous Sinner*. Let this matter, as it is of sufficient moment, be here carefully attended to.

In ch. 7; 20, 21 he says — *I have sinned; what shall I do unto thee, O thou preserver of men?—Why dost thou not pardon my transgression, and take away mine iniquity?* In 9, 20 — *If I justify myself, mine own mouth shall condemn me: if I say, I am perfect, it shall also prove me perverse.* — 28. *I know, that thou wilt not hold me innocent* — 30. *If I wash myself with snow-water;* 31. *Yet shalt thou plunge me in the ditch, and mine own clothes shall abhor me.* Lastly; in 42, 6 — *I abhor myself, and repent in dust and ashes.* Whereas, he says, in ch. 10, 7 — *Thou knowest, that I am not wicked.* 13, 15 — *I will maintain mine own ways before him.* — 18. *I know, that I shall be justified.* 23, 10 — *He knoweth the way that I take; when he hath tried me, I shall come forth as gold.* — 11. *My foot hath held his steps; his way have I kept, and not declined.* And lastly: in 27, 5 — *Till I die, I will not remove my integrity from me.* — 6. *My righteousness I hold fast, and will not let it go; my heart shall not reproach me, so long as I live.*

And now, if any one, ascribing these contrarieties to Job's inconsistency with himself, should pronounce him *right* in owning himself a great sinner, and *wrong* in pleading his own Integrity: he will soon see it necessary, to infer the contrary. Had Job really been, and owned himself to be, a *great Sinner*; his *great Sufferings* had been then accounted for, agreeably to the maxims of his Friends: and
all

all difficulty and dispute had then been at an end. But as the whole Poem turns on Job's uncommon *Goodness*, and yet uncommon *Misery*; so this *Goodness* or *Innocence*, this *Righteousness* or *Integrity*, is not only insisted upon by *Job*, but expressly admitted by GOD himself, both in the beginning of this book and at the end of it. See 1; 8, 21: 2, 3: and 42; 7, 8. That Job did not here plead *guilty*, or contradict the asseveration of his *Innocence*, appears further from the subsequent Speeches. So *Bildad*, who spoke next, understood him: ch. 8, 6. So *Zophar* understood him: 11, 34. So *Eliphaz*, to whom he spoke the former words, understood him likewise: 15; 13, 14. And lastly; *Elihu*, after hearing all the replies of Job to his friends, tells him (33; 8, 9) — *Surely thou hast spoken in mine hearing; and I have heard the voice of thy words, saying: I am clean, without transgression; I am innocent, neither is there iniquity in me.*

If therefore this Inconsistency, in Job's declarations concerning himself, cannot have obtained in this book at first; it must arise from some *misrepresentation* of the true Sense. And as it relates to Job's *confession of guilt*, expressed in the 3 chapters 7, 9, & 42; on these passages I shall here offer some remarks — in hopes of removing one of the greatest general difficulties, which now attend this Poem.

As to the first instance: Job appears, at least from our Eng. version of ch. 7, 20, to be confessing his sins to *God*; whereas he is really speaking there, in reply, to *Eliphaz*: and 'tis obvious, that the same words, applied thus differently, must carry very different ideas. Who does not see the *humility and sorrow*, with which Job would say, *I have sinned against thee*

thee, O God? and yet fee the refentment and force, with which he would fay to *Eliphaz* — *I have finned, you fay* — but, granting this, what is it to YOU? *to* (or againſt) *thee, O ELIPHAZ, what crime have I committed?* That Job, in other places, *repeats* ironically, and confutes by *quoting*, the fayings of his Friends, will appear hereafter.

Eliphaz had been attempting to terrify him by the recital of a *Vifion*, and the long fpeech of a *Spirit:* 4, 12—21. Job, in reply (6; 15—27) complains of the cruel treatment he had begun to experience from his nominal friends and falſe brethren: and (7, 14) particularly complains, that (Eliphaz) had terrified him with *dreams* and *vifions.* Job then goes on (7; 17 &c.) *What is a miſerable man,* like myſelf, *that thou makeſt ſo much of him!* (1 Sam. 26, 24) *that thou ſetteſt thy heart upon him! that,* with ſuch officious affection, *thou viſiteſt him every morning; and art trying him every moment! How long will it be, 'till thou depart from me; and leave me at liberty to* breathe, and even *ſwallow down my ſpittle!* You ſay, *I muſt have been a Sinner;* what then? I have not finned againſt *thee! O thou ſpy upon mankind! Why haſt thou ſet up me;* as a butt, or *mark, to ſhoot at? Why am I become a burden unto* thee*? Why not rather *overlook my tranſgreſſion,* and *paſs by mine iniquity? I am now ſinking to the duſt! To morrow, perhaps, I ſhall be ſought in vain!*

As the firſt part of this difficulty aroſe from Job's firſt reply to *Eliphaz*; the ſecond part of the ſame difficulty ariſes from Job's firſt reply to *Bildad,* in ch. 9: where Job is now made to ſay, as followeth

---

* So the *Greek* Verfion: and thus both *Grey* and *Houbigant*; with *Ladvocat*, in *Theſis Sorbon.* 1765, p. 21.

—v. 2 and 4: *How should man be just with God? Who hath hardened himself against Him, and prospered?*—ver. 20: *If I justify myself, mine own mouth shall condemn me*—with many other self-accusatory observations, which have been already quoted from verses 28, 30 and 31. Now this chapter, which in our present version of it, is very unintelligible, will perhaps recover its original meaning, and prove beautifully consistent, upon these two principles—that, from verse 2 to 22, Job is really *exposing his Friends*, by ironically quoting some of *their absurd maxims*—and that, in verses 28 and 31, he is speaking, *not to God*, but in reply to *Bildad*.

Thus, in ver. 2—*I know it is so of a truth* i.e. Verily I perceive, that (*with you*) the matter stands thus: As, *how shall man be just with God*—and again—*God is omnipotent*; which is granted, and enlarged upon. Verses 15 and 16 strongly confirm the idea of Job's *irony* on the maxims of his Friends: thus—*Whom* (i.e. GOD) *I am not to answer*, you say, *even tho' I were righteous*; but *I am to make supplication to my judge*. Nay: *if I have called to God, and he hath really answered me; I am not to believe, that he hath heard my voice. Because* &c. So again, as to verses 20, 21, 22: *If I justify myself*, then you say, *my own mouth proves me wicked! If I say, I am perfect*; then *it proves me perverse!* And even supposing, that *I am perfect and upright*; yet am *I not to know it!* In short: *My soul loatheth my very life* i.e. I am almost tired to death with such nonsense. Whereas the *one* sole true conclusion is *this, which therefore I* resolutely *maintain*—" GOD DESTROYETH "THE PERFECT AND THE WICKED." And, as to verses 28 and 31; the whole embarrasment attending them is removed, when we consider them as directed to *Bildad* — who, by the vehemence of his speech had shewn, that he would continue to insist upon Job's guilt. *If I wash myself in snow water; and make my hands ever so clean: yet wilt thou* (Bildad) *plunge me in the ditch* &c.

Let us proceed therefore to the 3d and last part of this general difficulty; which arises at present from Job's confession, in 42, 6: *I abhor myself, and repent in dust and ashes.* But, *repent* of what? * And why *abhor himself?* He was, at that instant, in the very situation he had been earnestly wishing, and often praying for: and was it possible for him not to seize that favourable moment? What he had so often wished was, that GOD would appear, and permit him to ask the reason of his uncommon Sufferings. See 10; 2: 13; 3 and 18 to 23: 19, 7: 23; 3—10: 31; 35—37: &c. And now, when GOD does appear; we see, that Job, immediately attentive to this matter, resolves to put the question and declares this resolution — *Hear, I beseech thee; and I will speak: I will demand of thee, and declare thou unto me. I have heard of thee by the hearing of the ear; but now mine eye seeth thee.* What now becomes of Job's *question?* Does he put any? Far, at present, are the next words from any such meaning; at least, in our present version: for there the verse expresses nothing but *sorrow for sin*, which sets the Poem at variance with itself: it also loses all sight of *the question,* for which the Poem had been prepa-

* *Si veras pœnitentiam egi, cum Deo mox locuturo pugnabis; qui bis testatur, nihil fecisse Job, aut vero dixisse, quod esset pœnitentiâ dignum.* Houbigant.

ring, and which Job himself declares he would now put! Add, that in the first of these 2 lines, the verb does not signify *I abhor myself* — that the first hemistic is evidently too short — and that the 2d is not properly IN *dust* (but UPON *dust*) *and ashes*.

It is therefore submitted to the Learned, whether the restoration of 2 Letters, which, at the same time that they lengthen the line, will remove the inconsistency, and give the very question here wanted, be not strongly and effectually recommended by *the Exigence of the Place*. As על כן is properly *therefore*, and על מה (10, 2) is *wherefore*; מה was easily dropped before כן: it not being recollected, that כן here is connected (not with the preposition before it, but) with the verb (after it) and signifies *hoc modo*. The true reading, therefore, and the true sense, I humbly conceive to stand thus —

4   שמע נא ואנכי אדבר
       אשאלך והודיעני :

5   לשמע אזן שמעתיך
       ועתה עיני ראתך :

6   על (מה) כן אמאס
       ונחמתי על עפר ואפר :

4. *Hear, I beseech thee, and I will speak;*
   I will demand of thee, and declare thou unto me.

5. *I have heard of thee by the hearing of the ear;*
   but now mine eye seeth thee.

6. WHEREFORE *am I thus become loathsome;*
   and am scorched up, upon dust and ashes? *

---

* See 7, 5: My flesh is clothed with worms, and clods of dust; my skin is broken, (וימאס) and *become loathsome*. And 30, 30: My skin is black upon me; and my bones are *burnt with heat*. See also 2, 8: 10, 2: 16, 15.

It will immediately be here objected, that the Poem could not poſſibly end with this Queſtion from *Job*: and, among other reaſons, for this in particular — becauſe we read in the very next verſe, *that, after* THE LORD *had ſpoken theſe words unto Job* &c. If therefore the laſt Speaker was not *Job*, but THE LORD; Job could not originally have concluded the Poem, as he does at preſent.

This objection I hold to be exceedingly important; and indeed to prove deciſively, that the Poem muſt have ended at firſt with ſome ſpeech from GOD. And this remark leads directly to a very intereſting enquiry — *What* was at firſt *the concluſion* of this Poem. This may, I preſume, be pointed out and determined, not by the alteration of any one word, but only by allowing a diſlocation of the 14 verſes, which now begin the 40th chapter. Chapters 38, 39, 40 and 41 contain a magnificent diſplay of the Divine Power and Wiſdom, in the works of the Creation; ſpecifying the *Lion, Raven, Wild-Goat, Wild-Aſs, Unicorn, Peacock, Oſtrich, Horſe, Hawk, Eagle, Behemoth* and *Leviathan*. Now it muſt have ſurprized moſt readers to find, that the deſcription of theſe Creatures is ſtrangely interrupted at ch. 40, 1; and as ſtrangely reſumed afterwards, at 40, 15. And therefore, if theſe 14 Verſes connect well with, and regularly follow, what now *ends* the Poem; we cannot much doubt, but that theſe 14 verſes have again found their true ſtation, and ſhould be reſtored to it. 'Tis not pretended, that the idea of this great Tranſpoſition is *new*, it having been mentioned by Mr *Heath*, pag. 163 &c: but I ſhall endeavour to ſupport it by the following arguments.

The *greatness* of the supposed Transposition is no objection: because so many Verses, as would fill *one piece of vellum* in an antient Roll, might be easily *sewed in*, before, or after, its proper place. In the case before us: the 25 lines, in the first 14 verses of chapter 40, seem to have been sewed in improperly, after 39, 30; instead of after 42, 6. That such large parts have been thus transposed in Rolls (to make which, the Parts were sewed together) is absolutely certain; see my 2d *Dissertat.* p. 342, 572 and *Dissert. Gen.* p. 72. And that this has been the case here, is still more probable, for the following reason.

The lines, here supposed to be out of place, are 25; and contain 92 words: which might be written on one piece, or page, of vellum. But the MS, in which these 25 lines made one page, must be supposed to have the same, or nearly the same, number of lines in each of the pages adjoining. And it would greatly strengthen this presumption; if these 25 would fall in regularly, at the end of any other set of lines nearly of the same number: if they would fall in after the next set of 25, or the 2d set, or the 3d, or 4th &c. Now this is actually the case here; for the lines, after these 25, being 100 or 101, make just 4 times 25. And therefore, if we consider these 125 lines, as written on 5 equal pieces of vellum; it follows, that the 5th piece might be carelesly sewed up, *before* the other 4.

Let us observe also *the present Disorder* of the Speeches, which is this. In chapters 38 and 39 God first speaks to Job. The end of ch. 39 is followed by *And the Lord answered Job, and said*; when

yet

yet Job had not replied. At 40, 3—5 Job anſwers; but he ſays, *he had* then *ſpoken* TWICE, and *he would add no more:* whereas this was his *firſt* reply, and he ſpeaks afterwards. From 40, 15 to 41, 34 are now the deſcriptions of *Behemoth* and *Leviathan*; which would regularly follow the deſcriptions of the *Horſe, Hawk,* and *Eagle.* And from 42, 1 to 42, 6 is now *Job's* ſpeech; after which we read in ver. 7 — *After the* LORD *had ſpoken theſe words unto Job!* Now all theſe confuſions are removed at once; if we only allow, that a piece of vellum containing the 25 lines (40, 1—14) originally followed 42, 6. For then, after GOD's firſt ſpeech, ending with *Leviathan*: *Job* replies. Then GOD —— to whom *Job* replies the 2d time, when *he added no more.* And then GOD addreſſes him the 3d time; when *Job* is ſilent, and the Poem concludes: upon which the Narrative opens regularly, with ſaying — *After* THE LORD *had ſpoken theſe words unto Job* &c. *

Some leſs Tranſpoſitions, in our copies of this Poem, have been obſerved by Dr *Grey;* p. 218. And there is one, which muſt not be here omitted; as it is intimately connected with Job's proteſtations of his Integrity, and his wiſhes to plead his cauſe before GOD. Chapters 29, 30 and 31 contain *Job's* animated *Self-Defence;* which was made neceſſary by the reiterated accuſations of his Friends. This Defence *now* concludes with 6 lines; which declare — that, if he had either enjoyed his eſtates *covetouſly,*

* See a clear Diſlocation of 10 verſes, containing 126 words (5 times 25) in the Heb. Text; at *Exod.* 30; 1—10: as ſtated in *Diſſert. General.* p. 11.

or procured them *unjuftly*, he wifhed them to prove *barren and unprofitable*. This part therefore feems naturally to follow verfe 25; where he fpeaks of his *gold*, and how *much his hand had gotten*. The remainder of the chapter will then confift of thefe 4 regular parts — 1ft: his *piety* to GOD, in his freedom from *Idolatry*; ver. 26—28 — 2dly: his *benevolence* to Men, in his *charity* both of temper and of behaviour; 29—32 * — 3dly: his folemn affurance, that he did not *conceal* his guilt, from fearing either *the violence of the poor*, or *the contempt of the rich*; 33, 34 — and then 4thly: (which muft have been the *laft* article, becaufe concluſive of the whole) he infers, that, being *thus fecured by his Integrity*, he may appeal fafely to GOD himfelf. This appeal he therefore makes boldly; and in fuch words as, when rightly tranflated, form an Image, which perhaps has no parallel. For, where is there an Image fo magnificent, or fo fplendid, as this? — JOB, thus confcious of Innocence, wifhing even GOD *himfelf* to draw up *his Indictment!* that very *Indictment* he would *bind round his Head*; and with that Indictment, as *his crown* of glory, he would with the dignity of *a Prince advance* to his Trial! Of this wonderful paffage I fhall firft give the prefent Englifh verfion; and then add a verfion more juft and more intelligible. *Oh that one would hear me! Behold, my*

---

* There feems no fenfe in the brutal wifh now expreffed in ver. 31 *Oh that we had of his flefh, we cannot be fatisfied*. Job is there affirming his *Hofpitality* to his neighbours: and the true meaning therefore feems to be, that *the men of his tabernacle* would teftify for him, faying, *Where is the man*, that *hath not been fatisfied with his flefh* i.e. fed to the full with *provifions* from his table. See *Prov*. 23, 20: *Ifai*. 22, 13: *Dan*. 10, 3: and *Obfervat. Mifcell. in Job*, p. 297.

desire is, that the Almighty would answer me, and that mine adversary had written a book. Surely I would take it upon my shoulder; and bind it as a crown to me. I would declare unto him the number of my steps; as a prince would I go near unto him.

35. Oh, that one would grant me a hearing!
Behold, my desire is, that the Almighty would answer me;
And, as plaintiff against me, draw up the indictment!
   With what earnestness, would I take it on my shoulders!
I would bind it upon me, as a diadem!
   The number of my steps would I set forth unto Him;
Even as a prince, would I approach before Him!

Before we lose sight of these several passages, expressive of Job's most ardent wish to plead his Innocence; this may perhaps be the most proper place for introducing that very important and most celebrated passage I KNOW THAT MY REDEEMER LIVETH &c. This passage is generally confined to verses 25, 26 & 27 in ch. 19; but should be extended to ver. 29. These 5 verses, tho' they contain but 12 lines, have occasioned controversies without number; as to the general meaning of Job in this place: whether he here expressed his firm belief of *a Resurrection to Happiness after Death*, or of *a Restoration to Prosperity during the remainder of his Life*. Each of these positions has found powerful, as well as numerous, advocates: and the short issue of the whole seems to be — that each party has confuted the opposite opinion, yet without establishing its own. For, how could Job here express his conviction of a reverse of things in *this* world, and of a restoration to *temporal Prosperity*; at the very time, when he strongly asserts, that his Miseries would be

soon

soon terminated by Death? See ch. 6, 11 : 7, 21 : 17, 11—15: 19, 10; and particularly, in 7, 7 — *O remember that my life is wind: mine eye shall no more see good.*

Still lefs could Job here exprefs an *Hope full of Immortality*; which fenfe cannot be extorted from the words, without very evident violence. And as the *poffeffion* of fuch belief is not to be reconciled with Job's fo bitterly *curfing the day of his Birth*, in ch. 3; fo the *declaration* of fuch belief would have folved at once the whole difficulty in difpute.

But, if neither of the preceding and oppofite opinions can be admitted; if the words are not meant to exprefs Job's belief either of a *Reftoration* or of a *Refurrection*: what then are we to do? It does not appear to me, that any other interpretation has been *yet* propofed by the learned: yet I will now venture to offer a *third* interpretation, different from both the former; and which, whilft it is free from the preceding difficulties, does not feem liable to equal objections. Let the Reader proceed to examine it with the fame candour, with which it is now propofed to him.

The conviction then, which I fuppofe Job to exprefs here, is this.—That, tho' his Diffolution was haftening on, amidft the unjuft accufations of his pretended Friends, and the cruel infults of his hoftile Relations; and tho', whilft he was thus fingularly oppreffed with anguifh of Mind, he was alfo tortured with pains of Body; torn by fores and ulcers from head to foot, and fitting upon duft and afhes: yet that ftill, out of that miferable Body, in his Flefh thus ftripped of Skin, and nearly dropping

ping into the grave, HE SHOULD SEE GOD; who would *appear in his favour,* and *vindicate* THE INTEGRITY *of his Character.* This opinion may, perhaps, be fairly and fully supported — by the sense of the Words themselves — by the Context — and by the following Remarks.

We read, in 2, 7 — that *Job* was smitten *with sore boils, from the sole of his foot unto his crown:* and (ver. 8) *he sat down among the* ASHES. In 7, 5 Job says — *My flesh is clothed with worms, and clods of* DUST: *my skin is broken, and become loathsome.* In 16, 19: *Also now, behold my witness is in heaven, and my record is on high.* Then come the words of Job, in 19, 25—29. And then, in opposition to what Job had just said — that GOD would soon appear to vindicate him — and that even his accusing *Friends* would acquit him — Zophar says (20, 27) that *the Heaven* would reveal his iniquity; and *the Earth* would rise up against him. Lastly: this opinion concerning Job's words (as to GOD's *vindication* of him) is confirmed strongly at the end of the book, which records the conclusion of Job's history. His firm hope is here supposed to be, that, *before his death,* he should *with his bodily eyes* see GOD *appearing and vindicating his character.* And from the conclusion we learn, that GOD did thus appear — *now* (says Job) *mine eye seeth thee.* And then did GOD most effectually, and for ever, brighten the glory of Job's fame, by four times calling him HIS SERVANT; and, as his anger was kindled against Job's friends, by speaking to them in the following words — *Ye have not spoken of me the thing that is right, as* MY SERVANT *Job hath* — *Go to* MY SERVANT *Job*
— *and*

—*and* MY SERVANT *Job shall pray for you* — *in that ye have not spoken of me the thing which is right, like* MY SERVANT *Job*. 42; 7, 8.

Our present version of this celebrated passage is this. 25. *For I know* that *my Redeemer liveth, and* that *he shall stand at the latter* (DAY) *upon the earth*. 26. *And* tho' *after my skin,* (WORMS) *destroy this* (BODY), *yet in my flesh shall I see God:* 27. *Whom I shall see for myself, and mine eyes shall behold, and not another:* tho' *my reins be consumed within me.* 28. *But ye should say, Why persecute we him, seeing the root of the matter is found in me?* 29. *Be ye afraid of the sword: for wrath* bringeth *the punishments of the sword, that ye may know* there is *a judgment.*

The new version of this passage now follows.

25. For I know, that my Vindicator liveth;
and He, at the last, shall arise over *this* dust.

26. And, after that mine adversaries have mangled *me* thus, even in my flesh shall I see GOD:

27. Whom I shall see on my side;
and mine eyes shall behold, but not estranged *from me:*
all this have I made up in mine own bosom.

28. Verily ye shall say, "Why have we persecuted him; "seeing, the truth of the matter is found with him?"

29. Tremble for yourselves, at the face of the sword; for the sword waxeth hot against iniquities:
therefore be assured, that judgment will take place. *

25. ואני ידעתי גאלי חי ואחרון על עפר יקום:
26. ואחר עורי נקפו זאת ומבשרי אחזה אלוה:
27. אשר אני אחזה לי ועיני ראו ולא זר כלו כליתי בחקי:
28. כי תאמרו מה נרדף לו ושרש דבר נמצא בי:
29. גורו לכם מפני חרב כי חמה עונות חרב למען תדעון [שדין]:

* [Note 10: see pages 38, 99, 112, 128.]

I do not attempt to regulate my detached remarks upon this book, by the order and succession of the several Chapters; and I shall now take notice of a matter of considerable moment, in chap. 27. The reader will allow the importance of it; because it relates to *eleven whole Verses*, now ascribed to *Job*, which were probably spoken by ZOPHAR. Let it be first observed, that the plan of the former part of the Poem is as follows.

Ch. 4 & 5 *Eliphaz*, 1st Speech ——— Job replies; ch. 6 & 7.
——— 8 *Bildad*, 1st Speech ——— Job replies —9 & 10.
——— 11 *Zophar*, 1st Speech ——— Job replies 12, 13, 14.

Ch. 15 *Eliphaz*, 2d Speech ——— Job replies; ch. 16, 17.
———18 *Bildad*, 2d Speech ——— Job replies — 19.
———20 *Zophar*, 2d Speech ——— Job replies — 21.

Ch. 22 *Eliphaz*, 3d Speech ——— Job replies; ch. 23, 24.
———25 *Bildad*, 3d Speech — Job rep. 26, & (now) 27.

It is therefore evident, that *Eliphaz* and *Bildad* speak 3 times; and are as often answered by Job: but, tho' the regular mechanism of the several parts leads us to expect a 3d Speech likewise *from Zophar*, yet we are greatly disappointed. But, that we really, even now, are in possession of a 3d Speech made by *Zophar*, will probably be allowed by most of those readers, who consider well the following remarks.

The *eleven Verses*, which conclude the 27th chapter, and are now given as the words of *Job*, cannot have been spoken by *Job*; because they contain such doctrine as *Job* himself could not hold, and which indeed he expressly denies: namely, that *great calamities* prove *great wickedness*. But these eleven verses perfectly express the sentiments of ZOPHAR, and are

are in his fierce manner of accufation; and they ftand in the very *place*, where Zophar's 3d Speech is naturally expected. We fhould obferve alfo, that if, in anfwer to Bildad's 3d Speech, Job's reply is contained in ch. 26 and in the firft 12 verfes of ch. 27; that reply ends there very properly, thus —— *Behold, all ye yourfelves have feen it; why then are you thus altogether vain?* But, which is a ftronger argument, the 13th verfe, here fuppofed to begin Zophar's 3d Speech, is the very fame maxim, and nearly in the fame words, with the conclufion of Zophar's 2d Speech: fo that he means to fay — *I abide by my laft pofition*; and what I before maintained, I maintain ftill. He had (20, 29) concluded, that *This* (fc. mifery) *is the portion of a wicked man from God; and the heritage appointed him by God.* And here he refumes the maxim, and perfifts in the juftnefs of his obfervation: *This is the portion of a wicked man with God; and the heritage of oppreffors, which they fhall receive of the Almighty.* How miferably the Commentators are tormented, at finding the maxims of Job's accufers here afcribed to *Job himfelf* — may be feen in the remarks of the learned *Alb. Schultens* on this book; p. 729, 744: and alfo *Obfervationes Mifcell. in Job*; 8°. *Amftel.* (Boullier) 1758, p. 252.

It will be however objected — that there is no authority either from *Heb. MSS* or *Antient Verfions*, for afcribing thefe 11 Verfes to *Zophar*. The anfwer is — that if the words *muft*, from their *internal* evidence, have come from *Zophar*, not from Job; then the Title, afcribing them to Zophar, was probably omitted before the Verfions were made: at a very early period, when feveral other corruptions took place likewise. And indeed there obtains at present, in the Titles of this and the next chapter, no little confusion. For instance: ch. 27 begins with *Job continued his parable*, when he had not been uttering any thing particularly parabolical. This Title is far more applicable to the next chapter, which contains the justly-celebrated panegyric upon *Wisdom:* for this might be very properly introduced with *And Job proceeded to take up his parable*; because he then pronounced an oblique charge of *Folly* on his 3 Friends, which was beautifully implied in *the great difficulty* of *finding* WISDOM. It is therefore presumed, that the Title, now beginning ch. 27, should begin ch. 28; and, that before verse 13 of ch. 27 should be read *Then answered Zophar, the Naamathite; and said.*

I shall conclude these remarks on the book of *Job*, with an observation relative (in general) to *our present Eng. Translation* of the Bible. This Translation, made by Royal Authority near 200 years ago, is supposed to have been delivered down to our time, in many different Editions, but all carefully conformable to the Royal Standard. Whereas, if this is not the case; if considerable alterations have been made, whether by design or thro' want of care, in *any* editions of this Translation; and especially, if made in *many* of them: this furnishes a strong additional argument, in favour of a *Review* of that Book, which is of such real importance to Mankind. Now, to my great surprize, I have lately discovered a considerable alteration, in the words of *Job* 4, 6; which, in different editions of our *present* Translation, are expressed no less than 4 different ways.

The common editions read thus — Is *not* this *thy fear, thy confidence, thy hope, and the uprightness of thy ways?* And the different methods, in which the latter part is expressed, are these ——

1. —confidence, the uprightness of thy ways, and THY HOPE.
2. ——————— the uprightness of thy ways,   THY HOPE.
3. ——————— and the uprightness of thy ways, THY HOPE.
4. ——————— THY HOPE, and the uprightness of thy ways.

The *first* of these 4 variations is the manner, in which this verse is expressed in the Standard copy; as printed in 1611, 1615, 1633, and 1640. The *second* is in a small edition by *Field*, 1658. The *third* obtains in *Barker*'s Bible, 1639; in *Field*'s 24°, 1653; and in the magnificent *Oxford* folio, in 1680. The *fourth* and last variation is found in the editions of 1638, 1639, 1660, 1661, 1665, 1668, 1671, 1678, 1682, 1686, 1695, 1697, 1704, 1706, 1717, 1747, 1769 &c.

PSALMS.

If any one book of the Old Testament calls for our more particular attention, and a more careful enquiry into its true sense; it is the book of PSALMS. For this book is much more in *common use*, than any other. And whilst it is animated with the sublimest strains of *Devotion*; it expresses the most just and rational *Piety*, and contains some of the most illustrious *Prophecies*. It is therefore no wonder, that these sacred Hymns have been so much commented upon, by the Learned; and that the world has been favoured with so many new Versions of this whole book, or the different parts of it. Nor yet will it be any wonder, if the *Corruptions* admitted into the

Text, together with the great *Difficulties* arising from obscurities of various kinds, have left it possible, that Improvements may be *still* made in an Eng. Translation. This, I presume, is in fact the case; and I hope to prove it, by an induction of various Particulars. My present design is, to submit to the Learned a translation of several *whole* Psalms; with remarks on others, in some *particular* places.

The Psalms, which I shall here attempt to translate entirely, in number 32, are these — 2, 8, 16, 18, 22, 25, 34, 36, 37, 40, 41, 42, 43, 45, 48, 49, 50, 55, 67, 68, 69, 80, 85, 87, 89, 110, 114, 117, 118, 120, 129, 132. And in determining upon these several Psalms, the *matter* as well as the *form* will frequently require *Notes:* some of which will give the authority for the Sense here attributed to the Words; whilst others will give the reason for the Division of the Hemistics. But these Critical Notes I shall reserve, for my *Appendix*; agreeably to the notice already given, in page 38. It must, however, be observed here — that the Heb. Poetry naturally resolves itself into *short Lines*, which in general are nearly of the same length; and that this length is in general clearly determined by *the Sense:* not by any imaginary succession of *Iambics* and *Trochaics*, or by a supposed regular number of feet in any succession of the lines. And it will certainly be granted, that no great stress ought to be laid on any scheme of Metre; which allows the same Syllables to be either long, or short — the same Words to contain either 2 syllables, or 3 — and the Lines to consist either of 6, or 8, or 10 syllables, or twice as many. But, an attention to the Heb. Poetry, so far as to distinguish it from *Prose*, according to an arrangement which at once shews it to be *Poetry*, this has been already found of great use in the discovery of *Corruptions*, and a just *Correction* of them. This is likewise of great use, in explaining one Hemistic by another; sometimes enforcing the same truth in different but *synonymous* words, and sometimes illustrating it by its *contrary*. And that this method of parallelism, already found serviceable, is capable of being made more extensively beneficial, will (I trust) appear from the following specimens. Let it be added, that the Reader, who has contracted a reverence for the Version in common use, will not much relish either *Changes in the Expression*, or *Corrections in the Sense*; till he has well considered, that several Alterations are *absolutely necessary* — partly, to render the Psalms themselves *intelligible*, which they are not at present, in various places — and partly, to prove that the Sense, which *The New Testament* ascribes to some of them, is ascribed fairly and with truth.

Introduction to The Second Psalm.

It has been often and justly observed, that, in *some* of the Psalms, different parts must be assigned to different Speakers. And this Psalm, commonly called *The Second*, naturally resolves itself into 4 parts; assignable to *the Psalmist*, *Jehovah*, *Messiah*, and *the Psalmist*. And these parts, taken together, constitute a very sublime Hymn, prophetically celebrating *The Universality of Messiah's Kingdom*; which, upon his *Resurrection*, was begun, and soon established thro' the earth: in defiance of all the opposition made to it both by *Jews* and *Gentiles*. See *Acts* 4; 25, 26, 27: 13, 33: and *Heb.* 1, 5.

Psalm 2.

Psalmist.

1. Why do the nations furiously confederate;
and the peoples meditate a vain thing?

2. Why will the kings of the earth set themselves in array;
and the rulers take counsel together,
against JEHOVAH and against his Messiah? (*saying*)

3. "Let us break asunder their fetters;
"and cast away from us their yoke."

JEHOVAH.

4. He, who sitteth in heaven, shall laugh to scorn;
JEHOVAH shall hold them in derision.

5. Then shall He speak to them, in his wrath;
and, in his displeasure, confound them: (*saying*)

6. "Yet have I anointed my king,
"upon Sion, the mountain of my holiness."

MESSIAH.

7. I will publish the decree of JEHOVAH:
He hath said unto me, "Thou art my son;
"this day have I begotten thee.

8. "Desire of me; and unto thee
"I will give the nations for thine inheritance,
"and for thy possession the extremities of the earth.

9. "Thou shalt rule them with a sceptre of iron;
"as a potter's vessel, shalt thou dash them in pieces."

Psalmist.

10. Now therefore, O ye kings, be wise;
be instructed, O ye judges of the earth.

11. Serve ye JEHOVAH, with fear;
and rejoice unto Him, with reverence.

12. Do homage to the Son; lest he be angry,
and ye perish from the right way:
when his wrath shall begin to kindle;
how blessed all they, who trust in Him!

Psalm 8.

Argument.

The Goodness of GOD in
The Creation and Dignity of *Man*.

---

2.   O JEHOVAH, OUR LORD!
HOW EXCELLENT IS THY NAME, IN ALL THE EARTH!

3. THOU, who hast set thy glory above the heavens,
out of the mouth of babes and of sucklings,
hast established strength, because of thine adversaries;
to still the enemy and the avenger.

4. When I view the heavens, the work of thy fingers;
the moon and the stars, which thou hast ordained:

5. What is man! that thou art mindful of him;
and the son of man! that thou visitest him?

6. For thou hast made him little lower than the angels;
and hast crowned him with glory and honour!

7. Thou hast given him dominion over the works of thy
all things hast thou put under his feet: [hands;

8. Sheep, and oxen, all of them;
and also the beasts of the field:

9. The fowls of heaven, and fishes of the sea;
all that passeth thro' the paths of the seas.

[Chorus]

10.   O JEHOVAH, OUR LORD!
HOW EXCELLENT IS THY NAME, IN ALL THE EARTH!

Psalm 16.

An Hymn, prophetically descriptive of *The Messiah*; as expressing his abhorrence of the general
Idolatry

Idolatry of Mankind, and his own zeal for the honour of JEHOVAH: with the full assurance of his being *raised from the dead*, before *his Body should be corrupted* in the Grave. That David did not here speak of *himself*, but of THE MESSIAH, and of him *only* — is asserted by S. Peter and S. Paul: see *Acts* 2, 25 — 32; with 13, 35 — 37. And if this Psalm speaks, in a literal sense, concerning *an actual and speedy Resurrection*; by that same literal sense, *David himself* is necessarily excluded.

1. Preserve me, O GOD; for I have trusted in thee:

2. I have said unto JEHOVAH, "Thou art my Lord; "my goodness is not without thee."

3. As for the divinities, which are upon the earth; these, and the heroes, my delight is not in them.

4. Their idols are multiplied, after them do men run: but I will not offer their drink-offerings of blood; nor will I take even their names upon my lips.

5. JEHOVAH! thou hast appointed my portion, and my thou hast maintained for me my lot.   [cup;

6. The lines are fallen to me very pleasantly; yea, mine inheritance is to me delightful.

7. I will bless JEHOVAH, who hath given me counsel; and by nights mine own thoughts instruct me.

8. I have set JEHOVAH before me continually; for He is on my right hand, I shall not be moved.

9. Therefore my heart is glad, and my glory rejoiceth; my flesh also shall rest in hope.

10. For thou wilt not abandon my life to the grave; thou wilt not give Thy Holy One to see corruption.

11. Thou shalt make me know the path of life; thou shalt make me full of joy with thy countenance: at thy right hand are pleasures for evermore.

Remarks on select Passages in
Psalm 18.

The *Messiah's* sublime Thanksgiving; composed by David, when his Wars were at an end, towards the conclusion of his Life. And in this sacred Song, the goodness of GOD is celebrated — 1st: for *Messiah's Resurrection* from the dead; with the wonders attending that awful Event, and soon following it: — 2dly: for the Punishments inflicted on the *Jews*, particularly by the destruction of Jerusalem — and 3dly: for the Obedience of the *Gentile* Nations. See *Rom.* 15, 9: *Heb.* 2, 13: and *Matt.* 28, 2—4; with 24, 7 and 29. See also the preceding pages 122—125. And that *the Title*, now prefixed to this Hymn, here and in 2 *Sam.* 22, describes only *The Time* of its composition, seems evident: for who can ascribe justly to *David himself*, as the subject, verses 5, 6, 8—17, 21—26, 30, 42, 44 &c.

To the chief Musician; a Psalm of David, the servant of the Lord, who spake unto the Lord the words of this song, in the day that the Lord delivered him from the hand of all his enemies, and from the hand of Saul: saying.

MESSIAH's Song; part 1.

2. I will love thee, O JEHOVAH, my strength!

3. JEHOVAH is my rock, and my fortress!
even my deliverer hath my GOD been!
GOD is my rock, in Him will I trust!
my buckler, the horn also of my salvation, and my refuge!

4. I called on JEHOVAH, who is worthy to be praised;
and from mine enemies I was saved.

5. When the waves of death compassed me;
and the floods of ungodliness made me afraid:

6. When the sorrows of the grave surrounded me;
and the toils of death were spread before me:

7. In my diſtreſs, I called on JEHOVAH;
and I cried unto my GOD:
and out of his temple he heard my voice;
and my cry entered into his ears.

Part 2.

8. Then the earth ſhook, and trembled;
even the foundations of the hills were moved,
and they ſhook themſelves, for He was wroth.

9. There went up a ſmoke, in his anger;
and at his command, the fire devoured:
coals were kindled at it.

10. He bowed the heavens alſo, and came down;
and darkneſs was under his feet.

11. And he rode upon a cherub, and did fly;
and he was ſeen upon the wings of the wind.

12. And he made darkneſs his pavilion,
even his tent round about him;
dark waters, and thick clouds of the ſkies.

13. At the brightneſs before him, his thick clouds paſſed;
they kindled into coals of fire.

14. And JEHOVAH thundered out of heaven;
and the moſt High uttered his voice.

15. And he ſhot forth arrows, and ſcattered them;
and he multiplied lightnings, and deſtroyed them.

16. And the channels of the ſea were ſeen;
and the foundations of the world were diſcovered:
at thy rebuke, O JEHOVAH!
at the blaſt of the breath of thy diſpleaſure!

Part 3.

17. He ſent down from on high, he took me;
he drew me out of many waters.

18. He delivered me from my mighty enemy,
and from them that hated me, when they were too ſtrong for [me.

19. They prevented me, in the day of my calamity;
but JEHOVAH was a ſtay to me.

20. He also brought me forth into a large place; he delivered me, because he delighted in me. [ness;

21. JEHOVAH rewarded me, according to my righteous-according to the cleanness of my hands, he requited me.

22. For I have kept the ways of JEHOVAH; and have not wickedly revolted from my GOD.

23. For all his judgments were before me; and his statutes I did not remove from me.

24. And I was perfect, before him; and preserved myself from iniquities. [righteousness;

25. Thus hath JEHOVAH requited me, according to my according to the cleanness of my hands, in his eye-sight.

Part 4.

26. With a merciful man, thou wilt shew thyself merciful; with a perfect man, thou wilt shew thyself perfect:

27. With a pure man, thou wilt shew thyself pure; but with a froward man, thou wilt shew thyself perverse.

28. For thou wilt save an afflicted people; but looks, that are haughty, thou wilt bring down.

29. For thou, JEHOVAH, wilt light up my lamp; my GOD will illuminate my darkness.

30. For by thee I shall break thro' a troop; and, by GOD's help, I shall leap over a wall.

31. As for GOD, perfect is his way; the word of JEHOVAH is tried: a buckler is He to all, that trust in Him.

32. For who is GOD, but JEHOVAH? and who is a rock, except our GOD?

33. It is GOD, who girdeth me with strength; and maketh my way perfect.

34. He maketh my feet like those of hinds; and on my high places he maketh me to stand.

35. He teacheth my hands to war; so that a bow of brass is broken by mine arms.

36. Thou hast also given me the shield of thy salvation; and thy right hand hath holden me up: even thine affliction of me hath made me great.

37. Thou haſt enlarged my ſteps under me;
ſo that my footſteps ſhall not ſlip.

38. I have purſued mine enemies, and overtaken them;
neither did I turn, till they were conſumed.

39. I have wounded them, ſo that they cannot riſe;
and they are fallen under my feet.

40. For thou haſt girded me with ſtrength unto battle;
thou haſt put under me thoſe, who roſe againſt me.

41. Thou haſt alſo given me the necks of mine enemies;
of thoſe who hate me, and I have deſtroyed them.

42. They cried, but there was no one to ſave them;
even to JEHOVAH, but he anſwered them not.

43. Then did I beat them ſmall, as the duſt before the
as the dirt of the ſtreets, did I caſt them out.   [wind;

Part 5.

44. Thou haſt reſcued me from the ſtrivings of my people;
thou haſt made me the head of the nations:
a people, whom I have not known, ſhall ſerve me.

45. As ſoon as they hear of me, they ſhall obey me;
but the ſtrange children ſhall diſſemble to me.

46. The ſtrange children ſhall fall away;
and be afraid, becauſe of their cloſe places.

47. JEHOVAH liveth! and bleſſed be my rock!
and exalted be the GOD of my ſalvation!

48. He is the GOD, who avengeth me;
and ſubdueth the peoples under me.

49. He delivereth me from mine enemies;
yea, thou lifteſt me up above thoſe, that riſe againſt me:
from the men of violence thou haſt delivered me.

50. Therefore will I praiſe thee, JEHOVAH, among the
and I will ſing unto thy name: (ſaying)   [nations;

51. " He magnifieth the ſalvation of his king!
" and ſheweth loving-kindneſs to his anointed!
" to David, and to his ſeed, for ever!"

Psalm 22.

Part the *first* prophetically sets forth THE MESSIAH, as in a state of violent Suffering; and *the beginning* was expressly spoken by JESUS, upon the Cross: *Matt.* 27, 46. The *insults* of the Jews, on that occasion, here predicted in verses 7 and 8, are recorded by the same Evangelist; 27, 43. The *Crucifixion* itself is foretold, in the words *they pierce my hands and my feet*; ver. 16. And the circumstances of *his garments parted* (i. e. divided in pieces among the soldiers) and *lots being cast for his vesture*, which was not divided — are recorded in *Matt.* 27, 35 and *John* 19; 23, 24. Note also, that these extraordinary particulars, thus predicted of *the Messiah*, and fulfilled in *Jesus*, and thus proving JESUS to be THE MESSIAH, do not admit any just application to *David*; nor derive the least countenance, as to *him*, from the very long history given of *him* in the Old Testament. It is equally impossible to apply properly to *David* the Second part of this Hymn; which expresses *the Triumph of the Messiah*, after his Resurrection, and *the Progress of Christianity thro' the World*. Unless we can suppose, that David could describe *himself*, as actually being King over all the nations under heaven; or could consider *all the ends of the earth*, as being within the limits of *Judea*.

Part 1: MESSIAH's *Supplication.*

2. My GOD! my GOD! why hast thou forsaken me! Far from my cry, and the words of my lamentation!

3. O my GOD! I call by day, but thou answerest not; and by night, but there is no intermission for me.

4. But thou, who dwellest in the sanctuary, and hast been the praise of Israel:

5. In thee our fathers trusted;
they trusted, and thou didst save them.

6. Unto thee they cried, and were delivered;
in thee they trusted, and were not disappointed.

7. But I am *treated as* a worm, and not a man;
a reproach of men, and despised of the people.

8. All they, who see me, laugh me to scorn;
they shoot out the lip, they shake the head (*saying:*)

9. " He trusted in JEHOVAH, let Him deliver him;
" let Him rescue him, since he delighteth in him."

10. But thou art he, who took me from the womb;
thou wast my confidence, upon the breasts of my mother.

11. Upon thee was I thrown, even from my birth;
from my mother's womb, thou wast my GOD.

12. Be not far from me, for I am in trouble;
draw nigh, for there is no helper.

13. Many bulls surround me;
the mighty ones of Bashan beset me about.

14. They gape upon me, with their mouths;
like a lion, ravening and roaring.

15. As water, am I poured out;
and all my bones are dissolved:
my heart is become like wax;
it is melted in the midst of my bowels.

16. As a potsherd, is my strength dried up;
and my tongue cleaveth to my gums:
even to the dust of death thou bringest me.

17. For dogs surround me;
an assembly of wicked men inclose me:
they pierce my hands and my feet.

18. I may number all my bones:
these same men look, they stare upon me.

19. They part my garments among them;
and upon my vesture do they cast lots.

20. But thou, O JEHOVAH, be not far off;
O my strength, make haste to mine assistance.

21. Deliver from the fword my life;
my foul from the power of the dog.

22. Save me from the mouth of the lion;
and deliver me from the horns of the unicorns.

Part 2: MESSIAH's *Thankfgiving*.

23. I will declare thy name unto my brethren;
in the midft of the congregation will I praife thee (*faying :*)

24. "Ye, who fear JEHOVAH, praife Him!
" all ye, the feed of Jacob, glorify Him!
" and ftand in awe of Him, all ye, the feed of Ifrael!

25. " For He hath not defpifed, nor abhorred, the af-
　　　　　　　[" fliction of the afflicted.
" neither hath He hid his face from him:
" but when he cried unto Him, He heard him." [tion;

26. From thee fhall my praife arife in many a congrega-
my vows will I perform before them, who fear thee.

27. The meek fhall eat, and be fatisfied;
they fhall praife JEHOVAH, who feek Him:
their heart fhall live for ever.　　　　　[to JEHOVAH;

28. All the ends of the earth fhall remember, and turn
and all the families of the nations fhall worfhip before Him.

29. For, to JEHOVAH belongeth the kingdom;
and He is governor over the nations.

30. All, who are fed from the earth, fhall eat and worfhip;
before Him fhall bow all, who defcend to the duft.

31. And my foul fhall live to Him; my feed fhall ferve
it fhall be counted to the Lord for a generation.　　[Him,

32. They fhall come, and declare his righteoufnefs
unto a people which fhall be born; for He hath done it.

Pfalm 25.

This is the firft of thofe 7 Pfalms, which are compofed in the *Acroftic*, or *Alphabetical*, form; according to which, the 22 Heb. Letters were prefixed, in their order of fucceffion, to the feveral
　　　　　　　　　　　　　　　　　　　　　Verfes.

Verses. But even in this form, which seems particularly guarded against mistakes, in *the beginning* of each verse, several mistakes have been made by transcribers: which mistakes are rendered most clear and evident, from the manner in which these Psalms are printed in my *Edition* of them. In the common Heb. Text, the 2d letter does not now begin the 2d verse. The 5th verse now contains the first part of the 6th verse; whilst the second part of this 6th verse is now subjoined to what should be called verse the 8th. And lastly; that verse, which should begin with the letter *Koph*, has lost that introductory letter; and begins with the very same word as the verse after it: so that the 19th letter has lost its station, and the 20th letter (*Resh*) begins *two* verses, this and the next. All these confusions are corrected in the following version.

1. Unto thee, O JEHOVAH, my GOD!
    do I lift up my soul in prayer.
2. In thee have I trusted, let me not be put to confusion;
    and let not mine enemies triumph over me.
3. Yea, let none, who wait on thee, be confounded;
    let them be confounded, who act basely without cause.
4. Shew me thy ways, O JEHOVAH!
    and teach me thy paths.
5. Lead me in thy truth, and teach me;
    for thou art the GOD of my salvation.
    And on thee have I waited every day;
    because of thy goodness, O Jehovah.   [cies;
6. Remember thy kindnesses, O JEHOVAH, and thy mer-
    for they have been ever, of old.   [not;
7. The sins of my youth, and my transgressions, remember
    according to thy mercy, be thou mindful of me.
8. Good and upright is JEHOVAH;
    therefore will he instruct sinners in the way.

9. He will guide the humble in judgment;
   and he will teach the humble his way.
10. All the paths of JEHOVAH are mercy and truth,
    to thofe who keep his covenant and his teftimonies.
11. For the fake of thy name, O JEHOVAH!
    pardon my fin, for it is great.
12. Who is the man, that feareth JEHOVAH?
    him fhall He teach, in the way he ought to choofe.
13. He himfelf fhall dwell in profperity;
    and his feed fhall inherit the land.
14. The fecret of JEHOVAH is for them that fear him;
    and he will make known to them his covenant.
15. Mine eyes are continually towards JEHOVAH;
    for he will pluck my feet out of the net.
16. Look upon me, and be gracious unto me;
    for I am folitary, and in affliction.
17. Relieve the forrows of my heart;
    and bring me out of my diftreffes.
18. Cut fhort mine affliction and my pain;
    and forgive me all my fins.
19. Behold mine enemies, for they are many;
    and they hate me with violent hatred,
20. Keep my foul, and deliver me;
    let me not be confounded, for I have trufted in thee,
21. Let integrity and uprightnefs preferve me;
    for I have waited for thee, O JEHOVAH!

---

22. Deliver Ifrael, O GOD, out of all his troubles.

Pfalm 34.

This fecond of the Alphabetical Pfalms is lefs irregular, in its initial Letters, than Pf. 25: and yet the Verfe, which fhould begin with the 6th letter, is now wanting. But, from my *Edition* of this Pfalm, it is feen at once, that the Verfe, which is wanting

ing in its proper place, is happily preserved *at the bottom* of the Psalm: after the Verse, beginning with the *last* letter, is compleated. It must also be observed, that it seems to have been another principle in the composition of this Psalm, to insert the word JEHOVAH in every one of the Verses; excepting Verses 13, 14 and 15: and in these the sacred name is omitted, probably for this reason — because these verses contain *that Moral Lesson*, on which *the fear of Jehovah* is here founded. That this word existed formerly in verses 6, 21, and 22, will appear hereafter. And when the last word of this last verse is properly corrected; it will furnish the very letter (*Vau*) to be prefixed to the word following, which compleats the fitness of that Verse for the place, where it is now wanted. It shall only be remarked further, at present; that verses 20 and 21 are of particular importance, as containing the famous prophecy, that *not a bone of The Just One* (Messiah) *should be broken*: *John* 19, 36. See this point stated, at large, in my *Dissert. General.* pag. 28, 29.

---

2. I will bless JEHOVAH at all times;
    ever shall his praise be in my mouth.
3. In JEHOVAH shall my soul boast itself;
    humble men shall hear, and be glad.
4. O magnify JEHOVAH with me;
    and let us exalt his name together.
5. I sought JEHOVAH, and he answered me;
    and out of all my fears he delivered me.
6. Look unto JEHOVAH, and be enlightened;
    and your faces shall not be ashamed.
    [*For Jehovah redeemeth the soul of his servants;
    and none shall be desolate, who trust in him.*]

7. This

7. This humble man cried, and JEHOVAH heard him;
   and out of all his troubles He saved him.
8. The angel of JEHOVAH pitcheth his camp,
   around them who fear Him, and delivereth them.
9. O taste, and see, that JEHOVAH is good;
   blessed is the man, who trusteth in Him.
10. O fear JEHOVAH, ye that are his saints;
    for there is no want to them, who fear Him.
11. Mighty men may be poor, and suffer hunger;
    but they, who seek JEHOVAH, shall want no good.
12. Come, ye children, hearken unto me;
    I will teach you the fear of JEHOVAH.
13. Who is the man, that is desirous of life;
    that loveth days, to see good?
14. Keep thy tongue from evil;
    and thy lips from speaking guile.
15. Depart from evil, and do good;
    seek peace, and pursue it.

} The Moral Lesson.

16. The eyes of JEHOVAH are towards righteous men;
    and his ears are (open) to their cry.
17. The face of JEHOVAH is against the doers of evil;
    to root out the remembrance of them from the earth.
18. The [righteous] cry, and JEHOVAH heareth:
    and delivereth them out of all their troubles.
19. Nigh is JEHOVAH to the broken in heart;
    and those, who are contrite in spirit, he will save.
20. Many are the afflictions of The Just One;
    but from them all JEHOVAH delivereth him.
21. JEHOVAH keepeth all his bones;
    not one of them shall be broken.
22. Misfortune shall slay wicked men;   [make desolate.
    and the haters of The Just One shall JEHOVAH

Psalm 36.

On the Folly of being so presumptuously wicked, as to *profess* a defiance of Divine Power. Because

God is able, as well as willing, to punish Vice, and protect Virtue. This subject is here beautifully illustrated by *the Fate of Mankind*, at *the General Deluge*: when the Apostates from true Religion were destroyed; whilst *Noah*, a preacher of righteousness, was (together with his *Family*, and the various *Animals* in the Ark) most wonderfully preserved.

2. The revolter to wickedness declareth solemnly:
" that *in the midst of his heart there is no fear*;
" that *God is not before his eyes.*"

3. Surely he flattereth himself in his own eyes;
to find out wickedness, and to repeat it.

4. The words of his mouth are iniquity and fraud;
he hath ceased to consider wisely, to do good.

5. He contriveth iniquity upon his bed;
he presenteth himself in the way not good,
and whatsoever is evil he doth not abhor.

6. O JEHOVAH! in the heavens is thy mercy;
and thy truth, the witness in the clouds.

7. Thy righteousness was on the strong mountains;
thy judgments were in the great deep:
when thou savedst man and beast, O JEHOVAH!

8. How excellent was thy mercy, O GOD! [wings.
therefore the sons of men shall trust in the shadow of thy

9. They shall be satiated with the plenty of thy house;
and the river of thy pleasures wilt thou make them to drink.

10. For with thee is the well of life;
in thy light we may behold light.

11. Extend thy mercy to those, who acknowledge thee;
and thy righteousness to those, who are true of heart.

12. Let not the foot of pride approach to me;
nor the hand of wicked men remove me.

13. There are they fallen, all the workers of iniquity;
they are cast down, and shall not be able to arise.

Psalm 37.

This third Alphabetical Pſalm contains further proof of the careleſneſs of Jewiſh tranſcribers. The plan here is — to give 4 hemiſtics to each of the 22 letters. But the ſtanza, beginning with the 4th letter, now wants one hemiſtic; which is happily preſerved in the ſtanza beginning with the 8th letter. And ſo, a ſimilar defect in ver. 20 may be ſupplied (after the correction of one word) from the redundant hemiſtic now in ver. 25. The alterations, neceſſary for a regular beginning of the Stanzas, are theſe — that a proper word be prefixed, at the ſtation, where a word is wanting that begins with the 16th letter: and that *the letter* be removed, which now, very improperly, begins the laſt ſtanza. The other corrections will be accounted for hereafter.

---

1. Fret not thyſelf, on account of evil-doers;
    nor be envious, againſt the workers of iniquity:
2.   for they ſhall ſoon be cut down, as the graſs;
    and wither away, as the green herb.
3. Truſt in JEHOVAH, and do good;
    ſo ſhalt thou dwell in the land, and verily be fed:
4.   delight thyſelf alſo in JEHOVAH;
    and he ſhall give thee the deſires of thine heart.
5. Commit to JEHOVAH thy way;
    truſt alſo in Him, and He will bring it to paſs:
6.   and He will bring forth thy righteouſneſs, as the
    and thy juſt dealings, as the days at noon. [light;
7. Wait for JEHOVAH, and ſhew thyſelf patient for Him;
    fret not thyſelf at him, who proſpereth in his way:
    becauſe of the man, who executeth wicked devices,
    to ſlay ſuch as are upright of conduct.
8. Deſiſt from anger, and leave off wrath;
    fret not thyſelf, only to do evil:

9. for evil-doers shall be cut off,   [herit the earth;
    but they who wait for JEHOVAH, these shall in-
10. For yet a little while, and the wicked man shall not be;
    yea, thou shalt diligently consider his place, yet he
11.   but meek men shall inherit the earth; [shall not be;
    and delight themselves in the abundance of peace.
12. The wicked man plotteth against the just;
    and gnasheth upon him with his teeth:
13.   the Lord will laugh him to scorn;
    for He seeth, that his day is coming.
14. The wicked have drawn the sword;
    and bent their bow, to cast down the poor and needy:
15.   their sword shall enter into their own heart;
    and their bows shall be broken.
16. Better is little to a righteous man,
    than the great abundance of wicked men:
17.   for the arms of wicked men shall be broken;
    but JEHOVAH upholdeth the righteous.
18. JEHOVAH knoweth the days of upright men;
    and their inheritance shall be for ever:
19.   they shall not be ashamed, in the time of evil;
    and in the days of famine, they shall be satisfied.
20. But wicked men shall perish;   [lambs;
    and the enemies of JEHOVAH shall be as the fat of
    they consume away, as smoke they consume away;
    and their seed shall seek after bread.
21. The wicked man borroweth, and payeth not again;
    but the righteous is merciful, and giveth:
22.   for such, as are blessed of him, shall inherit the earth;
    and such, as are cursed of him, shall be cut off.
23. From JEHOVAH are the goings of one, who is pure;
    he establisheth him, and his way pleaseth:
24.   though he fall, he shall not utterly be cast down;
    for JEHOVAH upholdeth his hand.
25. I have been young, and now am old;
    yet I have not seen the righteous man forsaken:

26. he

26. he is ever merciful, and lendeth;
and his feed is bleſſed.
27. Depart thou from evil, and do good;
and dwell for evermore:
28. for JEHOVAH loveth judgment;
and forſaketh not his ſaints.
*Tranſgreſſors are deſtroyed for ever;
but the ſeed of wicked men ſhall be cut off:*
29. the righteous ſhall inherit the land;
and dwell therein for ever.
30. The mouth of the righteous man ſpeaketh wiſdom;
and his tongue talketh of judgment:
31. the law of his GOD is in his heart;
his foot-ſteps ſhall not ſlide.
32. The wicked man watcheth for the righteous;
and ſeeketh occaſion to ſlay him:
33. JEHOVAH will not leave him in his hand;
nor condemn him, when he is judged.
34. Wait thou upon JEHOVAH;
and be obſervant of his way:
*and he will exalt thee, to inherit the land;
when the wicked are cut off, thou ſhalt ſee it.*
35. I have ſeen the wicked man in great power;
and ſpreading himſelf, like a green bay-tree:
36. yet I went by, and lo he was gone;
yea I ſought him, but he was not found.
37. Mark the perfect man, and behold the upright;
for the end of that man is peace:
38. but the tranſgreſſors ſhall be deſtroyed together;
and the end of wicked men ſhall be cut off.
39. The ſalvation of righteous men is from JEHOVAH;
he is their ſtrength in the time of trouble:
40. and JEHOVAH will help them, and deliver them;
and will ſave them, becauſe they truſted in Him.

Psalm 40.

The prophet here expresses the triumph of THE MESSIAH: first, on *his Resurrection*; and secondly, on having *put an End to the Sacrifice of Animals, by offering up Himself*. See this Psalm expressly thus ascribed to the Messiah, by the Author of the Epistle to the *Hebrews*; whose argument is evidently founded on thus opposing to the Bodies of Animals, then no longer to be offered, *the Body of Jesus Christ offered up once for all.* See Heb. 10; 5—10. The words of the Apostle, *Wherefore when he cometh into the world*, plainly exclude *David*; and as plainly point out *The Messiah:* and both, in exact consistency with the Psalm itself. There has long been one real and great difficulty, which will, for the future, be avoided; by considering — that the 7 verses, which *now* conclude this Psalm, *do not belong to it:* being a compleat copy of what is now the 70th Psalm, but preserved there very defectively.

Part 1.

2. With earnest expectation I looked unto JEHOVAH;
and he hath inclined unto me, and heard my cry.

3. And he hath brought me up out of the horrible pit, out of the deep mire;
and he hath set my feet upon a rock, he hath established my goings.

4. And he hath put in my mouth a new song of praise unto GOD;
many shall consider, and fear, and shall trust in JEHOVAH.

5. Blessed the man! who hath made JEHOVAH his confidence;
and hath not turned to the proud, and the favourers of imposture.

6. Manifold are thy works, O JEHOVAH my GOD!
thy wonders, and thy contrivances, there is no recounting unto thee:
I would shew, and would declare them; but they are numberless.

Part 2.

7. Sacrifice and offering thou didst not delight in;
then a body didst thou prepare for me:
burnt-offering and sin-offering thou didst not require;

8. Then said I, " Lo! I come;
" in the roll of the book it is written concerning me:

9. " To do thy will, O God, is my delight;
" yea, thy law is in the midst of my affections."

10. I have published righteousness, in the great congregation;
lo! my lips I will not restrain:
thou, O Jehovah my God, knowest.

11. Thy righteousness have I not concealed within my heart;
thy faithfulness and thy salvation have I declared:
I have not hidden thy mercy and thy truth from the great congregation.

A different Psalm, being now the 70th.

[12. *O Jehovah! withhold not thy compassions from me;
let thy mercy and thy truth always preserve me.*

13. *For evils without number have compassed me about;
mine afflictions have taken hold of me, so that I cannot look up;
they are more than the hairs of my head, so that my heart faileth me.*

14. *Be pleased*] O God, to deliver me; hasten, O Jehovah, to my assistance.

15. Let them be ashamed and confounded, who seek my life to destroy it;
let them be driven back, and put to confusion, who wish me evil.

16. Let them be desolate because of their shame, who say Aha! Aha!

17. Let all those, who seek thee, be joyful and glad in thee:
let those, who love thy salvation, say always, Jehovah be magnified!

18. But I am poor and needy; hasten, O Jehovah, unto me:
thou art my helper and deliverer; O my God, make no delay.

Pfalm 41.

Part 1.

1. Bleffings are on him, who attendeth to the humble man; in the day of evil JEHOVAH will deliver him. [earth;

2. He will keep him, and revive him, and blefs him upon and he will not give him up to the will of his enemies.

3. JEHOVAH will fupport him, on the bed of languifhing; and will make all his bed, in his infirmity.

Part 2.

4. I have faid: "O JEHOVAH! have pity upon me: "O heal my foul; HAVE I SINNED AGAINST THEE?"

5. Mine enemies fpeak evil againft me; (*faying*) "When fhall he die, and his name perifh?"

6. He, who cometh to fee me, fpeaketh vanity; and in his heart heapeth up iniquity to himfelf: then, going forth, he fpeaketh in the fame manner.

7. Againft me do all thofe whifper, who hate me; againft me do they contrive mifchief: (*faying*)

8. "The fentence of being guilty is pronounced upon him; "and now, that he lieth, let him rife no more."

9. Even the man of my peace, he whom I trufted; he, who did eat of my bread, hath lift up his heel againft me.

Part 3.

10. But thou, O JEHOVAH, have pity upon me; and raife me up again, and I fhall reward them.

11. By this I know, that in me thou art well-pleafed; that mine enemy fhall not triumph over me.

12. But I — for my Perfectnefs thou wilt fupport me; and thou wilt fet me before thy face for ever.

Pfalms 42 and 43.

Part 1.

1. As the hart panteth after ftreams of water; fo my foul panteth after thee, O GOD!

2. My foul thirfteth for GOD, for the living GOD; when fhall I come, and behold the prefence of GOD!

3. My tears have been food for me day and night;
while it is said to me all day long, "Where is thy GOD?"

4. These things I remember, and I pour out my soul by
myself: [house of GOD!
when shall I pass over, in company with the mighty, to the
with the voice of shouting, and the thanksgiving of the festival
multitude!

[Chorus]

5. *Why art thou dejected, O my soul? and why art thou dis-
quieted within me?*
put thy trust in God; for I shall yet praise Him,
the salvation of my countenance, and my God!

Part 2.

6. My soul is dejected within me: therefore I remember
thee my GOD; [this little hill.
from the country of Jordan, and of Hermon, and from

7. Deep calleth unto deep, at the voice of thy cataracts;
all thy breakers, and thy waves, have passed over me.

8. By day will JEHOVAH command his mercy;
and by night his song shall be with me, and prayer unto the
GOD of my life. [gotten me?

9. I will say unto GOD, my strong hold, why hast thou for-
why do I go mourning, thro' the oppression of the enemy?

10. Like a sword thro' my bones, is the reproach of mine
adversaries;
while they say to me all day long, "Where is thy GOD?"

[Chorus]

11. *Why art thou dejected, O my soul? and why art thou dis-
quieted within me?*
put thy trust in God; for I shall yet praise Him,
the salvation of my countenance, and my God.

Part 3.

12. Judge me, O GOD, and avenge my quarrel;
deliver me from the unmerciful people, from the man of fraud
and iniquity. [removed me far off?

13. For thou art the GOD of my strength; why hast thou
why do I go mourning, thro' the oppression of the enemy?

14. O

14. O send out thy light, and thy truth: these shall con-
    duct me;
they shall bring me to thy holy mountain, and to thy taber-

15. Then will I go unto the altar of GOD; [nacles.
unto the GOD of my joy and of my exultation:
and I will praise thee upon the harp, O GOD, my GOD!

[Chorus]

16. *Why art thou dejected, O my soul? and why art thou dis-*
    quieted within me?
    put thy trust in God; for I shall yet praise Him,
    the salvation of my countenance, and my God.

Psalm 45.

1. My heart hath meditated on a noble subject;
what I have done I will declare unto THE KING:
my tongue shall be the pen of a ready writer.

2. THOU art more beautiful than the sons of men!
grace is diffused over thy lips:
therefore GOD hath blessed thee for ever.

3. Gird thee with thy sword upon thy thigh;
powerful is thy glory and thy majesty.

4. Lead on therefore, ride on prosperously;
in the cause of truth, of meekness, and of righteousness:
and thy right hand shall teach thee terrible things.

5. Thine arrows are very sharp, O thou most mighty!
the nations shall fall under thee;
in the heart of thine enemies shalt thou be King.

6. Thy throne, O GOD, is for ever and ever;
a sceptre of righteousness is the sceptre of thy kingdom.

7. Thou hast loved righteousness, and hated wickedness;
therefore hath GOD, even thy GOD, anointed thee
with the oil of gladness above thy fellows.

8. Myrrh, aloes and cassia fill thy garments;
out of the wardrobes of ivory are these marks of thy joy.

9. Daughters of kings are amongst thy high honours;
on thy right hand is placed the queen, in gold of Ophir.

10. Hearken

10. Hearken, O daughter, and confider, and incline thine
and forget thine own people, and thy father's houfe.   [ear;

11. Then will the King admire thy beauty;
for He is thy Lord, therefore worfhip Him.   [offering;

12. Even the daughter of Tyre fhall attend with a facred-
the rich men of every nation fhall fupplicate thy favour.

13. Honourable is the King's daughter, in her appearance;
inwoven with gold are her robes.

14. In raiment of needlework fhall fhe be brought to the
the virgins fhall advance after her;   [King;
her companions alfo fhall be brought unto thee.

15. They fhall be conducted with joy and exultation;
and fhall enter into thy palace, O King!

16. Inftead of thy fathers, there fhall be thy children;
them fhalt thou make princes in all the earth.

17. They fhall celebrate thy name thro' all generations;
becaufe the nations will praife thee for ever and ever.

Pfalm 49.

1. Hear this, all ye peoples!
give ear, all ye inhabitants of the world!

2. As well the fons of the low, as of the high;
the rich man, and the poor, together.

3. My mouth fhall fpeak wifdom;
and the meditations of my heart fhall be underftanding.

4. I will incline to a parable mine ear;
I will open upon the harp my dark faying.

5. Wherefore fhould I fear, in the days of evil?
tho' furrounded by the wickednefs of mine enemies:

6. Of thofe, who truft in their wealth;
and boaft themfelves in the multitude of their riches.

7. No man can poffibly redeem his brother;
nor give unto GOD a ranfom for him.

8. For the redemption of his foul is precious;
and he ceafeth to be for ever.

9 But the HOLY ONE fhall live for ever;
he fhall not fee corruption.

10. Whereas

10. Whereas wife men shall die;
equally as the fool and the brute, they perish;
and they leave to others their riches.

11. Their sepulchres are their houses for ever;
their habitations to generation and generation:
even of them, who have given their names to countries.

12. AND MAN, THO' IN HONOUR, SHALL HAVE NO UNDERSTANDING;
BECOMING LIKE THE BEASTS, WHICH GO DOWN INTO SILENCE.

13. This is to them the way of stumbling;
and they, who come after them, run like them.

14. Like cattle, do they advance to the grave;
death is their shepherd, and they go down:
in straight rows, to his flock, he fasteneth them;
till the grave cease from being an habitation for them.

15. Verily GOD shall redeem my soul;
for he shall rescue me from the power of the grave.

16. Fear thou not, tho' a man become rich;
tho' the glory of his house be increased.

17. For when he dieth, he shall carry away nothing;
his glory shall not descend after him.

18. Tho', while he lived, he blessed his own soul;
and would praise thee, for indulging thyself likewise.

19. He goeth to the generation of his fathers;
who shall see the light no more for ever.

20. MAN, THO' IN HONOUR, SHALL HAVE NO UNDERSTANDING;
BECOMING LIKE THE BEASTS, WHICH GO DOWN INTO SILENCE.

Psalm 50.

1. The GOD of Gods is JEHOVAH!
he hath spoken, and called the world
from the rising of the sun to its going down.

2. Out of Sion, the perfection of beauty,
hath GOD manifested his splendour.

3. Our God cometh, and keepeth not silence;
before him goeth a devouring fire,
and round about him is a mighty tempest.

4. He calleth unto the heavens from above,
and unto the earth, that he may judge his people.

5. Gather yourselves unto Him, O ye his saints;
ye, who make a covenant with Him by sacrifice.

6. And the heavens shall declare his righteousness;
for God, He, is the judge.

7. Hear, O my people; for I speak:
O Israel; for I testify concerning thee:
God, even thy God, am I.

8. I reprove thee not, on account of thy sacrifices;
even thy burnt-offerings are before me continually.

9. I accept not a bullock from thy house,
nor he-goats out of thy folds.

10. For mine are all the beasts of the forest;
and the cattle, upon a thousand hills.

11. I know every fowl of the mountains;
and the abundance of the fields is with me.

12. If I were hungry, I would not tell thee;
for mine is the world, and the fulness thereof.

13. Do I eat the flesh of bulls?
or the blood of he-goats do I drink?

14. Sacrifice unto God a sacrifice of praise;
and pay to The most High thy vows.

15. Then call upon me, in the day of distress;
I will deliver thee, and thou shalt glorify me.

16. But unto the wicked man saith God:
What is it to thee, to recount my statutes?

17. For thou takest my covenant in thy mouth;
yet even thou hatest my instruction,
and castest my words behind thee.

18. If thou seest a thief, thou runnest with him;
and with adulterers art thou an associate.

19. Thy mouth poureth forth words with malice;
and thy tongue frameth deceit.

20. Thou

20. Thou fitteſt with thy brother, yet ſpeakeſt againſt him;
with the ſon of thy mother, and uttereſt ſlander.

21. Theſe things haſt thou done, and I was ſilent;
thou thoughteſt me altogether like thy ſelf:
I diſprove thee, and ſet the compariſon before thy eyes.

22. Underſtand now this, ye who forget GOD;
leſt I tear in pieces, and there be none to deliver.

23. He, who ſacrificeth praiſe, glorifieth me;
and to the upright in the way, to him will I ſhew my ſalvation.

Pſalm 14.
compared with Pſalm 53.

1. The fool hath ſaid in his heart, There is no GOD!
they have corrupted, they have made abominable, their beha-
there is none, that doeth good; not even one.   [viour;

2. JEHOVAH hath looked down from heaven,
upon the children of men;
to ſee, if any one underſtandeth,
or enquireth after GOD.

3. Every one goeth aſtray, together are they corrupted;
there is none, that doeth good; not even one.

    Their throat is an open ſepulchre;
    with their tongues do they practiſe guile.
    The poiſon of aſps is under their lips;
    their mouth is full of curſing and bitterneſs.
    Swift are their feet to ſhed blood;
    deſtruction and miſery are in their ways.
    But the way of peace they have not known;
    there is no fear of GOD before their eyes.

4. Have they no knowledge, all the workers of iniquity?
my people have eaten, they have eaten, angels' food;
yet called they not on the name of JEHOVAH.

5. They were greatly afraid, when no fear was (neceſſary);
for GOD was with the generation of the righteous.

6. { The counſel of the humble man ye mock at;
   { but JEHOVAH is his refuge.

or { They abuſed the ſtrong proofs of thy favour;
   { when yet JEHOVAH was their refuge.

7. Oh

7. Oh for a grant from Sion, for the deliverance of Israel!
when JEHOVAH bringeth back the captivity of his people;
Jacob shall rejoice, and Israel shall be glad.

Psalm 55.

1. Give ear, O GOD, unto my prayer;
and hide not thy self from my supplications.

2. Attend unto me, and answer me;
I am loud in my cry, and greatly distressed.

3. On account of the leader of the hostility;
and because of the oppression of the wicked man.

4. For they transfer upon me iniquity;
and prosecute their hatred of me with fury.

5. My heart is sore pained within me;
and terrours are fallen upon me.

6. Fear and trembling are come into me;
and horrour overwhelmeth me.

7. And I said: Oh, that I had strong wings;
as a dove would I flee away, and be at rest.

8. Lo, then would I wander far off;
I would remain in the wilderness for ever.

9. I would hasten to myself an escape;
from the stormy wind, and from the tempest.

10. Destroy the chiefs, dividing their counsels;
for I have seen violence and contention.

11. In the city, both by day and by night,
they go about upon her walls.

12. Iniquity and mischief are in the midst of her;
wickedness and deceit are in the midst of her:
and guile departeth not from her streets.

13. If an enemy reproacheth me, I can bear it;
if an hater of me had magnified himself against me,
then perhaps I might have hid myself from him.

14. But it was thou! a man after my own heart!
my guide! and one well-acquainted with my steps!

15. Together have we taken sweet counsel;
and walked to the house of GOD, in concord.

16. Let death seize upon them;
let them go down alive into the grave:
for wickednesses are in the midst of them.

17. I will call upon God;
and JEHOVAH will save me.

18. Evening, morning, and noon-day will I pray,
and cry aloud: and he will hear my voice.

19. Deliver in peace my soul;
that no evil come near unto me:
for they, who stand with me, are against the many.

20. God will hear, and humble them;
even He, who dwelleth from everlasting to everlasting.

21. Because they do not return to their duty;
neither do they stand in fear of God.

22. He hath stretched out his hand against my peace;
and he hath violated his covenant.

23. Flattering, even softer than butter, was his mouth;
and yet his heart was as instruments of war.

24. Smoother than oil were his words;
yet are they now drawn swords.

25. Oh, cast upon JEHOVAH thy care;
and he will sustain thee: he will not suffer,
that the just man be tossed to and fro for ever.

26. And do thou, O JEHOVAH my God!
bring them down to the pit of corruption.

27. Men of much blood and of deceit
shall not live out half their days:
but I trust in thee, O JEHOVAH!

Psalm 67.

1. May God be merciful unto us, and bless us;
may he cause his countenance to shine upon us!

2. So that his way may be known upon earth;
even his salvation, among all nations!

3. *Let the nations praise thee, O God;
let the nations, all of them, praise thee!*

4. Let the peoples be glad, and shout for joy;
for thou shalt judge the nations with equity,
and comfort the peoples thro' the earth!

5. *Let the nations praise thee, O God;
let the nations, all of them, praise thee!*

6. The earth giveth her offspring!
may GOD, our own GOD, bless us!

7. May GOD bless us!
and may all the ends of the earth fear Him!

Psalm 68.
In 9 Parts.

Part 1.

1. Let GOD arise, let his enemies be scattered;
and let them, that hate Him, flee from his presence.

2. As smoke is driven away, shall they be driven:
as wax melteth before the fire;
let the wicked perish at the presence of GOD.

3. But let the righteous rejoice, and exult;
at the presence of GOD let them rejoice exceedingly.

Part 2.

4. Oh sing ye unto GOD, celebrate his name;
clear the way for Him, who rideth thro' the desarts:
JEHOVAH is his name, exult ye before Him.

5. He is a father of orphans, and an avenger of widows;
even GOD, in the habitation of his holiness.

6. GOD restoreth to an house those, who were destitute;
he bringeth out with abundance those, who were bound:
but the rebellious dwell in a dry land.

Part 3.

7. O GOD! when thou didst go forth before thy people;
when thou didst march thro' the wilderness:

8. The earth trembled, and the heavens poured down;
[even the thick clouds poured down waters.

The mountains melted away] from before GOD;
thus did Sinai, from before the GOD of Israel.

9. Thou

9. Thou, O God, didst send a rain of plenteous manna;
thine inheritance fainted, and thou didst confirm them.

10. Thy quails were continued in the midst of them;
thus in thy goodness didst thou prepare for the poor.

Part 4.

11. God, even Jehovah, gave the word;
and many were the women, who sung the glad tidings—

12. "*The kings of armies flee away, flee away;*
"*and she, who staid at home, divideth the spoil.*

13. "*Tho' ye have lien down among the pots;*
"*ye are as the wings of a dove, which is covered with silver;*
"*and its feathers with burnished gold.*

14. "*Since the Almighty scattered these kings;*
"*as to her, she is white as the snow upon Tzalmon.*"

Part 5.

15. The hill of God — is it the hill of Bashan?
a craggy hill is the hill of Bashan.

16. Why look ye proudly, ye craggy hills?
this (Sion) is the hill, which God desireth to inhabit;
yea, Jehovah will inhabit it for ever.

17. The chariot of God is twenty thousand,
even thousands and thousands:
the Lord is among them, it is Sinai in holiness!   [captive;

18. Thou hast ascended on high, thou hast led captivity
thou hast given gifts amongst men:
that Jehovah God might dwell even with the rebellious.

Part 6.

19. Blessed be Jehovah, day after day;
the God of our salvation beareth our burdens.

20. The God for us is the God for salvations;
and to Jehovah belong the decrees, issued for death.

21. Verily God will smite the head of his enemies;
even the shaggy pate of him, who goeth on in his trespasses.

22. The Lord hath said: "*As from Bashan will I return* (tri-
"*I will return, as from the depths of the sea:*   [umphant)

23. "*So*

23. "*So that thou shalt wash thy foot in blood;*
"*and the tongue of thy dogs shall be red thro' the same.*"

Part 7.

24. Men have seen thy goings, O GOD!
the goings of my GOD, my king, in holiness!

25. Before go the singers, behind go the minstrels;
in the midst are the damsels, with the timbrels, singing —

26. "*In the assemblies bless ye God!*
"*even Jehovah! ye descendants of Israel!*"

27. There is Benjamin, the youngest (lately) their ruler;
the princes of Judah (now) their council:
the princes of Zebulon, and the princes of Naphtali.

Part 8.

28. Thy GOD hath commanded this thy strength;
strengthen still, O GOD, what thou hast wrought for us.

29. For the sake of thy temple at Jerusalem,
to thee shall kings bring an oblation.

30. Rebuke the beast of the reed (Egypt)
the assembly of the bulls, with the calves of the nations;
who dance to their silver instruments of music:
scatter these nations, which delight in wars.

31. Let the princes come up out of Egypt;
let Ethiopia hasten to spread out her hands to GOD.

Part 9.

32. O ye kingdoms of the earth, sing unto GOD;
O celebrate JEHOVAH for ever!

33. Him, who rideth on the everlasting heavens!
lo, he sendeth forth by his voice the voice of strength!

34. Ascribe ye strength to GOD over Israel;
his worship and strength are in the clouds.

35. Wonderful art thou, O GOD, out of thy sanctuary;
even the GOD of Israel!
he giveth strength and powers unto the people!
blessed be GOD!

Psalm 69.

1. Save me, O GOD!
for the waters are come in, even unto my life.

2. I sink in deep mire, where there is no standing;
I am come into deep waters, where the flood overflows me.

3. I am weary with my crying, my throat is dry;
mine eyes fail with waiting for my GOD.

4. More than the locks of my head are they, who hate me without a cause;
beyond my hairs are they, who are mine enemies wrongfully:
at the time that I am restoring what I have not taken away.

5. O GOD, thou knowest my plan of recovery;
and my offering-for-sin is not hidden from thee.

6. Let not those be ashamed at me, who wait for thee, O Lord of hosts! [Israel!
let not those be confounded at me, who seek thee, O God of

7. Because for thy sake have I suffered reproach;
for thy sake hath shame covered my face.

8. For thy sake I became a stranger unto my brethren;
and an alien unto the children of my mother.

9. For the zeal of thine house hath eaten me up;
and the reproaches of them, that reproached thee, fell on me.

10. When I humbled my soul by fasting;
even that was turned to my great reproach.

11. When I made my garment of sackcloth;
then became I to them for a by-word.

12. They said of me, that I sat at the gate;
and their songs were, that I drank strong drink. [ance;

13. But I pray to thee, O JEHOVAH! in a time of accept-
O GOD! in thy manifold kindness answer me, in the truth of thy salvation.

14. Deliver me out of the mire, and let me not sink;
let me be delivered from those who hate me, and out of the deep waters.

15. Let not the flood of waters overflow me;
neither let the deep swallow me up:
and let not the pit shut its mouth upon me.

16. Answer

16. Anſwer me, O Jehovah, according to the goodneſs of thy loving kindneſs;
according to the multitude of thy compaſſions, look upon me.

17. And hide not thy countenance from thy ſervant;
for I am in ſtraits, haſten, anſwer me.

18. Draw nigh unto my ſoul, and deliver it;
for the ſake of mine enemies, Oh ſave me.

19. Thou knoweſt my reproach, and my ſhame;
and my diſhonour is in the ſight of all mine adverſaries.

20. Oh heal the breaking of my heart, for I am in miſery;
for I looked for ſome one to have pity, but there was none:
and for comforters, but I found them not.

21. They alſo gave me, for my meat, gall;
and, for my thirſt, they have made me to drink vinegar.

22. Their proviſion, thus before them, will be for a ſnare;
and, by way of recompence to them, will be for a ſtumbling-block.

23. Their eyes will be darkened, ſo that they will not ſee;
and their backs wilt thou bow down continually.

24. Thou wilt pour out upon them thine indignation;
and thy wrathful diſpleaſure will take hold of them.

25. Their habitation will be deſolate;
and in their tents will be no inhabitant.

26. For him, whom thou haſt ſmitten, have they perſecuted;
and they have added to the grief of him, whom thou haſt wounded.

27. Behold the puniſhment, which will be on their iniquity;
for they will not come into thy righteouſneſs.

28. They will be blotted out of the book of life;
and with righteous men they will not be enrolled.

29. Tho' I am brought low by affliction, and am grieved;
thy ſalvation, O God, ſhall ſet me up on high.

30. I will praiſe the name of God with a ſong;
and I will magnify it with thankſgiving.

31. For I ſhall be pleaſing to Jehovah, beyond an ox;
more than any bullock, that hath horns and hoofs.

32. Conſider

32. Confider this, ye humble, and rejoice;
feek ye after GOD, and your heart fhall live.

33. For JEHOVAH hearkeneth to the poor;
and thofe, who are bound to him, he doth not defpife.

34. Heaven and earth fhall praife him;
the feas, and every thing that moveth therein.

35. For GOD will give falvation in Sion;
and he will build up the cities of Judah:
and they fhall return thither, and inherit it.

26. For the feed of his fervants fhall poffefs it;
and they, who love his name, fhall dwell therein.

Pfalm 80.

1. O fhepherd of Ifrael, give ear;
and lead the houfe of Jofeph, as a flock.

2. Thou, who inhabiteft the cherubim, fhine forth;
on the children of Ephraim and of Manaffeh.

3. Oh, raife up thy mighty power;
and come, for falvation, to us.

4. { *O God of hofts, make us to turn;*
{ *manifeft thy countenance, and we fhall be faved.*

5. O Jehovah, GOD of hofts!
how long wilt thou be angry with the prayer of thy people?

6. Thou haft made us to eat the bread of tears;
and haft made us to drink, with tears in abundance.

7. Thou makeft us a ftrife to our neighbours;
and our enemies laugh us to fcorn.

8. { *O God of hofts, make us to turn;*
{ *manifeft thy countenance, and we fhall be faved.*

9. A vine haft thou brought out of Egypt;
thou didft caft out the nations, and haft planted it.

10. Thou didft prepare the ground for it, and it took root;
and, when it had taken root, it filled the land.

11. The fhadow of it covered the hills;
and the boughs of it the goodly cedars.

12. It fhot forth its branches unto the fea;
and unto the river, the young fhoots thereof.

13. Why

13. Why haſt thou broken down its fences?.
ſo that all, who paſs on the way, pluck its fruit!

14. The boar, out of the wood, layeth it waſte;
and the wild beaſt of the field devoureth it.

15. O God of hoſts! turn, we beſeech thee;
look down from heaven, and behold;
and do thou viſit this whole vine.

16. O protect that, which thy right hand hath planted;
even on account of the ſon of man, whom thou makeſt ſtrong
    for thyſelf.

17. Conſume with fire thoſe, who are deſtroying it;
at the rebuke of thy countenance, let them periſh.

18. Let thy hand be over the man of thy right hand;
over the ſon of man, whom thou makeſt ſtrong for thyſelf.

19. Then ſhall we not draw back from thee, Oh quicken us!
and on thy name will we call, O JEHOVAH!

20. { O God of hoſts! make us to turn;
    manifeſt thy countenance, and we ſhall be ſaved.

Pſalm 85.

Alternately ſung by *the High-Prieſt* and *People*.

High Prieſt.

1. Thou haſt been gracious, O JEHOVAH, to thy land;
thou haſt turned the captivity of Jacob.

2. Thou haſt taken away the iniquity of thy people;
thou haſt covered all their ſin.

3. Thou haſt removed all thine anger;
thou haſt turned from thy wrathful indignation.

People.

4. TURN US, O GOD of our ſalvation!
and withdraw thy reſentment from us.

5. For ever wilt thou be diſpleaſed at us?
wilt thou protract thy wrath from generation to generation?

6. Wilt thou not once more quicken us?
ſo that thy people ſhall rejoice in thee.

7. Shew to us, O Jehovah, thy mercy;
and thy salvation grant unto us.

High Priest.

8. I will hear what the Almighty sayeth——
Jehovah by me sayeth "*Peace
" unto his people, even unto his saints:
" but let them not return to folly.*"

People.

9. Truly nigh to those, who fear him, is his salvation;
that glory may dwell in our land.

10. Mercy and truth are met together;
righteousness and peace have kissed each other.

11. Truth flourisheth out of the earth;
and righteousness looketh down from heaven.

12. Yea, Jehovah granteth *the blessing*;
and our land granteth *her offspring.*

13. Righteousness goeth before *Him,*
and directeth his goings in the way.

Psalm 87.

1. His foundation is upon the holy hills!
Jehovah loveth the gates of Sion,
above all the dwellings of Jacob.

2. Glorious things doth He speak of thee;
thou, city of God, for ever: (saying)

3. " *I will make Egypt and Babylon to remember;
" among those who know me, behold Philistia and Tyre;
" the people also of Cush, these shall be born there.*"

4. Even of Sion, as the mother, it shall be said;
such and such men shall be born in her:
for He establisheth her, even The most High.

5. In the register of the nations, it shall be written;
this, and that, shall be born there, for ever.

6. Thus *shall the princes be as the sand of the sea:
and all the fresh springs of my favour shall be in Thee.*

Psalm 107.

1. O give thanks to JEHOVAH, for he is good;
for his mercy is for ever.

2. Let the redeemed of JEHOVAH say so;
they, whom he hath redeemed from the hand of the enemy.

3. And he hath gathered them out of all lands;
from the east, and from the west,
from the north, and from the south.

4. They had wandered in the wilderness, in the desart;
they found not the way to a city of habitation.

5. Hungry were they, and thirsty;
their soul within them fainted.

6. *Then cried they to* JEHOVAH *in their distress;*
and out of their straits he hath delivered them.

7. And he hath led them forth, in the right way;
that they might go to a city of habitation.

8. OH, THAT [MEN] WOULD PRAISE JEHOVAH, FOR HIS MERCY;
AND HIS WONDERFUL DOINGS FOR THE SONS OF ADAM!

9. Verily he hath satisfied the doubtful soul;
and the hungry soul he hath filled with good:

10. Them, who sat in darkness and the shadow of death;
fast bound in misery and iron.

11. For they had rebelled against the words of GOD;
and the counsel of the most High they had despised.

12. But their heart was humbled thro' trouble;
they fell, and there was no helper.

13. *Then cried they to* JEHOVAH, *in their distress;*
and out of their straits he hath delivered them. [of death;

14. He hath brought them out of darkness and the shadow
and hath broken their bonds asunder.

15. OH, THAT [MEN] WOULD PRAISE JEHOVAH, FOR HIS MERCY;
AND HIS WONDERFUL DOINGS FOR THE SONS OF ADAM!

16. Verily he hath broken the gates of brass;
and hath cut asunder the bars of iron.

17. He hath brought them back, from the way of their transgression;
and for their iniquities have they been humbled.

18. All refreshment did their soul abhor;
and they drew near unto the gates of death.

19. *Then cried they to* JEHOVAH, *in their distress;*
and out of their straits he hath delivered them.

20. He hath sent his word, and healed them;
and hath delivered them from their pits of corruption.

21. OH, THAT [MEN] WOULD PRAISE JEHOVAH, FOR HIS MERCY;
AND HIS WONDERFUL DOINGS FOR THE SONS OF ADAM!

22. Oh, that [men] would sacrifice sacrifices of thanksgiving;
and declare his works, with loud rejoicing!

23. They, who go down to the sea in ships,
performing work on the mighty waters;

24. These men see the works of JEHOVAH,
and his wonders in the deep.

25. For he speaketh, and raiseth the stormy wind;
and it lifteth up the waves of the sea.

26. They go up to the heavens, they go down to the deeps;
their soul melteth away, at the trouble.

27. They reel to and fro, and stagger as a drunkard;
and all their wisdom is swallowed up.

28. *Then cry they to* JEHOVAH, *in their distress;*
and out of their straits he delivereth them.

29. He maketh the storm to stand silent;
and the waves of the sea are still.

30. Then are they glad, because they are quiet;
and he bringeth them to the haven of their desire.

31. OH, THAT [MEN] WOULD PRAISE JEHOVAH, FOR HIS MERCY;
AND HIS WONDERFUL DOINGS FOR THE SONS OF ADAM!

32. Oh, that [men] would exalt him, in the assembly of the people;
and celebrate him, in the seat of the elders!

33. He turneth rivers into a wilderness;
and springs of water into dry ground:

34. Also

34. Also a fruitful land to barrenness;
for the wickedness of them, who dwell therein.

35. He turneth a wilderness into a pool of water;
and dry land into springs of water.

36. And there maketh he the hungry to dwell;
and they prepare a city of habitation.

37. And they sow fields, and plant vineyards;
and they make a fruitful increase.

38. And he blesseth them, and they multiply exceedingly;
and even their cattle he doth not diminish. [low,

39. But when they sin; they are diminished and brought
thro' oppression, affliction, and sorrow.

40. He poureth out contempt upon princes;
and maketh them to wander in a pathless waste.

41. Yet lifteth he up the poor man out of misery;
and maketh (him) families as a flock.

42. *Oh, that the upright would consider this, and rejoice!*
then all iniquity would stop its mouth.

43. *Who is wise, and marketh well these things?*
Even he shall understand the mercies of JEHOVAH.

Psalm 110.

1. JEHOVAH said unto my Lord;
" *Sit thou on my right hand, 'till I make*
" *thy foes the footstool for thy feet.*"

2. The rod of thy power shall JEHOVAH send
from Sion, " *Rule amidst thine enemies.*"

3. With thee shall be royalty, in the day of thy power;
in majesty and holiness from the womb:
before the morning-star, I have begotten thee.

4. JEHOVAH hath sworn, and will not repent;
" *Thou art a priest for ever,*
" *after the order of Melchisedek.*"

5. The Lord is on thy right-hand (O GOD)
he smiteth kings in the day of his wrath.

6. He shall judge among the nations, filling the vallies;
he smiteth the head over many a country.

7. Of the brook in the way will he drink;
therefore shall his head be exalted.

Psalm 114.

1. When Israel came out of Egypt;
and the house of Jacob from a strange people:

2. Judah was his sanctuary;
and Israel was his dominion.

3. The sea saw, and it fled;
Jordan was driven backward:

4. The mountains skipped, like rams;
and the little hills, like young sheep.

5. What ailed thee, O sea, that thou fleddest?
O Jordan, that thou wast driven back?

6. Ye mountains, that ye skipped, like rams?
and ye little hills, like young sheep?

7. Tremble thou, earth! at the presence of THE LORD;
at the presence of THE GOD OF JACOB!

8. Who turned the rock into a standing water!
and the flint-stone into a springing-well!

Psalms 117 and 118 consider'd as One.

Part I. PSALMIST.

1. O praise JEHOVAH, all ye nations;
celebrate him, all ye peoples.

2. For great towards us is his mercy;
and the truth of JEHOVAH is for ever.

1. Give thanks unto JEHOVAH, for he is good;
for his mercy is for ever.

2. Let Israel say now, '
that his mercy is for ever.

3. Let

3. Let the houſe of Aaron ſay now,
that his mercy is for ever.

4. Let all, who fear JEHOVAH, ſay now,
that his mercy is for ever.

Part 2. MESSIAH.

5. Out of deep diſtreſs I called on JEHOVAH;
JEHOVAH hath anſwered, by granting me liberty.

6. JEHOVAH is for me, I will not fear;
what can man do unto me?

7. JEHOVAH is for me, to aſſiſt me;
and I ſee (my triumph) over thoſe, who hate me.

8. Better it is to truſt in JEHOVAH,
than to put confidence in man.

9. Better it is to truſt in JEHOVAH,
than to put confidence in princes.

10. All nations compaſs me about;
but in JEHOVAH's name ſhall I diſappoint them.

11. They compaſs me, yea they compaſs me about;
but in JEHOVAH's name ſhall I diſappoint them.

12. They compaſs me about, as bees;
but they will be extinguiſhed, as the fire of thorns:
for in JEHOVAH's name ſhall I diſappoint them.

13. They have thruſt ſore at me, that I might fall;
but JEHOVAH hath helped me.

14. JEHOVAH is my ſtrength and my ſong;
and he hath been to me for ſalvation.

15. The voice of joy and ſalvation is in the tents of juſt men;
the right hand of JEHOVAH hath done a mighty act!

16. The right hand of JEHOVAH is exalted;
the right hand of JEHOVAH hath done a mighty act!

17. I ſhall not die, but I ſhall live;
and declare the works of JEHOVAH.

18. JEHOVAH hath heavily chaſtiſed me;
but he hath not given me up to death.

19. Open to me the gates of righteouſneſs;
I will go in thro' them, I will celebrate JEHOVAH.

20. This is the gate (leading) to JEHOVAH;
just men shall go in thereby.

21. I will celebrate thee, for thou hast heard me;
and thou hast been to me for salvation.

Part 3. CHORUS.

22. The stone, which the builders rejected,
is become the head of the corner.

23. This is JEHOVAH's doing;
and it is marvellous in our eyes!

24. This is the day, which JEHOVAH hath made;
we will rejoice, and be glad, therein.

25. Save now, we beseech thee, O JEHOVAH;
we beseech thee, JEHOVAH, give now prosperity.

26. Blessed be He, who cometh in JEHOVAH's name;
we bless you, who are of JEHOVAH's family.

27. JEHOVAH is GOD, and he hath given us light;
they have bound the sacrifice with cords,
even unto the horns of the altar.

Part 4. PSALMIST.

28. Thou art my GOD, and I will celebrate thee;
thou art my GOD, and I will exalt thee.

29. O give thanks to JEHOVAH, for he is good;
for his mercy is for ever!

Psalm 120.

1. Unto JEHOVAH, when I was in trouble,
I called; and JEHOVAH heard me.

2. Deliver, O JEHOVAH, my soul;
from the lying lip, from the deceitful tongue.

3. What shall be given to thee, O lying lip?
and what done unto thee, O deceitful tongue?

4. Even the arrows of the Almighty, which are sharp;
with coals of fire not to be extinguished.

5. Woe is me, that I sojourn without rest;
that I dwell in my tents, mourning!

6. Long

6. Long hath my foul had its habitation, among thofe, who hated peace.

7. I was for peace; but when I mentioned it, they without caufe were for war.

Pfalm 129.

1. Greatly have they afflicted me, from my youth; may Ifrael now fay:

2. Greatly have they afflicted me, from my youth; yet they have not prevailed againft me.

3. Upon my back have the plowers ploughed; and they have made long their furrows.

4. JEHOVAH, He is juft; He hath cut afunder the cords of the wicked.

5. They fhall be confounded, and turned backward; even all thofe, who are haters of Sion.

6. They fhall be as the grafs, on the houfe tops; which, before it is full grown, withereth.

7. Wherewith the mower filleth not his hand; nor the binder filleth his grafp.

8. Nor fhall they, who pafs by, fay ——
"The bleffing of JEHOVAH be upon you!"
"We blefs you, in the name of JEHOVAH!"

Pfalm 132.

1. Remember, O JEHOVAH, to David all his piety;

2. How he fware unto JEHOVAH, how he vowed to the Mighty One of Jacob:

3. "*I will not go into the tabernacle of my houfe;*
"*nor go up upon the couch of my bed;*

4. "*I will not give fleep to mine eyes,*
"*nor to mine eye-lids flumber:*

5. "*Until I find a place for* JEHOVAH,
"*an habitation for the Mighty One of Jacob.*

6. "*Lo, we heard of the ark at Ephratbab;* (Shilo)
"*we found it in the fields of Jear;* (Kiriath jearim)

7. "We

7. " *We will go to his habitation;*
" *we will worship at his footstool.*"

8. Arise, JEHOVAH, into thy resting-place;
thou, and the ark of thy strength.

9. Let thy priests be clothed with righteousness;
and let thy saints shout for joy.

10. For the sake of David thy servant,
turn not away the face of thine anointed.

11. JEHOVAH hath sworn unto David;
truly he shall not turn from it:
" *Of the fruit of thy body will I place on thy throne.*"

12. " *If thy children will keep my covenant;*
" *and my testimonies, which I shall teach them:*
" *their children also, for evermore,*
" *shall sit upon thy throne.*"

13. Verily JEHOVAH hath chosen Sion;
he hath desired it for an habitation for Himself: (saying)

14. "*This is my resting-place for ever;*
" *here will I dwell, for I have desired it.*

15. " *Her victuals abundantly will I bless;*
" *her poor will I satisfy with bread.*

16. " *And her priests will I clothe with health;*
" *and her saints shall shout aloud for joy.*

17. " *There will I make to flourish a horn to David;*
" *I have ordained a lamp for mine anointed.*

18. " *His enemies will I clothe with shame;*
" *but upon Himself shall his crown flourish.*"

The

THE reader will obferve, that the Pfalms, of which the tranflations are now given to the world, are not exactly the fame with thofe mentioned in p. 173 of this volume.—But of the 48th and 89th no tranflations were to be found among Dr. *Kennicott*'s papers. And on the other hand, the Editors have thought it right to publifh the tranflations of Pf. 14 compared with Pf. 53, and Pf. 107, which appeared to have been fairly copied out by Dr. *Kennicott* for the prefs.

NOTES

NOTES

ON THE

PSALMS.

Notes on the Psalms.

I.

THE Preface, a Summary of the doctrine of the Psalms—Happiness the portion of the worshippers of Jehovah, misery that of the wicked. See Jerem. 17, 7, 8.

1. *Counsel* of the wicked or righteous—the system adopted—or the delusions of the wicked, עצת from the Arabic עצה *figmenta et mendacia protulit*——Hof. 10, 6. Israel shall be ashamed of its own *delusions*: i. e. idols — golden calves — &c. idolatry.

עמד refers to the same; expresses the worshippers of the true God, Ps. 134, 1; 135, 2; here worshippers of Idols. عمد *data opera fecit*. דרך *mos, consuetudo*. מושב *confessus, cœtus*— MSS. ובמושב.

2. הגה Ps. 63, 6, *musing*; meditate, when before ב, Josh. 1, 8. Ps. 77, 11; 143, 5; except Ps. 115, 7, where the particle is used differently.

3. ו *eodem plane modo*: Job 14, 19.

4. Job 21, 18.

5. קום. gain the victory. Ps. 89, 44, not given him the victory in battle: here, the wicked shall not carry their cause.

6. ידע from ودع *permansit, constitit* (Job 9, 5.)

II.

On Solomon's Inauguration. The making Adonijah king was contrary to GOD's appointment, 2 Sam. 12, 24, 25: 1 Chron. 22, 9, 10: 1 Chron. 28, 4—6. A Rebellion therefore against David and GOD. David therefore commands Solomon to be anointed, &c, to be brought to mount Sion, and seated in his throne. Probably 7—9 is the oracle in answer to the consultation: see 1 Kings 2, 24. The shout reaching the Rebels, they *trembled for fear*, יחרדו—This the primary sense. The secondary and higher relates to Christ.

1. גוים and לאמים frequently the people of Israel. Ps. 67. Gen. 25, 16, 23. the latter word denotes several nations or tribes from one common ancestor. Princes and people were in the conspiracy, 1 Kings 2, 15.

3. The fubſtance of their confpiracy. The fame temper in the people at Solomon's death.

5. אז *the very inſtant.* (Mudge.)

6. נסך *in folio collocavit.* I read with LXX at the end קדשו.

7. LXX probably read truly אספרה את חק יהוה אמר אלי Δίαγγελῶν τὸ πρόσταγμα Κυρίε, &c. Spoken in the perfon of Zadok or Nathan, as the anfwer of the Oracle on their enquiry.

8. גוים as in 1. אפסי ארץ land of Canaan, generally the weſt ſide, Pf. 72, 8; which Pfalm on the like occafion with this. Alfo Zech. 9, 10.

9. רוע *contrivit, comminuit, contudit*—pound them to powder with *a peſtle of iron,* שבט.

12. דרך *illico,* Nold. 1052. במעט *ever fo little.*

III.

Titles frequently wrong—here perhaps right. The laſt words are a pious wiſh for GOD's bleſſing on Ifrael — very frequent, Pf. 20, 25. &c.

2. His enemies thought he could not efcape, and made fure of his life, 2 Sam. 17, 2. נפשי *my perfon, me.* אין *vix,* 1 Sam. 21, 5. Exod. 12, 30. Selah, a bold fymphony.

5. הקיצותי — קוץ *tædio affectus eſt.* David made a forced march to pafs Jordan, (2 Sam. 17, 16—22) and his men were hungry, thirſty, and weary. See ver. 29.

IV.

בינצה *præpoſitus cantorum.* נגינות ſtring-inſtruments played on with the plectrum. On David's deliverance by fome extraordinary interpofition of Providence from a confpiracy, occaſioned by his zeal for Jehovah's worſhip.

1. Verbs all preter, the action paſt.

2. איש *a man of rank,* (Pf. 49, 2) above the level of אדם *mankind.* Vanity and lies, *i. e.* worſhip of Idols.

3. The mark of diſtinction is that GOD heareth him.

4. —They might mutter, but for their own fakes avoid outward ſignification of it, no, not in their moſt fecret retirements. Ecclef. 10, 20. אמר בלב fee Pf. 14, 1. See on Job 4, 6.

5. To the prieſt, to offer the facrifice.

6. The prayer accompanying the sacrifice. רבים the *many*, the word in general, in antithesis to *us* afterwards. See Mudge. נס *signum*.

7. The signal acceptance having been manifested, the 2 last verses contain the grateful acknowledgments of the Psalmist, and his resolution to depend only on JEHOVAH's goodness for future protection.

8. Houbigant reads rightly לבדך.

V.

David's thanksgiving for his deliverance from the conspiracy of Absalom; the man of blood, and the deceitful man, Achitophel, his counsellor, (Pf. 41, 9) who advised to shed his blood; 2 Sam. 17, 1, 2. הנחילות wind-instruments like the humming of bees.

3. ערך and אצפה sacrificial terms — first, setting the wood in order — second, the sacrifice properly on the wood, from צפף (ה affix) صفّ *ordine disposuit supra prunas*, &c, laying the victim on the altar, consuming it by fire, and the concomitant Prayer.

4. גור GOD's purity so great, that no evil shall *sojourn*, make the shortest abode, with him.

7. I would read כרב הסדך *such is the abundance of thy goodness*: see 2 Sam. 15, 25. The Tabernacle called היכל the *Temple*; 1 Sam. 1, 9.

8. Arabic sense שרר *cum aliquo rixavit, crimine arguit*.

9. I read (with the antient versions) בפיהם *in ore eorum*.

12. צון (Æthiop.) thence the noun, *arx, locus munitus*.

VI.

Composed for one grievously afflicted in body and mind, his enemies ascribing his afflictions to the judgment of GOD, for some heinous crime, and treating his dependance on GOD as vain; JEHOVAH restores his health, his enemies are confounded, and he rejoices in this Psalm. על השמנית to be accompanied with all manner of stringed instruments, as high as the 8 stringed harp.

2. עצם the whole structure, or frame; and as an aggregate for all the members, with a verb plural.

4. שיבה

4. שובה and חלצה run into one another by a common Hebraism: the former *once more*, see ver. 10. (Mudge.)

7. עתקה *bebescit*. Notwithstanding Mudge and myself (Job 21, 7) it here signifies *decay*. כל *plurimus*, Nold. Pf. 9, 2, &c.

VII.

Shiggaion from شَغَا, *anxius fuit*. Cush probably (the same as Shimei, 2 Sam. 16, 5—8) called him a man of blood; as if he had destroyed Saul's family, to reign in his stead: and now he had been requited by Absalom.

1. רֹדְפִי *ab omni persequente me.*
2. פרק *liberavit.*

4. If my professions of duty to Saul were not sincere, but I had evil designs against him: if provoked with much ill treatment, I have ever returned it: if, when I could have deprived him of his crown and life at once, I had the least thought of injuring him, though he was without cause my enemy. 1 Sam. 24 and 26. חלץ *liberum emisit*, as Job 36, 15. I read משלמי with Hare. Houbigant well reads ישפך *projiciat*, for ישכן.

6. בערפות perhaps the true reading, as Arab. *super colla.*

7. שובה see Num. 10, 36. The cloud resting, and Israel encamping, Moses sung, GIVE REST, O JEHOVAH, *to the myriads of thousands of Israel.*

8. עלי *intra me*; Job 30, 16; Hof. 11, 8. Ellipsis of אשר.

9. גמר Chal. and Syr. *consumsit*: so, Pf. 12, 2; 77, 9.

11. אל *nequaquam*: all the versions but Chald.

12. Hare well reads ישובו (Job 6, 29) GOD gives men time to recollect themselves, and repent of their evil ways.

13. Arabic right. I read הדלקים *urentes, inflammatos*. The Arrows of the Almighty, Deut. 32, 24; languishments of famine, the burnings of the carbuncle, and the bitter pestilence. Schultens, Prov. 26, 23. Lightenings are also called GOD's arrows, Pf. 18, 15, represented as the artillery of Heaven.

14. Absalom, displeased that he, David's eldest son living (Chileab or Daniel being probably dead) should be past over, and Solomon be the successor, resolves to defeat it by dethroning David. GOD blasts the hopeful project; and instead of destroying the father, the son perishes. The futures are here in the

present tense — הִנֵּה *behold!* the transaction is before the eye. I think with Hare ירד is crept in from the margin.

VIII.

The LXX read עַל הַגִּתּוֹת *pro torcularibus*, to be sung at the time of *vintage*. This Psalm is prophetical of Christ. Heb. 2, 7; Matt. 21, 16.

1. I read נתנה — The Imperative cannot signify the preter indicative. For in Pf. 56, 9 שׁוּבוּ אתה is the same as שִׂמְחָה and is preter Hiphil. The preter hath often the sense of the future, and the future and imperative are naturally analogous; but not *vice versa*; because the imperative is inconsistent with a preter sense. אֲשֶׁר *quamvis* Ecclef. 8, 12.

2. I read עֻזְּךָ with the Syriac, and take the Arabic sense of (עֹז) the noun, *gloria, dignitas*. I point לְמַעַן as the infinitive Kal of מוֹעֵן (in Arabic) *aliquem vilem ostendere*.

3. שָׁמֶיךָ corrupt — unquestionably שֶׁמֶשׁ *Sun* — the work of the fingers.

4. פקד used to express divine Providence, Job 10, 12.

7. One Fr. MS. reads צונה.

8. I read with Hare עֹבְרֵי אָרְחוֹת מִים.

IX.

Chaldee Paraphrast perhaps read מִיתְלַבֵּן from לבן (Arabic) *percussit saxo*. Hithpahel often passive. The Psalm a thanksgiving for some remarkable deliverance from the Nations, where the arm of GOD was manifest.

1. LXX read well אורך.

3. כשל not only *impegit*, but *corruit*, see Isai. 31, 3. Hof. 14, 2.

4. כי extends to the verb in the latter clause. עָשָׂה מִשְׁפָּט (or דִין) carrying sentences into execution.

5. רשע generally implies *idolatry*, denying JEHOVAH to be the sole object of worship: otherwise it denotes the last degree of profligacy: here some one person, perhaps Goliah. Houbigant is right in reading בהם *cum ipsis* — good sense now — ו *quantum ad*. As to the cities, *them* thou hast razed.

11. עלילה not only *actio*, but *studium, molimen*.

12. Two MSS. אתם.

13. I read

13. I read ורוממו in the last clause, and think with Hare, that הצילני is dropt.

16. Higgaion, Selah; Notes to the Musicians, one for soft, the other bold. See Mudge on Ps. 3, 2.

17. שוב *quievit*. I read with Hare לישאול.

19. עז (Arab.) *ne gloriam sibi vindicet homo.*

20. מורה *doctrina*, from ירה *docuit*.

X.

6. אשר (from שרר) *aspiciam*.

8. Houbigant right, חרצים *foveis*, large caves holding hundreds of men. 1 Sam. 22, 2; 24, 3. I read with Hare יצפון, and the meaning from the Arabic *selegit*.

9. יחטף עני necessary to mark the actual seizure of the poor man. I read ודכהו *omnino conteret eum*, from דכה *contrivit*.

10. ישחו and נפלו read plurally. Hare.

14. One MS. ראיתה another ראירת. Houbigant right, לתתם, and I render ל *donec*, Isai. 7, 15. Dan. 9, 34. Levit. 24, 12.

15. I read רשע ובל.

17. I take ו from ארץ and join it to תאות, and render it *quandoquidem*, extending its influence to the 3 verbs in ver. 17.

XI.

Under the persecution of David by Saul.

1. I read with Houbigant כמו צפור as the ancient versions. — איך *cur*, Prov. 5, 12. 2 Sam. 1, 14.

3. השתות *fundamenta*. Had David been guilty of any crime, he ought to have had a fair trial by the laws; but Saul tried to assassinate him, contrary to justice, and to the fundamental laws of all nations. I read with Hare יפעל.

The 2d and 3d verses are the answer of his friends, and David replies in the remaining 4 verses.

5. I read יבחר with the Syriac.

6. Schultens on Prov. 26, 21 פחם *congeries carbonum*; not a plural.

7. I read ישרי — Chald. and Arab.

XII.

2. I think, with Hare, this verse (the *last* in the present Heb.) should stand here, and the 7th in the Heb. ends the Psalm. I point כרם *sicut bubalus*, with heads aloft, without shame, exalting the horn. ולות (from the Arabic) *stupor ob mœrorem vel curam*.

3. Houbigant right, שפתי agreeably to the next verse.

6. I read אשית בישע עני *ponam afflictum in salute*.

7. Houbigant very right, וחרוץ *et aurum*.

XIII.

2. I read with Hare עצבות. Syr. and Arab. ולילה seems lost in the middle clause. LXX Alexand.

3. פן *ne.* Ex. 34, 15. Is. 36, 18. Ellipsis of שנה *somnum* in the latter clause. The phrase שנת שנה Jer. 51; 39, 57.

4. פן influences the 2d clause.

5. ו before אני *quia*, as Isai. 39, 1.

XIV.

During the captivity (last verse) on the murder of Gedaliah; when, notwithstanding all the assurances of GOD by Jeremiah, that the remaining Jews might safely stay in Judea, they fled into Egypt and carried Jeremiah. Jer. 41, 42, 43.

4. כל adverb *omnino.* I read אבלו עמי *my people eat* — the Jews GOD's people, though little disposed to obey him.

5. This Psalm and 53 nearly the same, except here. בדור the same as פזר chaldaized from בזר *dissipavit*, which (Chald. dialect) is בדר, and used Chald. in Ps. 53.

Perhaps it should be read,

שם פחדו פחד לא היה פחד
כי אלהים פזר עצמות חנף
הביש עצת עני
כי יהוה מחסהו

There were they afraid in good earnest, there was no fear but God would scatter the bones of the reprobate wretch, that ridiculed the counsel of the meek, because JEHOVAH *was his refuge.*

All the ancient Versions read לא היה פחד.

7. I read

THE OLD TESTAMENT.

7. I read יָשֻׁר אֵל Arab. ושר אשר et coruscavit fulmen et lucidum reddidit: see note on Job 37, 3.

XV.

3. As נשא פנים is *accepting the person*, so נשא חרפה is *accepting* or *encouraging the slander*.

4. I read נשבע לרעתו לא ימר *juratus in malum suum non mutat fidem*.

XVI.

2. Read כל all — טובה *prosperity*, so Job 9, 25.

3. He held all the divinities, *i.e.* Gods of the nations, in the utmost contempt. קדושים expresses the tutelar divinities of the nations, Job 5, 1. 1 Kings 15, 12; 22, 47. 2 K. 23, 7. To prevent the misapplication, the Psalmist adds here *those that are on the earth*, because the word sometimes is applied to the *angels* of GOD. אדירי probably an epithet given by the nations to their Gods, as אבירי and כבירי (Καβειροι), and signifies mighty, illustrious. ל often *quantum ad*, 1 Sam. 9, 20. Prov. 25, 2. חפץ (Arab.) *contempsit*, noun *contemptus*.

4. I read מחר—מחרו Arab. *domum meretricis frequentabat*—whoring after strange Gods.

9. Literally my glory exulteth. 1 MS. כבדי.

10. כי influences the verbs in this and the next verse.

11. I read with the Syriac אשבע.

XVII.

6. אני is *ego ipse*.

7. הפלא certainly the true reading. 1 MS. I read חסים בך with Hare, and all the versions.

9. Metaphor—Huntsmen spying Game, go round to see how most advantageously to pitch their nets to take it.

10. I read with Mudge חבלמו. I join עלי from ver. 9 to the beginning of this verse.

11. I read with Mudge אשרנו *nobis feliciter incessit*. Some MSS. אשרינו *O felices nos.* עתה *tandem*, 1 Sam. 27, 1. 1 Kings 12, 26. They drove the beast into the toils, and then shot him.

12. 2 MSS. יכסף.

14. חלד

14. חלד (Arab) *blood.* הוים *small towns and villages.* הוות term. masc. and fem. as others. The punishment next to death was banishment to their estates.

15. תמונה *δόξα* — alluding to the glorious appearance of GOD in the most holy place of the Temple. Ps. 4, 6.

XVIII.

2. צור *rupes,* also *arx* — Tyre צור και' εξοχην.
3. I and Hare read מהלל יה'.
4. משברי agrees better with נחלי than חבלי.
12. I read חשרת.
13. I point עֻבְּרוּ *gravidæ factæ sunt.* Job 21, 10.
14. The other copy omits the last clause here, but it is absolutely necessary to the sense: otherwise the hail and fire, with which the clouds were loaded, *doth* not appear to be discharged. Verb ברד equal to ברד ימטר Exod. 9, 23.
15. Chald. הםם *everrit.*
16. ים *sea.*
26. גבור See Job 15, 25; 36, 10.
27. ברד Arab. بَرَّ *pium morigerumque se gessit, et benefecit alicui.* תתפתל *luctaberis, donec viceris.*
29. כי *quidem, equidem* (ὅτι) Mudge.
35. נתתה (I' and Mudge) ιδη.
37. צעדי from صعد *per clivosum ivit locum.*
46. יבלו from בלל *perturbatus fuit* — יחרגו خرج *in angustiam redegit.*
49. The Man of violence is certainly *Saul.*
50. גוים *tribes of Israel,* as Ps. 2. David sung this in Jerusalem before all the tribes of Israel, probably at some great feast — not in a foreign land.
51. The former verse ends the Psalm — this an acclamation of the people, at the close. I suppose an ellipsis of יהו before the 2 participles.

XIX.

3. Ellipsis of ב, as Arab. version.
4. I make no doubt, the noun קוה signified *sonitus,* as قوة (Arab.) *clamavit.* Hence the utility of the Dialects, &c.
7. Mudge right — *restorative of life* — but *testimonies* right.

8. LXX

8. LXX read right בהרה τηλαυγης — *purity* is in the next verse.

11. Hare right — גם begins the 2d clause.

12. Hare right שניאותו.

13. מזרים (ellipsis of מ) in Chald. מְזִיר *arrogantia, superbia*. The Rabbins distinguish all sins into those committed בשוגג *ignorantly*, and במזיד *presumptuously*. I take the great *transgression* to be Idolatry. Hare right — אהי חם.

XX.

The first 5 verses the prayer of the people, on offering the sacrifice; probably (Mudge) before some expedition. 6th, by the Priest on the manifestation of GOD's acceptance. 7th and 8th, by the people after victory. 9th, is an Euphemismus for King and People.

3. דשן never signifies to *reduce to ashes*. Arab. *accepit munus altaris*.

9. I read וענט.

XXI.

1. מה מאד *quam maximè*.

6. כי *nonne?* Mic. 6, 4 — influences the 2d clause.

8—12. The Oracle concerning David.

9. בלע *membratim dilaceravit*. Job 10, 8.

11. נטו explained by Arab. נטו *vaniloquus fuit*.

12. שכם Arab. *momordit* — תכנן from כנן (Chald.) *circumligavit*.

XXII.

1. למה influences the 2d clause, with an ellipsis of תהי. I read מי — מי שועתי influences the last member of the 2d clause — מי for מ.

8. ילענו some MSS.

9. מבטיחי participle Hiphil, from Arab. *conjecit in faciem*; 8th conjugation, *concidere fecit in faciem*.

11. עזר a judicial term — *asserting the right of*. See Dr. Harris on Isai. 53, the 1st Dissertation.

17. ראה (with ב) *feasting the eyes with*.

19. אלהי (I with Hare) latter clause.

20. יחידה *only daughter* — here applied to his life; see Pf. 35, 17.

21. האמים.

21. ראמים see Job 39, 9 Note — see Hare — and Houbigant as to עניתני.

23. (Hare) this verse begins a new Psalm. Sometimes two Psalms joined together, when the latter had no title: see Ps. 27.

26. יחי from Arab. roots — *benedixit* — the common Arab. form of blessing — *Beet te regno Deus!* See ver. 30.

29. I read with LXX ונפשי לו חיה — *benedicat ei.* ו quod attinet ad, see Isa. 59, 21; Jer. 23, 24.

30. I read with LXX זרעי *my feed*.

XXIII.

1. לא μηδεν Job 6, 21; 36, 19.
3. ישבב Ps. 19, 8.
5. *Impinguasti caput meum oleo.* Perhaps *anointing him King.*

XXIV.

Probably on bringing the Ark into the city of David. 2 Sam. 6, 12, &c.

1. ארץ Canaan, Ps. 72, 8. from sea to sea East and West, from the river of Egypt to the river Euphrates North and South — founded by the seas, and bounded by the rivers. תבל limited in the same manner.

5. צדקה more than *Justice* — ελεημοσυνη *benevolentia.*

6. דור *habitaculum, domicilium.* A tribe of Arabs is now called a *Dour.*

9. הנשאו as in ver. 7.

10. Ever an ellipsis of שר or אדני before צבאות.

XXV.

Alphabetical Psalm of detached sentences, as usual.

1. I and Hare אלהי אתה — 2d verse must begin with ב.

3. Last clause — let them be put to the blush, who worship strange Gods, unable to help them. See Malac. 2, 11—16.

5. Two verses crammed into one, and order inverted — was doubtless thus:

| הדריכני באמתך | כי אתה אלהי ישעי |
| ולמדני כי אותך | קויתי כל היום: |

8. ירה בדרך *viam monstravit*—the *way*, the *law* of GOD.
9. I read במשפטיו *his judgments*, another word for *law of God*.
11. Hare right — some word wanting in the first clause — but rather חנני or רחמני.
14. סוד abbreviation of דברי סוד *decreta consilii*, Jer. 23, 18.
17. הרחיב I read — and join ו to the following clause.
18. Not קרב wanting (as Hare) but קומה as Pf. 17, 13—קרבה אל Pf. 69, 19, quite a different construction.
21. קויתיך same as ישועתך קויתי (see Gen. 49, 19) יהוה dropt, Κυριε.
22. General Acclamation.

XXVI.

4. נעלמים see note on Job 42, 3.
5. Evil doers and profligates generally mean Idolaters.
9. תאסף influences חיי in the 2d clause.

XXVII.

2. ל is here *quum*, as 2 Sam. 18, 29 — rather כ as in the 1st clause.
4. I take לבקר to be an abbreviation of להגיד בבקר חסדו Pf. 92, 3.
6. רום ראש *give victory*. Pf. 7, 3: 110, 7.
7. I think this verse begins a new Pfalm. Joining 2 Pfalms together no uncommon error of copyists. See Pf. 9 and 10 in LXX. Pf. 146 in Heb. where 2 Pfalms are plainly joined: to which add this, the 22d, and perhaps some others.
8. For לך read לך לך לך—Hare wrong supplied—the truth thus: לך לך אמר לבי
נבקוש פני יהוה See Gen. 12, 1.
12. I read the end of this, and the beginning of the next verse thus: ויפח חמס לו:
13. לא האמנתי לראת בטוב
LXX και εψευσατο η αδικια εαυτη—נפח Arab. *mutuo certavit, cum aliquo difceptavit*, &c. As this passage is strictly prophetical of the Messiah, much light is thrown on it from Mark 14, 56. A very commodious sense, without altering the text. Houbigant's conjecture is inconsistent with the verse following, which

supposes

supposes great despondency to have been expressed in this. As ס ראה with ב see note on Pf. 22, 17.

14. קוה אל יהוה the same as קוה אל ישועת יהוה *wait for the salvation of Jehovah.*

XXVIII.

3. משך Arab. *celeriter confodit*, in the 8th conjugat. *rapuit, celeriter abstulit.* In the 2d clause a verb wanting — LXX &c. perhaps אל תאבדני.

4. *Redire fac retributionem eorum eis.*

7. I read as LXX ויעלו בשרי. Hare right, not לבבי twice in 2 lines. I should read בטחה לבי in the former line — the noun both genders.

8. I read here לעמו with the ancient versions.

XXIX.

Grotius right — imagined this on David's victory over Hadadezer, King of Zobah, 2 Sam. 8. The mountains, mentioned, in that prince's country. The victory attended with a mighty storm of thunder, lightning, hail, and rain ⸺ and probably with an earthquake.

1. אילים 2 MSS. See 2 Kings 24, 15.

2. I read with LXX בחדרת קדשו Pf. 96, 9.

3. I take קול to be a verb, *tonitru edidit*, the perfect tense in Kal. *Waters* here a metaphor, to denote a mighty army. See Jer. 47, 2. Houbigant right, and הרעים should be repeated.

7. I think this verse hath lost an Hemistic between חצב and להבות אש — the thunder of JEHOVAH caused the hail to pour down, it darted forth flashes of fire (Pf. 18, 15) the reading might be ⸺ קול יהוה חצב ברד   רבב להבות אש : חצב (Arab.) *filiculis petivit*, and the noun *vehemens ventus.*

9. I read last clause קלו — Hare right, temple means the Heavens.

10. First clause (rides in the whirlwind, and directs the storm) JEHOVAH directs the inundation.

XXX.

Title misplaced here — belongs perhaps to Pf. 24. Thanksgiving for the author's recovery from a dangerous fit of sickness.

3. I read מְהוֹרְרִי inf. niphal : *ita ut non conjectus essem in foveam.*

4. Mudge right —— *memorial* and *name* the same thing. Exod. 3, 15.

7. I read with LXX להדרי.

9. The words of his supplication.

10. With LXX I make the verbs here of the perfect tense, and not imperatives. מחול *chorus tripudiantium.*

12. I read כבודי (LXX) — *that my glory may shout unto thee.* למען influences the latter clause.

XXXI.

Probably written by Jeremiah, so many Parts corresponding with his 18th and 20th chapters. Hence then, and from the 14th and 40th Psalms — the first book or collection of the Psalms was not made until the captivity, though many are by David. The Prophet here was not at Anathoth, (as Mudge), but at Jerusalem, during the whole transaction, and his enemies the nobility of Judah.

3. Three copies מעווי.

5. Three copies פרית.

6. *Lying vanities* — strange Gods, all application to heathen rites ; which were a lie and a fraud, &c.

7. אשר *quando* — he was not yet relieved.

9. A verb wanting after the nouns in the latter clause —— perhaps ימסו.

10. I join מכל צררי to the end of the verse. See Ps. 6, 7.

11—13. See Jer. 18, 18 to the end of the 19th, and 10 first verses of the 20th chapter.

17. Jerem. 18, 21 and 20, 12.

18. —— 18, 18.

20. —— 18, 18 and 20, 10.

21. With LXX I translate מצור *besieged.* See 2 Kings 24, 10, ותבא העיר במצור.

22. Jerem. 20; 7, 8.

XXXII.

1. נשוי (contrary to all analogy, if from נישא) from נשה *oblitus est.* So Houbigant.

5. Ellipsis

5. Ellipsis of אם *quando* (beginning of this verse) influences אמרתי. Pf. 139, 6. Prov. 11, 2.

6. מצא Syr. *defæcavit*, wash the ore from the earth, &c. through the Psalms allusions to refining of metals — the propriety of mentioning the inundations of waters; which, instead of refining, would carry the whole away. רק *præsertim*, Josh. 6, 18.

8. Houbigant wrong, איצה not *firmare*. I make עיני *aspice me*, a participle from עָוָן *posuit oculum, observavit*, (1 Sam. 18, 9) is right rendered, Saul *eyed* David. Imper. Hiph. ה often dropt at the end in verbs of this form.

9. I and Houbigant אל תהיה.

11. I and Hare — *this verse the beginning of the next Psalm*. The next Psalm hath no title, therefore this verse was easily separated.

XXXIII.

20. חכתה Arab. roots, *clamavit cum gemitu*. Job. 3, 21.

22. We desire it on no other terms, and in no other degree, but what is equal to the sincerity of our trust.

XXXIV.

The title does not agree with the Psalm. Perhaps Abimelech is the common title of the king of Gath (as Pharao of Egypt) and Achish his particular name. But the Psalm does not allude to that history. Alphabetical.

5. I read אלי — זה in the next verse is to be understood δεικτικως. I read (latter clause) with the old versions פניכם. Letters ה and ו both in this verse. But the sense is so compleat, that nothing seems lost, as Hare and Houbigant imagine.

10. כפירים *rich men, mighty*, as Ezek. 38, 13.

15. God always represented as looking towards that which is pleasing to him. In the latter clause a verb is necessary in English to compleat the sense.

16. This verse and the former changed places. If not, this in a parenthesis; or else the reading of the LXX must be admitted צעקו צדיקים.

XXXV.

3. סגר or סגור is the σαγαρις or *Scymitar*. הריק influences this

this word as well as the lance.

5. I read רחם *impellens eos.*

7. שחרת and רשתם have changed places—the next verse proves, it was the Net which was hidden.

8. שואה *fragor erumpens cum desolatione.* (Schultens). בעית שואה=בישואה *tempore tumultus.* ידע signifies *expecting*, being before informed what is to happen. Isa. 47, 13.

11. שאל (Arab.) *adversatus est, conviciis insectavit.*

13. My prayer dwelt upon my palate.

14. שחה *prostravit se humi* — קדר equivalent to *sordidatus.* See 2 Sam. 12, 16—22.

15. נכים *verberones,* whipt slaves, vile scoundrels.

16. I and Hare—the words should certainly be thus read: קרעוני בחנפי לעגי מעוג   ולא דמו הרק עלי שנימו קרע *laceravit,* here *dilaceriis.* Mudge right, that מלעוג=מעוג *sanna.* לעגי *subsannantes.*

20. Buxtorf right הלא = לא. דברי מרמורת accusations of the false witnesses, ver. 11. by *the quiet ones* of the land *himself,* so Ps. 34, *this poor man.*

21. ז *mox,* Nahum. 3, 12. Ps. 37, 36.

23. לריבי I take inf. Hiph. with an aphæresis of ה — see note on Job 13, 8.

25. I read נפשנוהו (or ת) Chald. נפם *delevit,* so 2 Sam. 5, 8 — and the lame and the blind, which had reviled him, David utterly destroyed.

XXXVI.

2. בעיניו marginal note, Hare — LXX had it, but not אליו. מצא *affecutus est.* לשנא *usque dum eam odio habeat.*

4. Metaphor, 2 armies in array—the wicked man ranges on the water-side. לא by *no manner of,* it answers to μηδέν. See Job 6, 21.

XXXVII.

Alphabetical. Each Letter 2 verses ——— except ד, כ, and ק, which have lost an Hemistic, ע half a one.

3. I read with all the versions המונה *copiam ejus.* Syr. and Ar. from ימן *felix.*

7. Latter Hemistic of the 1st verse plainly lost — no trace left to recover it.

10. אֵינֶנּוּ *non amplius ibi* (Gen. 37, 30) here ver. 36.
20. כִּי רְשָׁעִים יֹאבֵדוּ
     וְאֹיְבֵי יְהוָה כְלוּ
     בִיקַר בָּרוּמִים כָּלוּ
     בֶעָשָׁן כָּלוּ :

Sed impii peribunt, et inimici Jehovæ consumentur; simul ac eve‑ huntur ad honorem, tabescentes sicut fumus consumentur. LXX right.

21. Mudge right ——— not the *dispositions*, but *abilities*. The wicked so poor, as to be obliged to borrow without being able to re-pay: whereas the righteous shall have wherewithal to be generous and munificent. Therefore I read הוֹנֵן from הוֹן *suffecit*, ver. 26.

22. See Gen. 12, 3.

23. Law of JEHOVAH called *the way, his way*.

26. When any person would bless another, he will say, Mayest thou be as the seed of the righteous.

27. I read with the LXX שֹׁכֵן לְעוֹלָם וָעֵד (Symmach.) ηρε‑ μησις — parallel to Ps. 25, 13.

28. I read, with the LXX, and Houbigant, עוֹלִים נִשְׁמָדוּ ατομοι εκδιωχθησονται. Those words dropt out because like the 2 preceding words — without admitting them, we have no verse with ע at the beginning.

34. The former Hemistic of the 2d verse lost absolutely.

35. I read with the LXX מִתְעַלֶּה επαιρομενον, so Syr. & Arab.

36. I read with the LXX, Syr. & Arab. וָאֶעֱבֹר και παρηλθον.

37. אַחֲרִית *posterity* (Ps. 109, 13) the wicked and all his race to be destroyed, the pious man to have a numerous progeny, see his sons sons to the 3d and 4th generation. See Job 8, 19; 18, 13—20.

39. ו redundant, the verse must begin with רִי.

XXXVIII.

3. שָׁלוֹם *integritas, soliditas, perfectio*.

6. קֹדֵר (Ps. 35, 14) *sordidatus*.

13. לֹא μηδεν, as Job 6, 21.

14. תּוֹכָחוֹת a judicial term, denoting the reply to the accusation.

17. My anguish is continually in my presence.

19. I read with Hare הִנָּם. See Ps. 35, 19; 69, 5.

XXXIX.

1. The LXX near the fenfe in the 3d claufe, שמר *fervavit*.
2. Grotius right, in the 2d claufe, *abftinui a rebus lætis*.
Heb. verbs for *keeping filence* fignify to *abftain*. LXX If. 57,11 παρορω — טוב often *jucunditas*.

5. נצב one that ftandeth upright — that pofture denotes life — (the dead are *fallen*) LXX ζων.

6. Vatablus and Grotius obferve, fome books read כצלם — fame thought in Sophocles, *Ajax* v. 125.

10. The LXX απο της ισχυος nearly right. Chald. Syr. of the root *percuffit vehementer*.

11. כעש abbreviation of כבגד אכלו עש as in Job 13, 28. I read אך כל הבל as in the 5th verfe. Ver. 13 parallel to Job 10; 20, 21.

XL.

Mudge well conjectured, this Pfalm is Jeremiah's thankfgiving for his delivery from the dungeon, into which he had been thrown by the Princes, and taken out at Zedekiah's command by Ebed-melek the Æthiopian. He had preached JEHOVAH's intentions with regard to Jerufalem, and perfuaded the King and people to fubmit to the Chaldeans without further refiftance. *Roll* that written by Baruc at the mouth of Jeremiah. Secondary fenfe Chrift.

1. Waiting I waited for JEHOVAH. ים=אונו יט.

4. This is the new Song mentioned in the former verfe. See Jer. 37, 3—11. Pharaoh's army being marched out of Egypt, and the Chaldeans having raifed the fiege of Jerufalem, the prophet warned the king and people not to rely on Egypt, they would not help them. He therefore fuffered from the princes, and was caft into the dungeon. רהב note on Job 9, 13. שטה Chald. *infanivit*. Schultens (Prov. 7, 25) ڸهـــــــ *commorfo fræno ruit*. The Egyptians faithlefs allies to the Jews. 2 Kings 18; 20, 21.

6. I read (LXX. & Syr.) ואזנים, boring ears marking the perfon for a perpetual fervant. See Jer. 1, 4—10. Hammond right, rendering σωμα by *mancipium* (as frequently Ariftotle, Demofthenes, and Strabo) and reading σωμα δε κατηρτισω μοι σοι. See Jer. ch. 20.

7. Roll

7. Roll written by Baruch from Jeremiah's mouth, ch. 36. ב *cum*, Judg. 11, 34. Isai. 7; 24, 25. עלי *coram me*, Gen. 48, 7. Jer. 12, 11. Eccl. 2, 17.

9. Jer. 36, 3. I read (Lat. & Syr.) צדקך *benevolentiam tuam*.

10. I read (with LXX) צדקתי but at the end of the last verse.

11. I read with all the versions ואתה. Mudge wrong, supposes a new Psalm here. (If new, cannot begin till ver. 13. 2 in one). לא תכלא refer to לא אכלא 9th verse. *Psalm* 70 *the same as this from* v. 13, with few variations.

12. Houbigant right עונתי *ærumnas, miserias*, this more suitable than *iniquities*. عنا *calamitate affectus fuit*.

13. I read (as Ps. 70) אלהים. רצה from רוץ *cucurrit*, ה paragog.

15. LXX על עקב παραχρῆμα, *immediately*. ישובו (Ps. 70) right —expression רגע = ישובו יבישו רגע Ps. 6, so Syr. See Jerem. 20; 10, 11.

XLI.

8. This *cursed thing* is the wickedness they laid to his charge, ver. 7.

13. A Doxology, added probably by the collector of this 1st book of Psalms, which ends here. The Psalm plainly ends at ver. 12. Division of the Psalms into books *not* arbitrary. Collected at different times by different persons.

The Second Book.

Psalm XLII.

1. I read (Chald. & Syr.) כאיל היערג belling is the term for the cry of the Hart. See *Dictionarium Rusticum in voce* Hart. על *prope*, as Cant. 5, 12. Same expression.

3. I read as in ver. 10 באמרם.

4. Much pain to commentators. עלי as in Job 10, 1, relates to his *private* devotions, as the latter part does to the *public* thanksgiving. סך from Arab. *fremuit*; and אדדם זג *vociferatus est*; אדיר *clamor*, dancing and music in the Jewish thanksgivings.

5. מה dropt in the second clause, see here ver. 11; and ver. 5 of the next Psalm — the same verses prove פני ואלהי.

6. Perhaps אזכירך *I will put thee in remembrance*. Mountains

tains of Hermon, Tabor and Hermon. Mitfar an adjoining mountain, fmall, *the little mountain.* Retain the original word.

    8. יצוה (from Arab. root, *fplendor*) verb in Hiphil *illuminavit.*

    10. Arab. fenfe of רצח *confregit*, with ב refpecting the thing.

XLIII.

As in the former book 2 Pfalms are put into 1, here 1 is cut into 2. The Subject and Conclufion plainly fhew it.

XLIV.

    2. Houbigant right את בידך. The nations were removed, and Ifrael planted in their room; GOD made them to flourifh till they overfpread the land.

    4. I read with LXX ואלהי מצוה.

    5. The 1ft claufe, Deut. 33, 17 — expreffed at full length is נוגח יחדו אפסי ארץ *we could pufh our enemies one and all to the extremities of the land.*

    16. Relates to Senacherib. חרף and גדף ufed with refpect to *him*, 2 Kings, 19, 22.

    25. נפש often *corpus, cadaver*. Num. 9; 6, 7.

XLV.

Two titles put into one. *One of the fons of Korah, an inftruction* — not relating to the fubject of this Pfalm, belongs to fome other. ששנים from שש. On Solomon's marrying Pharaoh's daughter —— applicable to the Meffiah, whofe kingdom alone is for ever and ever. It has fuffered much from tranfcribers, more from interpreters.

    1. רחש denotes the conception of any thing in the mind, before committed to writing, or declared by fpeech.

    3. Hare right, a word wanting at the end: wrong in tranfplanting hither לעלם from the former verfe. Rather fupply with תלבש as Job 40, 10. Same expreffion.

    4. הדרך *bend alfo the bow*, Jer. 51, 3. צלח *to rufh violently on a perfon, or thing.* רכב *currus.* תורך Ar. ورك *invafit, percuffit in coxendice, fall on the rear of the enemies.*

    5. גבור (LXX) after שנונים. Houbigant right — יפלו fhould be repeated יפלו יפלו Hiph. & Kal.

                         Q   8. Mudge

8. Mudge wrong, הבלי not *cabinets* — שמחיך (I read) Arab. *altus fuit, superbus:* thence the noun *sublimis* — agrees with הבלי former part of the hemistic.

12. Wealthy people, *the Tyrians*; who probably among the presents to Solomon on renewing the league which his father had made with them, sent their prince's daughter to adorn his Seraglio. I make an ellipsis of באשר after מנחה.

17. שם *fame*, Ruth 4, 14. harsh to render it *name*, as he has not once mentioned it. Hare right, על כן at the beginning of this verse.

XLVI.

Alamoth, some musical instrument, see 1 Chr. 15, 20. Probably on Senacherib's army being destroyed before Jerusalem in *one night*. Very sublime.

4. נהר *illuxit* — this a sure presage of deliverance, as in the following verses. This probably the speech of the priest, attending the sanctuary, and presaging deliverances from the glory of GOD appearing.

10. אנכי often *ego solus*, Exod. 20, 2.

XLVII.

6. זמר *to shout*, and *play on instruments* (being repeated here) both included.

9. אלהים מגני ארץ almost literally, *the tutelar Gods of the earth* — Gods the protectors of the earth.

XLVIII.

Probably on Jerusalem delivered from the siege of Rezin king of Syria, and Pekah king of Israel. Isai. ch. 7.

2. נוף from Arab. ناف *procerus fuit*.

5. At the beginning an ellipsis of כאשר *simul ac*. חפו *festinanter se abripuit, metu periculi*.

7. כ at the end of the former verse influences here. Their fear and hurry compared to that of mariners whose vessel is driven upon the rocks by a violent storm.

10. קצוי certainly from קצו Arab. *longius abfuit*, thence قصو *extremitas*, the very word — the Lexicographers are all wrong in deriving it from קצה — contrary to all analogy.

13. פסגו

13. פםנו (Symmachus) *take the dimensions of.*

14. I think with Hare, and Mudge, that על מות belong to the title of the next Psalm: as well for the reasons they assign, as also that then the 2 hemistics will rhime, an ornament (as far as I can observe) never neglected by the Composers of the Psalms, when it fairly comes in their way.

XLIX.

8. חדל *vacavit alicui rei.* ו influences both clauses in the verse following.

14. חכמים (irony) *wise in their own opinion.*

11. Hare right, בקרבם = קרבם *this is at the bottom of their reasoning.*

12. נמשל *proverbium fit.* Niphal. Selah should be after this verse.

13. דרך *consilium, vivendi ratio.*

14. שתו from Arab. *pulverizavit.* I read with LXX and all the versions but Chal. למו at the end of this verse.

18. The 2d clause here, and 1st of the next verse, by way of apostrophe to the rich man. דור *domicilium,* as Ps. 24, 6 ——— means the grave.

20. ילין as in the 12th verse.

L.

1. ארץ *the land*—ver. 5, the judgment of God's own people, the children of Israel.

7. אעידה by *admonishing,* Jer. 42, 19.

10. Houbigant right, חיות היער.

11. זיז from Chal. זז *movit se.* שדי *plain,* opposed to hills. LXX frequently πεδίον.

18. תרץ from רצץ *confregit,* for גנב is the name for the housebreaker. Exod. 22, 2. חלק Chal. *communio, societas,* so here.

21. אהיה name of God, see Exod. 3, 14. *I am.*

23. שם דרך abbreviation of לדרך פעמיו שם ——— as Ps. 85, 14. the *way,* the *law* of Moses.

LI.

Title misplaced. From the last verse, it was written during the Captivity, and the cessation of Temple Worship. The author

author under great depreſſion of mind, ariſing from the guilt of ſome crime, probably ſome compliance with heathen idolatry. Not *murder*, or *adultery*, plain from the 4th verſe — *againſt* THEE ONLY *have I ſinned*.

4. Grotius right, דבר a judicial term, the ſentence on the criminal.

10. נכון *ſedatus* — freed from the agitations which guilt had cauſed in him.

12. Hare right, רוח נדיבה *mentem alacrem, non amplius depreſſam*.

14. Mudge דמים that debt of blood, by which a man is for any capital crime rendered ἔνοχος θανάτῳ, ſuch as was by the Jewiſh law all compliance with the idolatry of the nations.

LII.

2. I read with Syr. עַל חָסִיר the high prieſt was called חסיר אל *ſanctus Dei*, Deut. 33, 8, he is ſtiled איש חסידך *thy holy one*. מה or rather למה influences the 3 firſt verſes. I derive רמיה from רמה *projecit*, expreſſing the ſwiftneſs of the deſtruction.

6. ייראו certainly only with its original vowel, ראה — the righteous could not have occaſion for fear — therefore in the parallel places, Pſ. 69, 33; 107, 42; 119, 74; Job 22, 19; it is expreſſed by יִשְׂמְחוּ. In Pſ. 40, 4 indeed this ſentence is uſed in the ſenſe of *fear*; but it is there applied, not to the righteous, but the multitude; and it is on ſeeing the deliverance of the righteous, not the deſtruction of the wicked.

9. Arab. ſenſe of אקוה, قوء *clamavit*, ſomething *done* in *public*, not *hoping* in the mind — or אחוה *I will declare*.

LIII.

Nearly the ſame as the 14th. Two Titles, one the ſame as the 14th. מחלת *the dances*, part of the Jewiſh divine ſervice. See 2 Sam. 6, 14. Written during the captivity.

1. In 14 עלילה inſtead of עול.
2. יהוה inſtead of אלהים.
3. כלו חג inſtead of הכל סר.
4. כל פעלי — in the end יהוה inſtead of אלהים.

5. This

5. This verse very different now, at first the same. See note on Pf. 14.

6. In 14 ישועת instead of ישועות.

LIV.

No great relation between the title and Pfalm. The author in great diftrefs — prays — is delivered — and offers thanks.

1. According to thy might, execute my judgment.
3. I read here with Chald. וזדים, as Pf. 86, 14.
7. I read here with the LXX, Lat. Syr. תצילני.

LV.

Probably on Abfalom's rebellion, and the defection of Achitophel.

2. אריד a fyriafm, the imperative Aphel —— or elfe הריד from רדד *expandit.*

3. שטם *membratim dilaceravit,* note Job 16, 9.

4. Not in the Syriac.

6. Houbigant right, אשכנה the fenfe from Arab. سكن *recepit fe aliquo, quietis ergo.*

9. בלע *dilaceravit,* Job 10, 8.

10. על *juxta,* Pf. 110, 4. Ifa. 59, 18.

13. ערך rendered rightly by Le Clerc, *fecundum æftimationem meam, ut putabam.* I take the Arab. fenfe of אלף *fociavit.* Thence the nouns, *focius, familiaris,* &c.

14. אשר adverb *ita ut,* as in 1 Sam. 3, 11. Nold. p. 102.

15. ישיא (the Keri) from נשא *abripuit* —— בקרבם probably a marginal note crept in.

19. I read with the LXX קדם ישב. LXX right in rendering חליפות ανταλλαγμα, *permutatio, pretium redemptionis.*

21. I and Houbigant חלוק — Hare wrong in changing פיו into פניו for דבריו in the latter claufe is plainly exegetical of this word.

LVI.

1. שאף all the old verfions *conculcavit,* from שוף. א to exprefs Kametz.

2. I read with all the antient verfions שאפוני.

3. That this paffage is corrupt, is clear from the antient verfions

fions. The 2d verfe plainly ends at ל. So the LXX, who join מרום to יום in the verfe following, but no fenfe. The Syr. feems to have read מרומים *excelfi*, and couples it with לחמים, but then it is deficient in the next verfe.—I imagine the true reading to be מרום כל־היום אראה *I look upwards* (towards heaven) *all the day long*. Ellipfis of ל often, Ifa. 37, 23, and fo this Hemiftic agrees with the next.

4. I read with the LXX, Syr. דברי.

6. I read יצפוני *feligunt me*, fee note on Pf. 10, 8.

7. I read with the LXX, Vulg. & Syr. על אין פלט *eo quod non fit perfugium*.

8. אתה שימה the fame as שימת. I point בְּסִפְרָתְךָ *in decretis tuis*. ספרה is properly the record in which the decrees are enrolled.

10. I read here, as in ver. 4, דברי in both claufes. It is a repetition of the fame fentence. I fufpect *the latter Hemiftic was originally in*, and is now dropt out of *the 4th verfe*.

12. The 1ft claufe equivalent to the Lat. phrafe, *voti damnatus fum*.

13. מֻרְחָבִי fo I point it, *Partic. Pahul, in Pybal*, from נדח the fenfe from Arab. *dilatavit*, and as a noun, *terra fpatiofa et ampla*. Setting feet in a wide place a metaphor, through the Pfalms, to exprefs deliverances from affliction.

LVII.

The title feems rightly placed — the occafion, fee 1 Sam. 24.

2. The fenfe Arab. גמר *avertit*.

3. חרף Benon. שָׁאֲפִי (as in the former Pfalm) *conculcantem me*.

4. Difordered greatly. I think the 3d verfe ends with *Selah*. And at the beginning of the 2d claufe of the 4th verfe, I read with the LXX ויציל *et eripiet*. In the next claufe I read בתוך לאבים *in locis fiticulofis* לאב *fitivit*, hence תלאובה *ficcitas*, Hof. 13, 5 — David's fituation in the wildernefs. 3 MSS. read לבאים, ellipfis of מן (before בני אדם) frequent after נצל, 2 Sam. 20, 6.

6. I point כָּפַף fenfe from Arab. *claufit adftriétis vinculis*, infin. Kal. influenced by the particle ל before פְעָמָי.

7. The laft 5 verfes nearly the fame as the firft 5 in Pf. 108.

8. I read

8. I read כבורי some musical instrument. The Arab. *tympanum* —— the same instrument used in Church Music by the Æthiopians, and now called כבר.

LVIII.

2. אף *potius, quinimo*. פלס *trutinavit*, distributing by weight common as to administration of justice.

3. This and the 2 next verses I take to be the answer of JEHOVAH to the question in the 2 first verses, as the 6, 7, and 8, are the reply of the Psalmist; and the remainder are the decree of JEHOVAH. Subject the same as that of Ps. 73, and regards the dispensations of GOD's providence.

7. Acute distempers called the arrows of the Almighty, see Ps. 91; 5, 6. Deut. 32, 24. I read at the end of the second clause למו. I take the sense of יתמללו from Arab. מלל *cineribus calidis, aut prunis, supposuit coquendum panem, vel carnem* — noun metaphorical, *fever in the bones*, the verb is used for *calore febrili correptus*.

8. שבלול all the antient versions, except Chald. *wax*, makes best sense here. I read אשה *ignita*, often used in the books of Moses to express sacrifices burnt with fire.

9. Parallel to Job 27, 20 to the end.

LIX.

Title misplaced. Probably written at the siege of Jerusalem by Senacherib, in the reign of Hezekiah.

5. Hint at the treachery of Senacherib, who attacks Jerusalem after receiving 300 talents of silver, and 30 of gold, to buy peace of him.

6. שוב *sese convertere in hanc vel illam partem*. עֶרֶב *multitudo*, Ex. 12, 38. Rabshakeh endeavoured to breed a dissension between the people and their governors, 2 Kin. 18, 26—35.

7. שמע Arab. *diffamavit*.

9. I read עיו as in the last verse; which being better preserved will correct this. For the same reason I read אומרה *I will shout*, and add אלהי חסדי to the end of this verse, which are wrongly placed at the beginning of the next.

10. קדמני יראני naturally run one into another by a very common Hebraism.'

11. Let them not be slain in battle, lest the people forget the hand of GOD, and ascribe the success to their own valour; but let them be destroyed by such a miraculous exertion of power as will leave no room for dispute; but oblige every one to acknowledge it the immediate work of GOD. I take the sense of הניעמו from نوع *inclinavit*. The metaphor from felling a large tree, which first stoops, then falls.

12. Probably alludes to the Letter sent to Hezekiah by Senacherib, 2 Kings 19, 14: and 2 Chr. 32, 17—19.

13. I read with Syr. בלם *perde eos*, in both clauses.

14. Ellipsis of אשר before יהמו, making it refer to ערב in this, and the 6th verse.

15. This spoken of the multitude. One stratagem used to make the people surrender, was trying to raise a mutiny on the want of provisions. 2 Chr. 32, 11. Syr. reads יביעון as in the 6th verse.

LX.

שושן עדות always supposed the name of some musical instrument. The former, see note on Ps. 45; the latter, عود *chelys*, *testudo*, lute probably the instrument here meant. I think the right reading in the latter clause is שמונה עשר אלף 18000 men; for this title, and 2 Sam. 8, 13, 1 Chr. 18, 12, mutually correct one another; and shew that David smote the *Edomites*, (not the *Syrians*), in the valley of salt, and that the number slain was 18000, not 12000. This Psalm seems written on setting out on an expedition, immediately after an earthquake; which calamity was interpreted as a sure mark of GOD's displeasure. It is after the 4th verse the same as the 108th Psalm, with some small variations.

4. Syr. קשש *jaculatus est*, and the noun *sagittarius*. Probably the *archer* served for the banner of the *Assyrians* as well as it was the impression on their money. Selah should be at the end of the 3d verse.

6. I take אחלקה to be the same as אחלק השלל *I shall divide the spoil*. Prov. 29, 24. Probably, after a successful expedition, they used to divide the spoil among the army at Shechem, (as that place lay convenient, for encamping) before they were dismissed

to their own homes. This verb regards divisions by *tale*, as
כורד by *measure*.

8. Former clause *Moab is the wall of my confidence*, for I take
the Arab. sense of סיר in which سور is *murus urbis*. LXX render right, τας ελπιδος μου. נעל *compes*. I read אתרועע
Pf. 108.

9. 108th Psalm reads מבצר *the fenced city*, perhaps this rather than Hare's מצור.

10. הלא *si non*, abbreviation of הן לא.

LXI.

The 5 first verses by the king, the 4 first during his absence
from Jerusalem, the last on his return; 6th and 7th the
acclamation of the people, and the 8th by the king.
Thanksgiving for the king's safe return from some dangerous expedition.

5. The inheritance of them that fear GOD's name is his
constant favour and protection, and victory over all their enemies, to which they were entitled, by virtue of GOD's covenant
with their fathers, as long as they continued to keep his law.
See Deut. 28, 7.

7. מן *quaeso, utinam*, it is a Syriasm. See the Syriac version
of Judges 5, 11.

LXII.

על = על ידי 1 Chr. 25, 3. Jeduthun one of the 3 chief Musicians, and presided over the harpers. Probably written
after Absalom's defeat; when the great men, who had
joined him, came to reconcile themselves to David. One
of their excuses was, that they did not intend to take his
life, only to ease him of the cares of government. We
find 2 Sam. 15; 3,4, that David's inability, through age,
to administer justice with expedition, was made one pretence for their rebelliously setting up Absalom.

1. אך here, and in the next verse *tantummodo*, as Prov. 17, 11.

2. *I shall not be greatly moved*. The Psalms express utter
ruin by being moved.

3. תהותתו from Arab. هتت‎. התת *declivi cursu fluxit*. רצח
comminuit, collisit. The 2 verses naturally run into one another
by a very common Hebraism.

4. I read

4. I read with the LXX משאתי in the 1ft clause, and in the laft with all the verfions בפיהם.

7. GOD was in honour obliged to preferve him in his dignity, fince he placed his whole confidence in him.

8. The latter claufe, *God is our refuge*, the acclamation of the people.

10. הבל from Arab. *an anxious defire after gain*.

LXIII.

1. I and Hare עיפה.
2. כן *ficut.* Jarchi renders it כאשר.
5. Arab. هل הלל *exultavit*.
6. אם influences the 2d clause.
9. לשואה inf. Kal. & affix. *ad defolandum eam cum fragore*. See Schultens on Prov. I, 27.
10. The 1ft claufe, *may they cut him in pieces with the edge of the fword*, Syr. & Arab. fenfes of נגר. The latter claufe = Homer's ἑώρια κυνίσσι.
11. I read with Syr. & Arab. ויתהלל.

LXIV.

4. Firft claufe, latter Hemiftic, 1 MS. reads ירוהו; in the latter claufe I make יראו with Syr. fut. Niph. from ראה only written with its vowel.

5. יספרו Arab. *invicem juverunt*. In the end I read with the Syr. למו.

6. They even imputed to him for crimes what they imagined were his intentions, without any external evidence to fupport it. תמנו from מנה *paravit, conftituit*.

9. יראו here again with its vowel, and is the future Kal. of ראה.

10. יתהללו fame fenfe as in the 5th verfe of laft Pfalm.

LXV.

1. Vulg. Arab. Æthiop. and Alcala and Aldine editions of the LXX. read at the end, *in Jerufalem*. But as the fenfe is now compleat in the Heb. *although I think it the true reading*, I have made no alteration in the text.

3. דברי *gefta, acta*, as well as *verba*. I read with the LXX מנו, fo it anfwers to the latter claufe.

4. I make

4. I make נשבע partic. pref. Niph. so the construction is easy.

5. Houbigant right, ימים.

6. LXX and Syr. right, בכחך.

8. See Exod. 15, 14—16. I point מוּצָאיִ partic. Hoph. *eductos ex Ægypto*, as in Ezek. 14, 22.

9. I read with Symmachus דגנה.

10. I read with Syr. רוית *inebriasti*, and point נִחֵת *descendere fecisti*, with an ellipsis of גשם or something like it.

11. מעגל *orbita currus, vel plaustri*. GOD is represented as going the circuit of the heavens, Job 22, 14; and Pf. 104, 3, as making the clouds his chariots. Compare these.

13. Bp. Hare right, הרים *hills*, opposed to valleys.

LXVI.

2. Ellipsis of ב before כבוד in both clauses, which causes it to become an adverb: Nold. pag. 142 and 172.

4. Hare right, לך יזמרו the repetition of a transcriber.

7. אל *nequaquam*, Pf. 7, 11.

10. כי influences all the verbs as far as the 1st clause of the 12th verse.

12. I read with LXX לרוחה — from ver. 9 relates to transactions in Egypt, and at the red sea.

14. פצו Arab. قاص *clare extulit*.

15. קטרת *fumes* from burning the fat, perhaps better *the fat* itself.

16. Hare right, לכל.

17. I read with LXX ורוממתיו תחת לשני or ורוממתיהו בלשוני — תחת as ὑπο, *per*, the instrument.

18. I am inclined to read יהוה.

LXVII.

Mudge—for plentiful product of the Land—Deut. 26. Therefore the words *nations, people, tribes, kindreds*, can only be understood of Israel; for they alone could offer thanksgiving for the increase of their own land, and they were the only people over whom GOD exercised an equal Providence: for in that sense ought the 4th verse to be understood.

4. גוים,

4. גוים, לאמים, as in the 2d Pfalm, relate to the 12 tribes in Canaan. תנחם fut. Hiph. from נוח.

LXVIII.

Probably on the miraculous defeat of Zerah, the Ethiopian, who came up againſt *Aſa* with a mighty Army of Ethiopians and Lubim; deſtroyed at Mareſhah, 2 Chr. 14; 10—13.

2. I read with all the antient verſions, יתנדפו.

4. I read with all the antient verſions יה שמו — Cappellus כי יה *for Jah is his name.*

6. מושיב *domum ducens.* ה in ביתה motion to a place. יחידים *choſen ones,* properly *only ones,* from Iſaac ſo called, the only ſon of his father. This all relates to bringing Iſrael out of Egypt. In the 2d clauſe I read בקשרות (כו & ק).

12. נורת from Æthiopic גוי *ſupellectile inſtrumentum,* uſed ſo in the verſion of Matt. 12, 29.

13. The meaning of this puzzled place ſeems to be — the children of Iſrael (here compared to a Dove, becauſe יונה *a Dove,* ſignifies alſo *oppreſſion,* Zeph. 3, 1. alluding to their ſufferings in Egypt) after the paſſage of the red ſea, and the deſtruction of the Egyptians, ſaw them lying dead on the ſea ſhore, and had an opportunity to ſtrip them of their bravery, by which they acquired great ſpoils. But when the kings of Canaan were deſtroyed, it *ſnowed* plunder on them, they were quite covered with it, as Salmon with ſnow. שפתים from Syr. ſing. *littus maris.* I read with Symmachus בצלמון.

16. תרצדון from Arab. رصد *ſupellectilem diſpoſuit.* The mountains were all ambitious of being the habitation of JEHOVAH; they therefore adorned themſelves in the beſt manner, to attract his notice. He chooſes mount Zion.

18. Hare right, בסני ſhould begin the 18th verſe. St. Paul reads ἔδωκε; but all the preſent copies of the LXX ἐλαβεῖς, as the Heb. and indeed the ſenſe requires this. Ellipſis of אל in יה אלהים.

19. ברוך inf. Kal. as a gerund, *benedicendo onerat nos.* Probably יהוה.

20. I think ולאלהים יהוה. Conſtruction of the latter clauſe a little

a little perplexed, for fake of rhyme. Le Clerc.

23. Hare right, תרחץ. I read with Symmachus תלקק מנהו מאיבים belongs to the 1st claufe, Symmachus better אִיבִיךְ.

26. Houbigant במקוה *in conventu.* God not called *the fountain of Ifrael.*

27. רגמתם Arab. رجم *acer fuit et validus;* thence noble Arabians מרגום and thence *Regemmelech,* Zech. 7, 2. (Houbigant wrong) one of the ἄπαξ λ'.

28. מטה עוך = עוך Pf. 110, 2.

30. The beaft of the reed is the river horfe, denoting Egypt. Hare right, בעלי עמים as If. 16, 8 בעלי גוים. Fouling the filver ftreams a metaphor for raifing ftirs and commotions; Mudge. I read with LXX מתרפסים fee Ezek. 32, 2; 34, 18.

31. With Zerah were Lubim, the Lybians. He was probably king of *Egypt* and Ethiopia; which was not uncommon in thofe times. Egyptian dynafties place about this time 3 anonymous kings fucceffively; Zerah perhaps 1; probably, the Actifanes mentioned by Diodor. Siculus. The Chafmonim were probably the fame as the Calafyries, and Hermotybies, mentioned by Herodotus (in Euterpe, p. 153, Edit. Gronov.) the body guards of the king of Egypt. Stretch forth hands = implore mercy.

32. I read with LXX לאדני and for Selah סלו as in the 4th verfe.

35. I read with LXX, in the former claufe, ממקדשיו, and in the latter with all the verfions לעמו.

LXIX.

Written (fee 3 laft verfes) during the Captivity, probably towards the end of it. From ver. 30 and 31 it is plain that the Temple-worfhip had ceafed, and was not yet reftored.

1. I read with LXX נפשי.

3. I read with LXX מיחלי.

4. Hare right, מצמיתי *præ coma mea,* Cantic. 4; 1, 3 et 6, 7. Ifa. 47, 2. אז *mox, flatim,* Prov. 20, 14 & 1 Sam. 20, 12.

10. I read with LXX אדכה.

12. Arab. שיח *culpavit, arguit criminis,* applicable to the judges who fate in the gate.

22. לשלמים *integre, perfecte,* Jer. 13, 19.

26. I read

26. I read with all the versions (except Chald.) יוספו.
27. צדקה *benevolentia*, Pf. 24, 5.
31. פ מ influences.

LXX.

Same as Pf. 40, from ver. 13. few variations.

1. I read רצה as in Pf. 40.
2. See Pf. 40 — ver. 3 fee Ditto, and so on to the end.

LXXI.

The 3 first verses and the beginning of the 31st Pf. nearly the same.

2. Pf. 31 drops — תצילני ות in the 1st clause; and in the latter, in the room of והושיעני reads מהרה הצילני which seems the true reading: and Vander Hooght's Bible shews the occasion of the mistake.

3. Pf. 31 right, צור מעוז common — but צור מעון no where. In 2d clause, Pf. 31. reads also rightly לבית מצודות—but the other is no good sense, and is corrupted from the former, as under, לביא תמיד צוית.

6. גוי (from Arab.) Heb. גזה *corroboravit, remuneravit.*
17. Houbigant right, beginning here לבדך.
20. אשר *quamvis*, as Eccl. 8, 12.
22. Houbigant in the 1st clause right, אודה.

LXXII.

3. בשלום =שלום= in *felicitate, feliciter* — as בצדקה *in benevolentia, benevole.*

7. First clause, *germinet benevola = benevole.*

10. אשבר as well as פסת (v. 16) are Chald. therefore this Psalm is of late date.

11. מלכים in a *large* sense, as Pf. 2, 2. as I *limit* גוים to the tribes. Because though these words are in a secondary sense prophetical of Christ, (and then must be taken in the greatest latitude), yet as applicable to Solomon, they are confined necessarily to the land of Israel; and the following verses thus limit their signification.

18. The Psalm ends at the 17th verse. This and the next are the doxology of the compiler of this 2d Collection.

20. This probably has been added by some later transcriber.

The

The Third Book.

Psalm LXXIII.

2. Cethib right, former part of this verse, שפכה partic. pahul Kal, answering to נטוי.

3. כי influences the latter clause.

4. חרצבות once more found, If. 58, 6, where it should seem to denote oppression. I derive it from 2 roots, supposing it a compound (as I think most of the quadriliterals are). חרץ Arab. *fidit cutem, fregit caput.* רצב Arab. חרצה *contusio vel fractura,* and Arab. חריצה *nubes pluviam vehementiorem fundens, et terræ superficiem rumpens.* Storm of wind and rain, metaphor to express affliction, see Matt. 7, 24—27.

In the end of the 1st clause I read למושב —— not here speaking of the *death* of the wicked, (that follows in ver. 19), but of their flourishing state; besides that the supposing them to die in peace would overthrow all his reasoning. The sense of אול from Arab. اول *principium.*

6. Hare reads right, בשית *sicut vestem.* Robe and Chain probably the dress of the Judges among the Jews. The Chain worn by the Egyptian Judges, Diodor. Sic. vol. 1. p. 86. Edit. Wesseling.

8. ימיקו from Arab. موق *fatuus fuit.*

10. הלם a noun, from Arab. لام med. 1 *reprehendit,* thence لوم *culpa.* Latter clause, *dum aquæ abundantiæ exprimuntur iis.*

14. The whole from ver. 11 is the reflection of God's people on the apparent prosperity of the wicked, and the despairing inference they drew from it: it was so contrary to the usual face of things, under the Mosaic dispensation, and to all they had been taught to expect, that it tempted them to doubt even the first principles of all religion.

15. I read in the 1st clause with Chald. and Syr. כמוהו. Ellipsis of ב in the latter clause.

16. Hare reads right, ועמל.

17. עד influences the latter clause.

18. למשואות = לעת משואות *tempore fragoris erumpentis cum desolatione.* Schult. Prov. 1, 27.

20. Ellipsis

20. Ellipsis of ילך or some verb like it, in the former clause. צלמם from Arab. *oppressit*. The perversion of justice is made instrumental by Providence in causing revolutions in States, and ends in the ruin of tyrants.

28. The LXX, Vulg. and Arab. read in the end of the Psalm these words — *in the gates of the daughter of Zion* —— probably right. It ends abruptly in the Heb. now.

LXXIV.

1. Schultens, Prov. 21, 28. נצח *in purum putum*.

3. הרע *jubilavit*. I read in the end with LXX, Syr. and Arab. בקדשך.

4. The *Temple* continued to be the tabernacle of the Testimony. Lam. 2, 6. The enemy enters the Temple, first seizes the outer court, and plants his standard; then advances to the holy place, breaks down the doors, and burns the sanctuary.

5. *One* person *the Enemy* — (the Chaldean army *the adversaries*) probably from 2 Kin. 25, 8, Nebuzar-adan. Ellipsis of אנשי before קרדמית, and literally rendered *the ax-men*.

6. I read with the antient versions פתחיה *januas ejus* — general drift of the Psalm.

8. י paragogic in מועדי, not plural — never but one מועד or אהל מועד at once. And this word never signifies a synagogue, those assemblies were of later institution.

9. Hare right, begins this verse at בארץ. The signs are those miracles wrought by God for their deliverance.

11. למה influences the 2d clause. מ *in*: Job, 3, 11; Jer. 20, 17. כלה *omnino cessat*: Job 4, 9.

14. As to לציים Bochart Phaleg (l. 4. c. 29) the Troglodytes — so called probably from living in caves, from לצא Arab. *in speluncam confugit*. Crocodile is *Pharaob*, Isa. 27, 1.

15. Schultens, Prov. 3, 20 — original idea of בקע *cum crepitu findi*.

16. If there be any passage to justify it, I would render מאור the *moon*: LXX.

17. See note on Job 29, 4, on חרף.

19. חירת in the 1st clause from the sense of Arab. خانت *in prædam se dimisit accipiter, milvus, vel aquila*: thence خاتية *aquila*. Perhaps the English word *Kite* from hence.

20. מחשבי

20. מחשבי from the Arab. *abundavit.* נאורת ſheep cotes, moveable habitations — thence *Tents.*

22. See Deut. 32, 27.

23. שכח to *diſregard,* as well as *forget.* Calaſio.

LXXV.

By way of Dialogue — 2d and 3d Verſes by JEHOVAH — the reſt by the Pſalmiſt.

8. בלא מסך *abſque mixtura.*

9. I read with LXX אגיל.

10. LXX rightly render אגדע — more applicable to a horn, than cutting off.

LXXVI.

Probably on the deſtruction of Senacherib's army by that ſtupendous miracle.

3. I read with Chald. רישף וקישת — this agrees better with the other part of the verſe. Ellipſis of כלי before מלחמה.

4. אתה common to both the verb נאור, and the noun אדיר. Senſe of טרף from the Arab. *eminens, altus.*

5. מצא יד *occaſionem rei gerendæ invenire.* Judg. 9, 33. Eccl. 9, 10. [*find a handle.* Engl.]

6. I read with LXX and Syr. נרדמו רכבי סום.

10. The ſenſe of שארות (ſo I read) Arab. *conſuluit.* See 2 Kin. 19, 22 &c.

12. בצר ſometimes *obſtruxit, occluſit.* See Iſa. 22, 10. thus it expreſſes the fortifications of cities.

LXXVII.

2. נגר Arab. *ſecuit* — more ſuitable to the paſſage, and the Syr. verſion, the framers of which read ידו, and perhaps נגרה as if from גדד *laceravit.* The learned Mr. Green hath from Lam. 3, 49 amended this paſſage, and reads עיני נגרה *mine eye trickleth down,* and is therein favoured by the Chald. Paraphraſe. Either reading makes a good ſenſe.

4. אחז *bæſit, hærere fecit,* ſee 1 Kin. 6 : 6, 10.

8. I read with Syr. and Arab. אמרו *verbum ejus.*

9. קפץ *ſhutting up the band,* to withhold. Deut. 15, 7.

10. חלותי (απαξ ג.) *precatus eſt,* ellipſis of דברה. See Chald. שנות Arab. سنا *extulit.*

13. He always triumphed over his enemies. See Pf. 68, 25, alluding to the triumphal procession; we marched to the temple, on GOD's giving victory. I read באלהינו with the versions.

15. I read with all the antient versions בזרועך.

18. Houbigant right, כגלגל *sicut rota.*

LXXVIII.

2. I render חידות *histories.* LXX, Ezek. 17, 2, διηγημα. This Psalm is no riddle or mystery; but a succinct account of the Jewish history down to David: probably for the instruction of children, and learnt by heart.

4. I read לא נכחדם, see Job 15, 18.

9. כ in the former verse influences the beginning of this. One MS. reads ונשקי ורומי rightly. רומי partic. pref. kal from רמה *projecit*—probably alludes to some historical fact unknown.

15. Schultens, Prov. 3, 20, בקע *findendo scaturire fecit.* I read in the latter clause with the LXX &c, וישקם.

19. ו in the beginning influences אמרו in the 2d clause.

26. The wind was South-east; but the Heb. has no single word — only for winds from the 4 cardinal points.

27. Ludolfus right — these were *the Locusts.*

29. One MS. right, יביא.

30. *They were scarcely estranged from their longing:* see Num. 11, 33.

31. שמן (as Judg. 3, 29) *the most mighty men in their army.* [we say *the flower.*]

34. Hare right, אלו; ו from the beginning of the next verse.

38. I read with the Chald. &c. עונם.

41. ישובו and ינסו run into one another by a very common Hebraism. תוה — the great crime of the Israelites was their continual doubt of JEHOVAH's power.

44. *Their streams could not be drunk.*

45. ו in the beginning of the former verse influences this. History, Ex. 8, 14.

47. Houbigant right, יהגר *abscidit, ictibus repetitis,* הגר is still preserved in the Arab. in the same sense.

50. Syr. sense of פלם *semitam fecit, aperuit.*

51. I read with the antient versions אונם *fortitudinis eorum.* Pf. 105, 36.

61. עזו

61. עזו = עוז ארון *ark of his strength.* נתן influences the 2d clause.

63. הוללי pret. Hophal of ילל *ululavit.* So Vulg. and Arab. LXX Rom. επιθησαν, but Ald. and Alcala επιυθηθησαν; and the Scholiast observes other copies read the same.

65. Schultens right — this a sarcasm of the Philistines, on their routing the Israelites, and taking the Ark of GOD; that he was asleep, or perhaps had drank too plentifully of wine, and was stupified. It was usual for the worshippers of one GOD, to insult the GOD of their enemies. 1 Kin. 18, 27.

66. Alludes to the emerods inflicted on the Philistines; the disgrace of which they were obliged to perpetuate, by sending the golden emerods with the ark, when it returned home to Israel.

69. I read with Syr. במו רמים *in excelsis.*

71. עלורת properly *animalia lactantia.* See the antient versions.

LXXIX.

2. Houbigant right, חירת הארץ.
5. Schultens, Prov. 3, 31, אנף *iratus est naso ardente.*
7. Two MSS. and all the antient versions, אכלו.
8. יקדמונו, see Ps. 21, 3.
11. This verse points out the exact time of composing this Psalm — after the sacking Jerusalem, and before the princes had been presented to the king of Babylon at Riblah; where they were by his order put to death. 2 Kin. 25, 18—20. They were the persons appointed unto slaughter, as Zedekiah was the person in bonds, 2 Kin. 25, 7: and from the agreement of the 6th and 7th verses with Jer. 10, 25, Jeremiah may have been the author of this Psalm.

LXXX.

See the note on the title of Ps. 60. This sung alternately by the priests and people; who join in the chorus.

4. עשן Syr. *prævaluit* — all the versions (except Chald.) read in the end עבדך.

6. I read in the end, with the versions, לנו. After the establishment of the two mighty empires of Egypt and Babylon, the

land of Ifrael, lying between both, was the perpetual fource of quarrels between them.

10. I read with the LXX, Vulg. and Arab. כסה.

13. Senfe of יכרסמנה from Arab. كرنم *vorax*.

15. I read with the Arab. verfion שרפוה באש וכסחוה *qui eam combufferunt igne, et fpoliarunt eam*, taking the fenfe of the latter from the Arab. *fpoliavit opibus univerfis*.

LXXXI.

5. בעת צאתו = בצאתו, the particle influences the latter claufe, where I read שפת לא ידעה ישמע *linguam, quam non intellexit, audivit*.

6. Firft claufe, *I removed his fhoulder from the burden*: LXX read in the latter תעבדנה. דוד was a large veffel, in which the earth was mixed, and worked up for making the brick.

7. Arab. סתר *texit*.

8. The touchftone to try Ifrael, was their continuance in the worfhip of the One true GOD.

11. LXX render אבה προσιχε rightly — Arab. *recordatus fuit, attentus*.

12. I take the fenfe of שררות from שרר Arab. *malus fuit*.

15. עָתַם from עוה preferved in Arab. عما for عوا *pernicie, calamitate affectus fuit* — thence the noun عاثمة *pernicies*. The Syr. verfion renders it in this manner.

16. Houbigant right, מצוף דבש, and in the end (with Syr.) אשביעו.

LXXXIII.

Probably on the war of Jehofhaphat with the Edomites, Moabites, Ammonites &c. 2 Chr. 20 —

5. I read יחד ועליך ברית יכרתו, as Chald. and Syr.

11. I read שיתמו ונדיבמו *pone eos, et magnates eorum*. Chald.

12. I render נאות *pafcua*, for I cannot find it ever ufed for *habitaculum, domus*.

13. גלגל from Arab. جل, thence the noun *frumenti calamus, et ftipula*: fo If. 17, 13.

14. I make an ellipfis of אשר before the 2 verbs, as do all the antient verfions.

16. Schultens, Prov. 3, 35 — קלון is *inuftio infamiæ*, קלה *uffit*.

aſſit. I render י here, and at the beginning of the 18th verſe, by *donec:* a ſimilar uſe of it is in Gen. 18, 5, and Judg. 3, 11.

LXXXIV.

1. There is ever an ellipſis of שר, or אדני, before צבאות.

5. I read with Syr. מסלותך. Prov. 16, 17. Here the word means the journey to Jeruſalem thrice every year.

6. This and the next verſe deſcribe the journey. The valley of Baca probably the ſame as the valley of Rephaim mentioned 2 Sam. 5, 22 & 24: for we find that *Mulberries* grew there, (which is the meaning of Baca), and might give the name to the valley. This place had pools in it, to collect the rain water; and ſo was a convenient place for travellers to take up their quarters on the road. I read with LXX מעון *manſionem, hoſpitium.* They render it τόπον, as Pſ. 68, 6; 71, 3. גם *quoniam,* as in Mal. 3, 15, *nunc beatos dicimus arrogantes, quoniam ædificati ſunt facientes impietatem, quoniam tentaverunt Deum, et liberantur.* Nold. p. 202. יעשה Arab. غطا *plenus fuit.*

7. Chald. חיל *a valley.* The country round Jeruſalem was very mountainous, ſo that the reſting places for travellers were in the valleys: the meaning is, *from ſtage to ſtage.* The author was probably of Ephraim, and the valley of Baca his firſt ſtage. I read in the latter clauſe יראו, with an ellipſis of the particle עד. See alſo Gen. 13, 10.

10. Arab. سعى *tenuiora rerum ſectatus eſt.* דור Chald. *ordinavit,* thence דוור *præfectus,* probably the ſenſe here.

11. שמש partic. preſ. Kal Chald. *miniſtravit.* The ſame ſenſe in Syr. and Samar. מגן part. preſ. Hiphil.

LXXXV.

The firſt 3 verſes ſeem unconnected with the reſt of this Pſalm, and to be part of ſome other—perhaps ſhould begin the 60th Pſalm, and the 3 firſt verſes of the 60th ſhould begin this. That parts of different Pſalms are thus put together, ſee Pſ. 40 and 70—alſo 57 and 108—and 60 and 108.

8. This verſe is the demand of the perſon enquiring; and the anſwer of the high prieſt, or prophet, declaring the oracle of GOD.

13. I read with Syr. צדיק. *Walking before God* a common phraſe.

phrase. Isa 38,3. *The way*, in the latter clause, *the law of Moses*. The last 4 verses of this Psalm afford a positive proof of the actual exercise of the equal Providence promised in the Mosaic Dispensation.

LXXXVI.

2. I read with Syr. חסיד אתה *benignus tu*.
11. יחד from הדה *gavisus fuit*.
17. עמי *mea causa, propter me*; as Ps. 119, 65. and 2 Chr. 20, 17.

LXXXVII.

1. This Psalm is certainly no more than a fragment, as Hare hath observed. The beginning is lost, and probably the end also. The Chaldee Paraphrast was sensible of this, and hath made the 1st verse a part of the Title, beginning the Psalm at the 2d verse, but reading the 1st somewhat differently, probably thus: שיר יסוד בפי אבות מקדם *canticum fundatum in ore patrum priscorum*.

4. I make אזכיר pret. Hiph. a Chaldaism for הזכיר, and an ellipsis of אשר, *qui celebraret*. I point הגה *istas*. An ellipsis of יאמר in the latter clause, or the verb in the next verse hath a retrospective force.

5. Speaks here of some great prince, probably Solomon, who fixed the seat of empire at Jerusalem. I read in the end עליונה *iste stabilivit eam supremam*.

7. I read with LXX, Syr. &c. מעוני *habitationes*. Also וְשָׁרִים with Syr.

LXXXVIII.

This Psalm hath 3 titles, the last only belongs to it. Whence the other 2 have been taken, it is of no great moment to know; only it proves that the titles are not now to be depended on, as being of the same antiquity with the Psalms themselves, as Hare hath observed. — A Prayer of a person shut up in a separate house for the leprosy, who seems to be in the last stages of the distemper. This disease was understood under the Mosaic dispensation to be the immediate stroke of God.

1. Hare right, שיעתי, LXX right, יומם.
5. הפשי from Arab. جفش *capsa exigua, domus parva*: so

the Latins had their *domus exilis Plutonia*, THE GRAVE; here it marks the feparate houfe, where the fick perfon was fhut up. I read in the fecond claufe בכמו חללים. The laft claufe literally is, *fince they are cut off from thy Jurifdiction*, as יד often fignifies.

6. All the verfions, except Chald, read בצלמות *in umbra mortis*—certainly right.

7. סמך *irruit, incubuit*; as in Ezek. 24, 2. I read in the latter claufe with LXX, and Symmachus, עניתני, the metaphor of a ftorm at fea to exprefs affliction, is common in the Pfalms.

8. One MS. כלוא part. pahul, kal—ellipfis of the verb הייתי.

10. The Interrogations in this and the following verfes imply the ftrongeft negations.

15. Senfe of נער Arab. *infeftatus fuit ab afilis equus, vel afinus.* Chald. *ultro citroque movit fe.* The latter claufe, *I have borne thy horrors, I am diftracted.*

16. *Thine indignations have paffed over me.* Arab. צמרת *ad offa percuffit.*

18. Hare right, מחשבים, as in ver. 6. Hare right, that this is but a fragment, and wants the latter part: it being quite contrary to the cuftom of the Pfalms to conclude without either a prayer for deliverance, or thankfgiving for obtaining it.

LXXXIX.

Probably on the defeat and flaughter of Jofiah by Pharaoh Neco at Megiddo. See v. 38—45.

1. I read לעולם.

2. All the verfions, except Chald. read כי אמרת *quoniam dixifti*—2d claufe, *loving kindnefs fhall be built up for ever*—3d claufe, *the heavens, thou didft place the confirmation of thy faithfulnefs in them:* fee ver. 35, and 36, where it appears that the fun, the moon, and the bow in the fky, were the tokens of confirmation given by GOD to the covenant made with David. כי in the 1ft claufe influences תכן in the 3d.

10. Thou didft crufh Egypt with as much eafe, as a mighty warrior deftroyeth a fingle enemy, even at one blow.

15. I read with Syr. תרועך.

19. Two MSS. and all the verfions, read חסידיך plur. but fing. feems right; the holy one is Samuel, JEHOVAH's prophet.

22. LXX

22. LXX render ישׂיא rightly. I take the meaning from the Arab. נשׂא *crevit.*

29. שׂמתי influences the whole latter clause.

33. *Neither will I give the lye to my faithfulness*: so Aquila.

47. Hare right, מה חדל, as Ps. 39, 4.

50. Hare right, קול רבים עמים.

XC.

This Psalm is of much later date than Moses. The age of man then was not 70 and 80 years—he lived 120, Joshua 110, and their contemporaries in proportion. Probably it was written about the return from the captivity, when they were rebuilding the temple and city: and this was *the work of their hands*, which they pray GOD to *bless* and *prosper*.

Though (as the learned Mr. Green observes) the Psalmist laments the diminution of life, no one expression limits it to the shortened period of that generation, who were untimely cut off for their sins. But it plainly and wholly refers to the decrease of man's age from *a thousand* years, the original sum, to 70, or at most 80 —— a diminution sufficient to make him treat the present life of man as a phantom, or watch in the night.

1. מעון abbreviation of צור מעון, as in Ps. 31, 2.

2. I end this verse with אתה, (as in Ps. 93, 2), and begin the next with אל — as LXX, and Arab.

3. שׁובו in the latter clause, from Job 33, 25, *recovery from sickness* — here the Psalmist prays, that the years of the age of man may again be lengthened out to their original number. On reconsidering this passage I think Hare right, and that שׁובו is equivalent to שׁובו אל עפר *return to the dust*, Gen. 3, 19.

5. Arab. זרם *refecuit repetito ictu.* שׁנה inf. kal as a gerund. The same thought Job 14, 19—21.

7. I read here, with Mr. Green, כן *sic.*

9. Arab. sense of فنى *periit, consumptus fuit.* הגה from Syr. הגׂ *imaginatus fuit,* as מלה from מלל. Hare right, כלו.

10. I read רבתם *multitudo eorum,* with LXX, and all the versions.

12. Nothing can be more natural than this petition, after the complaint of the shortness of human life. But LXX join למות to the former verse, and read ימינך at the beginning of this.

XCI.

XCI.

1. אשרי seems lost at the beginning, *happy the man that dwelleth, that lodgeth, that faith.*
2. ל *quantum ad*, Job 28, 28. Judg. 21, 7.
3. מדבר הוות, as Pf. 38, 12. The falfity of the accufation fhould be providentially brought to light.
4. I read יסחרך with the verfions—ellipfis of כ before צנה, fee note on Pf. 5, 12.—Jofh. 9, 5. Ezek. 4, 12.
9. Hare right, כי אמרת—The fpeaker the fame till v. 14.
10. This plague generally interpreted a ftroke of the leprofy.
13. Bochart—שחל and כפיר *ferpents*, as well as *lions*. Lib. 3. c. 3.
14. I read with LXX, &c. כי חסה. Speech of JEHOVAH to the end.

XCII.

3. I read with LXX, בהגיון עלי כנור, *in a foft ftrain on the harp*. See Note Pf. 9, 16.
7. Ellipfis of כי in the beginning here, as Lam. 1, 10.
10. I and Symmachus בשמן, ως ελαια.

XCIII.

2. Though GOD exifted from all eternity, yet the throne of his government as to this earth, could not be fixed till its formation.
3. דכים from דכה *contrivit*.
4. Alludes to the thunder — מ influences the 2d claufe.

XCIV.

3. The particle עד־מתי extends to the end of the 7th verfe.
15. LXX rightly render כי עד, ιως ου.
17. Laft claufe — *my foul had well nigh inhabited filence.* So JEHOVAH is faid to inhabit eternity, *i. e.* to be eternal.
20. I render עלי חק *fub fpecie ftatuti*.

XCV.

Houbigant right, this Pfalm has 3 parts —— the 1ft part of the people, to the middle of ver. 7 — the reft of the 7th and 8th verfes fpoken by the prieft, or prophet, to the people — the remainder by JEHOVAH to the people.

7. I render

266 *Remarks on select Passages in*

7. I render יד *dominion*, or *jurisdiction*, as Pf. 88, 5.

9. אשר *certe*, as 1 Sam. 15, 20. גם *quamvis*, as Ruth 1,12. Though the Israelites had seen God's stupendous works in Egypt, and at the red sea, yet they desponded at every difficulty.

10. I read with all the versions בדור ההוא *with that generation.*

XCVI.

Delivered by David to Asaph, &c. to be sung at bringing the ark into the city of David. See 1 Chr. 16, 7 & 23.

1. First Hemistic wanting in the other copy.
2. First Hemistic wanting also in the other copy. In the 2d, the other has מיום אל יום.
3. The other את כבודו.
4. The other right, ונורא.
6. The other עז וחדוה במקומו.
8. The other לפניו.
9. The other in the latter clause מלפניו. In the former I read with LXX, בחדרת, εν αυλη.
10. First and last Hemistics both lost out of the other copy.
11. See the other copy — 12, 13, see the other.

XCVII.

1. איים not necessarily *islands*, but at large a region or country, so Is. 20, 6. Jerusalem and Judah. Chap. 23,2 and 6, Tyre, though then a city of the continent. Jer. 25, 22, the countries of the tribes of Arabs, beyond the dead sea, are so called, Dedan, &c.

3. Hare right, ולהבה תלהט, as Pf. 83, 15, and 106, 18.

10. I read with Syr. ומיד.

11. I read with the versions זרח *orta est*. Chald. endeavours to express both.

12. God's *name*, and *memorial*, the same, see Exod. 3, 15.

XCIX.

1. I read with all the versions ישב הכרובים, as Pf. 80, 1.

3. The Chorus; and I suspect it to be deficient, and that it should be read thus:

רוממו

רוממו יהוה אלהינו
יודו שמו גדול ונורא
כי קדוש יהוה אלהינו

The first Hemistic is justified by the 5th and 9th verses. The last by the 9th.

4. I read יהוה מלך — ועז has no commodious sense, and the word יהוה is wanting, to which אתה may be referred.

5. I read here also in the end כי קדוש יהוה אלהינו.

8. The sense of נקם from Arab. *objurgavit — he spared them, but shewed his displeasure at their misdoings.*

C.

3. הוא *solus*, as it would be best rendered, Deut. 4; 35, 39: also ch. 32, 39. 1 Kin. 18, 39. In the 3d clause I read with Chald. ולו אנחנו — there is either an ellipsis of another אנחנו before עמו, or it hath dropt out of the text—this was easy, the same word being repeated.

4. I read with Syr. וברכו.

CI.

4. The sense of רע from رَوغ *versutia, dolo usus est.*

5. Houbigant right, רהב לבב. Here, and v. 8, צמת Arab. *siluit.* Syr. thus in v. 8.

6. הוא requires *ille solus*, as in the last Psalm.

CII.

Evidently about the end of the Captivity. Pathetically sets forth the melancholy condition of the Jews, as one single person.

3. בעשן 2 MSS, and all the versions, except Syr.

5. I read דבחה, as Job 19, 20, see note there.

6. קאת and כום see Bochart l.2. c.20 and 24. p.272 & 292.

8. The antient Oath was — GOD do unto me, as he hath done unto such an one, (Jerusalem, for instance), and more also, if &c. So Abraham and his seed are said to be made a *blessing*, i.e. the highest wish of any man in favour of another should be, GOD bless thee as he blessed Abraham.

17. כי influences from ver. 16 to the 2 verbs here.

23. Ellipsis of אם before both these verbs.

24. Hare right, אל תערני, all the versions *ne abripias me.*
28. I read with Chald. and Syr. ישכונו בארץ.

CIV.

Houbigant right — sung alternately by 2 Choruses. One addresses itself *to* JEHOVAH, the other speaks *of* him.

3. Ellipsis of הוא in the beginning; or rather המקרה a contraction of הוא מקרה. As to the thought in the latter part of the verse, see Ps. 18, 12.

4. I read אש ולהט *ignis et flamma.*

11. Syr. reads excellently — וישבעו פראים צמאים *et saturantur onagri sitientes.* The phrase שבר צמא is not a little uncouth.

13. I read מעליותיך *e cœnaculis tuis* — thus it answers to the latter clause.

15. Hare right, להצהיר. צהר Arab. *unxit caput liquamine.*

16. Arab. שבע *profusus fuit.*

18. שפן not the conie, but the αρκτομυς of the Greeks, and the Aljarbuo of the Arabs. We have no name for it. A drawing of it, (from a creature brought over by Dr. Sherard), and descriptions, are in Haym's Tesoro Brittanico, vol. 2. p. 124 &c. See also Bochart 3, 33.

20. תשת from שתת *egressus est.* The root is still preserved in this sense in the Ethiopic.

21. אל *planities,* as Gen. 14, 6, *the plain of Paran.* Properly the υπωρεια, the skirts of the forest.

25. זה *tale,* as Judg. 18, 4.

33. שיח *devotio,* from Arab. שאה *peregrinavit religionis ergo.* Schultens, Prov. 6, 22.

CV.

This as far as v. 15. is said, 1 Chr. 16, 7, to have been given by David to Asaph — there another copy. *We compare.*

4. עזו abbreviation of עזון ארון, Ps. 78, 61.

12. כמעט *quasi nihil,* Prov. 10, 20.

16. וַיִּקְרָא I point fut. hiph. Jer. 32, 23.

18. I read with Syr. בברזל *propter ferrum.* באה often *abivit, occubuit,* applied to the Sun: *occubuit anima ejus propter ferrum.* Judg. 19, 26 —— *and towards the morning the woman fainted and fell at the door of the house.*

19. The

19. The first clause refers to the completion of his interpretations of the dreams of the chief butler, and baker; the second to the interpretation of Pharaoh's dreams, called the oracle of JEHOVAH, because sent by him to Pharaoh. Gen. 41, 25.

22. I read with the versions ליסור *ut castigaret*.

25. The latter clause, see Exod. 1, 10.

27. I read with the versions שם בם. דברי often *acta, gesta*, so 1 Kin. 11, 41, and other passages.

28. Hare right, ולא שמרו *tamen non observaverunt*.

35. I read with Syr. ויאכלו in both clauses.

40. I read with all the versions שאלו. שלו I render *quail*, tho' Ludolfus, p. 169, &c. makes it probable that they were *locusts*.

41. I read with LXX נהרות.

CVI.

2. I read with Arab. גבורת *omnipotentiam, fortitudinem*.

3. I read with the Syr. in the first clause משפטי, and in the latter (with all the versions) עשי *facientes*.

4. The former clause is explained by the 47th verse. For this Psalm was probably written when the captivity drew towards an end.

5. Hare right, גאוליך *thy redeemed ones*. Compare v. 47 with the 2d verse of the next Psalm.

7. I read with LXX עלים. The march Exod. 13, 18. ב *versus*, as Num. 13, 17. The rebellion here spoken of, see Exod. 14; 10—12, before they reached the red sea.

14. Compare Pf. 78, 17—20. Clear illustration.

15. All the versions, except Chald. render רזון *saturitatem*—I think the true reading דרון *fastidium*, found with its original vowel דראון, Isa. 66, 24.

26. Compare Ezek. 20, 23. *Lift up the hand* = *swear*. Deut. 32, 40. Num. 14, 30—32.

27. נפל in hiphil often *sorte possidendum dedit*, [*fell* to such a one], Ezek. 45, 1: 47, 22, and 48, 29.

28. The Syr. and some other versions intimate some obscene ceremonies practised with the idol of that Deity.

30. He did not pray, but executed judgment; putting Zimri to death according to the sentence, Num. 25; 4, 5.

37. שרים synonimous to Baalim, *the gods of the land*. Arab. سيد *dominus, princeps*.

43. Arab.

43. Arab. لَعَسَ *rebellavit*.
47. Syr. שבח *hymnum cecinit*, Matt. 26, 30. Mar. 14, 26.

The Fifth Book.

Psalm CVII.

3. Hare right, מימין *a meridie*.
10. *Miserably fettered with iron.*
17. Houbigant right, אֱוִלִים, but the sense, Syr. *irruentes*. So used Act. 19, 29. Leprosy seems aimed at; and as persons so afflicted by God, were by the law to be shut up; a recovery from that distemper might well be called *breaking the doors of brass*, and *cutting asunder the bars of iron*. In this participle is the original vowel.
20. I read with the versions וימלטם.
25. יעמור and יקם in this, and v. 29, have changed their places, as Hare rightly conjectures. Confirmed by the Syr. version.
28. I think יושיעם right here, and v. 27.
29. I read with Syr. גלי הים.
41. I read with Syr. משפחיתם *familias eorum*.
43. I read with the versions ויתבונן.

CVIII = LVII, and LX.

First 5 verses nearly the same as the last 5 of Ps. 57—compare.
1. נכון לבי supplied from the other copy — all the versions except Chald.
6. The remaining 8 verses are the same as the last 8 of Ps. 60, with some small variations. For the notes, see on Ps. 57, and 60.

CIX.

The thanksgiving of an innocent man, against whom an accusation had been brought by his adversaries for some capital crime, and whose ruin was thought so certain, that they already began to triumph over him, as if condemned; when by some remarkable interposition of providence, his innocence is made to appear, the falsity of the accusation accufation is manifefted, and his adverfaries are covered with fhame and difgrace.

1. I read with Æthiop. תפלתי, ellipfis of אל.

2. Hare right, רשע — latter claufe *they have spoken against me a slander of falsity*, for לשון, Ezek. 36, 3.

4. תפלה equivalent to, or an abbreviation of, תפלתי לך, as Pf. 69, 14.

5. I render with the Arab. verfion, *imprecati sunt*. Arab. סום or שום *flagitavit*. This rendering makes the Pfalm confiftent; the curfes being put in the mouth of the enemies of the Pfalmift, to whom they certainly belong.

7. תפלה here *deprecatio*, the cry for mercy from the criminal on condemnation. The phrafe תהיה לחטאה properly *frustra fit*, fee LXX.

10. I read with LXX יורשו fut. Hoph. *ejiciantur*.

19. I read with the verfions כמוח *ficut cingulum*.

20. The literal rendering is, *hæc eſt actio adverſariorum meorum apud Jehovam*. For פעלה fignifies *actio, molimen*. This is the fubject matter of their prayer.

21. I read with LXX. Alexan. עשה חסד אתי.

24. *Caro mea abnegavit pinguedinem*. מִשָּׁמֶן a noun, as If. 17, 4.

31. I read מִשְׁפָּט *a pœnis judicialibus*.

CX.

Probably written on David's war with the Ammonites, which ended in taking Rabbah; but in its fecondary and trueft fenfe is applicable to the Meffiah; and is fo applied Act. 2, 34, and Heb. 7; and indeed fome paffages feem only applicable to HIM.

2. I read with the LXX, Syr. and Arab. מטה עז לך ישלח. See Ezek. 19; 11, 12, 14.

3. I read in the firft claufe בחדרי קדש *in atriis sanctuarii*. This was probably the place, where the army was muftered at Jerufalem. In the latter claufe I read with Hare כטל *ficut ros*.

5. I think the antient verfions read here יהוה.

6. I read with Hare, and Cappellus, מלא גאיות גויית *implens valles cadaveribus*.

7. I point

7. I point יִשְׁתֶּה with Mudge, fut. hiph. *potandum dabit*. על כן *ut*, so Lam. 3, 21. The phrase ירים ראש in the latter clause frequently put for giving the victory: Pf. 27, 6.

CXI.

Alphabetical, each Hemistic a different letter — detached sentences.

2. The latter clause from Mudge. דרש Æthiop. *composuit, concinnavit* — had this sense in Hebrew; as it is rendered by a version quoted by Chrysostom on this passage. חפץ must be *institutum*.

10. I read with LXX, עשיה.

CXII.

Alphabetical, as the last.

2. דור *habitation*, as Pf. 24, 6. See the note there.

4. I read with LXX. Alex. יה, or יהוה, in the end of this verse. The 3 adjectives now want a substantive.

5. טוב איש = אשרי איש in ver. 1.

9. נָתַן a participle.

10. כָּעַם a participle.

CXIII.

In 2 parts. The Priest begins in the first verse; 2d and 3d belong to the people; 4th to the priest; the rest to the people.

5. Hare right — בשמים belongs to לשבת, and בארץ to לראות; the structure of the period uncommon.

CXIV.

2. Hare thinks this a fragment, because there is no antecedent to the relative in the first clause. But the reading seems faulty — perhaps היתה יהודה קדש ליהוה *Judah was holiness to Jehovah*, i. e. was consecrated to Him, as *the tribe*, among whom he would dwell: for now קדשו לו = לקדשו. But *Quære*.

7. I read with the versions חלה הארץ, or חול, *contremuit terra*: answer to the question in the foregoing verses — Do you ask why the sea fled, why Jordan ran back to its source? The very earth trembled. But *Quære*, I think the compilers of the versions read יהוה not אדון.

8. I read

8. I read with the versions in the end מים למעיני *in fontes aquarum.*

CXV.

1. I read with all the versions ועל אמתך.
4. I read with the versions עצבי הגוים *simulacra gentium.*
7. I read with all the versions (except Syr.) ידים להם and אף אין יש —רגלים להם.— Æthiop. reads here, as Pf. 135, 17, רוח בפיהם.
8. I read with the versions וכל, in the beginning of the second clause.
9. I read with the versions בית ישראל, so Pf. 135, 19.
12. I read with the versions וברכנו *et benedixit nobis.*

CXVI.

For recovery from a desperate fit of sickness, probably the leprosy; the leper confined, by the direction of the law.

2. I read with Syr. ביום אקרא. [*Quære*].
9. I read with Syr. ואתהלך.
10. אֲדַבֵּר fut. niph. דבר *perdidit*; *credidi quod perditus essem.*
12. One MS. right, תגמולױ.
14. יקר *gravis.* Schult. Prov. 1, 13.
16. ואני in the beginning. The repetition of אני עבדך an error of the transcriber. I read with Hare.

CXVII.

1. שבחי rendered as Pf. 106, 47. Israel was divided into tribes שבטי — lineages משפחות — households בתים — families אמות or אמים: see Num. 25, 15. Josh. 7; 16—18.

CXVIII.

6. I read with all the versions יהוה לי בעזרי, as in the beginning of the verse following.
12. כ *antequam,* as Deut. 24, 13. Isai. 18, 5.
13. It does not appear, to whom the Psalmist here speaks. From all the versions it seems probable, that the true reading was דחה הרהיתי *impellendo impulsus eram.*
14. I read with all the versions זמרתי.
20. This verse spoken by the priest — the next by the king — the

—the three next a Chorus by the people—the 25th by the king—the two next by the prieſt—the 28th by the king, and the laſt the grand Chorus of the whole.

27. חג (Ex. 23, 18) *the victim*. Houbigant therefore wrong.

CXIX.

3. I read with Syr. ובדרכיו.
9. I read with the verſions לשמר דבריך.
14. I read with Syr. מעל.
23. I read with the verſions ועבדך.
24. In the end חקיך is dropt, but preſerved by the LXX.
26. ספר from Syr. ſenſe, *inquiſivit*.
29. I read with Syr. הורני *doce me*.
30. שויתי ſenſe from Arab. שיי *voluit*.
34. I read with the verſions בכל לבי.
38. Houbigant right, ואשר, *et incedam feliciter*.
43. עד מאד belong certainly to ver. 47. Syr. does not acknowledge them here. LXX. and Arab. have them *there*.
48. Hare right, אשר אהבתי crept in from the former verſe.
49. I read with the verſions דברך.
51. I read with the verſions וכתורתך.
56. I read with Syr. זאת היתה לי נחמה — a word wanting is there preſerved.
57. I read with LXX, חלקי אתה.
58. I read with the verſions בכל לבי.
61. I read with the verſions ותורתך.
68. I read with LXX. and Syr. טוב אתה יהוה.
69. I read with the verſions ואני בכל לבי.
70. I read with the verſions ואני.
75. I read with Chald. and Vulg. ובאמונה.
77. עוה *torſit*, (*torquere filum* uſual), *torquere fraudes*, *mendacia*, frequent in Heb.
85. Houbigant right, כרו from Arab. כרר *repetivit*. LXX. render right, שיחות ἀδολεσχίας.
90. I point כֹּנַנְתָּ, and read with LXX, הארץ.
95. I read with Syr. ועדותיך.
103. I read with all the verſions אמרתיך.
113. סעפים, ſee 1 Kings 18, 21.

118. I read

118. I read with Aquila, and Symmachus, חשבת *reputasti.* LXX. חשבתי.

128. I read with Mudge לכל פקודיך ישרתי, and all the versions, but Chald. None have the second כל.

130. I read with Chald. יאיר חשכים *illuminat obscuros.*

131. I read with the versions ואשאפה רוח *et traxi spiritum.*

137. I read with Chald. LXX. and Syr. וישרים.

145. I read with the versions בכל לבי.

148. I read with the versions (except Arab.) לשיחי. [*Quære.*]

CXX.

This and the fourteen following Psalms are called Songs of ascent, or of the steps. Why—is not clear. Syr. hints—they were on coming up from Babylon. The phraseology is much of that age: perhaps some were on this occasion, and others on *the coming up* of the Jews three times a year to Jerusalem. See Mudge.

1. I read with all the versions בצרה לי.
3. See Mudge.
4. שנן Chald. sense *explicit.* Version of Jerem. 51, 11.
5. I point גַּרְתִּי *incolatio mea :* and read with the versions גרתי משכה.
6. I read with the versions עם שנאי.

CXXI.

5. The right hand in the Scripture is the south; whence the propriety of the Metaphor here. [*Quære.*]

CXXII.

3. This is the first instance in the Psalms, of the abbreviation of אשר into ש. The internal marks of several of the following Psalms, particularly the 123d, and 137th, will make it probable, that this abbreviation is the work of a later age, and at least as recent as the captivity. חבר Arab. *pulchrum fecit.*

9. I read אבקשה נא.

CXXIV.

5. I read with Syr. עברו. All the Fr. MSS. הזדונים.

CXXVI.

4. Houbigant right, שובה partic. pahul *reducta est.* With
a full

a full stream, as the rivers southward. For all the rivers near Babylon run southward, consequently grow larger as they go farther south. [Perhaps made at Jerusalem after the return of part.]

7. Aben Ezra interprets מישך *canistrum, sportula*, perhaps right—it is a small quantity, and is opposed to the sheaves in the end of the verse. Or from the Arab. sense, *tenuit, apprehendit, continuit*, as much as the hand can take up and hold.

CXXVII.

2. I point יֻתַּן fut. hoph. and read פן *vix*. The alteration is small, and the sense much better. *Sleep is scarcely bestowed on his beloved one*. This particle, Prov. 5, 6: *Thou canst scarcely take life into consideration*—death being so certain a consequence of following her, the chance of life is not worth putting into the balance against it.

3. Hare right, שכרו necessary.

5. ידברו a forensic term, *cum causam egerint*, Schultens, Prov. 27, 11.

CXXX.

6. ל (לאדני) *coram*, 2 Sam. 18, 28. I read in the second clause with the LXX, Vulg. and Arab. versions, מושמרים לבקר עדי לילה *a matutina vigilia usque ad noctem*. Houbigant's reading is good.

CXXXI.

2. The sense *I have no desire*, see Ps. 119, 30; *sed silere feci animam meam*.

CXXXII.

1. ינורת sense from Arab. عني *cum cura incubuit rei*.

2. אשר influences the 2d clause.

6. The field of the forest is the territory of Kirjath-jearim, where the Ark was, and whence David fetched it.

8. Ellipsis of עם *set forward*. See Num. 10, 35.

9. The holy ones here, and ver. 16, are the high priests, of whom there were two in the time of David, Zadok and Abiathar. See Note on Ps. 52, 2.

CXXXIII.

1. גב a noun, its sense from Arab. جم *multus fuit*, thence the noun *turba, cœtus*. 2. I read

2. I read with all the versions שירד על-זקן.
3. Houbigant right—the mountain here not *Zion*, but *Sioun*, Deut. 4, 48, as part of Hermon, should be שִׂיאן.

CXXXIV.
1. גשו הנה or באו הנה = הִנָּה.
2. Ellipsis of ב before קדש, *in sanctitate*.

CXXXVI.
9. I read with all the versions לממשלת בלילה *in dominium noctis*.
25. I read שׁנֻתן *qui dat*.

CXXXVII.
3. I point תִּילָלֵינוּ thus—it is a Chaldaism for שׁוללינו *spoliarunt nos*. I read also שבחה *hymnum*. The former from all the versions—the latter from the LXX.
5. I read with Syr. תשכחני ימיני or תשכחי *obliviscatur mei dextra mea*.
8. I read with Chald. and Syr. שׁוֹרְדָה *devastatrix*: if Babylon had been already wasted, the wish were useless.

CXXXVIII.
1. I read with all the versions אודך יהוה.
2. גדל hiph. *magnificavit*—he preferred *faithfulness to his promise* to the attribute of his *power*.
3. I read with Syr. תענני ותרהיב *respondisti mihi, et roborasti*.
6. I read יודע benoni kal, with an ellipsis of יש.
8. *Jehovah will make an end in my behalf.*

CXXXIX.
1. I read with the versions ותדעני *et cognoscis me*.
3. רבעי a Chaldaism for רבצי *cubile meum*. The sense of זרית from Arab. זר *visitavit*.
6. I read פלאי הדעת *mirabilis est scientia*.
9. Hare reads beautifully אשא כנפי כנפי שחר.
11. ישיפני the sense from Arab. *abiit, evanuit*. Houbigant right, יעור *occæcabit*.
16. The last clause *dum nondum esset unio inter eos*.
17. Hare right, אלי *Deus meus*.
18. עמך *on thy side*, see Job 31, 5, and 2 Kings 10, 15.

19. אנשי דמים are ινδρες θανάτου, men, who for their crimes deserve to die.

20. I read נשאו = נשאו ידיהם and so all the versions. צריך a Chaldaism for צריך *inimici tui.*

21. Houbigant right, ובמתקוממיך in the latter clause.

24. דרך עצב *via idoli,* the worship of idols, opposed here to דרך עולם, the way which was to continue for ever, the worship of the one true God.

CXL.

2. I read with LXX, כל היום.

5. I read with Syr. in the 3d clause ליד מעגלי.

9. Selah must be either after תפק, or after מסבי, in the next verse. I read with Arab. אל ירומו.

10. I read in the beginning ימטיר, see Ps. 11, 6.

CXLI.

Mudge right — this Psalm by Jeremiah, on the death of Gedaliah and his Company, slain by Ishmael. The Prophet was probably invited, but was warned not to partake of the entertainment, which was accompanied with some idolatrous practices; and thereby escaped sharing in the dismal catastrophe which befel those present.

3. I read with LXX. שמרה and with Mudge make נצרה a noun. דל *reciprocatio,* Schultens, Prov. 26, 7.

5. I read with the versions יעלמנו *scientiam doceat.* In the 2d clause I read ושמן רשע, with the versions. I render אל יני *non impinguet,* from Arab. נוי *pinguis evasit.* In the latter clause I read כי עוד תפלתי, the ו in its proper place.

6. נעם the Arab. sense *commodum, vel opportunum fuit aliquid.*

7. I read with Alex. &c. copies of the LXX. עצמיהם, αυτων, so Syr. and Arab.

10. I read במכמרי רשעים.

CXLII.

2. This verse ends with רוחי.

4. I read with all the versions מביט, ellipsis of אהיה before this and the following participle ראה.

CXLIII.

CXLIII.

9. I read here חסיתי, with LXX, &c.

CXLIV.

2. I render חסדי as אלהי חסדי in Pf. 59, 17.

8. *Sons of the ſtranger* the Philiſtines; who had broken the league to which they had ſworn. The author had in view the 18th Pſalm to this verſe: and indeed this verſe ſeems to end the Pſalm, and the next verſe to begin a new one.

10. I read with Syr. and Vulg. את דוד עבדך.

11. I point רָעָה *a gladio vorante.*

12. Le Clerc here rightly ſupplies the אמרו; for thoſe were the boaſts of the ſons of the ſtranger, to which the latter hemiſtic of the laſt verſe is an anſwer. [Q.]

CXLV.

Alphabetical, but has ſome connection.

5. I read at the end of the firſt clauſe ידברו, and of the 2d ישיחו, on the authority of the verſions.

6. I read with the verſions (except Syr.) תספרנה.

9. I read with LXX, לכל קויו. (LXX Alex.)

14. At this verſe נ has been dropt, but is retained in all the verſions except Chald. See Houbigant.

CXLVI.

4. עשתנתיו ſee note Job 12, 8.

5. Hare right, שׁשׂברו *cujus ſpes.*

CXLVII.

1. Hare right, זמרו in the 2d clauſe, and in the laſt לישרים נאוה. The ſenſe requires the firſt; and the word wanting in the ſecond is ſupplied from the ſame Hemiſtic, Pſ. 33, 1.

3. The ſenſe of עצבותם from Arab. *fractum habuit ovis cornu.*

8. An hemiſtic loſt, but preſerved by the LXX, ועשב לעבדת אדם *et herbam in utilitatem hominis*, ſee Pſ. 104, 14.

11. Here, according to all the antient verſions, except Chald. endeth this Pſalm; the next verſe beginning another. Probably, as the following Pſalm hath no title, it has careleſsly been added to the former.

CXLVIII.

CXLVIII.

6. Hare right, יעברו, see Jer. 5, 22.
8. I read with Syr. רוח וסערה.

CL.

4. מנים here = מנענעים, 2 Sam. 6, 5, there rendered *Cornets.* But being derived from נוע *motitavit*, it was probably the fame, or like the Siftrum of the Egyptians.

Deut. XXXII.

The following Translation, though new in several parts of it, is not here inserted, as being finished or perfect. But since two sentences in it are quoted in the New Testament as foretelling *the Adoption of the Gentiles*; it is necessary to the evidence for Christianity, as depending upon Prophecy, that this Divine Song be here considered: and the following State of it, though capable of much improvement, will give some general idea of the whole.

1. Give ear, O ye heavens! and I will speak;
   and hear, O earth! the words of my mouth.
2. Let my doctrine drop, as the rain;
   let my speech distil, as the dew:
   as the small rain, upon the tender herb;
   and as the showers upon the grass.
3. Verily I will proclaim the name of JEHOVAH:
   ascribe ye greatness unto our GOD.
4. The rock! perfect is his work;
   verily all his ways are judgment:
   a GOD of truth, and without iniquity;
   just and upright is He!
5. They are corrupted; they are not His; sons of pollution!
   a generation perverse and crooked!
6. Is this the return ye make to JEHOVAH?
   O people, foolish and unwise!
   Is not He thy father, thy redeemer?
   He, who made thee, and established thee!
7. Remember thou the days of old;
   consider the years of many generations:
   ask thy father, and he will shew thee;
   thy elders, and they will tell thee.

8. When

8. When the Highest gave inheritance to the nations;
when He separated the sons of Adam:
when He appointed the bounds of the peoples;
small was the number of the sons of Israel.

9. But the portion of JEHOVAH was his people;
Jacob was the lot of his inheritance.

10. He sustained him in a desert land;
even in the waste howling wilderness.
He led him about, He instructed him;
He kept him, as the apple of his eye.

11. As an eagle stirreth up her nest;
fluttereth over her young:
spreadeth abroad her wings, taketh them,
beareth them upon her wings:

12. So JEHOVAH alone did lead him;
and with Him was no strange GOD.

13. He made him ride on the high places of the earth;
that he might eat the increase of the fields:
and He made him to suck honey out of the stone;
and oil out of the flinty rock.

14. Butter of kine, and the fat of sheep;
with the fat of lambs, and of rams:
of young bulls, and of goats;
with the fat, the finest flour of wheat:
He drank also the pure blood of the grape:
thus did Jacob eat, and was filled.

15. But Jeshurun waxed fat, and kicked;
(thou didst wax fat, grow thick, wast cover'd with fatness:)
then he forsook GOD, who made him;
and lightly esteemed the rock of his salvation.

16. They provoked Him to jealousy with strange (gods):
with abominations they exasperated Him.

17. They sacrificed to devils, not to GOD;
to gods, which they knew not:
to new (gods), which came of late;
which your fathers did not tremble at.

18. Of the rock, that begat thee, thou art unmindful;
and hast forgotten GOD, who formed thee.

19. Then

19. Then JEHOVAH faw, and He abhorred;
for the provocation of his fons and of his daughters.
20. And He faid, "I WILL HIDE MY FACE FROM THEM;
 " I WILL SEE, WHAT SHALL BE THEIR END:
 " FOR A GENERATION VERY FROWARD ARE THEY;
 " CHILDREN, IN WHOM THERE IS NO FAITH.
21. " THEY HAVE MOVED ME TO JEALOUSY WITH WHAT
  " IS NOT GOD;
 " THEY HAVE PROVOKED ME TO ANGER WITH THEIR
  " VANITIES:
 " AND I WILL MOVE THEM TO JEALOUSY WITH
  " THOSE, WHO ARE NOT A PEOPLE;
 " WITH A FOOLISH NATION WILL I PROVOKE THEM
  " TO ANGER.
22. " VERILY A FIRE IS KINDLED IN MY WRATH;
 " AND IT SHALL BURN UNTO THE LOWEST HELL;
 " AND IT SHALL CONSUME THE EARTH, WITH ITS
  " INCREASE;
 " AND IT SHALL FIRE THE FOUNDATIONS OF THE
  " MOUNTAINS.
23. " I WILL HEAP UPON THEM MISFORTUNES;
 " MINE ARROWS I WILL EXHAUST UPON THEM.
24. " SCORCHED WITH HUNGER, AND DEVOURED WITH
  " BURNING HEAT;
 " THE BIRD OF DESTRUCTION SHALL BE BITTER
  " TO THEM:
 " AND THE TOOTH OF BEASTS WILL I SEND UPON
  " THEM;
 " WITH THE POISON OF SERPENTS OF THE DUST.
25. " FROM WITHOUT THE SWORD SHALL DESTROY,
 " AND FROM WITHIN TERROR,
 " BOTH THE YOUNG MAN, AND THE VIRGIN;
 " THE SUCKLING, WITH THE MAN OF GRAY HAIRS.
26. " I SAID, I WOULD SCATTER THEM INTO CORNERS;
 " I WOULD MAKE THE REMEMBRANCE OF THEM TO
  " CEASE FROM AMONG MEN:
27. " WERE IT NOT THAT I AVOIDED THE WRATH OF
  " THE ENEMY;
 " LEST THEIR ADVERSARIES SHOULD BEHAVE
  " THEMSELVES STRANGELY:
 " LEST THEY SHOULD SAY, [*Our hand is high;*
 " *and Jehovah hath not done all this.*]"

MOSES.

MOSES.

28. Verily they are a nation loft to all counfel;
neither is there any underftanding in them.
29. O that they were wife, and would underftand this!
and would confider their latter end!
30. How fhould one chafe a thoufand;
and two put ten thoufand to flight:
except that their rock had fold them;
and JEHOVAH had fhut them up.
31. For not, like our rock, is their rock;
our enemies themfelves being judges.
32. But, from the vine of Sodom, is their vine;
and from the fields of Gomorrah:
their grapes are grapes of gall;
and the clufters are bitter to them.
33. The poifon of dragons is their wine;
and the venom of afps moft cruel.

JEHOVAH.

34. "IS NOT THIS LAID UP IN STORE WITH ME;
"AND SEALED UP AMONG MY TREASURES?
35. "VENGEANCE IS MINE, AND IT SHALL BE REPAID;
"IN A SHORT TIME THEIR FOOT SHALL SLIDE:
"FOR AT HAND IS THE DAY OF THEIR CALAMITY;
"AND WHAT IS PREPARED FOR THEM MAKETH
"HASTE."

MOSES.

36. Yet fhall JEHOVAH protect his people;
and he fhall be comforted in his fervants:
when He feeth, that their power is gone;
and there is none fhut up, or left.
37. When men fhall fay — *Where is their God?*
their rock, in whom they trufted?
38. *Who did eat the fat of their facrifices;*
and drank the wine of their drink-offerings.
Let him rife up, and help you;
let him be a protection over you.

JEHOVAH.

THE OLD TESTAMENT. 285

JEHOVAH.

39. " SEE NOW, THAT I, I AM HE!
    " AND THERE IS NO GOD WITH ME.
    " I KILL, AND I MAKE ALIVE;
    " I WOUND, AND I HEAL:
    " AND NONE DELIVERETH OUT OF MY HAND.
40. " FOR I LIFT UP MY HAND TO HEAVEN;
    " AND SAY: AS I LIVE FOR EVER;
41. " I WILL WHET MY GLITTERING SWORD;
    " AND MY HAND SHALL TAKE HOLD ON JUDGMENT:
    " I WILL RENDER VENGEANCE TO MINE ADVER-
        " SARIES;
    " AND THEM, WHO HATE ME, WILL I RECOMPENSE.
42. " I WILL MAKE MINE ARROWS DRUNK WITH BLOOD;
    " AND MY SWORD SHALL DEVOUR FLESH:
    " WITH THE BLOOD OF THE SLAIN, AND OF THE
        " CAPTIVES;
    " FROM THE HEAD OF THE PRINCES OF THE ENEMY.

MOSES.

43. Rejoice, O ye nations, with His people!
    for He will avenge the blood of his servants:
    and He will render vengeance to his adversaries;
    but will be merciful to his land and to his people.

HOSEA XI, 1.

In our interpretations of the holy Scriptures, we ought to admit this as an infallible Canon of Criticism — that whatever is *declared to be the true sense* of any passage, and so declared by a man whom GOD has enabled to work Miracles; *that*, if the words can possibly admit of it, *must be allowed to be the true sense*: though that sense should not be the most obvious; and though it would not perhaps have been discovered at all, without the assistance of such a sacred interpreter.

The

The application of this Rule may be neceſſary, in vindication of St. Matthew's uſe of the words — *Out of Egypt have I called my ſon*: the Apoſtle having quoted them, as originally meant of CHRIST *the ſon of God*; and as a prophecy, that *He* was to be called by GOD out of Egypt. A very careful examination of this point is the more expedient: becauſe, while *Julian*, with other *unbelievers*, has charged the Evangeliſt as *guilty* of a *falſe quotation*; even ſome *Chriſtians* have allowed that nothing more can be meant here than *an Accommodation of Words* owing to *a Similitude of Circumſtances*. But all Chriſtians ſhould conſider, what not a few ſeem to have forgotten — how abſolutely neceſſary it is, that *many expreſs Prophecies* ſhould have been *fulfilled* in *Chriſt*, in order to prove him *The True Meſſiah*: and that ſcarce any paſſage is quoted as a Prophecy of this kind, in more direct and poſitive terms, than the paſſage before us — *that it might be fulfilled, which was ſpoken of the Lord by the prophet, ſaying*, OUT OF EGYPT, &c. *Matt.* 2, 15.

Let it then be obſerved firſt, that Hoſea has *certainly* prophecied of Chriſt in ſome other paſſages; and 2dly, that it is *probable*, or at leaſt *poſſible*, he may have done ſo in the paſſage now before us. Chapters 1 and 2 clearly foretell the rejection of the Jews, with the adoption of the Gentiles. And chap. 3 foretells, that *in the latter days the children of Iſrael ſhall return, and ſeek the Lord their God, and* DAVID THEIR KING: by whom both Jews and Chriſtians underſtand here *The Meſſiah, David's ſon*.

Let

Let us now attend to the celebrated paſſage, quoted by St. Matthew; and learn, from the words themſelves and the context, whether it be not *probable*, or at leaſt *poſſible*, that Hoſea did here prophecy of CHRIST.

HOSEA X, 12.

12. Sow to yourſelves in righteouſneſs,
 reap in mercy,
 break up your fallow ground:
 for it is time to ſeek the Lord,
 ᵃ till he come, and rain righteouſneſs upon you.

 ᵃ This verſe clearly relates to the coming of Meſſiah. For, after the days of Hoſea, when did RIGHTEOUSNESS *rain*, or pour down *upon Iſrael*, but in the days of Chriſt? And of whom, but *Him*, could it properly be ſaid—*till He come* for this great purpoſe? But the words *it is time to ſeek the Lord* ſeem to recommend another, and very juſt tranſlation of this hemiſtic—*till he come*, WHO *ſhall teach you righteouſneſs*. As to the verb and the pronoun ſee *Gen*. 46, 28. and *Deut*. 33, 10: and that 1 may, as equivalent to אשר, be rendered *who*; ſee *Jerem*. 36, 32. &c. The Syr. verſion ſignifies—*donec veniat et* OSTENDAT *vobis juſtitiam ſuam*: and the vulgate is—*cum venerit*, QUI DOCEBIT *vos juſtitiam*. As to the propriety of thus rendering the ſecond verb and the 1, ſee *Pocock* on this place, vol.2. p. 483. In p. 484. this learned author ſays—*Ribera, with many more, following Jerom, reſtrains it to Chriſt, who ſhould teach them the true way of righteouſneſs; ſo that what is required of them is, that they ſhould prepare their hearts for the coming of Chriſt.* But the words here, expreſſive of this preparation, may be more exactly rendered thus—*Sow to yourſelves* FOR *righteouſneſs*; *reap* (or ſo that ye may reap) *at the mouth of mercy*. The line preceding this verſe ſpeaks of *Judah* as well as *Iſrael*: on which therefore Pocock remarks, p. 475—*it will be ſufficient to underſtand, that* ALL ISRAEL, THE WHOLE TWELVE TRIBES, *are ſhewed to be concerned in what is ſaid hath been done, or ſhall be done.*

13. Ye

13. Ye have plowed wickedness, ye have reaped iniquity;
ye have eaten the fruit of lies:
because thou didst trust in thy way, in the multitude of
thy mighty men.
14. Therefore shall a tumult arise among thy people, and
all thy fortresses shall be spoiled:
as Shalman spoiled Beth-arbel, in the day of battle;
^a the mother was dashed in pieces upon her children:
15. ^b So shall Beth-el do unto you,
^c *because of your great wickedness:*
in the morning shall the king of Israel utterly be cut off.

^a The punishment for your Idolatries at Beth-el shall be as great and severe, as those inflicted by Shalmanezer; when he cruelly laid waste Beth-arbel, destroying the inhabitants without distinction of Age or Sex.

^b As the place, called *Beth-el*, was twice before in this chapter called by the reproachful name of *Beth-aven* and *Aven*, (see ver. 5 and 8), it is not likely it should be here called by it's true and honourable name *Beth-el*. Probably, therefore, the words בית אל *(house of God)* which are used for *the Temple at Jerusalem* in Zac. 7, 2, may have the same signification here.

^c But great as the Idolatries of all Israel had been, and how provoking soever their past wickedness: they would afterwards be guilty of one crime, emphatically stiled here *the wickedness of their wickedness*, or the crime of crimes, the *extremum omnium malorum*—so Pocock, p. 496. In the same page this Critic justly observes—that a pause may be put after *Beth-el*; and *because of your great wickedness* may be connected with *in the morning*, &c. This different connection is here adopted; and for this reason: because every one knows, that the crime of all crimes amongst the Jews, or the greatest act of their wickedness, was *putting to death the Messiah*—which seems evidently to be here intended by *The king of Israel shall utterly be cut off*. These words cannot well relate to Hoshea, the last king of Israel; who *did evil in the sight of the Lord*: and therefore, if he had been cut off, the death of a wicked prince could not have been described as an *extraordinary judgment* occasioned by their *extraordinary wickedness*. But, had the prophecy meant the *death* of Hoshea;

XI. 1. *When Israel was a child, then I loved him;*
AND I CALLED MY SON OUT OF EGYPT.

2. As they called them, so they went from them;
they sacrificed unto Baalim, and burnt incense to graven images.

we should have found that death mentioned in his history: whereas it is said, on the contrary, (2 *Kin.* 17, 4), that the king of Assyria *shut him up and bound him in prison*; and *Josephus* says expressly, that Salmanasser took him alive. lib. ix. c. 14, 1.

But who then could be here meant by *the King of Israel*, to be *surely cut off?* Who, but *the Messiah*—before, by this same prophet, described as *King of Israel*. For, since *Messiah* is confessedly meant (3, 5) by *David their King*; if Messiah, the second David, was to be what the first David had been, he was to be *King over all Israel*. And it is surprizing, that this very title had not, long before, secured the appropriation of this passage to the Messiah. For where else in the Old Testament shall we find the Messiah foretold, under this title? And yet it seems necessary to find it somewhere in the Old Testament; because it is quoted in the New Testament as one of Messiah's well known characters. *If he be the king of Israel*, say the chief priests, &c. *Mat.* 27, 42 — *Let Christ, the king of Israel, descend now from the cross,* &c. *Mar.* 15, 32 — *Thou art the Son of God; thou art the king of Israel.* Joh. 1, 49 — and lastly: *Blessed is the king of Israel, that cometh in the name of the Lord.* Joh. 12, 13. These are full and express authorities for applying this Title to the Messiah. And as to his being cut off *in the morning*, or *early in life*; this also is properly descriptive of Messiah, cut off by the Jews very soon after the entrance upon his public ministry. The word שחר is now rendered *early* Ps. 57, 9; 108, 3. And Pocock says — בשחר *statim, cito, perexiguo tempore*; p. 496 — he adds, that if we read בשחר, it would make no difference in the meaning.

But, if the *Messiah* be here meant by *the King of Israel*; who then is meant by *Israel* in the words following? I answer, *the Messiah* likewise. For, why may he not be called *Israel*, as well as *David?* This difficulty is however removed by *Isaiah*;

T   where

where the name *Israel* is unquestionably given to the Messiah:
Lowth, 49, 3. It is also remarkable, that Isaiah uses *Israel* both
for *Messiah* (the son of Israel) in ver. 3; and also for *all the
children of Israel*, in verse 5, &c. — just as Hosea in this xith
chapter, uses the word *Israel*, in verses 1 and 8 — and just as
he varies the sense of the word *Jacob*, in chap. 12; using it
for Jacob's descendants in ver. 2, and for Jacob himself in verses 3 and 4. And as to the word *Israel* he uses it for Israel
himself in xii, 12, and in the very next verse for all his
children. The general meaning therefore of the Prophet seems
here to be — that though the Messiah would be cut off by the
wicked Jews, yet he was still *the beloved of God*; who would
manifest his love to him, even whilst a child, and would
call him out of Egypt: and that this would God do; though,
when he had before called out of Egypt all Israel, they had
repaid his kindness with ingratitude and rebellion.

For thus it follows, in the Prophet; though some of the
words now, either from accident or design, are not capable of
any regular construction and connexion — *they called them, so
they went from them*, &c. But here, we are happily extricated
from our distress, by the united authorities of the Greek,
Syriac, and Arabic versions; agreeably to which, instead of

קראו להם כן הלכו מפניהם לבעלים יזבחו

the antient and true reading seems to have been this —

כקראי להם כן הלכו מפני הם לבעלים יזבחו

As I *called* THEM, *so they went from* MY FACE; THEY *sacrificed to Baalim*, &c.

Since writing the preceding remarks, I was agreeably surprized at finding a Dissertation on this subject, by the learned
Mr. *Peirce*, subjoined to his Comment on *Galatians*; in which
Dissertation several of the preceding points are stated in the
same manner — particularly — the *necessity* of this passage being
a *prophecy of Christ* — ascertaining to *Christ* the name *Israel*,
from Isaiah — *Bethaven* and *Aven* being Bethel — rendering
Bethel here agreeably to Zachariah — and Christ expected under the title *of King of Israel*. But, as I have offered some
remarks of consequence, not in Mr. *Peirce*; he has others, not
noted

Hosea VI, 2.

The truth of the Religion of Christ depending on his resurrection; it is no wonder, that that event was so often and so carefully foretold by Christ himself, (*Mat.* 16, 21; 17, 23; 20, 19: *Mar.* 9,31; 10,34: *Luk.* 9, 22; 18, 33), and that it should have been the subject of prophecy also in the Old Testament. And indeed it must have been foretold in the ancient Scriptures, not only that the Messiah should rise from the dead, but rise upon the third day: because *Christ* himself and St. *Paul* have mentioned this *rising on the third day* as a circumstance *necessary* to be fulfilled, *according to the Scriptures.*

Jesus began to shew to his disciples, how that he MUST *be killed, and be raised again* THE THIRD DAY. *Mat.* 16, 21—*The son of man* MUST *suffer, and be slain, and be raised again* THE THIRD DAY. *Luk.* 9, 22—*Then opened he their understandings, that they might understand the Scriptures: and said, Thus* IT IS WRITTEN, *and thus it behoved Christ to suffer, and to rise from the dead,* THE THIRD DAY. *Luk.* 24; 45,46 —*Destroy this temple, and* IN THREE DAYS *I will raise it up: which, when he was risen, his disciples remem-*

---

noted by me: particularly—on GOD's *calling* out of Egypt—on the *time* of this prophecy—on *Shalman*—and on *Israel* being equivalent to *King of Israel*. But see that curious Dissertation.

See also (Jeffery's) Review of the Controversy, &c. p. 278, &c.

See Zeph. chap. 3.—after prophecying the call of *the Gentiles, (all nations)*, to Christianity, (ver. 8. and 9.), and calling upon Israel and Judah to rejoice, (ver. 14.), in ver. 15. he says —*the King of Israel, even Jehovah, is in the midst of thee.*

bered, and they believed THE SCRIPTURES; *Joh.* 2; 19, 22 — And thus also St. Paul: *how that Christ died for our sins, according to the Scriptures; and that he was buried, and rose again* THE THIRD DAY, *according to the Scriptures*: 1 *Cor.* 15; 3, 4.

Now, to what passage in the Old Testament are we to refer, on this important occasion; and where can we find any prophecy; which names the very day of the Resurrection? The truth is, there is but *one place*, where we can at all expect it; and though we are generally directed thither, yet sadly are we disappointed in our hopes of satisfaction from it: the place is *Hosea* 6, 2. Mention indeed is there made of reviving after two days, and of being raised on the third. But as this is affirmed of more than one; and as the subject is *us*, not *him*; it is scarce possible, that any advantage can be derived to Christianity from such a reference; or rather, that any sound argument can be formed on *plural* terms in favour of the Resurrection of *one person*. Yet, when these words have been illustrated by a single remark; our hope will take place of our despair. And the remark is — that the suffixed pronoun נו, added to both the verbs *he will revive*, and *he will raise*, (which pronoun is now rendered *us*), may justly be rendered HIM. There cannot be a proof more decisive, as to the second verb, than the very same verb with the same pronoun in *Gen.* 49, 9, יקימנו or יקימנו *shall raise* HIM *up*. In general, the pronoun for *him*, added to verbs, and also in the future tense, may be נו as well as הו; and is therefore (where the points are not attended to) to

be

be distinguished from the *plural* pronoun by the Context only. One verb will furnish sufficient instances: thus, though ויצונו *(Deut.* 6, 24) be properly rendered *command* us; and though (in *Gen.* 28, 1) ויצוהו be *command him*; yet (*Deut.* 18, 18 and 31, 14) *command* HIM אצונו; and the same, in *Isai.* 10, 6. If then the pronoun here suffixed may be, and is, the third person singular, as grammatically as the first person plural; how came the latter sense to have been preferred to the former in this very remarkable place? It appears to me, that this may have arisen from an improper deference to *the points here* wrongly conformed to the *points* under the two other pronouns *preceding*, without any design to pervert the true sense: or it may have been owing to the zeal of the same set of men with those, who formerly said to Pilate — *Sir, we remember that that deceiver said, after three days I will rise again.* Mat. 27, 63.

Let us now consider the words in question, with the Context.

Hos. v. 15 —— vi. 3.

15. אלך אשובה אל מקומי-
עד אשר יאשמו ובקשו פני
בצר להם ישחרנני :

vi. 1. לכו ונשובה אל יהוה
כי הוא טרף וירפאנו
יך ויחבשנו :

2. יחיינו מימים

ביום

בְּיוֹם הַשְּׁלִישִׁי יְקִמֵנוּ
וְנִחְיֶה לְפָנָיו :
3. וְנֵדְעָה נִרְדְּפָה לָדַעַת אֶת יהוה
כְּשַׁחַר נָכוֹן מֹצָאוֹ
וְיָבוֹא כַגֶּשֶׁם לָנוּ
כְּמַלְקוֹשׁ יוֹרֶה אָרֶץ :

I will go and return to my place, till they acknowledge their offence, and seek my face: in their affliction they will seek me early. Come, and let us return unto the Lord: for he hath torn, and he will heal us; he hath smitten, and he will bind us up. AFTER TWO DAYS *will he revive* US, IN THE THIRD DAY *he will raise* US *up, and we shall live in his sight. Then shall we know,* (if), *we follow on to know the Lord: his going forth is prepared as the morning; and he shall come unto us as the rain; as the latter* (and) *former rain unto the earth.*

As to the verse first here cited; the true sense seems to be what is given by Pocock (p. 247, &c.) in these words — *God saith, that after he hath executed his threatened judgments on Ephraim and Judah, he will return unto his place, to Heaven, the place of his glorious residence* — *yet doth he limit his absence by adding, till they acknowledge their offence, and seek my face; till that they, perceiving all other help to fail them, return to me by repentance, and seek my favour* — *in their affliction they will seek me in the morning,* that is, *early. We may well look on this prophecy as fulfilled in all those, who (amidst their troubles and sorrows) waited for the consolation of Israel, and looked for redemption in Jerusalem,* i. e. *longed and sought for the appearing of* CHRIST, *in whom God's face is revealed most clearly.*

The

The next verse, (VI.1), which now begins in the Hebrew Text scarce intelligibly, is well introduced in the Greek, Syriac, and Arabic versions, and also in the Chaldee paraphrase, with the word for *saying*; and then the connection stands thus — *They will seek me early:* SAYING, *Come, and let us return unto the Lord, &c. The words, so coupled, will*, (says Pocock p. 250), *found as a form by God himself prescribed for them to use. In the remainder of the verse* (says he) *are expressed their acknowledgment of God's overruling power, with a confidence in his future mercy.* — *What is here spoken concerns both Judah and Israel; and it was not fulfilled, till they were gathered together under that* ONE HEAD *spoken of chapter* 1, 11; *and then salvation was reached forth to them both. But of that time the next words give us more occasion to enquire. And here, though the words are capable of such a general interpretation, as that God would* SOON *revive, and deliver them after he had afflicted them*, FOR A SHORT TIME: *yet surely the express mentioning of two days, and a third day, seems to intimate something more particular; and that is, the laying of* CHRIST *dead in the grave for two days, and rising again on the third day. This application of the words* (says he) *is the more to be attended to; because I know not how, or when, otherwise, (applied to Judah and Israel), they will be found to be made good:. or what is of prophecy in them may be said to have been fulfilled to them, but in* HIM — *For, when was* THAT THIRD DAY, *in which* THEY *were again raised up? Certainly, if we look on the words, according to their bare* LITERAL *sound; we cannot but see them so punctually made good in Christ, that we may say* — Hosea,

sea, being a prophet, and knowing that God would send Christ so to die, and so to remain for such a space and no longer, he, seeing this before hand, spake of the resurrection of Christ." After these words this learned Hebrean shews, that he is aware of the objection, from the prophet's speaking here of *us*, and *not as of a single person*. And yet he does not answer the objection properly; being probably prevented, by the vowel points, from attending to *the double sense of the suffixed pronoun*; which has been here enlarged upon already.

There yet remains one great difficulty; which is —how to justify the application of this second verse to Christ, by making the pronoun twice here *singular*, when it is still allowed to be twice *plural* in the verse preceding. And to me it appears, that this justification can be derived only from *the context* here, as *explained* by the words of this same prophet in chapter 3, 5—*Afterward shall the children of Israel return, and seek* THE LORD THEIR GOD, AND DAVID THEIR KING; *and shall fear the Lord and his goodness in the latter days.*

To this former passage Hosea seems clearly to allude, and partly to quote it, in the latter. The former says—*they shall return, and seek the Lord their God:* the latter says—*they shall seek me early, saying;* Come, *let us return unto the Lord:* or, according to the Greek and Arabic versions, *to the Lord our God.* And then, as the former says — they shall not only seek *the Lord their God*, but also DAVID THEIR KING; so the latter passage, though it does not express, yet evidently alludes to, *David their future king:* and this David was of course the HE, the single person,

who

who was after two days to be revived, and raised again to life on the third day. Such then I take to be the real solution of this (hitherto unsolved) difficulty—that this latter passage being a clear allusion to the former, when the same *Lord God* had been introduced nearly in the same manner in both; the same *Messiah*, which follows and is named in the first passage, follows and is meant, though not named, in the second.

It is very observable, that the word ונחיה *and we shall live* immediately follows, and seems mentioned as the consequence of, *the resurrection of Christ*, which is perfectly the language of the New Testament. And *living in his sight* may mean either *living here*, in the sight of Christ ever present with his church: or in the sight of *God, hereafter*, in a state of happiness. It follows—ונדעה *and we shall know*. And is not this also clearly allusive to the gospel dispensation; under which, (as Jeremiah says), *they should all know the Lord?* The New Testament also says— *this is* LIFE *eternal, that they might* KNOW *thee the only true God, and Jesus Christ, whom thou hast sent.* After which we read — that, if *we thus follow* on, and strive diligently, *to know the Lord*; then will *the going forth of the Messiah be prepared as the morning: and he shall come unto us*, fruitful and refreshing, *as the rain*; *as the latter and the former rain unto the earth.* Thus — *though heaviness may endure for a night, yet joy cometh in the morning.* The Messiah (says the Psalmist) *shall come down like rain upon the mown grass, as showers that water the Earth.* And lastly; *the dayspring from on high hath visited us*; *to give light to them that sit in darkness and the shadow of death*; *to guide our feet into the way of peace.*

SERMONS.

SERMON I.

St. MATT. I, 1.

THE BOOK OF THE GENERATION OF JESUS CHRIST, THE SON OF DAVID, THE SON OF ABRAHAM.

THUS begins *the everlasting Gospel*; the Gospel, sent *from Heaven to every nation, and tongue, and people.* In this manner opens the volume of that *New Testament*, that *Second Covenant*, which GOD made with man through Jesus Christ. And, must it not be highly worthy of our attention; that the very *first* thing asserted in the *first* of the four Evangelists is—that *Jesus Christ* was *the son of David?* Certainly, on this foundation we may build with safety. This is the first and chief Stone, in the magnificent Temple of Christianity; that Stone; which though other *Builders* have *rejected*, is here made *the head of the corner.*

No apology can be necessary *here*; for still considering this first chapter, as a genuine part of
St.

St. Matthew's Gospel. For, though objections to it have been lately made; no sufficient proof seems yet produced against it. So that the great truth, which I shall now consider, may be said to begin, as well as to conclude, the New Testament. It begins here, with *St. Matthew*, the first Evangelist. And it concludes the book of the *Revelation*; in the very last chapter of which, Christ himself is introduced as saying—*I (Jesus) am the root and the offspring of David.*[a]

Blessed for ever, therefore, be the Lord our GOD, who hath *visited and redeemed his people* Israel; and hath also *raised up an horn of salvation for us* Gentiles, *in the house of his servant David!* For *unto You*, as well as unto Them, was *born in the city of David a Saviour, which is Christ, the Lord*—agreeably to that prophecy of Isaiah, delivered to *the house of David*, above seven hundred years before the miraculous event, that a *Virgin should bring forth a son*, and *call his name Immanuel*.

This celebrated passage of the Evangelical prophet I attempted to explain, in a former Discourse before *this Audience*. And now, as I know of no other particular point of equal importance to Christianity, which yet so much wants illustration, as *the promise of God to David concerning the Messiah*; I shall make this the subject of our present meditation: submitting it, as a second part to the Discourse before mentioned.

[a] Rev. 22. 16.

That Chrift *was to be*, and *was*, David's fon — we Chriftians do not permit ourfelves to doubt. But, though a direct promife to *David*, that the Meffiah fhould defcend from *him*, is taken for granted in the Pfalms, and the Prophets in the Old Teftament; and is exprefsly affirmed in the New: yet it is certain, that Unbelievers have urged the want of proof in this cafe, as one great caufe of their difbelief of the Gofpel. Many Chriftians muft have felt the force of this objection; and I am apprehenfive, that a full and fufficient anfwer may not have as yet been given to it.

Nor will this appear to *You* an enquiry merely fpeculative; but, as having a direct and powerful influence upon *practice*. For in vain fhall we look for the fruits of Chriftianity, in the lives of it's profeffors; unlefs they *do in fact believe* what they profefs. And in vain do men *pretend* to believe, unlefs their belief be founded on reafon; till they fee and know, *how*, and *on what proofs*, Chriftianity is eftablifhed: and are convinced clearly, that this *foundation of God ftandeth fure*.

The method, which I propofe in the remainder of this Difcourfe, is ———

Firft: Briefly to fhew the ftrefs laid, in the New Teftament, on the *promife*, and the *fact*, of Chrift being David's Son.

Secondly: to point out *the promife itfelf*, as made to David.

Thirdly:

Thirdly: to prove, that David himself understood it of the Messiah. And,

Lastly: to clear the Prophecy from *some great difficulties*; which make it scarce possible to be so understood, from our present English Translation.

As to the *New* Testament; we have seen, that the very first words are—*The book of the generation* (that is — the history of the birth, &c.) *of Jesus Christ* THE SON OF DAVID. And we have also seen, that Christ claims to himself this title, at the *end* of the New Testament.

Indeed we find this to have been the common belief among the Jews. For in the 9th chapter of St. *Matthew* we read, that two blind men, taking Christ to be the Messiah, followed him; crying—*Thou* SON OF DAVID, *have mercy on us*. And, in the 7th chapter of St. *John*, we find some of the people asking, (the rest assenting), *Hath not the scripture said, That Christ cometh of the seed of David?* And (without quoting other passages of the New Testament, which are numerous to the same purpose) I shall only remark further from thence, that *this belief* must have been founded upon some *solemn and express promise* made to David. St. *Peter*, immediately after the descent of the Holy Ghost, speaks of David—as *knowing, that God had sworn, that of the fruit of his loins, according to the flesh, he would raise up Christ to sit on his throne*. And St. *Paul*, in his

SERMON I.

his sermon at Antioch, has the words following—*Of this man's seed hath God,* ACCORDING TO HIS PROMISE, *raised unto Israel a Saviour, Jesus.*

Let us then proceed, secondly, to enquire—where—and what—*the promise itself* is, as given in the *Old* Testament. Now, though such a promise is often mentioned in the *Prophets,* and the *Psalms;* yet it is there mentioned, not as the original promise then given, but in reference to such a promise given long before. Thus, in the 33d chapter of *Jeremiah*—*Behold, the days come, saith the Lord, that I will perform that good thing, which I* HAVE PROMISED—*I will raise up unto David a branch of righteousness,* (and a king shall reign and prosper), *and he shall execute judgment and justice in the earth.* I have inserted the words *and a king shall reign and prosper;* which, though not in our common Bibles here, may be proved genuine, especially by many MSS.

From the *Prophetical* books we may refer now to the *Historical;* which, as to the present case, may be divided into two parts, the history of *David,* and that of *Solomon.* In Solomon's history we find him mentioning two promises made to his father: the first *absolute*—that *Solomon was to build the Temple;* which, Solomon observes,[a] he himself had fulfilled: and the second *conditional*[b]—that *the regal succession should continue in David's family,* provided they

[a] 1 Kings 8, 20.   [b] 1 Kings 8, 25, and 2 Chr. 6, 16.

proved worthy of GOD's favour; for, if not, they were to be *plucked up by the roots.* [a]

But, as neither of these two promises related to the Messiah; we must refer to the history of *David himself*. And indeed, where so properly as in David's history, (an history longer by far than that of any other man in the Old Testament), *where* should *we so properly* as in *David's history* look for a *promise made to David*; and a promise of much greater moment, than all the other things recorded concerning him?

When we read, as in the Text of this Discourse, that *Christ* was *the son of Abraham*, we refer to the history of *Abraham*, in *Genesis*, for the promise, that thus it should be. And accordingly we find it there promised to Abraham, that *in* HIS *seed all the nations of the earth should be blessed*: the everlasting covenant being made, with him, in *Isaac*. [b]

This was the *first* restriction of the birth of Christ to any particular family. And this was foretold, when the world was advanced about half way between the Creation, and the Redemption; near 2000 years between the former and the latter. And, when about half of the last 2000 years was passed; then was foretold the *last* restriction of the great blessing; namely, to the family of David. And as that first restriction *is recorded*, as was necessary, in the *history of* ABRAHAM; so was it equally necessary, that the last restriction should be recorded in *the history of* DAVID.

[a] 2 Chron. 7, 20.   [b] Gen. 17, 19: 22, 18.

Now

SERMON I.

Now in David's history we find two promises from GOD; the first delivered *to Nathan for David*,[a] near the beginning of David's reign; and the second delivered to David near the end of his reign, either by GOD himself,[b] or by the prophet Gad.[c]

The second contains a promise, that *Solomon*, (mentioned by name), and not David, should build the temple at Jerusalem; together with the reason —because *David* had been a *man of war*, but *Solomon* was to be *a man of peace*. It related also to the *conditional* prosperity of Solomon, and his kingdom over *Israel*; and the phrase here, very remarkably is —*he shall be my son, and I will be his father*, i.e. let him act, if he act, as *my son*; then *will I act as his father*.[d] But, in a promise sent by Nathan, the phrase is—I WILL BE *his father*, and HE SHALL BE *my son*.[e] The reason is; that in *this* prophecy, to which alone we are now left for a promise of the Messiah, the style is, and might well be, *absolute*: the obedience of *Christ as a son* being *certain*, and consequently the affection of *God as a father*. And let us remember, that in HEB. 1, 5 it is affirmed, that these words, *I will be to him a father, and he shall be to me a son*, were spoken OF CHRIST.

[a] 2 Sam. 7;—and 1 Chr. 17;—referred to by David, in 2 SAM. 23; 1—7. [b] 1 Chron. 28; 3, and 6. [c] See the whole 22d chapter of 1 Chron; particularly v. 8, in the *Syriac* and ARABIC Versions. Note in ver. 9—the Hebrew speaks of *Solomon as then born*. [d] 1 Chron. 22, 10: 28, 6. [e] 2 Sam. 7, 14, and 1 Chron. 17, 13.

Here then we are arrived at (what will, I hope, soon appear to be) *the great promise*, uniformly and consistently relating to the Messiah; as to his descent from David. The prophecy is contained at large in *the seventh chapter of the second book of Samuel*; and recorded again (as a matter of such high importance well deserved) in the parallel place in *Chronicles*.[a]

I proceed therefore, thirdly, to shew—that David himself understood this message by Nathan, as containing a promise of the Messiah.

David, soon after he was crowned at Jerusalem, obtained two victories over the Philistines; and, being then at leisure, built for himself *houses*, or *palaces*, one of which was of cedar: he also prepared on mount Zion a place for *the ark of God*, which was conducted thither with great devotion and joy. The King, struck with *the mean habitation*, in which the ark even then was, compared with *the grandeur of his own residence*, consulted Nathan, about building for the ark a magnificent house likewise.

The piety of this proposal was so pleasing to GOD (especially, as no such thing had been commanded) that, though *David* himself was not allowed to execute his design of building *an house for* GOD ; he received a promise, that *God* would build *an house for* HIM; I say, though *David* was not to build an house for GOD, yet would *God* build an house for

---

[a] 2 Sam. 7; 4—16, and 1 Chron. 17; 3—14.

DAVID.

DAVID. And it is certain, that this house, or building, could not be *material, an house made with hands*; but must be figurative and spiritual: because it was to be *established for ever*; and it is explained by GOD's setting up *an everlasting kingdom*, under *one of David's sons, or descendants*, who should be raised up, not, like Solomon, during David's life, but after *David slept with his fathers*.

For, *what else* could David infer from such a promise as this? Were not his thoughts by this description led naturally, must they not have been directed almost necessarily, to the grand object of his hopes—*the future Saviour, and King of the world?* That the answer to this may be the more satisfactory, let us endeavour to determine, what might be, and probably were, David's ideas concerning the Messiah.

The Redeemer, who was (according to the promise made to *Adam*) to be *the seed*, or son, *of the woman*, had been restrained to the family of Abraham, in the tribe of Judah. So far David must know. Again: whether it was, or was not, understood *universally* by those who sacrificed animals, that *the deaths of such creatures represented the future death of the Messiah*; though the nature of such sacrifices was not understood by *all*, yet it certainly was by David. For *he* has declared, that GOD would accept *such sacrifices for sin* no longer; when the Messiah, in the fulness of time, should say, *Lo! I come*. And this same David foretold, not only the

U 3   Messiah's

SERMON I.

Messiah's *sufferings* and *death*, with very particular circumstances attending *his crucifixion*; but also, his *speedy resurrection*, and *regal government over all mankind*.

With such sentiments as *these* about him, was it possible for David to consider this promise in any other light, than as fixing to *his particular family* the honour of that *everlasting kingdom*, of that *universal blessing*; which, till that time, was open in general to *the whole tribe* of JUDAH?

And that David actually understood it so, will soon appear from his own words, when properly translated. The words, which sum up his opinion, are in *the 2d book of Samuel, chapter 7th, verse 19th*; and literally express this sense—*Thou hast spoken of thy servant's house at a great distance*; AND THIS IS THE LAW OF THE MAN, OR THE ADAM.[a] In our present translation the last words are—*and is this the manner of man?* But the original, which has not the least mark of a question, directly affirms thus—*this is the law of the man*, or *the Adam*: meaning either, that this great promise did, and must, relate to *the law* and appointment, vouchsafed to *Adam* himself,[b] namely, that of redemption by *the seed of the woman*; or (which in effect is the same) that it related to the divine appointment concerning *the second Adam, who was to come*. This latter is the meaning of the words

---

[a] See 2 Sam. 7, 19. and 1 Chron. 17, 17.   [b] *Adam* is האדם Gen. 2; 19, 20, 21, 22, 23, 25: 3; 8, 9, 12, 20: 4; 1, compared with 25.

in

SERMON I.

in the parallel place, in *Chronicles*; where David's sentiments on this occasion are expressed thus—*Thou hast spoken of thy servant's house at a great distance; and thou hast regarded me according to the order of* THE FUTURE ADAM, *or* THE ADAM FROM ABOVE.[a] Here again our own translation is wrong; for it reads—*according to the estate of a man of high degree:* whereas the literal rendering is—*according to the order of the future Adam*, or *the Adam from above*. The word, here connected with Adam, implies both *time* and *space*;[b] and therefore may here signify *the Adam* WHO IS TO COME, or *the Adam* FROM ABOVE—characters these, applicable here to no one person, but *the Messiah*; and in *Him* they wonderfully unite. For Christ in the New Testament is not only called *He that cometh from above*, and *he that is from above*;[c] but also, *the second Man*, and *the future Adam*.[d] For St. Paul saith—*The first Adam was a figure of* THE FUTURE—and again, *The first man Adam was made a living soul*, THE LAST ADAM *a quickening spirit*; *the first man is of the earth, earthy,* THE SECOND MAN *is the Lord from heaven*.

Having thus shewn, that the promise from GOD by Nathan was understood by *David* himself of THE

---

[a] See 1 Chron. 17, 17.   [b] מעלה—*de loco et tempore*. Buxt.
[c] Jo. 3, 31, and 8, 23—ὁ ἀνωθεν ἐρχομενος—εγω εκ των ανω ειμι
—— המעלה   [d] Rom. 5, 14, παραβασεως Ἀδαμ, ὁς ἐστι τυπος ΤΟΥ ΜΕΛΛΟΝΤΟΣ.— 1 Cor. 15, 45, Ὁ πρωτος ανθρωπος Ἀδαμ —Ὁ ΕΣΧΑΤΟΣ ΑΔΑΜ.— 1 Cor. 15, 47, Ὁ πρωτος ανθρωπος —— Ὁ ΔΕΥΤΕΡΟΣ ΑΝΘΡΩΠΟΣ Ὁ ΚΥΡΙΟΣ ΕΞ ΟΥΡΑΝΟΥ.

MESSIAH; I proceed, laſtly, to remove *thoſe difficulties*, which ſtill obſcure this important ſubject: which difficulties ariſe chiefly from the improper manner in which *the original words* of this paſſage are at preſent *tranſlated*.

Indeed this meſſage from GOD is one of thoſe paſſages, on which infidelity has violently laid hands; inſiſting upon the abſolute impoſſibility of it's at all relating to Jeſus Chriſt. The Author of *the Scheme of Literal Prophecy* [a] has offered three objections, which appear to him invincible. And as I do not know, that they have been yet confuted; I ſhall now conſider them.

His firſt objection is this—" This prophecy can-
" not agree to Jeſus the Meſſias; ſince it is expreſsly
" ſaid by GOD in it—*I* WILL APPOINT *a place for my*
" *people*; and WILL PLANT *them*; *that they may dwell*
" *in a place of their own, and move no more: neither*
" *ſhall the children of wickedneſs afflict them any more*—
" which (ſays he) is ſo far from being true, if refer-
" red to *Jeſus*, that ſince his time the Jews have
" been more afflicted, and more diſperſed, than ever
" they had been before."

The anſwer to this is — that the objector hath formed his argument entirely upon the Engliſh Verſion; in which *ſome verbs* are rendered *future*, which have here *a paſt* ſignification. For Nathan, ſo far from ſpeaking of the Jews, *at*, or *after* the coming of the Meſſiah, is ſetting forth the then paſt Good-

[a] Pag. 288, 289.

SERMON I.

ness of God to *David* and *his people*; as having raised *Him* from a sheepfold to the throne; and as having fixed *Them* happily in a country of their own: free from the distresses felt by their fathers, when wandering in the *wilderness*; or when lorded over by the *Philistines*, in the times of the *Judges*. For the two first verbs in verse the tenth, ought to be, in this construction, (agreeably to the idiom of the Hebrew language), rendered as *past*, not as *future*: just as the verb immediately preceding in verse the ninth, and another immediately following in verse the eleventh, both in the very same form, are both rendered now in the same English Version.

With this necessary correction, our Version of the first part of Nathan's Message will run thus—*Thus saith the Lord: I took thee from the sheep-cote, to be ruler over my people Israel. And I was with thee, and have cut off all thine enemies, and* HAVE MADE *thee a great name, like unto the name of the great men that are in the earth. Moreover I* HAVE APPOINTED *a place for my people Israel, and* HAVE PLANTED *them, that they dwell in a place of their own, and move no more. Neither do the children of wickedness afflict them any more, as beforetime; and as since the time that I commanded judges to be over my people: and I* HAVE CAUSED THEE *to rest from all thine enemies.*

Nathan, having thus set forth the divine favour, as already manifested to David and his people; proceeds to the higher part of his commission: namely,

that

that God's paſt favour, though thus great, was to be ſucceeded by greater. For, *the Lord alſo telleth thee, that he will make thee an houſe. And when thou ſhalt ſleep with thy fathers, I will ſet up thy ſeed after thee, and I will eſtabliſh his kingdom. He ſhall build an houſe for my name; and I will eſtabliſh the throne of his kingdom for ever. I will be his father, and he ſhall be my ſon:* IF HE COMMIT INIQUITY, *I will chaſten him with the rod of men, and with the ſtripes of the children of men.*

But here we are to encounter the ſecond objection of the Unbeliever beforementioned; and his argument is this. *Since it is ſaid of the perſon here ſpoken of,* IF HE COMMIT INIQUITY; *this Prophecy cannot agree to Jeſus, who did no ſin.* This is the objection; and it is indeed ſufficiently formidable. For, what is the point, here in queſtion? No leſs than an enquiry, whether there be, or be not, *any* HISTORICAL RECORD *of God's promiſe, that Chriſt ſhould be David's ſon:* for this record we muſt find here, or no where.

But, ſays the Deiſt; "how then are your Scrip-"tures reconciled? Do not Chriſtians hold; that "Chriſt, *doing no ſin,* deſerved no puniſhment? "And can Chriſtians then ſuppoſe, that God ſpeaks "of Chriſt in theſe words, *if he commit iniquity, I* "*will chaſten him?* And, if Chriſt be not meant in "this verſe; he cannot, in the verſes before and "after: conſequently, he cannot be meant in this "paſſage at all."

What

SERMON I.

What now *has been* the reply to this *adversary?* Or rather, what *can be* the reply from the *friends* of revelation? Among those who have ventured upon this subject, the general way has been—to assert *a double sense* of this, in common with other *prophecies relative to Christ:* and to say, that what does *not agree with Christ* must be spoken of some *other*, of some *primary and typical person*; as, *David,* for instance; or, in this particular case, of *Solomon.* But it seems to be quite forgotten; that, if, in any such double prophecy, you allow certain parts not to agree properly with *both* persons, and confine any one expression therein to *one person* exclusive of the other, the *sense* is then so far SINGLE: and of course, the *double* sense, said to pervade the whole, is given up, and gone, entirely.

But then; if, from the suppositions here made *of doing sin*, and *suffering punishment*, the Messiah cannot be here spoken of; what are we to do? How are we to bring to just disgrace this triumph of infidelity? Not that believers are bound to contradict whatever unbelievers shall advance: but yet, it must be the duty of those, who are *set for the defence of the Gospel*, carefully to *search the Scriptures*; and to see, whether things are so, as represented by our adversaries.

I proceed therefore to lay before you what seems to be the true sense of this important passage. And I remark first, that the original words do not properly

SERMON I.

perly fignify—*if he commit iniquity*—but—*yea,*[a] *when he fuffers, for iniquity.* The noun, from the verb here ufed, is often and properly rendered in our own tranflation *the punifhment of iniquity:*[b] confequently the verb, which when active fignifies to *commit iniquity*, muft when paffive fignify to *fuffer for iniquity*. The verb is *paffive* here; and therefore it means here *the fuffering for iniquity.*[c]

You have probably gone before me, in applying this to the Meffiah; fince *He* certainly *fuffered*, and was *punifhed*, not indeed for his own, but for *our iniquities.* For *the Lord laid on him the iniquity of us all*; and *by his ftripes*, by the ftripes laid on *him*, though due to *us*, by his ftripes *we are healed.* Let us now review the paffage. *I will be his father, and he fhall be my fon:* BECAUSE, or *yea*, IN HIS BEING PUNISHED FOR INIQUITY, *even* when he fuffereth the punifhment of iniquity, *then*[d] *fhall I chaftize him with the rod of men, and with the ftripes of the fons of Adam,* i. e. with the rod *due* to men, and with the ftripes *due* to the children of Adam. This is an exact verfion of the words; and perfectly do they re-

---

[a] 1 Sam. 15, 20, (*for* Deut. 3, 24), *becaufe* Jof. 22, 31, &c.
[b] Lev. 26; 41, 43. Lam. 4; 6 and 22. Ezek. 14, 10. See alfo Gen. 4, 13. 1 Sam. 28, 10. 2 Kings 7, 9. Job 19, 29. And חטאה Lam. 3, 39; Zech. 14, 19 twice.
[c] See Gen. 2, 4: בהבראם *when they were created.* Ezek. 43, 18: ביום העשותו *in die fieri illud.* NIPH. Infin. *fieri illud*— Buxt. Thefaur. 274. Num. 35, 19: בפגעו בו *when he meeteth* with him. Pfal. 3, 1: בברחו *when he fled.*
[d] Pf. 78, 34 (*yet* Job 24, 12) only converfive: fee Englifh.

prefent

SERMON I.

present *the Messiah*, as still *the son of God*, and well worthy that high character; because, even when *punished*, it was not on *his own* account but that of *men*. Let us remember, that *our chastisement was laid upon him*: and as to the words *I will chastize him with the rod of men, and the stripes of the sons of Adam* —with what clearness do they express, with what force of colouring do they delineate THE MESSIAH, suffering that *rod*, and those *stripes*, which were due to mankind! No wonder therefore, that the words following are—*But* (notwithstanding these his sufferings) *my loving kindness shall not depart away from him*.

There yet remains a third objection; which is— that *this passage cannot agree to Jesus*, because HE *never built* ANY HOUSE, OR TEMPLE, *to the Lord*; *as Solomon did*; *and as the prophecy expressly declares, the person spoken of therein shall*. But every man knows, that the word *house* does not always denote *a fabric made with hands for an habitation*. The objector might have heard of *devouring widows houses*; and of the Jews, as *a rebellious house*. Probably he had read of Moses, as *faithful in all his house*; but *the house of David*, in the common sense of *family*, he must have been acquainted with. In this very passage, David says—*Who am I, O Lord! and what is my* HOUSE, *that thou hast brought me hitherto! And this was yet a small thing in thy sight; but thou hast spoken also of thy servant's* HOUSE *for a great while to come*. *The house* therefore, spoken of here, *as to be built by God*; or by some descendant

from

SERMON I.

from David, whom GOD would raise up *after David was dead*—*might* be a figurative house, or family: and it *must* be so, because it is here expressly said, that *this house* was to be *established for ever*. By this son of David therefore, namely the Messiah, might GOD raise up an *house* infinitely magnificent; the *house, or family* of Jesus; the *temple* of Christianity: a *building* this, far greater, and more august, than *that of Solomon in all its glory*.

Should such an application of the words *house*, and *building*, and *temple*, appear at all strange; let us recollect the language elsewhere in the *Old* as well as in the New Testament. See particularly what ZACHARIAH prophecies of the *house*, or *building* by the MESSIAH; and as pertinently as if he meant to explain this very passage. [a] *Behold the man, whose name is* צמח *the branch; and he shall grow up out of his place,* (ומתחתיו *and from under him*), *and he* SHALL BUILD THE TEMPLE OF THE LORD. EVEN HE SHALL SURELY BUILD THE TEMPLE OF THE LORD, *and he shall bear the glory* הוד &c. *And they that are afar off* (the Gentiles) *shall come, and* BUILD IN THE TEMPLE OF THE LORD. The *New* Testament is equally strong with the *Old*. We read in 1 *Pet.* 2, 5, 6 *Ye also* (ye Christians) *as lively stones, are built up* A SPIRITUAL HOUSE —(Christ) *being the chief corner stone. Know ye not,* saith St. Paul, *that ye* (Christians) *are the* TEMPLE *of God?* —*The temple of God is holy; which* TEMPLE *Ye are.* —*Ye are the* TEMPLE *of the living God; ye are God's*

[a] Zech. 6; 12, 13.

BUILDING.

SERMON I.

BUILDING.—*Moses was faithful in all his* HOUSE, *as a servant; but Christ as a son, over his own* HOUSE : WHOSE HOUSE *we are.*— And lastly :— *Now therefore ye are of the houshold of God;* BUILT *upon the* FOUNDATION *of the Apostles and Prophets, Jesus Christ himself being the chief corner stone.*

From the preceding observations on the promise of GOD to David, concerning THE MESSIAH, and *him only*, there arises this inference : — That we be very cautious, in advancing the doctrine of *A double sense of such prophecies in the Old Testament*, as were meant to describe the Messiah. As to *deliverances*; it is allowed, that *one* may shadow forth *another*, because a less may give some idea of a greater — and therefore, that the deliverance of the Jews out of *Egypt*, or from *Babylon*, may shadow forth the deliverance of ALL MANKIND from *sin, and death,* by Jesus Christ.

But the case is widely different, as to the *person* of the Messiah — his office was *singular* — his character *had no parallel*— and he was to be known, and proved, to be different from all other men, by a set of prophetic marks, descriptive of *him*, and of him *only*: which set of marks, the more they are applied to others, the less they can prove with regard to him ; and indeed, if almost all of them are to be applied to others, they can with regard to him prove little, if any thing at all.

In particular, as to the important passage now before us : since the whole cannot be taken in a

double

double sense, let us consider it, as meant of one subject only.

If then our *common* translation of this message from GOD be just; the son here promised could be only *Solomon*: consequently, the Messiah is excluded. If the translation *now* offered be just; the son here promised could be only THE MESSIAH. So that, either way, *this* at least must be a prophecy intended in *one single sense.*

The New Testament sends us to the Old for *the testimonies* concerning *Jesus*; for all those descriptive marks, which were to prove *him the true Messiah:* and which were of course to constitute one great proof of the truth of Christianity. But, what would become of this proof; if the prophecies were all *primarily* meant of *other persons*; and only *secondarily*, or *ultimately*, of the MESSIAH? For, such a secondary sense being only discoverable *in the New Testament*; the *truth* of the New Testament must be *first proved*, before such secondary sense can be admitted: and then, of course, Christianity is proved without the assistance of such prophecies.

It is therefore no wonder at all, that the unbeliever should assert—that *Jesus is not* PRIMARILY *foretold any where*; and that *such a promised person has no* LITERAL *foundation in the Old Testament.* Yet surely, it must create some wonder, that Christians should undesignedly countenance (some in a less, some in a greater degree) this favourite principle of infidelity. But, as this doctrine has a direct tendency

dency to weaken the evidence for Christianity; there must be *some general reason*, which has led many wise and good men to *allow* what they could not *approve of*. And this reason has been—the difficulty, or rather the apparent impossibility, of *their applying solely to Christ* some Prophecies in the *Old* Testament, *so applied* in the *New*. Now this difficulty has been founded on the wrong ideas of *every thing being expressed rightly* in the *Text and Version* of the Old Testament; or, on the incapacity of such readers to discover and correct the mistakes. That there are *great mistakes in our present Version*, has been proved by *four important instances* in this one Discourse. And, as to the other and higher source of error, the *variation* of some words in *the original*, even in the Prophetic parts, and in places materially affecting the sense; proofs of several such instances will be soon communicated to the public. If then the obscurity, *now* so visible in some of the chief Prophecies concerning Christ, be in fact owing, partly to the errors in our common *Text*, and partly to the errors in our common *Version*;—and if it is for the honour of *this place* to have manifested *peculiar* zeal for *restoring the purity of the original*; may it soon have a large share in the *general* honour of *correcting our translation* likewise!

In the mean time may we, taught as we are in the New Testament to look for CHRIST, and *him only*, in the Prophecies of the Old Testament relative to the Messiah, may we in such wise read, mark, and learn, as to find *him*, who is *the way,*

the truth, and the life; him, who was, and is—
THE SON OF GOD—THE SON OF ABRAHAM—
THE SON OF DAVID—THE TRUE MESSIAH, AND
SAVIOUR OF MANKIND.

SERMON II.

Hebrews X; the 5th, 6th, and part of the 7th verses.

5. *Wherefore, when he cometh into the world, he saith, Sacrifice and offering thou wouldest not, but a body hast thou prepared me:*
6. *In burnt-offerings and sacrifices for sin thou hast had no pleasure:*
7. *Then said I, Lo! I come.*——

ST. Paul assures us, that *all Scripture is given by inspiration of God; and is profitable for doctrine, for reproof,* (rather confutation), *for correction, for instruction in righteousness.*

The contents of the whole book of Revelation could not have been summed up more concisely, and yet more clearly, than in these four articles. The *Doctrines*, we are to receive as *true*, is the
first

first article; and the second, the *Doctrines* we are to reject as *false:* the *Vices,* we are to *correct,* is the third article; and the fourth is the *Virtues,* we are to *cultivate.*

A right *faith* then is taught here, as the proper foundation of a right *practice.* The first general article, in which *holy Scripture* is here said to be *profitable,* is the *Doctrine,* which it contains. And yet, even this article is not introduced by the Apostle, without previously asserting *The Divine Inspiration of Scripture.*

It must therefore be an excellent rule for *the man of God,* who, as such, is desirous of being *perfect,* and *throughly furnished unto* all sound doctrine, as well as *all good works,* to have this Apostolical arrangement carefully in view: that so he may consult the honour, the dignity, and the certainty of Scripture, by advancing nothing as even likely to be true, which tends to *invalidate the reasoning,* and of course to *shake the authority,* of an Evangelist, or an Apostle.

The Author of the Epistle to the Hebrews, generally allowed to have been St. *Paul,* advances in the chapter from whence my Text is taken such doctrine, as several Writers have been pleased (either in plain words, or by consequence) to deny. And it has appeared to other Writers, that a defence of this chapter is very difficult, if not quite impossible.

And what now should be the consequence of reflections, like these;. reflections cast upon so

masterly

masterly a writer, as well as so diftinguished an Apoftle: as if he, who was an *Hebrew of the Hebrews*, and brought up *at the feet of Gamaliel*, could have been unacquainted with his Hebrew Bible! Or as if so exact a reasoner, as well as so good a man, could be convicted of using a false argument in support of a true doctrine! What, I say, should be the consequence; but that those, who are *set for the defence of the gospel*, should *give the more earneft heed* on such an occasion: and consider with particular attention — what it is St. Paul here afferts — how he reasons upon the affertion — and whether the Apoftle's argument, and consequently the Apoftle himself, be not here juftly defensible.

An enquiry, tending to eftablish the authority of *St. Paul*, in quoting from the Old Teftament an important paffage as relating to the *Incarnation of Chrift*, will scarce appear at any time, certainly it will not at prefent appear, *unfeafonable*. For when can we, more properly, vindicate to our Apoftle the honours illuftriously his due? When confirm one another, so feafonably, in our belief of *his infpiration*; as on *this day*, facred to *his fame*?

At prefent therefore I propofe

Firft: to ftate, what is the fubject of St. Paul's difcourfe in this chapter; and

Secondly: to what purpofe he quotes the celebrated paffage from the fortieth Pfalm:

X 3   Thirdly:

SERMON II.

Thirdly: to consider the particular passage thus quoted, as it stands in the Psalm; and

Lastly: to shew, that the affirmation of the Apostle concerning these words, as spoken by the Messiah, is by no means inconsistent with the Psalm itself: because the objections, which now lie against it, may be satisfactorily removed.

First then, as to *the subject of the Apostle's discourse*, in the chapter, from whence the Text is taken.

This was — that, from the nature of the service under the law of Moses, it must appear, that *that* law was not able, of itself, to *perfect* the worshippers of God — that the legal sacrifices were only *shadows* of substantial good things, then future — that, only shadowing forth future blessings, they were not what God principally aimed at, and *took pleasure in*; though God had indeed commanded them — but that those shadowy representations, which it was necessary should be often made, were all to cease, when the substance itself appeared; as soon as that *great sacrifice* of the MESSIAH *had been offered*: since it was from their relation to *him*, that these typical rites derived the virtue and efficacy belonging to them.

The law (says he) *having* only *a shadow of good things, cannot*, (even by its principal sacrifices, by those offered yearly on the great day of atonement), *make the comers thereunto perfect* — *For it was not possible*

fible (he adds) *that the blood of bulls and of goats should take away sin*; i. e. by any virtue of their own, and by any other efficacy than their shadowing forth the sacrifice of Christ: which former were therefore to cease of course, when the latter should in the fulness of time take place.

Having in these few remarks stated the Apostle's subject, I proceed to consider,

Secondly, to what purpose he here quotes the words of the Psalm. Let us just recollect, that his point was — the insufficiency of the Mosaic sacrifices, of themselves, to recover God's favour: consequently, that these must cease, when Christ, whose death they represented, was himself sacrificed for us.

Now, as the abolition of animal sacrifices greatly affected the honour of the law of Moses, upon the mistaken prejudices of the later Jews; St. Paul, writing to these Jews, thought it absolutely necessary to confirm his doctrine from the *Old Testament*, the divine authority of which those Jews allowed. And surely it was impossible, that any part of the Old Testament could confirm his doctrine more fully, than the following passage of the Psalm — *Sacrifice and offering thou wouldest not, but* A BODY DIDST THOU PREPARE FOR ME: *in burnt-offerings and sacrifices for sin thou hadst no pleasure; then said I, Lo! I come: in the roll of the book it is written* (or prophecied) *concerning me. To do thy will, O God &c.*

SERMON II.

&c. where, after quoting sufficient for his purpose, he breaks off, without finishing the last sentence which is — *To do thy will, O God, is my delight.*

Now, as nothing of this kind was foretold in the law, or *written in the roll of that book, concerning any person but the Messiah*; and as no other person ever *came into the world*, to set aside the use of animal sacrifices, but the *Messiah* only, who was to supersede all these by the one *sacrifice of himself*: so, to make him capable of this, it was necessary that he should have *a body* of his own to offer up. *A body* therefore was *prepared for* him; not indeed by man, but by *God* himself: for Christ was born of a *Virgin*, (and strictly therefore *the seed of the woman*), through the miraculous *power of God*. In that *body of flesh* he suffered and died; setting aside thereby all the preparatory and representative sacrifices of brute creatures. These indeed, as a temporary service, God had *required*, and must have *taken pleasure in*, so long as they were intended by him to last: which therefore was *the first will of God*. And Christ, by offering up his own body, agreeably to the good pleasure of his father, established *the second will of God*, in making atonement for mankind, once for all.

The Apostle therefore comments on the Psalm thus — *Above when he said, Sacrifice,* &c. *thou didst not require,* or *delight in,* (i.e. any longer), *then said he, Lo! I come: to do thy Will, O God,* &c: *he taketh away the first,* (the *first* will, or appointment of GOD,

GOD, by the law), *that he may establish the second* (the *second* will, or appointment of God by the Gospel): and then the Apostle adds—*By the which will* (the second) *we are sanctified, through the offering of the body*—the body—*of Jesus Christ, once for all.*

I shall add here two short remarks on this passage of the Apostle. The first is—that the word for *body,* (in the passage *a body didst thou prepare for me*), which seems to be there necessary to St. Paul's argument, is his true and genuine word; as appears from all the Greek copies of this Epistle, confirmed by all the antient versions. And it derives additional confirmation from verse the tenth; where the word is repeated—*through the offering of the* BODY *of Jesus Christ.* Nor is this at all contradictory to other passages, which speak of our redemption by *Christ's* BLOOD; for surely *that blood* must be the blood of *that body.* Christ himself speaks of his *body,* as *given for us:* St. Peter says, that *Christ bore our sins in his body:* and St. Paul, elsewhere—that *Christ hath reconciled us by the body of his flesh.*

The other remark is, that the Apostle here directly and positively affirms, (and shall not *we* believe him?), that the words [*Sacrifice,* &c. *thou wouldest not; then said I, Lo! I come*] that *these* are the very words of the MESSIAH; and therefore must have been prophetically meant and intended for *the Messiah* by the Psalmist. For the Apostle's words are extremely remarkable; *When* HE *cometh into the world,* HE *saith, Sacrifice,* &c. *thou wouldest not*—LO! I COME.

All

All this seems rational and consistent; indeed so clearly rational, and so entirely consistent, that probably no objection would ever have been made to the Apostle's reasoning here; had it not been very difficult to reconcile what is here quoted, with the words now found in the Psalm.

I proceed therefore, thirdly, to consider the passage, as it stands in the Psalm itself: and this I shall endeavour to do as plainly, as the nature of the subject will allow.

The present Hebrew words are thus expressed in our last (which is the Bible) translation.

Sacrifice and offering thou didst not desire;
   MINE EARS *hast thou opened:*
burnt offering and sin-offering hast thou not required.
   Then said I, Lo, I come:
in the volume of the book it is written of me:
   I delight to do thy will, &c.

Now here the words agree with those of the Apostle; excepting in the second clause, where the variation is indeed very considerable: for the words, which the Apostle quotes, as signifying *but* (or *then*) *a body didst thou prepare for me*, are here rendered, (what indeed they do not signify), MINE EARS *hast thou opened.* How widely different soever these two renderings may appear in English; yet, with the variation of only a small part (at the bottom) of three adjoining letters, the present Hebrew words would express

the

SERMON II.

the very sense of the Apostle; which now they evidently do not. So that either the Apostle has *misquoted*, if the Hebrew words were in his days what they are *now*; or *else*, the Hebrew words are *not now* what they were in his days: but the Hebrew Text must have since suffered some alteration *here*, as it has in many other places.

It has indeed been asserted, that St. Paul might, and did, adopt the words of the *Greek version*; though he saw, that the sense of that version was here widely different from that of the Hebrew Text. And what has been thus advanced by some, has been admitted by others; yet possibly neither advanced, nor admitted, for any better reason, than as being the only solution which occurred: and as if an account, though very unsatisfactory, was preferable to none at all.

But, is it reasonable to suppose — can it be for the interest of Christianity to admit — that either Christ himself, or any one of his Apostles, ever quoted out of the Old Testament what was not in it — quoted, as being there, what was not there; either in words express, or in sense equivalent? And yet such differences there are, at present, between *some* of the quotations in the New Testament, and the passages themselves as found in the common Hebrew Text.

But I do not so ill consult the honour of *St. Paul*, as to suppose it possible, that he could adopt the words of a *translation*, where *false*; and yet,

reason

reason upon them as *true*; and put them into the very mouth of CHRIST HIMSELF. Admit but this principle; and there follows necessarily this conclusion — that, either *the word in St. Paul* has been corrupted, or else *a part of three letters in the Psalm*: and if we attend carefully, the case will be clear in favour of the New Testament.

The word *body* in the Epistle is confirmed (as far as appears) by *all the Greek copies*, and by *all the antient versions*, of this Epistle; the word makes excellent *sense* here, *as Greek*; and it is in perfect harmony with the *context*.

Whereas the word in the Psalm, rendered *ears*, (instead of *body*), even though it should be (which is not yet certain) found in *all* the present *Hebrew* copies, does *not make sense* where it now stands; is not capable of a regular construction, *as Hebrew*; does not agree with the *context*; and is contradicted by *almost all the antient versions*, which even here in the Psalm confirm the reading of the Apostle. So many and so strong would these authorities be found, if they were produced at large, and permitted to appear in their full force; that probably but little opposition would have been made to the conclusion before drawn; had not some objections, much more powerful, and which have generally been thought insuperable, arisen from *other parts* of this Psalm.

These objections therefore I proceed, *lastly*, to point out, and (I hope) effectually to remove; in order

to

SERMON II.

to shew *the consistent propriety of the Psalm*, when considered as containing the words of *the Messiah*, agreeably to the Apostle's assertion.

One great objection is this—If the words, quoted by St. Paul, are the words of *the Messiah*; his must be also the words before and after the quotation, because there is no change of the speaker. But, say the objectors, *the latter part* of the Psalm cannot have been spoken by the Messiah; because *He* could not say, or be prophetically represented as saying,—MINE INIQUITIES *have taken hold upon me — they are more in number than the hairs of my head; therefore my heart faileth me.*

It is also objected, that several other expressions in the latter part of the Psalm, *wishing destruction to enemies*, are quite inconsistent with the true character of *Jesus Christ*.

And it is objected still farther, that the *beginning and end* of the Psalm are so far from agreeing uniformly to any one person, that they are *flatly inconsistent*; the former being a *thanksgiving* for *a deliverance out of all trouble*; and the latter being *a prayer* from one under *so much trouble*, as to be almost in *despair*.

Now, with regard to these three objections: though it should be possible to remove the first (as I think may be done) by rendering the word MINE AFFLICTIONS, which is now rendered *mine iniquities* — and *if it were* possible to remove the second objection, by rendering some of the other words, not as *wish-*

ing,

ing, but as FORETELLING, the *destruction of enemies* — yet I apprehend the third and last objection to be decisive, upon the present state of this Psalm.

Had this psalm been formed like the twenty-second, which contains also the words of *the Messiah*; describing him first as *suffering*, and praying for deliverance; and afterwards as *delivered,* and full of praise: had this same been the plan here, then had this Psalm (so far) been, like the other, *natural* and *noble.* But, that the first *ten* verses here should describe *Christ,* as *delivered* from his *sufferings*; nay, as *brought up out of the pit,* namely in his rising from the grave, and as *set upon a rock* for ever, safe from all suffering; and yet, that he should close this *new song of praise,* close this very triumph, with representing himself as even then *compassed about with evils numberless,* and just *sinking under them* — this appears to be impossible; so clearly inconsistent this with every principle of composition, and indeed with common sense, as scarce to be imagined of any common writer: much less, of the sacred poet *David*; and yet, behold, *a greater than* David *is here* — for it is a song of THE MESSIAH!

But as to this, and every other objection against the former part of this Psalm, as being *a song of Christ,* on account of the latter part; and as to the impossibility of ascribing this latter part, with the former, to *any one* person, as speaking the whole at *any one* time: all such objections will probably be removed to satisfaction by observing — that *this Psalm*

SERMON II.

Pſalm *is now made up of* TWO PSALMS; and two Pſalms certainly may be applicable to *different perſons*.

The ſeven laſt verſes originally made a diſtinct Pſalm; compoſed by a perſon under heavy diſtreſs, and imploring immediate aſſiſtance. Now Pſalm THE SEVENTIETH is the very *concluſion* of this *fortieth* Pſalm; but with this difference, that the ſeventieth Pſalm is preſerved *complete* at the end of the fortieth — whereas the ſeventieth itſelf wants the beginning; for the firſt words now (very aſtoniſhingly!) ſignify —

——— O GOD, TO DELIVER ME.

The beginning therefore being wanting, at the head of the ſeventieth Pſalm; we muſt learn how much is there wanting, by conſulting Pſalm the fortieth. If then we allow the five laſt verſes there to belong to a ſeparate Pſalm; we ſhall ſee, that the thirteenth verſe, which prays for deliverance, muſt have been preceded by the twelfth, which mentions the evils to be delivered from; and that the twelfth, beginning with *for*, muſt have been preceded by verſe the eleventh: and there we have what begins this ſeventieth Pſalm, with an invocation and addreſs to the Lord. So that the laſt ſeven verſes of this fortieth Pſalm are quite a different compoſition; and very improperly ſubjoined to the other *ten* verſes.

Several accidents of the ſame kind have happened elſewhere; making two Pſalms out of one, and one

Pſalm

Pſalm out of two. Thus, what are now the ninth and tenth Pſalms in the Hebrew, are but one Pſalm in the Greek verſion; and what is now Pſalm the hundred and forty-ſeventh in the Hebrew, is in the Greek two Pſalms. Thus again, it may be proved from many MSS. as well as the compoſition itſelf, that what are now the *forty-ſecond and forty-third* Pſalms were originally one Pſalm only. And it is highly probable, that the improper ſeparation of this forty-third Pſalm into a forty-third and a forty-ſecond occaſioned, that the original forty-ſecond became the forty-firſt — and then, as to the original forty-firſt; ſome joined it on *at the end of the fortieth*, whilſt others removed it to another place; (perhaps, to fill up a vacancy, owing to a ſimilar miſtake); and thus it made, and makes ſtill, *Pſalm the ſeventieth.*

Having ſeen it to be highly probable, that the ſeven laſt verſes, now added to the fortieth Pſalm, are *a diſtinct Pſalm*, and had at firſt no connection with the former ten verſes; let us ſee now, whether *the whole* of what is properly the fortieth Pſalm be not *a prophetical Hymn of the Meſſiah* — as St. Paul affirms of *the part*, which he has quoted.

When this Pſalm ſhall be thus properly attended to, as containing ten verſes only; the determination (I apprehend) muſt be — that it belongs to *the Meſſiah*, and can belong to no other perſon. It ſeems clearly to be meant as *a ſong of praiſe* from *Chriſt*, at his *reſurrection*; after he *had put an end* to other

bloody

bloody facrifices by his own death; and when GOD had *brought him up out of the horrible pit,* and *set his feet upon a rock, establishing his goings.* As he had, during his sufferings, offered up *prayers* and *songs of supplication;* so now, GOD had *put into his mouth a new song,* not of prayer, but of *praise,* a sacred song of triumph and thankfgiving.

He declares, that *men ought to learn* from that amazing event (meaning his own *resurrection*) the *blessedness* of *trusting in Jehovah* — that the contrivances of Jehovah's love were not only *wonderful,* but also *numberless* — though he could *not* therefore *recount them all,* yet he would not conceal the astonishing scheme of MAN's REDEMPTION, which he himself had accomplished, by offering up that *body,* which *God* had *prepared for him* — that he had declared his perfect readiness to perform *the will of God,* in doing and suffering what was *written* prophetically *concerning him* — that he *had published righteousness* (everlasting righteousness) by the Gospel dispensation — and that he would continue still more and more to proclaim *God's faithfulness and salvation to the great congregation;* or, as some translate, *to many a congregation.* For since *many* is frequently put for *all* (as in *Isai.* 53; 12, *he bare the sin of many*) there seems to *them* a beautiful opposition intended here, as well as in *Psalm the* 22*d,* between the *one local* congregation of the *Jews,* and the *universal assemblies of Christians over all the earth.* But, as *the great congregation* may signify *the universal congregation of Christians;* perhaps that phrase may be here continued with great propriety.

Y   Having

SERMON II.

Having thus shewn the nature of St. Paul's reasoning in the *Tenth Chapter* of *the Epistle to the Hebrews*—having vindicated the pertinency of his very celebrated *Quotation*, there made — and having freed *the fortieth Psalm* from what had hitherto prevented the just application of it to *the Messiah* —I shall conclude this Discourse with offering (what seems to be) an exact *translation* of *this important Psalm*.

Psalm XL.

Ver. 1. *With earnest expectation I looked unto* JEHOVAH; *and he hath inclined unto me, and heard my cry.*

2. *And he hath brought me up out of the horrible pit, out of the deep mire;*
and he hath set my feet upon a rock, he hath established my goings.

3. *And he hath put in my mouth a new song, even praise to our God;*
many shall consider it, and fear; and put their trust in JEHOVAH.

4. *Blessed is the man, who hath made* JEHOVAH *his confidence;*
and hath not turned to the proud, and to the followers of imposture.

5. *Manifold are thy works, O* JEHOVAH, *my God!*
thy wonders and thy contrivances there is no recounting unto thee:
I would shew, and declare them; but they are great beyond number.

6. *Sacrifice and offering thou didst not delight in;*
THEN A BODY DIDST THOU PREPARE FOR ME:
Burnt-offering and sin-offering thou didst not require;

7. *Then said I, Lo! I come;*
in the roll of the book it is written concerning me.

8. *To do thy will, O my God, is my delight;*
yea, thy law is in the midst of my affections.

9. *I have published righteousness in the great congregation;*
lo! my lips I will not restrain:
thou, O JEHOVAH, *my God, knowest.*

10. *Thy righteousness have I not hidden in the midst of my heart;*
thy faithfulness and thy salvation have I not concealed:
I have declared thy mercy and thy truth to the great congregation.

SERMON III.

I͞s a i a h IX; ver. 5, and 6.

5. *For every battle of the warriour* is *with confused noise, and garments rolled in blood;* but this *shall be with burning and fuel of fire.*

6. *For unto us a Child is born, unto us a Son is given; and the government shall be upon his shoulder: and his name shall be called Wonderful — Counsellor — The mighty God — The everlasting Father — The Prince of Peace.*

WE are told by St. Luke, that our blessed Saviour, on a very important occasion, *beginning at Moses and all the Prophets, expounded in all the Scriptures the things concerning himself.* And it is no wonder, that they, who heard such a teacher, upon such a subject, should afterwards say — *Did not our heart burn within us, while he opened to us the Scriptures?*

SERMON III.

We are sometimes apt to wish, that *we ourselves* had been *present* at this infallible explanation of Moses and the Prophets: or, at least, that the particulars of a discourse so highly interesting had been *written* for *our* instruction. In either of these cases, we should (I am fully persuaded) have found *the words of the Text* among those very Scriptures, which Christ expounded concerning himself: and we should then have seen the direct tendency, and the clear connexion of every link in the chain of this Prophecy.

But we are left (for wise reasons no doubt) to *enquire and search diligently* into the meaning of this, and of some other passages, which *prophesied* of our salvation by Christ; left to search *what, and what manner* of things were *revealed* unto the Prophets, and have been by them recorded, concerning *the Messiah*. And if his humiliation and glory be things, which *the Angels desire to look into*; well may *we* conclude it *our* duty, to consider with care all the passages prophetically descriptive of *him*. I call it our duty, to *consider all these passages with care*: for certainly, where any Scriptural matters are of particular moment, and yet attended with no small difficulty, there every Christian should earnestly wish to understand: and, more especially, every teacher of the Gospel, who is both to understand, and to explain.

On the subject of Prophecy, however important in itself, there have been various mistakes; and

two,

SERMON III.

two, which are oppofite to each other; leaving truth in the golden mean, as ufual, equally removed from both. The one extreme is — that of finding Chrift *almoft every where* in the Old Teftament; and the other is — the finding him *fcarce any where*: and I apprehend, that the difguft, naturally arifing from the former opinion, has encreafed the latter. For, whilft one fays — *Lo, here is Chrift*; and another, *Lo, he is there*; and both pretend to find him in paffages, where common fenfe determines that he could not have been intended: others, revolting at thefe abfurdities, will fcarce own Chrift to be meant where he really is. And, whether owing to this alone, or to whatever other concurrent caufe, the event feems to have been — that *Chrift* is not *now* feen and acknowledged in feveral paffages of the Old Teftament, where *He*, and perhaps *He alone*, is the perfon fpoken of. And, with every man *of this* opinion, it can be no wonder at all, that Chrift, *beginning at Mofes and all the Prophets, expounded in all the Scriptures the things concerning himfelf.*

It cannot be denied, that our Saviour and his Apoftles appealed frequently to *the Old Teftament* for proofs of his being *the Meffiah*; of his being the true and the only perfon there foretold, as to be *the light of the Gentiles*, and *the glory of Ifrael*; and of his being marked out with fuch very ftriking particulars of *life, death, and refurrection*, as concentered all in *him*, and never met in any other

other *person*. The conclusion, therefore, with every Christian, is, that such Prophecies must have *existed*, and existed *plainly*, in the Old Testament. And if such passages do not appear *at present* in their former splendour; if they do not strike *now*, with the same clearness of evidence, and with the same power of conviction, as they did 1700 years ago: it must be our duty, to find out (if we can) the causes of this difference.

Now there are two general causes, which may have operated, singly or together, in making passages obscure at present, which formerly were clear; and these are — either, that *some alteration may have happened in the Hebrew copies* — or else, if the text be still in such places pure, *our translation may not express the sense of the original.*

Both these causes have concurred, though in very different degrees, in throwing deep shades, and even thick darkness, upon the illustrious Prophecy referred to in my Text. I say, in *very different degrees*; because, though the errors here in our translation are *neither few nor inconsiderable*, there seems to be no greater corruption here of the Hebrew text, than the alteration of *one single letter*. And I remark this, with the greater satisfaction, because it has been repeatedly asserted, that strange *dislocations and corruptions* must be here admitted: if we would make the Prophet consistent, and at unity with himself.

It is, however, to *mistranslation*, that we owe here the chief inconsistencies, and that want of connection

SERMON III.

tion so very obvious to every man. Indeed, the justly celebrated *Mr. Mede*,[a] who has long led the way to a true explanation of the passage here *in the general*, has not at all touched upon *the fifth verse*, which contains the chief difficulty; and by which the connection of the four first verses with the sixth is *now*, in our translation, entirely destroyed. And yet, it is that very sixth verse, which gives to this Prophecy its principal glory; and stamps it with the seal of heaven, in favour of the then future Messiah.

Those Prophecies, which are generally allowed to relate to Christ, as they form one of the grand evidences for the truth of Christianity, have (and no wonder) proved *rocks of offence* to the advocates for Infidelity. And, in opposition to *this particular* Prophecy, it has been urged with great confidence of boasting, that *the rules of language* forbid us to consider THE MESSIAH as meant by the *child* here said to be *born*; because *the Messiah cannot be meant in the other words immediately connected with them* — whereas, say the objectors, all is regular, all consistent, on supposition that the Prophet speaks here of *Hezekiah*, or of *his own son*, or of *some other child* of common extraction, though described with uncommon magnificence.[b]

But, the truth is — that *several circumstances* in this illustrious Prophecy *are by no means* applicable

[a] Book 1, Disc. 25; and Book 3, ad Cap.7. pag. 101, 457.
[b] Collins's *Literal Prophecy*, pag. 140.

to

any *common* child — that *all* the circumstances *are* applicable to THE MESSIAH, and some to *him only*. And therefore it is no wonder, that our Church hath selected this very passage, for *the first lesson*, on the day sacred to the *nativity of Christ*.

It cannot therefore be useless, to take a more particular view of this distinguished Prophecy; and especially, to clear the connection from those difficulties, which (it must be confessed) render some parts of it, in our present translation, quite unintelligible.

THE ALMIGHTY is said, *in the midst of judgment*, to *remember mercy*. In conformity with this character, the holy *Prophets*, the ancient messengers from GOD, if commissioned to denounce *vengeance* on the Jews, were commissioned also to proclaim *consolation*; and frequently, to proclaim the latter at the very time that they denounced the former. We therefore find the severest threats mixed with the most reviving promises: and in the same prophetic volume that we read, *Behold the Lord will render his anger with fury*; we read also, *Comfort ye, comfort ye my people, saith your God*.

This interesting appeal both to the hopes and fears of the Jewish people, alarming them with the approach of national miseries due to their *sins*, yet supporting them with repeated promises of *the Messiah*, the chief glory of that people: *this* is the true key to the general meaning of the Prophet, in those passages, which are immediately connected with the Text.

St. Jerom

SERMON III.

St. Jerom has observed, that ISAIAH is not so properly a *Prophet*, as an *Evangelist*. But yet, though Isaiah did record, 700 years before the several events, many prophecies wonderfully descriptive of the Messiah's *Birth*, *Life* and *Death*; in some of which passages *Poetry* hath appeared in perfect beauty, as well as *Prophecy* in perfect dignity; and though it hath been justly remarked, that Isaiah is *oftner* the messenger of *glad* than of *gloomy* tidings: yet even in *his* prophecies, vengeance and pity, justice and mercy, threatnings and promises, sometimes *meet together*.

From the beginning of the seventh chapter to the end of the twelfth the Prophet describes the fate of the Jews, with respect to the hostile nations round about them; concluding with a description of *the Kingdom of the Messiah*: concerning whom, some very remarkable prophecies are also interspersed. Chapter the seventh describes the consternation of the Jews from the combined armies of *Israel and Syria*; with a promise of safety to *Jerusalem* at that time, and protection of the *family of David*, till the birth of *the Messiah* — who should be *born of a Virgin*, and be both *God and Man*.

But, though the scheme *then* formed against the royal house of David should certainly be frustrated; and though the two Kings, then advancing against Jerusalem, should be themselves cut off; and this, in less time than the little son of Isaiah, then present, could grow up to know good from evil: yet,

such

such was the impiety of Ahaz, and so general the wickedness of his subjects, that the Prophet (at the same time) declares, they were to suffer exemplary punishment; and from the hands of those very *Assyrians*, to whom Ahaz was then about to apply for assistance against his adversaries.

Very similar to this is the mixed nature of the eighth chapter, introductory to the ninth from whence the Text is taken. The destruction of the kings of Israel and Syria now drawing *nearer*, than at the time of the seventh chapter; the eighth opens with an account of *another son of the Prophet*, called by a name signifying *hasten spoil*; and it is declared, that before *this son* should be able to pronounce *Father*, and *Mother*, the cities of Samaria and Damascus should be plundered by the king of Assyria.[a] It then follows, that this Assyrian, whose assistance Ahaz preferred to that of God himself, should enter Judea as an adversary; and, like *an over-flowing stream, reach even to the neck*, i. e. advance to the head and capital city of Jerusalem. But still, that, as the land was *Immanuel's*, as it belonged to that *Messiah*, who was to be *God with us*; he (the Messiah) should be for a *sanctuary* to those, who feared

---

[a] On this eighth chapter see the excellent remarks of Mr. Peirce (Heb. 2, 13) from verse five, &c. particularly, as to verse sixteen, to which verse seems evidently to belong what now begins verse seventeen, not only in the *Greek*, but also in the *Arabic* and in the *Chaldee Par*. See also on this eighth chapter (Jeffery's) Review of the Controv. p. 124, &c.

SERMON III.

the Lord, and became his true disciples: whereas to all those, who should reject him and his doctrine, he should prove a *stone of stumbling, and rock of offence* — words, expressly quoted of Christ, in several parts of the New Testament.

The Prophet, having addressed himself *to* the Messiah in verse the eighth, in verse the eighteenth introduces *the Messiah* speaking of *himself and his* [a] *disciples*; as to be for *signs and for wonders*; as recommending the doctrines they taught, by *the signs, and wonders, and miracles,* which they performed. After which he closes the eighth chapter with the most expressive description of that misery, in which the Jews were to be involved — for attempting to consult the dead — for practising the worst rites of the idolatrous heathens — for blaspheming that GOD, whom they had forsaken — and for rejecting that teacher, the Messiah, whom GOD is represented as having sent. And the sum of their misery is, that, looking towards *Heaven,* they saw nothing but vengeance; and, upon *Earth,* behold all was distress and darkness.

The eighth chapter being thus ended, the ninth begins with the exultation and rapture of the Prophet; as if he then actually saw *the Light of the Gospel,* and *the Sun of righteousness* then risen *with healing in his wings.* And his triumph opens with looking towards *those parts* of Judea, which were to be chiefly honoured with the residence, and enlightened by the doctrine, of the Messiah: and these were the

---

[a] Not of his (Isaiah's) own sons; as Collins, *Grounds,* &c. pag. 42.

northern parts, which lay moſt expoſed, and had therefore ſuffered moſt from the incurſions of their foreign adverſaries.

Verſe the firſt (as numbered in our Engliſh Bible) is at preſent tranſlated, with a wonderful want of ſenſe, in the manner following — *Nevertheleſs, the dimneſs ſhall not be ſuch, as was in her vexation; when at the firſt he lightly afflicted the land of Zebulun and the land of Naphtali; and afterward did more grievouſly afflict her, by the way of the ſea, beyond Jordan, in Galilee of the nations.* Perhaps the true ſenſe of the original may be expreſſed thus — *But, darkneſs is not there, where there hath been diſtreſs.* As the former time made vile *the land of Zebulun, and the land of Naphtali;* ſo the latter time hath made it honourable: *by the way of the ſea, beyond Jordan, Galilee of the Gentiles.* Then follows verſe the ſecond — *The people* (rather *this* people) *that walked in darkneſs, have ſeen a great light; they, that dwelt in the land of the ſhadow of death, upon them hath the light ſhined.*

After this *partial* view of the mighty bleſſing, the Prophet congratulates the *whole nation*; all thoſe Jews, who *waited for redemption,* and rejoiced at the publication of the Goſpel. To all of *theſe* this publication was indeed *glad tidings, and of great joy*; Joy, ſays the Prophet, great as that of *Harveſt!* Joy, ſays he, great as that of *Victory!* — great, as that of *Plenty,* ſecured by *Peace* — as that of *Riches,* acquired by the *Spoils* of thoſe who wanted to plunder and to enſlave.

But

SERMON III.

But though the *latter* part of this verse clearly expresses most abundant joy; yet, to our great surprize, we read at present in the *former* part of the verse — *Thou haſt* NOT *increaſed the joy*. This is evidently the true rendering of the words in the preſent *text*. And if it be ſaid, that though the negative particle be in the *text*, yet there is another reading in the *margin*; the reply is, that, as it has not been agreed, whether *the marginal words* in the Hebrew Bible, are really *various readings*, or merely *conjectures*, they can have no authority, till they are proved to exiſt in *the text of MSS*. And therefore, in a caſe ſo important as the preſent, the learned will receive great ſatisfaction from knowing, that the marginal word, ſo neceſſary to the ſenſe here, is found in *the text* of ſeveral Hebrew MSS.

If then the Prophet ſpeaks here of ſuch exuberant joy; let us ſee, what foundation he lays, and what cauſe he aſſigns for this glory, and the crown of this rejoicing. [a] His reaſons are three, firſt, that *ſlavery was no more*: ſecondly, that *war was at an end*: and, thirdly, that *now commenced the kingdom of the Meſſiah, the Prince of peace*.

What this *ſlavery* was, which was thus terminated; and what the *hoſtilities*, thus ended; will be learnt from the nature of the *kingdom*, thus eſtabliſhed: and this kingdom muſt be *ſpiritual*, becauſe it is *everlaſting* — becauſe *of the increaſe of this government, and its peace, there ſhall be no end*.

The firſt reaſon for this joy is expreſſed in verſe the fourth, which repreſents *their being freed* from

[a] Compare Jer. xxx. particularly 7—9, and 19—22.

the yoke of sin, and *the tyranny of* Satan; which freedom the Prophet celebrates, as effected by a deliverance eminently the work of *God alone*; just as was the victory over the *Midianites*, when (as the seventh chapter of *Judges* informs us) care was taken, that Israel should not say — *Mine own hand hath saved me.*

In verse the fifth Isaiah expresses the effect of this victory and deliverance by the Messiah; and that effect is *peace*. But, in our *present* English translation, it is expressed in the following words; which convey either no meaning, or a meaning plainly inconsistent with the context — *For every battle of the warriour is with confused noise, and garments rolled in blood, but this shall be with burning and fuel of fire.* And then it follows — *for unto us is born* THE PRINCE OF PEACE.

But if the victory, here spoken of, be *spiritual*; can it be with *burning*, and with *fuel of fire?* And if this verse really did (which it does not) speak of any battle of the Messiah, as opposed to other battles; yet, was it possible for Isaiah to say, that other battles are attended with *noise and blood*, but this with *burning* and *fire*; because there is born *the Prince of peace?* The words have no opposition in the original, as in our present translation; but they describe the destruction of *all the instruments of war*; and of these as of no further use, because *the kingdom of everlasting peace* was then begun.

Thus, in the words of the Psalmist — when GOD *maketh wars to cease in all the world*, it is said, that

he

he breaketh the bow, and knappeth the spear in sunder, AND BURNETH THE CHARIOTS IN THE FIRE. And thus Isaiah (who elsewhere says, that, under Messiah's reign, SWORDS *shall be turned into plowshares, and* SPEARS *into pruning-hooks*) says here — as I apprehend the words should be translated — that *every* WEAPON *of the warrior used in* BATTLE, *and the garment rolled in* MUCH *blood* (or, *often* rolled in blood) *is for burning, even fuel of the fire.*

Without entering critically here into the authorities for this version, it may be only necessary at present to say in general, that there are authorities sufficient: and in particular, that the latter part of this verse is thus construed, not only in the *Syriac and Vulgate* versions, but also in at least *three editions* of our ENGLISH *translation,* as it stood above two hundred years ago — in which the words are, *shall be burnt, and feed the fire.*

Taking with us then this necessary idea, that *all the instruments of war were to be destroyed*; then, with the most exact regularity follows the Prophet's illustrious description of *King Messiah*: a description filled with words the most magnificent; yet true of *Christ,* and of him *only,* and therefore most comfortable to *us:* and words, where in general the meaning is so obvious, that the explanation *here* necessary may be very short. *Unto us* (says the Prophet, still speaking of the future with the certainty of the time present) *a child is born, unto us a son is given; and the government shall be upon his shoulder:*
and

SERMON III.

and his name shall be called Wonderful, Counsellor, the mighty God, the everlasting Father, the Prince of peace. And *wonderful* indeed is *the Child* thus *born,* as born of *a Virgin:* wonderful *the Son* thus *given,* as being *the Son of God*: and wonderful this *Immanuel (God with us)* in every circumstance of his life, his death, and his resurrection — COUNSELLOR; as being a teacher from heaven, sent to declare and *reveal* to man *the secret Council of God* — Himself the MIGHTY GOD; or *God the mighty,* the conqueror, the captain of our salvation — THE EVERLASTING FATHER; but these words (with more conformity to the original, and without *confounding* the Divine Persons of *Father and Son*) should be rendered, *The father of eternity, or of the everlasting age*; as being founder of the *age* and *dispensation,* which was to *know no end*; as publisher of the *everlasting Gospel,* which was to lead men to *life eternal* — and lastly, THE PRINCE OF PEACE; the author of that faith, which makes *Jew and Gentile* to love one another; which forms into *one family* of benevolence *all mankind*; which, when it cannot *reconcile* the world, *overcometh* it: which teaches, what no other doctrine ever taught effectually, *peace of mind*; and gives, what the favour of no other Prince ever gave, *peace with God.*

Having thus attempted, from a variety of particulars, to illustrate this celebrated Prophecy; and having vindicated the application of it to Jesus Christ, and to him only, by removing the difficulties

ties arising from the context; I shall conclude with a connected and regular translation of the words of the Prophet — when, with an holy triumph at the prospect of Messiah and his Gospel, he here says — *Nevertheless, darkness is not there* [in that part of the country] *where there hath been* [the chief] *distress. As the former time made vile the land of Zebulun, and the land of Naphtali* [being most exposed to hostilities] *so the latter time hath made it honourable* [by the chief residence and preaching of the Messiah] *even by the way of the sea, beyond Jordan, Galilee of the Gentiles.* THIS *people, who walked in darkness, have seen a great light; they, who* DWELT *in the land of the shadow of death, the light hath shined upon* THEM. *Thou* [O GOD] *hast multiplied the nation;* TO THEM *hast thou encreased the joy: they joy before thee, according to the joy in harvest; and as men rejoice, when they divide the spoil.* FOR *the yoke of their burden, and the staff of their shoulder, the rod of him that oppressed them, hast thou broken; as in the day of Midian.* FOR *every weapon of the warriour used in battle, and the garment often rolled in blood, is for burning, even fuel of the fire.* FOR *unto us a Child is born, unto us a Son is given; and the government shall be upon his shoulder: and his name shall be called* WONDERFUL — COUNSELLOR — THE MIGHTY GOD — THE FATHER OF THE EVERLASTING AGE — THE PRINCE OF PEACE.

Z

Psalm LXXXV; ver. 9, and 10.

Surely his salvation is nigh them that fear him; that glory may dwell in our land.

Mercy and truth are met together; righteousness and peace have kissed each other.

IT may possibly admit some doubt, which of the two is more astonishing—a man, who hears *the glad tidings of the Gospel*; yet will not embrace Christianity, will not put on the *form* and the *profession* of it—or a man, who, having the form of Christianity, and professing it in his *words*, denies the *power* of it; and disgraces both Christianity, and himself, by his *actions*.

SERMON IV.

We have in general (GOD be praised!) so much zeal still left, as to be shocked at a professed unbeliever, when we chance to meet with him: but the other appearance is so very common, I mean — that of *Christians* in name, yet *Heathens* in conduct — that we do not often attempt to account for the inconsistency.

But the truth is, that not a few make this fatal mistake — they *call* themselves Christians, and they take themselves *to be* Christians; yet are they not able to *give one good reason, for the hope that is in them.* Revelation itself is not yet revealed to such men as these. *Though all Scripture was written for our learning*; yet are there some, learned in almost every thing except the Scripture. And though they alone are truly wise, who are *wise unto salvation*; how many are ignorant, lamentably ignorant, where ignorance leads to folly, and folly leads to death. Obedience must be founded on faith. But a belief of the Gospel will not, amidst the storms of life, prove *an anchor of the soul sure and stedfast*; unless it be well grounded. Men must learn *the principles* of the doctrine of Christ; before they can *go on to perfection*. And in vain shall we exhort them to act as Christians, till they *know in whom* they have *believed*; till they see clearly, that Christ is of a truth *that Prophet, which should come into the world.*

Now the evidence for this great truth stands briefly thus. Christ, as a teacher, *might* come from GOD; because his *doctrine* was worthy of GOD —

Christ

SERMON IV.

Christ *did* come from GOD; because his *miracles* proved his divine mission—but, as to his being *the true Messiah*; THAT could only be proved by his answering to, and fulfilling, *the numerous prophecies*, which had marked out and described him. In other words; *the doctrine of the Gospel* is far superior to the best, taught by the Greeks or Romans: and yet Jesus might be only *a Philosopher*, though much wiser than *Socrates* or *Cicero*. The *miracles* of Jesus were as great, perhaps greater than any upon record among *the Jews:* and yet, though sent from GOD, he might be only *a Prophet*; equal, perhaps superior, to *Moses* or *Elijah*. But he was THE CHRIST, THE MESSIAH, so long promised, and so much expected; because he filled up in his own *singular* character *all the prophecies*, which had been given to distinguish *him* from every other man.

These prophecies, concerning the Messiah, are of two sorts; some more *particular*, others more *general*. And while there are many, which point out Messiah's *family*, and the *place* of his birth, with other characteristic circumstances of his *life, death,* and *resurrection*; there are many others, which describe the general circumstances, and consequences, of his coming—*the knowledge* derived to mankind from his *doctrine*—the *happiness* resulting to the whole world, from the redemption wrought by his *sufferings*—and the *honour* done to *Judea*, by his *birth* in that particular country: so that, though he was to be *a light to lighten the Gentiles* also, he was to be

THE GLORY of *God's people Israel.* And thus, in the words of the text—*Surely,* (say the Jews), *surely* HIS SALVATION *is nigh them that fear him; that* GLORY *may dwell in* OUR *land.* Nay, it dwells already: for—*mercy and truth* ARE *met together; righteousness and peace* HAVE *kissed each other.*

The Psalm, from which these words are taken, is read as a part of the *morning service* on *Christmas* day; selected by our church, as particularly pertinent to that sacred solemnity. And yet the pertinence of it, as relating to the Messiah, is at present by no means clear: *some parts* of it are really obscure; *other parts* have been thought quite inconsistent; and *one part* is, in both our English translations, deprived of that genuine meaning, which would give lustre, and dignity, and sense to the rest.

I propose therefore to offer, for your meditation at this time, a short explanation of this truly divine Psalm. For, as the several books of the Old Testament excel each other in their degrees of importance; and as no one book informs the head, and warms the heart, more effectually than this *of the Psalms:* so, even in this book, *as one star differeth from another star in glory,* those Psalms are indeed the most excellent, and demand our principal attention, which relate prophetically to *Christ and his Gospel*—and such we shall soon find *that Psalm* to be, which is now before us.

The

SERMON IV.

The Jews, when brought back from their seventy years captivity, seem to have considered that favour from heaven, though great indeed in itself, yet as still greater in its consequences: for they looked upon it as *confirming* every promise before made to them, concerning *that Son of David*, who was *to reign over them for ever*, namely, KING MESSIAH.

The Psalm begins with celebrating the divine goodness, in pardoning their sins, and restoring them to their own country.

LORD! Thou hast been favourable unto thy land:
  thou hast brought back the captivity of Jacob.
Thou hast forgiven the iniquity of thy people:
  thou hast covered all their sin.
Thou hast taken away all thy wrath:
  thou hast turned thyself from the fierceness of thine
    anger.

Thus far all is clear. But how then agree the words following?

Turn us, O God of our Salvation!
  and cause thine anger towards us to cease.
Wilt thou be angry with us for ever?
  Wilt thou draw out thine anger to all generations?
Wilt thou not revive us again,
  that thy people may rejoice in thee?

But, did not the Psalmist say just before, that GOD *had covered all* THEIR SIN, *and taken away all*

HIS WRATH? And could he then pray here, that GOD *would* remove what *was* withdrawn; and that he would *not be angry for ever*, when his anger was *at an end?* This is indeed a difficulty; but it may be solved, to satisfaction, in the manner following.

Their captivity had been a punishment for their many *sins*; especially, that of *idolatry*: and this they well knew. They knew likewise, that their future *prosperity* depended on their future *obedience*. They were also afraid, and with great reason, that, if GOD did not work a marvellous *conversion* in their *hearts*; if he did not cause those, who had returned to their country, to return to their *duty*; the anger of GOD would be again kindled, and be at least as lasting as their rebellion.

The meaning therefore of the 4th, 5th, and 6th, verses seems, very consistently, to be this — *Turn us*; turn our hearts, *O God,* the author of our salvation: and thus *shall thine anger towards us cease* entirely. *Wilt thou be angry with us, for ever? Wilt thou draw out thine anger to all generations?* Yes; if we continue unreformed; and, as such, objects still of thy displeasure. *But, wilt thou not quicken us again; that thy people may rejoice in thee?* Oh, revive us! Raise us *from the death of sin to a life of righteousness!* Kindle again in our souls the most awful ideas of thy *power*, and yet of thy *goodness*; of thy *justice*, and yet of thy *mercy!* And, when thus revived, and thus converted; then may we see that greatest of all blessings, *thy mercy* in and by

MESSIAH — even *thy salvation, according to thy word!*

That this sense of *turn us*, and *revive*, or quicken us, is not only a natural, but the true sense here, is further evident from *Psalm the eightieth*; where we read — *So will not we go back from thee: quicken us, and we will call upon thy name.* TURN US, *O Lord; cause thy face to shine, and we shall be saved.* And thus, in St. Paul to the Colossians — *You, being dead in your sins, hath he* QUICKENED *together with him.*

This Psalm therefore may be thus divided: Verses the 1st, 2d, and 3d, express the thanks of the people, for their return from captivity — Verses the 4th, 5th, and 6th, their prayer, for their own *reformation* — In verse the 7th, they pray for the coming of *Messiah* — Verse the 8th, contains the *words* of the *High-priest*, with *God's gracious answer*: which answer is followed by the grateful acclamations *of the people*, to the end of the Psalm.

To prepare for this interpretation, let us observe, how very strangely the words are expressed at present — *I will hear what the Lord God will say*; FOR *he shall speak peace unto his people.* But surely, GOD could not be consulted, BECAUSE it was unnecessary; nor could the High-priest possibly say, that he would ask of GOD, BECAUSE he knew what GOD would answer; especially, as we have now a *question to God* proposed, and yet no *answer from God* given at all. Under these difficulties we are happily relieved; since it appears, on satisfactory authorities, that,

that, instead of the particle rendered *for*, the word here originally signified *in* or *by me*; which slight variation removes the obscurity, and restores that very light which has long been wanted. After this necessary remark, let us now resume the consideration of the words in the context.

The *people* having prayed for the speedy arrival of their great *salvation*; the *High-priest* says, (as it should be here expressed), *I will hear what the Almighty sayeth.—Jehovah* BY ME *sayeth,* PEACE *unto his people, even unto his saints; but let them not return to folly.* Whereupon, as the Jews understood *peace* to comprehend *every* blessing, and of course *their greatest* blessing; they at once acknowledge the *certainty* of this salvation, the *glory* of their land—they proclaim it, as *nigh* at hand—and then, in rapture truly prophetical, they see this glory as actually arrived, as already *dwelling* in Judea—they behold GOD fulfilling most strictly what he had promised most graciously—they see therefore the *mercy* of GOD and the *truth* of GOD met together—they see that scheme perfected, in which the *righteousness* (i. e. the justice) of GOD harmonizes with the *peace* (i. e. the happiness) of man; so that righteousness and peace *salute* each other with the tenderest affection. In short, they see TRUTH *flourishing out of the earth*; i. e. they see *him*, who is *the way, the truth,* and *the life,* born here on *earth*; and they see even the *righteousness*, or justice of GOD, looking down from *heaven*, as being well pleased.

Surely

SERMON IV.

Surely his salvation is nigh them that fear him;
  that glory may dwell in our land.
Mercy and truth are met together;
  righteousness and peace have kissed each other.
Truth springeth up out of the earth;
  and righteousness looketh down from heaven.

Then follows verse the 12th, which is at present translated so unhappily, that it is quite despoiled of all its genuine glory. For, could the prophet, after all the rapturous things said before, coldly say here, that GOD *would give what was good* — and, that *Judea* should have *a plentiful harvest?* No: consistency and good sense forbid it; and truth confirms their protest against it. The words here express the reason of all the preceding energies, and properly signify—*Yea, Jehovah granteth* THE BLESSING; *and our land granteth* HER OFFSPRING. And what can be *the blessing*—what, amidst these sublime images, can be *Judea's offspring*—but he, and he only, who was *the blessing of all lands* in general, and *the glory of Judea* in particular? And what says the verse following? *Righteousness goeth before* HIM—certainly, not before *the fruits of the earth*—but certainly before that illustrious person, even the MESSIAH — *Righteousness goeth before* HIM, *and directeth his goings in the way.*

As to the word before rendered offspring, and referred to *the Messiah*, much might be said to establish that point: but the present occasion will not admit of

it,

it, notwithstanding its real importance; and this importance arises, not merely from the nature of *the Psalm before us*, but because there is *another Psalm*, also relative to the redemption by Christ, where the principal scope of it is nearly lost; and chiefly, through our wrong translation of the same word in the original.

As to the word here rendered *the blessing*, and applied to the redemption; the same word is so used by Jeremiah, thus — *Behold, the days come, that I will perform* THAT GOOD THING (the blessing) *which I have promised — at that time will I cause to grow up unto David the branch of righteousness:* 33, 14. And as to *Messiah* being here described, partly as springing up from the earth: so says Isaiah — *In that day shall the branch of the Lord be beautiful and glorious; and* THE FRUIT OF THE EARTH *shall be excellent and comely.* But this evangelical Prophet, in another place, has the very same complication of images, with that found in the Psalm before us. For *Isaiah* also has *the heavens*, with *their righteousness*; and *the earth*, with *its salvation — Drop down, ye* HEAVENS *from above, and let the skies pour down righteousness: let* THE EARTH *open, and let* THEM *bring forth salvation.* But, let THEM *bring forth* — Who, or what can be here meant by *them*, but the *heavens* and the *earth?* It is heaven and earth, which are here represented as *bringing forth*, and introducing the Saviour of the world. For what else can be here meant as

brought

brought forth by *them?* What, but HE alone; who, deriving his *divine* nature from heaven, and his *human* from the earth, was (what no other being ever was) both GOD and MAN.

Thus have I endeavoured briefly to explain this Pſalm — ſhewn *the conſiſtency* of the former parts of it with each other — ſtated the pertinency of the latter part, as relating to *the Meſſiah* — and conſequently vindicated the appointment of it by our Church, when we devoutly celebrate *the birth of Chriſt*. But, in order to celebrate this mighty bleſſing, or any other, with due propriety; we muſt, as St. Paul ſays, *ſing with the* SPIRIT, *and ſing with the* UNDERSTANDING *alſo*. If therefore, as the Apoſtle adds, *the whole Church be come together, and every one hath* A PSALM; unleſs he underſtand *the interpretation*, he will *ſpeak unto himſelf*, and not *to God*; but, LET ALL THINGS BE DONE TO EDIFYING.

In obedience to this Apoſtolical injunction, and in hopes of fixing in your minds a juſt idea of the bleſſing here prophetically celebrated; I ſhall firſt give the whole of this ſacred Hymn together; and then conclude, with a very ſhort application.

THE PEOPLE.

1. *Thou haſt been gracious*, O JEHOVAH, *to thy land;*
thou haſt turned back the captivity of Jacob.

2. *Thou*

2. *Thou haſt taken away the iniquity of thy people;
thou haſt covered all their ſin.*
3. *Thou haſt removed all thine anger;
thou haſt turned from thy wrathful indignation.*

4. TURN US, *O God of our ſalvation;
and withdraw thy reſentment from us;*
5. FOR EVER *wilt thou be diſpleaſed at us?
Wilt thou protract thy wrath from generation to generation?*
6. *Wilt thou not once more quicken us;
ſo that thy people ſhall rejoice in thee?*
7. *Shew us, O Jehovah, thy mercy;
and thy ſalvation grant unto* US*!*

THE HIGH-PRIEST.

8. *I will bear what the Almighty ſayeth—
Jehovah* BY ME *ſayeth,* " PEACE
" UNTO HIS PEOPLE, EVEN UNTO HIS SAINTS;
" BUT LET THEM NOT RETURN TO FOLLY."

THE PEOPLE.

9. *Truly nigh to thoſe, who fear him, is his ſalvation;
that glory may dwell in our land.*
10. *Mercy and truth are met together;
righteouſneſs and peace have kiſſed each other.*
11. *Truth ſpringeth up, out of the earth;
and righteouſneſs looketh down from heaven.*

12. *Yea,*

12. *Yea, Jehovah granteth* THE BLESSING;
and our land granteth HER OFFSPRING.
13. *Righteousness goeth before* HIM;
and directeth his goings in the way.

To Conclude.

If then *the anger of God* against the Jews was to *cease*; it was—when his rebel subjects returned to their allegiance. Did *God speak peace unto his people?* It was—provided *they did not return to folly:* it was *peace*, but—only *to his saints.* Was *the salvation of God nigh?* It was—only *to them, who feared* HIM.

And, does GOD *speak peace* to us? It is only—by *turning us from our iniquities.* Though *mercy* and *truth*, though *righteousness* and *peace, meet* in our redemption; this redemption itself saves us, by *saving us from our sins.* The very chariot of mercy is preceded by the sword of justice. CHRIST is *mighty to save*; but he speaks, and acts by *righteousness: righteousness directeth* all *his goings in the way.*

On *earth* there will be *universal peace*; but it will be—when there is given universally *glory to God in the highest.* Yet, at present, *unto* THE GODLY *there ariseth light, in the darkness*; consolation, in the worst of times: and, whatever be the fate of this world at large; though *nation should* again *rise against nation*, and *kingdom against kingdom*; and though this kingdom of ours should be still more *divided against itself:* yet—with all true
Christians

Christians—*their* kingdom, like their master's, is *not of this world*—they are subjects of a *kingdom*, which *cannot be shaken*—they are, they must be happy, as THE SONS OF GOD; because they are disciples of THE PRINCE OF PEACE. And such may *we all* be!—Grant it, O GOD, for the sake of thy Son our Saviour JESUS CHRIST: to whom, with the FATHER, and the HOLY GHOST—be ascribed all honour and glory, now and for ever. Amen.

SERMON V.

1 CORINTHIANS XI. 1.

Be ye followers of me, even as I also am of Christ.

AMONG all the various branches of knowledge, there is none more worthy of our cultivation than the knowledge of ourselves; a lesson this, not indeed the most easy, but truly excellent and valuable. That happiness is the end for which we were created, appears from the constitution of our nature; and that holiness is the only means of happiness, is fairly deducible from a view of the whole constitution of things. Here then is the point, (a point infinitely important!), how are we to attain this necessary holiness? Are we, of ourselves, sufficient for this mighty acquisition? If not, who will point out the path, and guide us through grace to glory?

SERMON V.

God, who at sundry times, and in divers manners, spake in times past unto the fathers by the Prophets, hath in these last days spoken unto us by his Son; who *was made flesh, and dwelt among us,* and at last died, for us men, and for our salvation. And, as we wanted, not only to be made *free from* the guilt and slavery of *sin*, but to *become the servants of righteousness;* how did he heighten this miracle of mercy, by giving us a system of the most exalted holiness, and exemplifying in his own spotless life the beauty of perfect virtue!

But yet, as *he knew what was in man*, he knew, that his own example, though it would teach all men what perfection was, would yet discourage some men from attempting to copy after it, because it was perfection. He knew, that virtue, when made to appear most excellent, appears hardest to be attained; and that he, who sets it as high as our nature can go, as much dissuades from it by its difficulty, as he invites to it by its worth and excellence. Knowing also, that the divinity of his own character would be an objection with some to the imitation of it, and that it was necessary to soften down the splendor of his own bright example, and present it to the world in a milder light, in the examples of holy men—for this, doubtless, among other reasons, he appointed a standing ministry, the Apostles and their successors to the end of time. These were to spread the religion of their great master through the world. These were, not only

to

SERMON V.

to display its excellence and necessity in idea, but also its possibility and amiableness in real life; for they were to point out the true path by their preaching, and they were to lead men by the hand in it by their practice. This was our Saviour's scheme for *the perfecting of the saints by the work of the ministry: whosoever* (says he) *shall both do and teach, the same shall be called great in the kingdom of Heaven.*

As to example in general, the great influence of it is undeniable. Good examples are consequently so beneficial, that they should be enforced frequently and strongly; and, in this age of coldness and indifference to things sacred, the best examples are absolutely necessary, to awaken the sentiments of what we can do, if we will; and what we must do, if we will be happy: and to fire us with an emulation of the zeal of those worthies, whose names are recorded with honour in the book of GOD.

And now — does not our attention fix at once on the character of him, who calls upon us in the Text? Amidst such an assemblage of bright examples in holy writ, where *one star differeth from another star in glory,* how readily do we acknowledge the superior excellence of the Apostle Saint Paul! An Apostle, in whose behaviour the warmest zeal for religion was tempered with the coolest reason, and in whose preaching *the words of truth and soberness* were delivered with the utmost fervour of oratory: an example therefore, greatly beneficial to all, but particularly so to those, who are admitted *ministers of Christ, and stewards of the mysteries of God.*

It may not then be unsuitable to the importance of this solemn occasion, and to the nature of this venerable assembly, to offer some observations,

 first: on *St. Paul's preaching*; and

 secondly: on *his practice*;

in order to recommend his example in both to the present ministers of the Gospel.

If we consider the *matter* of St. Paul's sermons, and also the *manner* of his preaching them; it will be difficult to say, in which article the Apostle was greater, or is more worthy of our imitation.

As to the former, we find, that, during a longer stay with any of the churches, his care was to teach them a compleat system of duty, both as to faith and practice — that *he kept back no profitable doctrine,* but declared unto them *the whole counsel of God.* Thus our Apostle, like *a wise master-builder,* not only laid the foundation, *Jesus Christ himself being the chief corner stone*; but in his preaching *the whole body* of Christian virtues was *so fitly joined together, and so compacted by that which every joint supplieth, that the holy building was compleatly formed into an habitation of God through the spirit.*

Not that he neglected those duties, which are coeval with human nature; and which oblige all rational creatures, as such. He knew, that his hearers could not be good Christians, without being good men; and that moral duties are the only solid foundation of Christian virtues. What therefore his great master *came to fulfill,* he took care *not to destroy,* but to maintain and establish.

For

SERMON V.

For—not to insist upon the moral conclusions of his Epistles—what else but a beautiful compendium of morality is that exhortation of his to the Philippians—*Finally, Brethren, whatsoever things are true, whatsoever things are honest, whatsoever things are just, whatsoever things are pure, whatsoever things are lovely, whatsoever things are of good report; if there be any virtue, and if there be any praise, think on these things.*

But though morality was our Apostle's care, yet Christianity was *the crown of his rejoicing*. For the Gospel, in his eye, was infinitely valuable; as it gave perfection to the morality of reason, by compleating it with the discovery of new relations, and consequently, new duties; and because it at once taught men the necessity of more and higher virtues, and gave them the only comfortable assurance of pardon for their failings, together with the sure method of obtaining it.

This then was the great subject, that engaged his affections, and lay nearest his heart. He felt the full consolation of the *glad tidings* of salvation, and knew them to be tidings of the *greatest joy* to all mankind. In short; he was so transported with this amazing instance of God's goodness, that he labours for words to express himself with energy equal to the dignity of his theme. And, notwithstanding all the fire of his imagination, all the fluency of his elocution, he almost sinks under the weight of his argument; as *not being able to comprehend the breadth, and length, and depth, and height of this love of Christ, which passeth knowledge.* Yet

Yet — what he could neither fully comprehend, nor sufficiently adore, he most zealously taught his followers; and no wonder, since *out of the abundance of the heart the mouth speaketh.* No wonder, that an Apostle, who knew, that duty was not rightly stated, and not at all secured by the systems of the philosophers, (however *wise in their own conceits*), nor yet compleatly provided for by the religion of the Jews, (however opinionated they were of its perfection and eternal obligation), should determine to *know nothing* — to appear among his followers as knowing nothing — because he was determined to preach nothing — i. e. nothing so constantly and fervently, as *Jesus Christ, and him crucified.* No wonder, that, as he declared Jew and Gentile both *under sin, and coming short of the glory of God,* his great topic should be universally — *Repentance towards God, and faith in our Lord Jesus Christ.*

No man had a more perfect knowledge of the long history of mankind, and the whole of human duty; no man was better acquainted with the true genius of Christianity, than St. Paul; and therefore, when *he spoke, he spoke as the oracles of God;* and the lessons, which he taught, were always the most interesting and important. Such as — the corruption of human nature, introduced by the transgression of the *first Adam*; in consequence of which we became not only mortal, but miserable, *and poor, and blind, and naked* — and the recovery of human nature by the death of the *second Adam,* who is

made

unto us wifdom, and righteoufnefs, and fanctification, and redemption — Such as — the infirmity of man, and the power of God — the poverty of nature, and the riches of grace — the weaknefs of human reafon — the wickednefs of the heathen — the deficiency of the Jew — and, in fhort, the wretchednefs of the whole world, without a Saviour; a Saviour to expiate their fins, to enlighten them with a clearer knowledge of their duty, and by eftablifhing *the means of grace*, to animate them with *the hopes of glory*.

Thefe were the important fubjects of St. Paul's preaching; *not wood, hay, and ftubble*; but *gold, filver, and precious ftones:* for he knew, that *in the day of trial every man's work would be made manifeft.*

To the preceding general enumeration I fhall add one obfervation in particular, on that mixture of *the ferious* and *the chearful*, which he recommended to his Chriftian converts — two things entirely confiftent; both, under the prefent frame of things, abfolutely neceffary; and in the due regulation of which feems to confift the great art of living happily.

To poffefs their minds with a ferious fenfe of religion, of its difficulty, and yet of its neceffity; he calls upon them to *work out their falvation with fear and trembling*. But then, to correct all fournefs of difpofition, and to preferve the beautiful face of religion undeformed, an index of the happy fweetnefs of temper within, he exhorts them to *rejoice evermore*.

more. And, as he knew, that true chearfulness in life was the privilege, and the privilege only of the good man, he exhorts with a peculiar emphasis — *rejoice in the Lord always*; *and again I say, rejoice.* He knew that a gloomy, melancholy, lonely picture would be drawn of the lovely and social religion of Christianity; a representation, which none can give it with any justice, and which none should give it, who would recommend it to the love of mankind.

That St. Paul did recommend it most effectually is certain; and his success can be no wonder to those who consider, not only *the doctrines* which he taught, but also *the manner* of his teaching them; on the latter of which I proceed now to make some observations.

That this great preacher carefully adapted his oratory to his audience (a lesson of the first consequence) is demonstrable, among other proofs, from the difference of his reasoning with the Jews at Antioch, and with the Gentiles at Lystra. And that he did this, with a most happy attention to circumstances, has frequently been proved from his discourse to the philosophers at Athens, and is clear also from his sermon to Felix.

In Felix he had for his hearer a Roman governor, that was remarkably lustful and unjust; a man, very unlikely to bear, much less to reform by, an home-reproof from his own prisoner. This then was a case, which required great art as well as great courage;

courage; and accordingly we find our Apostle mingling *the wisdom of the serpent* with *the innocence of the dove*. He had honesty enough, to rebuke the sins; and yet prudence enough, not to offend the sinner. He had the courage, to put even his judge in mind of his crimes; yet with so much address, as not to affront his person — an example, the most worthy of our imitation; as it would greatly contribute to make the bitter potion of reproof, if not palatable, at least salutary and successful.

How artfully then does our Apostle insinuate himself into the soul of this great sinner, and shake his conscience at the remembrance of his vices! — not by denouncing vengeance against him, for his lust and injustice; but by placing in the strongest point of light the opposite virtues — shewing their reasonableness in themselves, and their rewards at the day of judgment. For *he reasoned* — not of unrighteousness — not of incontinency — but of *righteousness* and *chastity*; and by holding forth a beautiful picture of these necessary virtues, he left it to Felix to form the contrast, and to infer the blackness of his own vices. A masterly stroke! and it effectually succeeded: for, as *the Prisoner spoke — the Judge trembled.*

The wisdom of our Apostle is farther evident from *the intelligible manner*, in which he always addressed the people. In his Epistles indeed, which were to remain for the examination of the learned, there were *some things hard to be understood*; but in his discourses

ses to the people he used *great plainness of speech.* And his stile was (the only proper stile of popular discourses) a noble simplicity, which cloathed the most important and awakening sentiments in language the most easy and intelligible. For he knew it to be one of the triumphs of Christianity, that it *preached the Gospel to the poor*; a commendation, which expresses not only the condescension, but the clearness also of the Gospel doctrines.

Thus he copied his great master in the plainness of his speech, and thus he preserved the honour of the Gospel; not being so unnatural, when his followers *asked bread*, as to *give them a stone*. And indeed to *give them a stone*—exhortation so unintelligible as to do them no service, is an instance of cruelty only to be exceeded by *giving them a serpent*—preaching such false doctrine as will do them real injury.

Another excellence of St. Paul's manner was his art of *interesting the passions,* and *engaging the affections* of his hearers. Under the present depravity of human nature, our reason being enfeebled, and our passions consequently grown powerful; it must be of great service to engage these in the cause we would serve; and therefore his constant endeavour was — not only to convince the reason of his hearers, but to alarm and interest their passions. And, as hope and fear are (with the bulk of mankind) the main springs of human action, to these he addressed himself most effectually — not by a cold speculation upon

abstract

abstract fitnesses, but by the awful assurances of a resurrection of the dead to an eternity of happiness or misery. As to the latter, who can hear without trembling, that — *the Lord Jesus shall be revealed from heaven, with his mighty angels, in flaming fire, taking vengeance on the ungodly; who shall be punished with everlasting destruction from the presence of the Lord, and from the glory of his power.* And as to the happiness of heaven, that he describes by words so strong, as to baffle the expression of all language but his own — by *a weight of glory infinite and eternal beyond all hyperbole*, or conception.

Thus then he secured the passions; and the affections he engaged by his endearing manner of address. And who could resist the force of such applications as these — *Brethren, my heart's desire and prayer to God for you is, that ye may be saved — I say the truth in Christ, I lie not; I could wish myself devoted to an accursed death, after the example of Christ, if by that means I might be assisting to your salvation — I beseech you then, be ye followers of me —* Forms of address these, so replete with paternal tenderness, that they are at once heard, and answered: the hearts of his hearers must have been so softened, as to be incapable of resisting petitions thus affectionately preferred for their own welfare. This is an example highly worthy of imitation in all ages, but especially in ours; in which though we can say, that the people have *ten thousand instructors in Christ*, yet who will say, that they *have many fathers?*

We

We have now taken a view of St. Paul, as a *preacher of the Gospel*; and find *the matter* of his sermons to have been the most interesting and important, and his *manner* of delivering them the most affectionate and engaging. But there is yet wanting one circumstance, to compleat the orator — the reputation of being *a good man*; a circumstance insisted upon by Aristotle, Tully, and Quintilian; and reason readily subscribes to their decision: since we may admire, but can never fully confide in, the persuasion of any man, till we are convinced of his honesty and integrity. And therefore, *though a man could speak with the tongues of men and of angels, and had not* goodness; *it would profit* himself *nothing*, and others but very little. He may fail, for want of other qualifications, even with the character of real goodness; but he cannot succeed without it. Now there is but one effectual and certain way to be thought good, and that is, by being so; and if ever any one became a finished orator by means of his goodness, *St. Paul was the man*.

This then leads from our Apostle's *preaching* to his *practice*; and on this second part of his character, though not less material, the observations must be few and short.

If we consider St. Paul in his Apostolical capacity, we shall find his zeal in propagating the Gospel greater than the fury, with which he once persecuted it. We shall find him *going forth, like the sun, from the uttermost part of heaven, and running about unto the end*

end of it again, while there is nothing hid from the heat thereof. We shall see him travelling with an undaunted and victorious pace, *from one nation to another, from one kingdom to another people,* through infinite dangers and distresses, which served only to inflame his courage, because he knew they would increase his reward.

But if we descend from this exalted point of view, and consider him as a private minister of the Gospel, (the character in which, under this settled state of the church, he is imitable by us), we find his zeal too great to be satisfied with public exhortations, however important and well-adapted; but it led him with great sollicitude *from house to house,* to compleat there by more particular and personal applications what he had delivered (as must necessarily be the case) more in the general in public.

And at these private interviews how effectually did he conciliate love and esteem, by readily conforming his own behaviour to that of his followers! —by *pleasing his neighbour for his good to edification*— and by thus (innocently) *becoming all things, to all men,* he took the surest method to *gain many.*

Perfectly read in the knowledge of the law, he remembered, that for the sin of the priest God had required as great a sacrifice as for the sins of the whole congregation—and that there was inscribed, by divine command, upon Aaron's Mitre *holiness to the Lord*—whence he rightly inferred, that if the *mi-*
nisters

nifters of condemnation were to be thus holy, much more ought the *minifters of righteoufnefs* to exceed in holinefs.

And, how forcibly does he defcribe his endeavours to accomplifh the grand point of human duty—the mortifying the powers of fenfe and paffion, and bringing them into fubjection to the nobler principle of reafon; *left, by any means, while he preached to others, he himfelf fhould be a caft-away!* How effectually did he render *his confcience void of offence,* by (the only fuccefsful method) the conftant *exercife of himfelf,* and a ftrict examination of his own conduct! How unfailing in his applications to the throne of grace; bowing his knees, with the utmoft fervour of devotion, for bleffings on himfelf and his fellow Chriftians! Equally conftant in the public, as in the private worfhip of God, we find him, *as his manner was,* going to the Synagogue. We find him, not only praying, but finging praifes to GOD, in the darknefs of midnight, and amidft the horrors of a dungeon. And we find him not neglecting to look up to heaven for a bleffing on the food, which it was become neceffary fhould be taken, even amidft the terrors of a tempeft, and under the expectation of immediate fhipwreck; when, though furrounded with Roman foldiers, *he gave thanks to God in the prefence of them all*—and it muft be added, that this act of thankfgiving was practifed by religious Heathens, and is only laid afide,

or

or (what is worse) is irreverently performed by our modern Christians.

There are other articles in St. Paul's character and behaviour, which might be recommended to imitation; such as his warmly maintaining his religious and civil privileges—asserting boldly the advantages of his birthright—and insisting upon the right, which he had (though not always exerted, and never rigorously) to his *living of the Gospel* where he *preached the Gospel.*

I shall only add, in justice to his civil as well as sacred character—that he lived in a dutiful *subjection to the higher powers.*

Tertullus indeed accused him of being a *pestilent fellow,* and *a mover of sedition.* But how improbable is it, that so good a man should be so bad a subject—or that he, who established obedience to the higher powers by the strongest sanctions, should act in notorious defiance to his own doctrines! So absolutely improbable this, that we can easily believe—that, as he had *not offended against the law of the Jews, nor against the temple, so neither against Cæsar had he offended any thing at all.*

This then is an imperfect description of that venerable man, and illustrious Apostle, who proposes himself for our imitation—an example of every virtue, that can finish the Christian, and adorn the minister of the Gospel—an example, in which it is impossible to say, which part does most honour to *himself*; but easy to say, which is the most

moſt ſeaſonable for *us*—Need it be mentioned? At leaſt to any, who have conſidered the languor and unanimated indifference, that prevail at preſent *in things pertaining to God!*—It is HIS ZEAL! A zeal, that made him *exceeding jealous for the Lord his God*; and yet a zeal, regulated by reaſon, and free from every ſymptom of enthuſiaſm—a zeal, that was not exerted to inflame the minds of his brethren one againſt another, by names that were invidious, or by diſtinctions that might be dangerous; but a zeal, that breathed univerſal charity, and the warmeſt brotherly kindneſs, and called upon all to unite heartily for the public good—particularly, in that grand point, the promotion of GOD's glory, by ſupporting his true religion, in order to the ſalvation of mankind.

If there was never leſs of this zeal amongſt us, it is equally true at leaſt, that there never was more occaſion for it. *To whom* then *ſhall we go*, and from whoſe example ſhall we catch the holy flame ſo effectually, as from that of our Apoſtle? Certainly while we are *muſing* on his virtue, *the fire will kindle* in our own breaſts, and give life to all our labours.

How uſeful then muſt it be, to examine ourſelves by his behaviour!—frequently to examine, how far *we*, his ſons and ſucceſſors in the care of theſe churches, fall ſhort of the ſtandard of his example! If we cannot be as extenſive in our miniſtration, if we cannot ſpread the Goſpel through

the

the world, like him; we may, we muſt be, like him in zeal for the ſalvation of mankind: and, as our fervour is more contracted, it ſhould warm with the more lively influences.

That our natural opportunities of acquiring neceſſary knowledge have been, at leaſt equal, I may well ſay ſuperior, to St. Paul's, will readily be granted: unleſs it can be ſuppoſed, which will not eaſily be admitted, that he muſt have received more human literature from the academy (which Strabo tells us there was) at Tarſus, and more theological learning from the inſtructions of Gamaliel, than we may enjoy in this illuſtrious univerſity.

Indeed our Apoſtle's abilities were very greatly augmented by ſupernatural aſſiſtance; but then, his dangers, and his difficulties were proportionate: we, if our powers are leſs, have leſs difficulties to ſtruggle with. And we ſhall be certainly equal to any difficulties, if we apply devoutly to that GOD, *who hath made us miniſters of the New Teſtament*, and *who will make his grace abound in us, that we may have all ſufficiency in all things.*

Seeing then that we may, in proportion to our different ſpheres of action, not only imitate, but equal our Apoſtle—*Would to God, that all, who hear me this day, were both almoſt, and altogether ſuch as he was, except his bonds and perſecutions!* The clergy of the church of England are a body of men, whoſe *faith is ſpoken of throughout the world*; and whoſe practice has in general been as illuſtrious as

their

their faith—and *I am perfuaded, that neither death, nor life, nor angels, nor principalities, nor powers, nor difficulties prefent, nor dangers to come, will be able to feparate* many minifters of this church, any more than our Apoftle himfelf, *from the love of God, which is in Chrift Jefus their Lord.*

And fhould there be, among fo numerous a body fome of a very different complexion; inftead of endeavouring to draw a vail over fuch mifbehaviour, as is too public to be concealed, it may be more in the fpirit of the Gofpel to fay —— *It muft needs be, that offences come; but woe to that man, by whom the offence cometh.* And, when we fee thofe, who have voluntarily bound themfelves by the moft folemn engagements to *feed the church of God, which he hath purchafed with his own blood*, delivering the moft important doctrines of the Gofpel with great unconcernednefs of foul— preaching the duties of falvation to the people, in a manner they cannot underftand—or deftroying by their example what they build by their exhortation—or laftly, not zealoufly attending to the welfare of the flocks, *over which the Holy Ghoft hath made them overfeers* — we naturally remember that faying of St. Chryfoftom, *Though I would not willingly urge painful reflections, yet I wonder, how fuch men can compare themfelves with St. Paul, without trembling!*

But, to excite thefe to repentance, and all to zeal and diligence, let it be obferved—that, if ever

there

there was an age, since the establishment of Christianity, that required eminent qualifications most prudently and most warmly exerted in the cause of the Gospel, it is this age of ours—an age of impiety, infidelity, *rebuke and blasphemy*. The teachers of Christianity have been always reviled by the infidel and the libertine; but to treat Christianity with the same rude insolence, was reserved for these days of ours. Infidelity is now propagated, not only with the utmost cunning, but with the greatest openness; *the pestilence, that walked in darkness, now destroyeth by noon day*. It is not superstition or popery, it is not persecution or priestcraft, that are now the subjects of invective—these were only introductions to a larger work. For, infidels now confessedly attack Christianity itself, by declaring publickly and without reserve—that prophecies are nonsense—and miracles impossible—that faith is an affront to reason—and religion to common sense—in short; they will be bold to say, God cannot make a revelation, if he would; and, if he could, it would be of no use, of no service at all to mankind!

―― *Let God arise, and let his enemies be scattered!*
But, *though the waves of the sea are mighty, and rage horribly; yet, the Lord, who dwelleth on high is mightier*. And Christianity, which *is founded on the rock of ages*, shall stand firm and unshaken; *though the rains should descend, and the floods come, and the winds blow:* and though all together should break upon it in one furious storm—yet shall it

lift up its sacred head beautiful and triumphant, for *it is founded upon a rock.*

And yet, we must remember—that, though Christ will always have a church, a number of true disciples upon earth; yet, we must remember,—that he can remove his Gospel to a more worthy people, when we have *filled up the measure of our iniquities.* For, where are now the once famous churches of Ephesus and Smyrna, Pergamus and Thyatyra, and others both Asian and European, planted by St. Paul himself?

They were——but are not.

That *ours* may be delivered, let us, the guardians of Christianity, who are *set for the defence of the Gospel,* unite as one man, to oppose the dreadful progress of infidelity and of impiety. Let infidelity be confuted by such writings, as prove—that, while *wisdom* is rudely insulted by her enemies, she is fully *justified by her children.* And let impiety be opposed by the sanctity of our own lives, and by our boldly rebuking the vices of the times.

As to the latter, the denunciation of God to the Prophet Ezekiel demands our most serious attention—*Son of Man, I have made thee a watchman to the house of Israel; therefore hear the word at my mouth, and give them warning from me. When I say unto the wicked, thou shalt surely die; and thou givest him not warning, nor speakest to warn the wicked from his wicked way to save his life; the same wicked man shall die in his iniquity, but his blood will I require at thine hand.* And at the same time let us remember the reward

reward of thofe, who *turn many to righteoufnefs— they fhall fhine as the ftars for ever and ever.* And though we fhould even *labour in vain,* and *Ifrael be not gathered;* yet fhall *we be glorious in the eyes of the Lord, our judgment is with the Lord, and our reward with our God.*

A great point will be gained at prefent, in thefe evil days, if we ftand our ground; and when we find, we can certainly keep men from growing worfe, we may foon be able to make them better. The fureft way to get more influence and power is—to make the beft ufe of what we have. For when men fee, that our labours are warmly directed for the promotion of their trueft intereft, they will ftrengthen us out of regard to themfelves. For however numerous our enemies may be, yet at prefent we truft, that *they that be* heartily *with us* are *more than they that are* in appearance *with them.*

And were we, the minifters of the Gofpel, altogether fuch as St. Paul was—or rather—could we but fuppofe, that *ten thoufand minifters of the Gofpel,* I will not fay with abilities equal to St. Paul's, but with his goodnefs of heart, and with his zeal, were ftationed through this kingdom—how would *the work of the Lord profper in their hands—*how *mightily would grow the word of the Lord, and prevail—*foon would infidelity and profanenefs hide their guilty heads—and the Church of England would be (in a nobler fenfe, than it has ever yet been) *the perfection of beauty, and the joy of the whole earth!*

This

This fuppofal, however pleafing in theory, is not at prefent to be expected in real life. And yet, every man can anfwer for one. And every man fhould remember—he muft anfwer, at leaft, for himfelf, in that next, everlafting fcene of things, to which we are (and may we ever remember that we are) all haftening.

Permit me then, by way of conclufion, moft earneftly to exhort and befeech you to be followers of St. Paul—with a fixed attention to view his great example, and to review it frequently, till you tranfcribe that fpirit, till you are inflamed with that zeal, which animated him in every action. Should we take but one tranfient view of him, we fhall be *like a man beholding his natural face in a glafs; he beholdeth himfelf, and goeth his way, and ftraightway forgetteth what manner of man he was.* No: let his image never forfake us, till we are *transformed into his likenefs;* till, like him, we preach in public, and exhort in private; and till, like him, we alfo become examples to the brethren. And then fhall we receive from the people the fame honourable teftimony, that was given to him and Silas—*Thefe men are the fervants of the moft High God, which fhew unto us the way of falvation.*

The *fervants of the moft High God* is a title exceedingly magnificent; but yet, not equal to fome others, which are known to be given us in the holy fcriptures; and given, not only to infpire us with noble images, but to make us *be* what we we are *called:* fince they are marks of honour, which we can then only wear with credit, when we have well deferved them. *What carefulnefs* then fhould the remembrance of thefe titles work in all of us? *Yea, what clearing of ourfelves! Yea, what indignation* againſt vice! *Yea, what vehement defire* of virtue! *Yea, what zeal!*

Watch ye therefore; quit yourfelves like men; be ſtrong: contend earneſtly for the faith once delivered to the faints, in nothing terrified by your adverfaries. Let the word of Chriſt dwell in you richly, in all wifdom. Meditate day and night in that facred volume, *wherein are hid* certainly the chief *treafures*, though not all the *ornaments of wifdom and knowledge*. Thus *furniſhed unto every good work, ſhine as lights in the world*. *In all things approving yourfelves as the miniſters of God, by purenefs, by knowledge, by love unfeigned, by the armour of righteoufnefs on the right hand and on the left, by honour and diſhonour*—and *by evil report, as well as good report*.

For both thefe we muſt expect; feeing we are *fet forth a ſpectacle* to God—and *angels*—and *men*. Bad men have their eye upon us, to mifreprefent us and triumph at our failings—good men, to applaud and imitate our virtues—evil angels, not imaginary but real beings, who are permitted to tempt us, particularly contrive our fall—good angels, thofe *miniſtering ſpirits ſent forth to miniſter to the heirs of falvation*, will rejoice at our victory—and laſtly, (a reflection that muſt fire our fouls, and *make us more than conquerors!*), GOD himself beholds us with a peculiar attention, having made us *workers together with him,* in the salvation of a world of creatures—a character, which if we sincerely endeavour to fulfil (and dreadful will be our condemnation, if we do not) he will both *confirm us with his grace,* and *crown us with his glory.*

Wherefore, *seeing we are compassed about with so great a cloud of witnesses, let us lay aside every weight, and run with patience the race that is set before us—looking unto Jesus, the author and finisher of our faith,* and to his blessed Apostle St. Paul, the nearest follower of *the great captain of our salvation.* And let us all imitate him now, even *as he did Christ,* that we may follow them both afterwards to *the general assembly and church of the first-born in heaven;* that *where they are, we may be also.*

SERMON VI.

2 PETER III; ver. 10, 11, 12, and 14.

The day of the Lord will come as a thief in the night; in the which the heavens shall pass away with a great noise, and the elements shall melt with fervent heat; the earth also, and the works that are therein, shall be burned up.

Seeing then that all these things shall be dissolved, what manner of persons ought ye to be in all holy conversation and godliness,

Looking for, and hasting unto the coming of the day of God, wherein the heavens being on fire shall be dissolved, and the elements shall melt with fervent heat? —

Wherefore, beloved, seeing that ye look for such things, be diligent, that ye may be found of him in peace, without spot and blameless.

THESE solemn words, with which St. Peter concludes his second Epistle to the Christians, contain an argument every way qualified to leave

SERMON VI.

the moſt laſting impreſſion on their minds. And as I am at this time to conclude my exhortations to you of this place, what words are more proper to engage your preſent attention—what words are more likely to be for ever remembered by you, than theſe words of the Apoſtle? Words, which one cannot read, or hear, without trembling! Words, that in the moſt alarming manner deſcribe to us that great and univerſal deſtruction, which will take place at the day of judgment; when *the heavens*, which now ſurround us with ſo much beauty and order, ſhall paſs away with a mighty noiſe; when *the earth*, with every thing we ſee magnificent and ſplendid, ſhall totter and tumble into ruins; and when *all mankind* ſhall be ſentenced, either to everlaſting happineſs, or everlaſting miſery.

But, let me aſk you, does not your blood run cold, and even freeze within you, when you hear of ſorrows inexpreſſible, and torments without end? Can your hearts be unmoved, when you think of everlaſting joys? Were we to read, that GOD had prepared *ſo much happineſs*, or *ſo much miſery*, for any other world of creatures, ſhould we not feel ourſelves affected ſtrongly; ſhould we not wiſh, ſhould we not pray, that this world of creatures might be ſo wiſe as to ſave themſelves from that miſery, and be rewarded with that happineſs? Should we not, I ſay, be thus affected, with reſpect to *other* creatures?

How

SERMON VI.

How then muſt our hearts beat, how muſt we ſtartle and be alarmed, when this reflection comes home to ourſelves—*We are the men!—We are theſe very creatures!—You*, and *I*, with all thoſe we have known, or heard of; with all thoſe, who have lived, or ſhall live, on this wide theatre of the earth, *we* ſhall be hereafter raiſed from our graves by the awakening voice of an Archangel—from theſe graves ſhall we be ſummoned to the tribunal of *him*, who once deſcended to be our Saviour, but who will be then our Judge—and before him, and to ,n, muſt we render a ſtrict account of the thoughts— of the words—and of the actions of our paſt lives— and particularly, as I ſhall be accountable for the inſtructions I have given *you*; ſo will *you* be accountable for the good or bad uſe you have made of ſuch inſtructions — whether, by being abſent, you have refuſed to hear them—or, if preſent, whether you have diligently attended to them — and, if having attended, whether you have been careful to practiſe, or whether you ſoon forgot the inſtructions you thus received in this houſe of God.

In the courſe of my exhortations to you, I have ſometimes expreſſed a ſolemn diſapprobation of the behaviour of many in this place; and as I ſhall do the ſame friendly office ſomewhat more particularly at preſent; it may be proper, before I proceed further, to ſhew you, that it is the expreſs duty of the miniſter to reprove and rebuke, as well as to praiſe

and

and exhort; and that I should not execute my own important office, if I were not to perform both.

Hear then what St. Paul commands all Christian ministers, in the person of Timothy—*Preach the word, be instant in season and out of season, reprove, rebuke*; and to Titus, *exhort and rebuke with all authority.* Hear also what God commands the prophet Isaiah—*Cry aloud, spare not; lift up thy voice, like a trumpet, and shew my people their transgressions, and the house of Jacob their sins.* And lastly, hear the most awakening charge of GOD to the prophet Ezekiel—*Son of man, I have made thee a watchman unto the house of Israel: therefore bear the word at my mouth, and give them warning from me. When I say unto the wicked, thou shalt surely die, and thou givest him not warning, nor speakest to warn the wicked from his wicked way, to save his life; the same wicked man shall die in his iniquity, but his blood will I require at thine hand.*

And now consider seriously with yourselves — if the blood of the congregation shall be required of the minister, that neglects to warn, and shake the conscience of the sinner; is it not wise in him, is he not obliged to cry aloud, and (however disagreeable it may chance to be to the people—and some men are not fond of being roundly admonished, even though their salvation be at stake) I say, however unwelcome truth may be, yet, if such be the minister's commission—I appeal to your own hearts, if he be not indispensably obliged to discharge it;

and

SERMON VI.

and at his peril be it, if he be so meanly fearful, or so absurdly complaisant, as to neglect this his duty.

But then, as the blood of the people will be required of the minister, who does not warn them; so, on the contrary, God declares in the next words—*But, if thou warn the wicked, and he turn not from his wickedness, nor from his wicked way; he shall die in his iniquity; but thou hast delivered thine own soul.*

In order therefore to discharge my own duty, that I may be *free from the blood of this congregation,* and that I may be once more instrumental in persuading you to work out your salvation; I shall now repeat the alarming words of the text, and then proceed to draw such observations as the Apostle recommends, and which my leaving you at this time makes more particularly necessary.

The day of the Lord will come as a thief in the night; in the which the heavens shall pass away with a great noise, and the elements shall melt with fervent heat; the earth also, and the works that are therein, shall be burned up.

Seeing then that all these things shall be dissolved, what manner of persons ought ye to be in all holy conversation and godliness,

Looking for and hasting unto the coming of the day of God, wherein the heavens being on fire shall be dissolved, and the elements shall melt with fervent heat?

Where-

SERMON VI.

Wherefore, beloved, seeing that ye look for such things, be diligent, that ye may be found of him in peace, without spot and blameless.

The Apostle's great argument, you see, is (of all arguments the greatest) that of—*a judgment to come!* An argument, that must make every son of Adam, as it did Felix, *tremble.* For *the day of the Lord is great and very terrible—Who may abide the day of his coming, and who shall stand when he appeareth? When the heaven shall depart as a scrowl rolled together, and every mountain and island shall be moved out of their places—when the whole earth shall quake, and the heavens shall tremble, when the sun and the moon shall be dark, and the stars shall withdraw their shining—Then shall the kings of the earth, and the great men, and the rich men, and the chief captains, and the mighty men, and every poor man—hide themselves in the dens, and in the rocks of the mountains; and shall say to the mountains, fall on us, and hide us from the face of him that sitteth on the throne, and from the wrath of the Lamb: for the great day of his wrath is come, and who is able to stand?*

This is the language, in which the terrors of that last dreadful day are described in the holy Scriptures; and may it sink so deep in our memories, as never, never, to be forgotten by us; but so influence our lives, that we may look forward to this decisive day with joy and not with grief! For this is the only wise reflection; and this therefore is the inference in the text—*Seeing then that all these things shall be dissolved, what manner of persons ought ye to be*

in

in all holy converſation and godlineſs?—Being *diligent, that ye may be found without ſpot and blameleſs.*

From theſe words we may infer this intereſting truth—that the only way for us to ſtand boldly in the day of judgment, and to ſecure the favour of the judge, is—*to give all diligence, to make it our principal care and ſtudy, that our lives be truly religious, and that we be perſons of all holy converſation and godlineſs.*

This then being a point of infinite conſequence to you all, that you may judge how far you are, or are not, thus happily qualified and prepared; I ſhall now ſuppoſe this pariſh divided into *three ſorts of people:*

Firſt, *Such as are Chriſtians only in name*;
2dly, *Such as are but Chriſtians in part;* and
3dly, *Such as are altogether Chriſtians:*

To each of theſe three ſorts of people I ſhall now addreſs myſelf with all poſſible plainneſs. But remember, that I diſtinguiſh no man; and therefore only recommend to every perſon in this congregation, to lay his hand upon his heart, and aſk himſelf—*to which of theſe three ſorts of people he belongs*; as I ſhall now addreſs myſelf to each, in their order.

Firſt then I ſhall addreſs myſelf to the *moſt wicked* ſort—that is—to thoſe, *who are only Chriſtians in name*: and to theſe I ſpeak firſt, becauſe their danger is greateſt.

Now

Now by *Christians in name only* I mean such men, as having in their infancy been admitted by baptism into Christ's church, are therefore called *Christians*; but who do not trouble their heads at all, or very little, about the doctrines and duties prescribed in the Gospel of Christ; not only, not knowing, nor desiring to learn the way to heaven and happiness, but perhaps scoffing at their neighbours for being more religious than themselves. But are there any persons so desperately wretched and wicked in *this place?*—It is to be feared, considering the general great wickedness of the present age, that there are some men of this very black character in *every* parish; and I wish I had no reason for thinking, that there are *some few* in *this.*

Our Saviour's rule is—*by their fruits ye shall know them.* And if we may judge of men by their practice, or by what they do not practise, may we not conclude that men, who come not to the house of GOD above once or twice in a year, come not from devotion but curiosity; and that men, who will not receive the sacrament, and perform the other public duties expressly commanded by Christ, are Christians by accident only, and not by choice; and therefore are in effect, no Christians at all?

If any one person of this sort should be now present, he will give me leave to expostulate with him. And first I would ask, *whether he believes the Bible to be the word of God,* and *Christ to be the Son of God*—if he does not, let him know, that, if *the Bible*

be

be *God's word, and Christ be his Son*, as we have the strongest reasons for believing, then he and all others, who live in a Christian country, and yet do not believe these truths, are in dreadful circumstances: since Christ has expresly declared, that, *he who hath opportunity to know his Gospel*, and *yet believeth it not, shall be damned*.

But perhaps, he has no objection to the Bible, and believes it *may be* the word of God; yet, as he never reads it, and will not come to church to hear it, he knows very little what it contains; and therefore, as to *a resurrection from the dead*, and *a day of judgment*, why—for what he can tell—there may be nothing in either of them: and so he even resolves to live on carelesly and wickedly, in defiance of all such notions. Just such men there were in St. Peter's days, whom he calls scoffers, who walked after their own lusts, and mocked at the doctrine of God's judging the world, saying —*where is the promise of his coming?*

To these profane men he answers in the words of the text——*The day of the Lord will come*, &c. And what saith Daniel—*They that sleep in the dust of the earth shall awake; some to everlasting life, and some to shame, and everlasting contempt*—St. Paul says—*God commandeth all men every where to repent, because he hath appointed a day, in the which he will judge the world in righteousness*. But Christ himself has informed us particularly—that, at the last day, he shall descend from heaven, and *all the holy angels*

SERMON VI.

angels with him; when he shall sit upon the throne of his glory: and before him shall be gathered all nations; and he shall separate them one from another, as a shepherd divideth the sheep from the goats; when he shall set the sheep (the holy) on his right hand, and the goats (the wicked) on his left. And then shall the king say unto them on his right hand — Come ye blessed of my father, inherit the kingdom prepared for you from the foundation of the world — and then shall he say to them on his left hand, Depart from me, ye cursed, into everlasting fire, prepared for the devil and his angels.

But perhaps these men believe a GOD, and a future judgment; and yet resolve to do as they please, whatever be the consequence. But has GOD commanded, and shall man dare to refuse obedience? *Who art thou, O man, that rebellest against God? Hast thou an arm like God, or canst thou thunder with a voice like him?* Will poor dust and ashes oppose itself to an almighty power? Insolent and ignorant beyond description! *Oh! consider this, ye that despise God, lest he pluck you away, and there be none to deliver you!* Let *the goodness of God*, who as yet giveth you life and time to reform, *lead you to sincere repentance*; and may you see *the things that belong unto your peace*, here and hereafter —*before they be for ever hid from your eyes!*

Leaving then those *nominal Christians*, but desperate sinners, which I hope, and indeed believe, are but *few* in this place: let us now consider the case

of

of the *half Christians*, which I fear *are many*.

By an *half Christian* is meant a man, who has been made a Christian by baptism, and, when grown up, conforms in some things to the religion of Christ, as practised in his country — who frequents the public worship of God, unless prevented by a shower of rain, or the opportunity of making a good bargain; and who, if he attends the public worship in the morning, thinks he may very well be excused, if he devotes the afternoon to visiting — or drinking — or sleeping.

But, *awake to righteousness, and sin not;—for such men have not the knowledge of God—I speak this to their shame.* I know not what your particular excuses may be; but this I know, and think it my indispensable duty to declare thus publickly—that if one were to estimate the number of true Christians in this parish from those, who have, for this year past, been constantly, or generally, present in this house of GOD—*the number would be very small indeed.*

True it is, that sometimes *necessity* will prevent a good Christian; but then he will be extremely sorry at being prevented from worshipping the Lord his God, and hearing *the words of eternal life* — but I press it upon your own consciences, and leave it to GOD who seeth the heart—whether choice has not prevented most of you; and whether you might not have been more constantly present, if you had strongly desired it. Remember, that most of you have but one day in the week to learn those doctrines

trines and duties, which alone can make you wife unto falvation: and that, if you refufe to hear thefe preached and explained, your ignorance will be fo far from being an excufe for your fins, that it will greatly aggravate your condemnation.

The thing is—religion is not your delight—and becaufe it is not your delight—therefore you are not true Chriftians—therefore it is plain—you do not love the Lord your God, with all your heart, and with all your mind, and with all your foul, and with all your ftrength.

But as the half Chriftian, though he is fometimes at church, is thus eafily prevented—fo as to other articles of his behaviour, he is in general ferious in his converfation, unlefs when provoked by any crofs accident; and then he will blafpheme God, and curfe his relations or his fervants—but perhaps he never fwears, nor abufes his neighbours, and yet he will now and then drink even to drunkennefs, and be guilty of fornication and adultery.——But can thefe perfons be the true fincere difciples of Chrift Jefus?—Do fuch men, in their ferious hours, do they, can they think themfelves the fervants of the moft high God; or after a life of fo little religion, and fo much wilful wickednefs, do they madly hope, do they impudently prefume to expect *a crown of glory*, and *everlafting happinefs?*

But—be not deceived—you know, that whatfoever a *man foweth, that fhall he alfo reap*. What! *know ye not that the unrighteous fhall not inherit the king-*

kingdom of God? St. Paul tells us, that the works of the flesh are these—*adultery, fornication, hatred, variance, murders, drunkenness—and such like; of the which, says he, I tell you now, as I have also told you in time past, that they who do such things shall not inherit the kingdom of God.*

Such imperfect and defective Christians would do well to consider the words of the apostle St. James—*whosoever shall keep the whole law, and yet offend in one point, he is guilty of all,* i.e. whosoever conforms his life to the rules of his religion, in general, and yet knowingly and wilfully indulges himself, from time to time, in the commission of any one sin, proves, that he has not a true desire of pleasing GOD, and therefore is not sincerely obedient to his laws; which are all established by the same high authority.

For, says the Apostle, *he that said, do not commit adultery, said also, do not kill: now if thou commit no adultery, yet if thou kill, thou art become a transgressor of the law.* By this same rule we may say—he that said, thou shalt not take the name of the Lord thy GOD in vain, said also—remember to keep holy the sabbath day—now if thou do not take God's name in vain, yet if thou dost not keep holy the sabbath, thou art become a transgressor of the law—so again, Christ, that commanded men to be received into his church by the sacrament of baptism, hath commanded all the members of his church to receive the sacrament of his body and blood; now, if thou art baptized, but wilt not receive the sacrament of the Lord's Supper, thou art become a transgressor of the law: and confequently, in all thefe, and other cafes, wherever there is a wilful tranfgreffion of any known law of God, and that tranfgreffion frequently repeated, fuch a man can be no fincere Chriftian; and, therefore, as he will not be owned by Chrift as his true and faithful difciple, he muft at the day of judgment have his portion with hypocrites and unbelievers, in that dreadful place, where there will be punifhment great as GOD can inflict, and man can fuffer, torments without meafure, and miferies without end.

And now, leaving this fecond fort of Chriftians to the moft penitent reflections for their paft violations of God's laws, and to refolutions of a more holy converfation; I fhall proceed to addrefs myfelf to the third fort of Chriftians amongft you— thofe who ferve GOD in fincerity and truth; who are therefore not only *almoft*, but *altogether*, Chriftians: and of thefe there are (I hope) *not a few* in this parifh — and GOD almighty grant, that their number may increafe daily!

By *a perfect Chriftian* is not here meant a man, that lives without fin; for in this fenfe no man ever was, or ever will be perfect; but—a man that is *fincerely religious*, and whofe mind is fet upon righteoufnefs—a man, who follows indeed the bufinefs of his calling, and endeavours by an honeft induftry to provide for this world, but whofe thoughts are ftill fixed upon another and better world, referved for him in the heavens—whofe chief ftudy

is

SERMON VI.

is to pleafe God, and to fave his own foul;—who earneftly defires, and diligently endeavours to know the will of God; and, when he knows it, ftrives to perform it to the beft of his knowledge, and to the utmoft of his ability.

Such then is the fincere and good Chriftian, and fuch I believe there are amongft you, in this place: to thefe therefore, with great pleafure, I, in the laft place, addrefs myfelf.

And as thefe have been almoft conftantly prefent in this holy place, to worfhip the Lord their God, and to be inftructed in their duty; they will gladly receive fome farther inftructions, efpecially as thefe may be the laft they will receive from me as their minifter in Chrift Jefus.

To you therefore, dearly beloved in the Lord, I now addrefs my exhortations—to you, who, however mean in your fituation, and humble in your prefent fortunes, have the noble ambition to confider yourfelves as the children of a God, that is almighty, and heirs of an inheritance in the heavens——*of an exceeding and eternal weight of glory.*

You have learnt how fhort, and how precarious life is, by the deaths of others—and you have learnt how little true fatisfaction there is here, from your own difficulties and troubles—and you find that the only folid and true happinefs enjoyed in this fhort, troublefome ftate of things, arifes from the filent joy of your own minds, confcious of the well-meant fincerity sincerity of your actions, and from the prospect of uninterrupted and endless joys hereafter.

Yet a little while, and your troubles will be all at an end—dare to be religious, in the midst of a crooked and perverse generation—and then—though distress and sickness should every way surround you—though *your feet should stumble upon the dark mountains*—though you *walk through the valley of the shadow of death*—yet, even then shall you *fear no evil*; for GOD being with you, his countenance shall comfort you; he will *make all your bed in your sickness*—and will give you to look forward, through all the astonishing circumstances of a resurrection from the dead, to the terrors of a day of judgment, *with joy unspeakable and full of glory.*

Having thus addressed myself, with all plainness, to the different sorts of Christians in this place, I shall now give a short character of a good Christian, drawn in such a manner that the most ignorant may understand it, the wicked be reformed, and the religious be confirmed by the description—and then conclude, with a few serious reflections and exhortations.

The good Christian then, (I shall suppose him born in such a parish as this, and in humble circumstances) is one, who was in his infancy admitted into the church of Christ by the sacrament of Baptism—when, he being too young to promise for himself, his Godfathers and Godmothers promised for him, that he should believe the doctrines, and perform the duties prescribed by Christ his

Saviour

SERMON VI.

Saviour—when arrived at years of discretion, he considers seriously, that as this life is but short, and he is to live for ever in happiness or misery hereafter, accordingly as he lives righteously or wickedly in this present world, he resolves to be holy in order to be happy—and therefore, the first step he takes is—to fulfill, in his own name, the promise made for him by others at his baptism—and this sacred engagement, he makes to GOD, before the Bishop, in the solemn office of confirmation, and compleats it by receiving the Lord's Supper.— Having made this promise to believe, and to do, what was promised in his name, he first regulates *his belief*, and then *his practice*.

His belief is readily granted to the doctrines clearly contained in the Bible; and his practice is regulated by its precepts.

He believes that there is a GOD—a Being that existed from all eternity, infinite in holiness, and goodness, wisdom, and power—that God is every where present, and views with strict attention his actions—his words—and his very thoughts—that, as GOD made this world by his power, so he governs it by his providence—and therefore, as there is no evil but by his permission, so there is no good but from his bounty: and that, as GOD provides him with the conveniencies of life here, so he desires he should be happy also hereafter—he believes that there is but one GOD, though consisting of three persons—that *God the Father* is the maker of heaven and earth, of him, and all things;

that

God the Son became man, and died upon the cross, for *his* salvation; that, after his resurrection from the dead, he ascended into heaven, there to remain till the day of judgment—that awful day, when he shall once again descend, to judge those whom before he redeemed; when they who have complied with his Gospel, shall be received into everlasting happiness; and they, who have not, shall depart into everlasting fire—and lastly he believes, that God the Holy Ghost sanctifieth him, i. e. by the secret methods of his grace helps on, and animates his endeavours after holiness of life; being always ready to comfort and support such as devoutly pray for his assistance.

These then are the articles of the good Christian's *belief*; things easy to be believed, and highly necessary to be constantly remembered. And as to his *practice*, he considers that he has duties to perform towards *God*—towards *his Neighbour*—and towards *himself*.

As he is convinced, that he was created, is constantly preserved and protected, and has been redeemed by God; and that all his happiness here and hereafter depends on God alone—so his heart is fired with gratitude for these blessings, and he frequently sends to Heaven his thanksgivings for blessings received, and prayers for the continuance of them, as well as for the pardon of all his sins—but though this be his general practice, constantly, and every where, in the shop, and in the field; yet particularly

SERMON VI.

particularly does he begin and end every day with a short prayer to GOD: at least, though he *rise up early, and late take rest, and eat the bread of carefulness,* he always falls down and repeats the Lord's prayer, the first thing in the morning, to derive a blessing on his daily labours; and the last thing in the evening for a protection against the dangers of the night.

But though this be his daily practice, yet every Sabbath day he devotes almost entirely to religion, to the worship of GOD, and to the promoting his own salvation—having therefore risen early enough to dispatch such business as is absolutely necessary, he scarce ever omits going to the house of GOD—praising GOD as he goes, for the happiness of being born in a Protestant land, and at a time when he can go to church without being in danger of his life, as was the case of the first Christians. At church he reflects with Jacob——*This surely is the house of God, this is the gate of Heaven!* And accordingly his solemn devotion during the prayers, his silent attention during the sermon, shew him to be then engaged in the most important business of his life. And that the instructions then received may have their due influence, he considers them over by himself, or with his friends, or in his family, afterwards. And that his servants and children, may equally enjoy the happy advantages of religious instruction, and receive the holy sacrament

equally

equally neceffary to their falvation, and to his own; he is prudent fo to contrive the neceffaries of that day, as not to interrupt the religious obfervation of it. And happy would it be both for mafter and fervant, if this point of prudence was more generally ftudied—for how can the one expect thofe under him to be good fervants, if he will not fuffer them to be good Chriftians?

He remembers—that GOD has commanded him to devote the whole fabbath day to religious purpofes; and therefore to thefe fame purpofes he devotes the afternoon as the morning; and as he renews his progrefs to this houfe of GOD, he is concerned to fee any of his neighbours removing, the *one to his farm, and another to his merchandize*, and a third to fome public merriment, or perhaps drunken company.

Having thus twice performed the public worfhip of GOD, he retires to his family or ferious friends; and concludes the facred bufinefs of the day, by reading the word of GOD, or by religious converfation or reflection.

Thus he confcientioufly difcharges his duty towards GOD; and this leads him to difcharge alfo the duties he owes to his neighbours. As a fon, he is dutiful and refpectful to his parents—as a parent, he is kind to his children; and particularly by bringing them up in the nurture and admonition of the Lord—by teaching them the words, and afterwards the meaning, of our excellent Church Catechifm,

SERMON VI.

Catechism, by bringing them regularly to church, and teaching them every thing virtuous and praiseworthy—As a *servant* he is faithful to his master—as a *master* he is gentle to his servants; not hindering them from, but requiring them to frequent the church, and seeing that they behave there with decency, and devotion—as a *magistrate*, he considers from whom he received his power, and what mighty consequences to others and himself, depend on the religious execution of his office—as a *subject*, he is loyal to the King, for the blessings of his religion and his liberty being happily secured to him—as a *neighbour*, he is kind and goodnatured, ever ready to serve and oblige, never quarrelsome nor contentious; being particularly careful not to injure either his neighbour's character by unjust censure, or his neighbour's estate by any unfair dealing—as a *poor man*, he pays all dutiful respect to his superiors—as a rich man, he considers the necessity of his various charities, and the extensive consequence of his example—and whether poor or rich, yet as *the father of a family*, knowing he is to be answerable (in some measure) for the behaviour of his children and servants, as well as for his own, he declares with Joshua—*As for me, and my house, we will serve the Lord.*

This then is the character, the amiable character, of a good Christian; but there is one thing yet remaining, with which I shall conclude these observations.

As

SERMON VI.

As he knows that he is not able, of himself, to perform these several duties, but that his sufficiency must be derived from God—and as he knows, that God has instituted two sacraments to convey his grace and assistance to every worthy receiver of them: so, as he was baptized in his infancy, he thinks it an invaluable happiness to receive the sacrament of bread and wine, signifying the body and blood of his Redeemer; being sensible of the mighty benefits of the death of Christ, and that his holy sacrament is a means whereby he receives the same, and a pledge to assure him thereof.

Hither, fully conscious of the imperfection of his best services, and deeply penitent for his sins, hither with the most lively faith in God's mercies to him through Christ, and with the most extensive charity to man, hither, to this table of the Lord, does he repair, as to *a fountain opened for sin and for uncleanness*: hither for the forgiveness of his sins, and for the increase of his virtues: in a word, hither does he come, most joyfully, and most thankfully, in hopes that God will confirm him with his grace, and hereafter crown him with his glory.

Such then is the character of the good man, of the true and sincere disciple of Jesus Christ: and such must *we* be—or else—good had it been for us, if we had never been born. This solemn sacrament of the Lord's supper we have now an opportunity of receiving; thither let us repair; and with one heart, and with one soul, vow the most

sincere

SERMON VI. 415

sincere obedience to all GOD's laws—never afterwards forgetting these our solemn vows and resolutions.

And how will it curb the improper gaieties of youth, restrain the violent passions of age, and prevent vices of every kind—to reflect upon the covenant made with GOD in this holy sacrament! Must we not reflect, when we are hereafter tempted, How can I do this great wickedness, and sin against GOD!—How break the covenant I then entered into so solemnly!—How, either cowardly or presumptuously violate that fidelity, which (by my sacramental oath) I swore to Jesus Christ the great captain of my salvation!

Bound by this solemn covenant, let me now leave you, freed from sin, and servants of righteousness; in the path that leads from holiness here to happiness hereafter.—Behold then, ye are witnesses against yourselves that ye have chosen you the Lord, to serve him—behold! ye are witnesses, not only against yourselves, but also against one another, that ye have sworn this day to serve the Lord, and to obey his voice — and, as Joshua said to the Israelites, *behold the stone, which I have set up, shall be a witness*; so may we say — Behold these walls shall be witnesses, and that altar shall be a witness against you, if ye shall forsake or deny the Lord your GOD.

And now, what shall I say more? The time makes it necessary to conclude, and yet my concern

cern for you would almost persuade me to begin again. In the short course of my ministry in this place, I have endeavoured to declare unto you the whole counsel of God, every doctrine and duty necessary to your salvation; and if you do not endeavour to remember these doctrines, and to practise these duties, so necessary to your peace here and hereafter, you will have reason to be both ashamed to live, and afraid to die.—*Ashamed to live*; for you will be the abhorrence of all good and valuable men—and *afraid to die*; because *after death comes judgment*—a day of judgment, when we all shall once more meet, either to our unspeakable joy, or to our utter confusion—Good God! what a day of meeting!—words cannot describe it—let your astonishment, let your most serious thoughts supply the rest—but you have heard it already, and may the consideration be deeply engraven on your hearts never, never to be forgotten.—*Let it be in thine heart, and teach it diligently unto thy children, and talk of it, when thou sittest in thine house, and when thou walkest by the way, and when thou liest down, and when thou risest up.*

There cannot be a more alarming, there cannot be a more useful consideration—than the frequent, than the serious consideration of a judgment so certain, and a sentence so decisive. For—as our Apostle in the text assures us,

The day of the Lord will come, as a thief in the night; in the which the Heavens shall pass away with
a great

great noife, and the elements fhall melt with fervent heat; the earth alfo, and the works that are therein fhall be burned up.

Seeing then that all thefe things fhall be diffolved, what manner of perfons ought ye to be in all holy converfation and godlinefs,

Looking for and hafting unto the coming of the day of God, wherein the heavens being on fire fhall be diffolved, and the elements fhall melt with fervent heat?

Wherefore, beloved, feeing that ye look for such things; be diligent, that ye may be found of him in peace, without fpot, and blamelefs.

And, finally, my beloved brethren, may the GOD of peace, who brought again from the dead our Lord Jefus Chrift, that great fhepherd of the fheep, through the blood of the everlafting covenant, make you perfect in every good work to do his will; working in you that which is well pleafing in his fight, through Jefus Chrift; to whom be glory for ever and ever. Amen.

SERMON VII.

DEUTERONOMY XXXII; ver. 46, 47.

—— *Set your hearts unto all the words, which I testify among you this day; which ye shall command your children to observe to do, all the words of this law: for it is not a vain thing for you, because it is your life.*——

THESE are the words of Moses to the children of Israel just before his death; and we cannot conceive words more proper for Moses to deliver on so solemn an occasion, or more worthy of the people to receive, and to engrave upon their hearts. Moses had been chosen to bring them up out of Egypt, and GOD had made him not only their *leader* to march before them, but also *a preacher of righteousness* unto his brethren.

SERMON VII.

This office he had difcharged with zeal and watchfulnefs; but, though this had been his conftant care, yet when he came to take leave of them for ever—*then* his concern for them was increafed, *then* his affection for them was enlarged; and therefore we find him *then* particularly laying before them the *reafonablenefs* and the *neceffity* of their duty, and commanding them, and exhorting them, and preffing them to the practice of it. And as this exhortation of his was the moft pertinent, the moft affectionate, and the moft fublime too, that ever appeared in the world; fo to meditate upon it will not only raife the admiration of men of learning, but will furnifh the moft ufeful reflections to men of all capacities.

The words of the text are the conclufion of that exhortation; and they are words, which command your attention—*Set your hearts unto all the words which I teftify among you this day, which ye fhall command your children to obferve to do, all the words of this law: for it is not a vain thing for you, becaufe it is your life.*

I fhall take occafion from thefe words, to felect out of this exhortation fuch paffages as are the moft ufeful and awakening — fuch as may raife your minds to a pitch of ferioufnefs anfwerable to the importance of a Chriftian congregation.

After which, I fhall proceed to offer you fome important admonitions for the religious conduct of your own lives.

Firft,

SERMON VII.

 Firſt, then, let us obſerve in how ſtriking a manner Moſes addreſſes himſelf to the children of Iſrael—*See! I have ſet before thee this day life and good—and death and evil*; *in that I command thee to love the Lord thy God, to walk in his ways, and to keep his commandments—that thou mayeſt live, and the Lord thy God ſhall bleſs thee: but if thine heart turn away, ſo that thou wilt not hear, I denounce unto thee this day that thou ſhalt ſurely periſh.* Moſes here addreſſes himſelf to the Iſraelites, as if the whole congregation was but one man; that ſo every man in that congregation might look upon *himſelf* as principally addreſſed to—*See! I have ſet before thee life and good—and death and evil*—I have now propoſed to thy choice *life and good* (i. e.) life as the certain reward of goodneſs; *and death and evil* (i. e.) death as the ſure puniſhment of evil.

For I command thee to love the Lord thy God, to walk in his ways, and to keep his commandments. Moſes, you ſee, begins with commanding them to love the Lord their GOD—*this* being the beſt and moſt powerful principle to lead them to their duty; for he that truly loves GOD, will certainly do the things which GOD commands him. To encourage them to this, he adds—*then mayeſt thou live, and the Lord thy God ſhall bleſs thee*; and this was encouragement ſtrong enough (one would think) to have ſecured their compliance. But, that no motive might be wanting, as he before endeavoured to allure them by the hopes of happineſs, he proceeds to alarm them

them by the fears of misery—*But if thine heart turn away, so that thou wilt not hear; I denounce unto thee this day, that thou shalt surely perish.*

There is one thing in this exhortation that must not be forgotten, because it may be too necessary in every congregation. Moses apprehended there might be among the people *some*, whose hearts were hardened; and who were resolved to continue in their evil ways, whatever admonitions he might give them to the contrary—men, who laughed at the miseries he denounced against them as a false alarm, and only capable of imposing upon the ignorant. Should there be any such now present, let them hear what follows with a very serious attention—*If* (says Moses) *there be among you any man whose heart turneth away from the Lord our God; and, when he heareth these words, bless himself in his heart, saying, I shall have peace, though I walk in the imagination of mine own heart—the anger of the Lord and his jealousy shall smoke against that man, and the Lord shall blot out his name from under Heaven: if he will not observe to do all these words, and fear this glorious and fearful name the Lord his God; then the Lord will make his plagues wonderful, even great plagues and of long continuance, and sore sicknesses and of long continuance—O! that they were wise, that they understood this, that they would consider their latter end!* But lest his own words should not have their proper weight with such offenders, Moses introduces *God himself*, speaking in all his majesty and thunder—

See

SERMON VII.

See now! that I, even I am he; and there is no God with me: I kill, and I make alive; neither can any deliver out of my hand. For I lift up my hand to Heaven, and say—I live for ever: if I whet my glittering sword, and my hand take hold on judgment; I will render vengeance to mine enemies, and mine anger shall burn unto the lowest hell. Dreadful words these, words which should confound the stoutest sinner in the world, and make him tremble at the thoughts of his transgressions!

Having thus plainly told the Israelites, what would be the certain consequences of their good or evil behaviour; Moses now makes the most solemn appeal that words can express—*I call Heaven and Earth to record this day against you, that I have set before you life and death, blessing and cursing;* and then he adds in the most engaging manner, therefore *choose life, that both thou and thy seed may live.* After this, in the very next verse, he reminds them of that powerful principle of holiness—the love of God —*that thou mayest love the Lord thy God with all thy heart, and with all thy soul, and with all thy might.* This was the solid foundation which *he* laid for the obedience of his brethren; and these the motives, by which he enforced *holiness unto the Lord.*

But as he knew it was their duty, not only to love God and keep his commandments themselves, but to teach the same carefully to their children; this also he inculcates in the strongest manner—*Hear, O Israel! The words, which I command thee this day,*

D d 4 *shall*

shall be in thine heart, and thou shalt teach them diligently unto thy children; and shalt talk of them, when thou sittest in thine house, and when thou walkest by the way, and when thou liest down, and when thou risest up.

And now—having given them the most lively, the most affecting instructions for supporting the true worship of GOD themselves, and for continuing the same after their deaths in the good lives of their children; having pressed them with all the motives, which his heart (overflowing with concern for their welfare) could suggest; he takes his solemn leave in the words of the text—*Set your hearts unto all the words, which I testify among you this day*; &c.

This was an exhortation worthy of the man that made it; and wisely adapted to the benefit, not only of those who heard it at first, but of all mankind. For why may not the lessons of this great Prophet be useful to *us* Christians now, as to the Israelites of old?—At least this is certain, that the great truth, which he delivered unto *them* in the words of the text, is written for *our* admonition (and it is a truth never to be forgotten)—that *religion is not a vain thing, because it is our life*—(i. e.) without religion we are really dead to every thing truly great and valuable; and our life, our happiness, now and to all eternity, depends upon our Christian obedience.

As religion then is of infinite consequence to us all; and as we must answer at the day of judgment,

I for

SERMON VII.

I for my inftruction, and *you* for your improvement by it: I fhall now ftate your *whole* duty, in the *plaineft* manner.

The firft truth which you ought to be put in mind of, becaufe it moft effectually prepares the foul for wifdom, is—that *you are perifhable, dying creatures*. You fee your friends conftantly dropping on every fide, and feel yourfelves all haftening after them to the grave. I fay—*all*; for though the *old* are the only perfons ufually confidered in that light, yet the *young* are haftening thither too, only (perhaps) at a greater diftance. And as you muft foon leave this world, with all its real troubles and unfatisfying pleafures; you muft then enter upon another, where your happinefs or mifery will be fubftantial and eternal. And as *your happinefs there* can only be fecured by *your holinefs here*; I fhall remind you of the true *faith* and *practice* of *Chriftianity:* I fay, *faith* and *practice*; becaufe there are in it things neceffary to be believed, as well as things neceffary to be performed; and of each of thefe I fhall briefly mention the moft material articles.

You are to believe then—that there is a GOD, a being that exifted from all eternity, infinite in holinefs, wifdom, and goodnefs—that he is every where prefent, and views with ftrict attention our actions, our words, nay and our very thoughts— that as he made this world by his power, he governs

verns it by his providence; and therefore, as there is no evil but by his permission, so there is no good but from his bounty: and as he provideth us, not only with the conveniences, but the comforts of life here, so he desires we should be happy also hereafter — You are also to believe — that there is but one GOD, though consisting of three Persons; each of which is represented in Scripture as taking a distinct office in the grand scheme of human happiness — that *God the Father* is the maker of heaven and earth, of us and all things — that *God the Son* became man, and died upon the cross, *for us men and for our salvation*; that, after his triumph over death and the grave, he ascended into heaven, there to remain till the day of judgment — that awful day, when he shall once again descend, to *judge* those whom he before *redeemed*; when they, who have complyed with the terms of his gospel, shall be received into joy unspeakable, and full of glory; and they, who have not, shall depart into everlasting fire — And lastly; that *God the Holy Ghost* sanctifieth us, i. e. by the secret methods of his grace helps on and animates our endeavours after holiness of life; and is always ready to comfort and support such as devoutly pray for his assistance.

These then are the chief things you are to believe; things very easy to be believed, and highly necessary to be constantly remembered. And now, as to the rule of practice, *that* may be (in a great measure)

measure) learnt from those commandments, which God gave unto the Israelites; and which oblige us Christians, also, because *Christ came not to destroy this moral law, but to fulfill it.*

You are to remember then — *you must have no other Gods but one*; you must worship none but that one Almighty God, who created, and preserves you; and him you must serve without admitting any thing to be preferred before him in your hearts; for if you do, that thing which you prefer before him, you make your God. So St. Paul tells us of some, *whose God was their belly*, i. e. they preferred drunkenness and gluttony to temperance and sobriety — virtues, which God had strictly commanded them.

And as you must worship *no false Gods*, so neither are you to worship *the true God after a false manner.* For you must not make any image of God, or indeed of any other being, in order to kneel down to it and worship it. This was an injunction very necessary to *the Jews*, who were addicted to the worship of idols; and the charge of idolatry seems justly to be laid against *the Papists*, who certainly transgress this commandment, if not in worshipping images, yet at least in falling down before them. But there is very little occasion, at present, however, (and God grant there never may be more!) for us to guard one another against worshipping images; since *our* danger is, not lest we should worship images too much, but lest we should not worship the true God at all — or, at most, not so devoutly and constantly as we ought to do.

If

If then GOD be a jealous GOD, *and will not give his glory to another*, surely he will not suffer himself to be treated lightly or profanely; what wonder therefore, that we are so strictly forbidden all *taking the name of God in vain*, all rash and common swearing, and cursing, and even the using the name of *God*, without awe and veneration? Let it be then seriously laid to heart—that though the breach of this commandment is grown amazingly common, and has therefore lost much of its guilt in the opinion of the world; yet GOD, whose honour is concerned, has expresIy declared—*he will not hold him guiltless*, that continues to profane his holy name.

As you are reverently to use GOD's holy name, so you are devoutly to observe GOD's holy day; *and if you do not remember to keep holy that one day* in the week, which from the beginning of the world was set apart by GOD, for his glory, and your own progress in duty; with what modesty can you pretend to be in earnest about religion, or to expect the divine favour? Six days out of seven are allowed for the bulk of mankind *to labour for the meat that perisheth*—the things of this short and transitory life; and surely one day must be little enough to provide for *that meat which endureth unto everlasting life*—to furnish your souls with those graces and virtues, which are absolutely necessary to their future happiness. Besides, as God has reserved so small a portion of your time; how can any presume to rob him of that, by spending it in unnecessary visits, in drinking, or

(perhaps)

SERMON VII. 429

(perhaps) in sleeping? *Awake to righteousness, and sin not*, by devoting to such unworthy purposes that holy day, which is peculiarly dedicated to the public worship of GOD, and therefore to his glory; and to the public instruction of man, and therefore to his happiness. To keep holy the Lord's day is, to lay aside (as much as possible) all worldly business, and to raise our affections from things on earth to things in heaven; to attend constantly the prayers and praises of the church, and at the beginning of service, unless prevented by any call of necessity or charity; and to spend the remainder of the day in reading, meditation, religious conversation, and every other method of promoting that holiness of life, which is the end of all religious institutions.

From your duty to GOD, the next step is your duty to one another; for you are all brethren, children of the same almighty and gracious Creator. And, in the duties arising from the nearer relations of life, *children* are most solemnly commanded to love, honour, and obey their parents; and *parents* as solemnly commanded to take care of, and love their children; and especially to *bring them up in the nurture and admonition of the Lord*. For this will be the strongest evidence of parental love and care. And indeed the training up your children for heaven, by laying early the seeds of virtue, and instilling into their tender minds a love and veneration for things sacred, will be not only the surest testimony of your affection for your children; but it will

prove

prove your wisdom, in distinguishing their best and truest interest; and will prove your zeal for GOD's glory, by transmitting his religion to the children which are yet unborn.

The following commandments oblige you, as being social creatures, not to injure your neighbour in his *life or health* — not in his *relations* — not in his *goods and property* — and not in his *name and character*; and indeed not to bear witness at all against him, unless before a magistrate, and upon a lawful occasion: and then, and always when an oath is required, you are to act with the utmost seriousness; because an oath is the most solemn obligation in the world, though we see it every day administered with so little solemnity, and taken (if possible) with less concern than it is administered.

The last commandment enjoins nothing new, but is only a guard to secure the preceding; for this forbids you to desire improperly what is your neighbour's; and certainly, if you do not desire it improperly, you will not take it from him by unlawful means.

In a still shorter view of the several important duties here enjoined, you are to make *God* the supreme object both of your love and fear; his name you must use devoutly; his scriptures you must examine carefully, and treat reverently; and GOD himself you must worship constantly, but especially upon his own day. It is farther required — that you do always to your neighbour, as you would be

willing

willing he should do to you; were you in his case, and he in yours—that you behave with due respect to your superiors, with condescension to your inferiors, and good nature to your equals — forgiving your enemies, and loving your friends. And as to *yourselves* — you are to be *sober*, and *temperate*, *and chaste*; because particular marks of GOD's displeasure are fixed upon the adulterer, the glutton, and the drunkard.

I have now mentioned the duties which you owe to *God*, your *neighbours*, and *yourselves*; and to discharge the whole with a true Christian sincerity is certainly your wisdom, and will be your exceeding great reward. Not that you are able of yourselves to perform these duties, but your sufficiency must be derived from God.

And this leads me to observe—that *prayer to God* is your indispensable duty, your highest interest, and your greatest privilege. Had you any great friend here on earth, who was both able and willing to redress all your wants; how would you flock to him constantly, and how would you bless the goodness of such a benefactor! Such, nay an infinitely greater friend have you all in GOD; who is best pleased, when you come to him most frequently, and with the greatest earnestness. And yet — how strangely do men deprive themselves of this, the greatest of advantages! How slow — how backward to address themselves to him, who is the source of happiness! What! Is the privilege of praying to the Creator a

less

less privilege than applying to a creature? Or, is the favour to be slighted, because it is the favour of GOD? Certainly men must reason in some such a strange manner; or else, what pretence can there be for the general neglect of (not to say, aversion to, and contempt of) prayer? Greater encouragements we cannot have, than these two reflections—that we are dark, indigent, and guilty creatures; and —that God, who is all-sufficient, has assured us that he will grant all we pray for, if it be convenient, and we ask it in a proper manner.

The manner then of our praying regards both the frame of *the mind*, and the posture of *the body*. The mind should be — humble — devout — and attentive in the highest degree. For should we pray, without thinking to whom we pray, and on what we pray for, (if that be not a contradiction), surely we shall affront GOD, and bring a curse upon us instead of a blessing. And as to the body, that should assist, and express the devotion of the mind, by the most supplicating posture, which certainly is kneeling. And indeed this posture is so strongly recommended not only by reason, but example, particularly that of St. Paul, and of Christ himself; that it is amazing in many places to see men, who come and worship, but will not fall down and *kneel* before the Lord their maker.

This then should be the manner of your praying, and that both in public and in private. For it is your duty, not only to attend the public worship one day

SERMON VII.

in the week, (or oftener if convenient), but to worship GOD alſo in private, at the outgoing of the morning and the evening. As you every day want GOD's bleſſing and protection; you ſhould begin and end every day with ſome ſhort and ſolemn prayer, at leaſt with that prayer, which Chriſt himſelf hath taught you. And, unleſs you will live without GOD in the world, a few minutes (at leaſt) *may — muſt* be allowed for ſo neceſſary a duty, tho' you *riſe up early, and late take reſt, and eat the bread of carefulneſs.* For this practice is ſtrictly commanded in the book of GOD, has been obſerved by all good men, and is only neglected by Chriſtian Heathens.

There remains now but one thing, which I ſhall preſs upon you the obſervation of, (and it can ſcarce be preſſed too frequently), and that is—the conſtant receiving the *ſacrament of the Lord's ſupper.* As for the ſacrament of *baptiſm, that*, I preſume, you have all received by the care of your parents, and the benefits of that you are careful to ſecure to your children: but why?—Becauſe Chriſt has abſolutely commanded it, and you know they are not Chriſtians without it. But then—is not the other *ſacrament, that of the body and blood of Chriſt*, equally commanded, and is not *that* as generally neceſſary to ſalvation? And how is it then, that *this* is (almoſt every where) ſo ſurprizingly neglected? Whatever unhappy notions ſome may have entertained of it, ſurely there can be nothing terrible

rible in the nature of it; becaufe it was ordained by our beſt friend, for our greateſt benefit and confolation. What then? Is it a thing burdenfome to eat bread, and drink wine, in obedience to the command, in compliance with the dying requeſt of Jefus Chriſt? Can it be a thing difagreeable, to remember by this holy feaſt the greateſt benefactor you ever had, your bleſſed Saviour and Redeemer? —Why do not thofe, who conſtantly neglect it, declare themfelves to be *Heathens?* Or—do they not in fact *proclaim themfelves* fuch by this neglect? It is certainly difficult, perhaps impoffible, to fay, how men can be Chriſtians, if they conſtantly neglect this inſtitution, which is fo folemnly enjoined by Chriſt himfelf in perpetual remembrance of his death and fufferings. To fuch perfons our Saviour addreſſes himfelf thus—*Why call ye me Lord, Lord, and do not the things which I fay?*—That Chriſt has exprefsly commanded this, appears clearly from the word of GOD; and therefore he who knows it to be commanded, and yet will not obey the command, *may as well renounce all his religion*—as to live in a determined contempt of this one great principle of it: for St. James has aſſured him—that *he, who offends wilfully and refolutely in one point, is guilty of all.*

Give me leave then to entreat you, as you value your falvation, if you would be *Chriſtians in reality* —that you will frequently receive this bleſſed facrament, as the beſt means of grace you can enjoy
—that

— that all young persons, when arrived at years of discretion and seriousness, would begin and continue to receive it to their lives end; and that these, and all others, would consider not only the *necessity*, but the *benefits* of receiving this sacrament; and also, what holiness should go before, attend, and follow it. Not that you must necessarily set apart just so much time to prepare for it: but yet, every one must have some solemn times of reflection on his past life, and this can never be more seasonable. The duties previous to the Lord's supper are fully expressed in our excellent Church Catechism— and therefore, if you come with true sorrow for your past sins, resolved to act more wisely for the future, and desirous of God's grace to confirm your resolutions; if you are thankful for the benefits of Christ's death, and in real charity with all the world — then, you are worthy partakers of this holy sacrament.

These then are the worthy dispositions of mind, which constitute a good Christian, and therefore prepare properly for the Lord's supper; and I must add this weighty truth (and may it sink down into your hearts!) that, as this sincere holiness is always necessary, and especially on such solemn occasions; so, without this sincere holiness, you have reason to be both — *ashamed to live* — *and afraid to die*.

I have now gone through the several articles of your duty; and *God grant*, you may all sincerely practice them.—Indeed, if you are refolved to live carelefs and indifferent, coming to this holy place only by way of cuftomary decency, and returning to your habitation forgetful of the inftructions you receive—if you think *heaven* not worth your regarding; or, that happinefs there may be obtained without holinefs here—— but, as the Apoftle fays, *Beloved, I hope better things of you, and things that accompany falvation*; and therefore I fhall clofe this difcourfe with a few fhort obfervations to encourage you to be altogether Chriftians.

If then *you know thefe things, happy,* infinitely happy, *are you, if you do them*; and furely you will be wife enough to do them, if you confider your duty as *reafonable* — as *pleafant* — and as *necef fary.*

Your duty is a *reafonable fervice,* becaufe GOD has commanded you to avoid nothing but what will hurt you, and only to follow after what will encreafe your happinefs; and this — with all proper allowances for the infirmity of human nature; and this too — with a due regard to the difference of your feveral abilities.

Your duty is alfo a *pleafant fervice,* becaufe the *good man* has the beft, nay the only title to be pleafed and *fatisfied from himfelf.* Chriftianity is a religion of chearfulnefs; and commands its true difciples to *rejoice evermore.* And *well* they may; fince *they* tafte all the proper joys of life with unembittered relifh, and have nothing gloomy within to difturb them upon reflection.

And

SERMON VII.

And laſtly, your religion is *a ſervice abſolutely neceſſary*. Things are ſo ordered, that life and good are inſeparable, as well as death and evil. The neceſſity therefore of being virtuous ariſes from the impoſſibility of a ſinner's being happy hereafter; ſo ſordid his mind, and ſo vile his inclinations, that if GOD did not exclude him heaven —*even there* he muſt be miſerable. Not that GOD will admit him into that place of glory; for, as the honeſt ſincerity of the heart is the beſt thing to recommend us to thinking men in this world, it is the only thing to recommend us to GOD in the world to come.

In a word: ſince *our duty is reaſonable — pleaſant — and neceſſary*, let each of us lay his hand upon his heart, and reſolve to-day, (while it be called to-day), to practiſe it ſincerely — to be juſt to his own high character, as a reaſonable creature — to be juſt to his own true pleaſures, as heightened by religion — and to be juſt to his own conviction of what is abſolutely neceſſary to his ſalvation.

Then will our characters be honourable and amiable in the eyes of all worthy men on earth — — then ſhall we kindle joy in the breaſt of every angel in the court of heaven — then ſhall we paſs through life chearful and ſerene; and die reſigned, and with hope full of immortality — and, when the trumpet, at the great morning of the reſurrection, ſhall call us forth to glory, we ſhall ſtand before our judge with conſcious dignity and transport tranfport — fhoot away triumphant through ten thoufand worlds — and enter upon that fcene of infinite and unbounded happinefs, which GOD hath prepared for us from the foundation of the world.

Set your hearts (then) *unto all the words, which I have teftified among you this day; which ye fhall command your children to obferve to do, all the words of this law: for it is not a vain thing for you, becaufe it is your life.*

This that you may all do, GOD of his infinite mercy grant, for Jefus Chrift his fake. *Amen.*

SERMON VIII.

PSALM VIII. 4, 5.

What is man, that thou art mindful of him; or the son of man, that thou visitest him! Thou hast made him a little lower than the angels; and hast crowned him with glory and honour.

THAT this short psalm contains a noble anthem of praise to the sovereign of the universe, for his goodness to his creature — man; is allowed universally. But it seems to have an amiable and mixed colouring from the rich display of the divine favour in the *redemption*, as well as the *creation*, of mankind. And therefore, as our attention to it, at this time, may be particularly seasonable; permit me to conduct your minds through the several parts of it, whilst I attempt a short explanation of it.

It

It begins thus—O JEHOVAH, *our Lord, how excellent is thy name in all the* EARTH! *Thou, that haft fet thy glory above the* HEAVENS! How warmly does the infpired poet exprefs here his gratitude and his wonder, that God fhould vouchfafe to look down upon, and to regard this lower world — vouchfafe to extend his mercies, and be gracious, even unto this earth—amidſt his attention to fcenes infinitely brighter and more magnificent, when his glory was eſtabliſhed, and difplayed, not only *through*, but *above* the very heavens themfelves!

The next verfe is this, *Out of the mouth of babes and fucklings haft thou ordained ſtrength*, (or perfected praife), *becaufe of thine enemies; that thou mighteſt ſtill the enemy and the avenger.* The chief difficulty of the pfalm lying in this verfe, let us obferve carefully,—that the words, *babes and fucklings*, muſt not be here taken literally: becaufe *babes* cannot celebrate God's glory, neither can *fucklings* proclaim his praife. The word babes is ufed by our Saviour to fignify men; but fuch men as are humble in mind, and mean in condition; and therefore, as the word does not neceſſarily in other places, and cannot here, fignify infants, the following is (perhaps) the true fenfe.

The Pfalmift having faid—*O Lord, thou haft fet thy glory above the heavens*; and yet *how excellent is thy name!* How exalted fhould be thy honour

SERMON VIII.

honour, for the care extended to this earth!—he adds here—Out of the mouths of *men*, creatures mean and low in the scale of thy creation; mere babes when compared with angels, which so far excel in strength; mere sucklings, beings of but yesterday, compared with their elder brethren, those *sons of God*, who existed long before, and *shouted for joy* at the creation of man—even by this human race hast thou also *ordained strength*, or established thy praise: and this—*because of thine enemies.* By the enemies of GOD, thus mentioned in the celebration of his goodness to man, are probably meant the rebel angels—those apostate spirits who, having themselves forfeited the favour of God, became, from the beginning of this world, enemies and tempters of mankind. One of these, called in the holy scriptures *the Devil,* or *Satan,* is generally allowed to have been the seducer of our first parents: and it is certain, that the Jews understood it so, in the time of the author of the book of Wisdom; who tells us,—*by the envy of the* DEVIL *came death into the world.* Perhaps this one evil being is alluded to in the next words of this verse—*that thou mightest still the enemy, and the avenger*—as if he had said—Out of the mouths of frail, humble, helpless *men* hast thou ordained strength, praise, and glory to thyself; because of thine enemies—ordained praise from men (perhaps) created to fill those habitations

tions of glory forfeited by rebel angels: and thou haft ordained men to ferve, and praife thee, that thou mighteſt ſtill—reſtrain—defeat the defigns of the grand enemy, and the avenger.

If the preceding obfervations exprefs the fenfe of this verfe, the next words will be very intelligible—*When I confider thy heavens, the work of thy fingers; the moon, and the ſtars, which thou haſt ordained*, that is, when I contemplate by night thy wonders in the expanfe of heaven; when I behold the *moon walking in brightneſs*, and the numberlefs and refplendent ſtars which adorn the footſtool of thy throne: then I am filled with aſtoniſhment at thy condefcenſion; and cannot but cry out—*What is man—that thou (O Jehovah) art mindful of him! And what the ſon of man, that thou ſhouldeſt viſit him!* Or; more literally, *that thou* WILT *viſit him*. The word *viſit* feems here prophetically to relate to the goodnefs of God *ſo viſiting*, as *to redeem*, mankind: agreeably to the ufe of this word in feveral parts of fcripture, particularly where St. Luke fays—that Zacharias was filled with the Holy Ghoſt, and faid—*Bleſſed be the Lord God of Iſrael; for he hath* VISITED, *and* REDEEMED *his people*.

The next verfe is—*Thou haſt made him a little lower than the angels, and haſt crowned him with glory and honour*. The particle for *little* may relate to *time*; and is thus ufed, in the quotation of thefe very

SERMON VIII.

very words, made by the author of the Epistle to the Hebrews. For the Apostle applies them to *Christ*, saying, that *Christ was lower than the Angels*, for a *little time*, during his abode as man here on earth. Take the word then with the same idea in the psalm, and there will arise this sense—*Thou hast made man (for a little time) lower than the angels*; and yet, even in his inferior and present state, *thou hast crowned him with glory and honour.* For thou hast constituted him the Lord of this creation, *thou madest him to have dominion over the works of thy hands*; *thou hast put all things under his feet: all sheep and oxen*; *yea and the beasts of the field: the fowl of the air, and the fish of the sea, and whatsoever passeth through the paths of the seas. Jehovah, our Lord, how excellent is thy name, in all the earth!*

The psalm, thus explained, furnishing us with exalted notions of God's goodness in the redemption, as well as the creation, of man; I shall from thence take occasion to offer some farther observations on these important subjects.

That we may be properly thankful for any benefit, it is necessary that we should understand its value. And we cannot be fully sensible of the blessing of *man's redemption* unless we are acquainted with the nature of man's fall. Now the only true account of this, as well as of the creation of man, is given by Moses: and as his account of the creation

tion is explained *literally* by the beſt interpreters, ſo likewiſe is his account of the fall. There are in ſcripture ſo many alluſions to the circumſtances of the fall *literally* taken as the matter ſtands *hiſtorically* recorded, that we do not ſeem to be at liberty to conſider it otherwiſe.

On the contrary, take the matter allegorically, and it lies ſo open to all the reveries of fancy, as to mean almoſt whatever the interpreter of the allegory ſhall pleaſe.

Certainly, a tranſaction of ſuch vaſt importance ſhould be explained according to the letter of the ſacred narrative; unleſs the literal and obvious ſenſe of the fact ſhould ſtand chargeable with abſurdities unworthy of an inſpired writer. But, that this is not the caſe, will (in ſome meaſure) appear from the remainder of this diſcourſe.

When we conſider this earth, with all the magnificence of its furniture, as prepared for the accommodation of Adam and his poſterity—when we conſider *man*, this great inhabitant, as a free and rational agent; as conſtituted the high prieſt of nature, to offer up the incenſe of thanks for himſelf, and the leſs perfect creatures round about him; and as created to advance the glory of his maker, and by perſonal holineſs perpetuate his own happineſs: we find it ſuch a plan of almighty ſuperintendency, as the more we contemplate it the more we muſt admire, and the more we admire,

the

the more we muft adore: efpecially, when we confider our felves as the happy beings thus wonderfully provided for. *Lord, what is man, that thou shouldest be so gracious unto him! That thou shouldest create him but little lower* (or for a *little time* lower) *than the angels*; and thus *crown him with glory and honour!*

But as all derivative perfection is finite, it muft be attended with fome degree of imperfection; and what is in any degree imperfect, muft be capable of mifcarrying. The ftate, as well as glory, of human nature, was, confequently, free agency; and man, becaufe free, being capable of choofing good, muft be alfo capable of doing evil. It is a wife ufe of this power which conftitutes virtue; and as man's happinefs was to correfpond with his holinefs, (between which there is an infeparable connexion), fo his obedience could not be made manifeft, but by fomething enjoined to which he might be difobedient.

It is alfo evident, that none can be independent but God: man therefore being neceffarily a dependent creature, muft expect fome mark of his dependency. This then God gave him, but in a reftriction the moft mild, in a prohibition the moft gracious: and as this was to be the teft of his obedience, on which depended his happinefs and immortality, it was delivered in the cleareft terms. No moral precept could have been proper

on

on this occasion. The memory of the creation being fresh and strong on the minds of the first pair, and God's manifestation of himself to them being frequent, to impart things necessary to be known, could they possibly have turned idolaters? Being only two, and these affectionate to each other, could they be forbidden to violate any of those social commandments, which were afterwards so necessary upon the encrease of mankind, and the multiplication of their vices? Food was all they wanted; and here too there was no danger from intemperance, their drink being pure water, and their meat the fruits of the earth, in the first of which nature afforded them no variety, in the latter there was much. *Here* therefore the restraint was laid; and one *particular tree*, a tree in the centre of the garden, was singled out, of the fruit of which they were forbidden to eat, upon pain of death. And what so natural, so agreeable to the state of our first parents in a *garden*, as forbidding them to taste the fruit of one certain tree, distinguishable by its station; and (because near at hand) giving them a constant opportunity of shewing obedience to the divine authority, by their abstaining from it?

This tree God called *the tree of the knowledge of good and evil*—not that this implies any change, which by their eating would be made in their intellectual faculties: but the original signifies—*the tree which was to be the test of good and evil*—by which

which it should be *known*, whether they would prove good or evil, obedient or disobedient to their maker.

This one tree, the tree of trial, being guarded by the divine prohibition, and fenced round with death, man could not well have manifested his virtue, nor have been allured from his duty, without some temptation, which might possibly prove an over-balance to the danger of forfeiting the divine favour. But who then was to be the tempter? On earth there were yet but two persons of the human species; and they perfect and uncorrupt, loving and beloved: these therefore would not attempt to seduce, and to destroy each other. A superior good being would not undertake an office so malicious. A mere brute creature had not the power to accomplish, or motive to engage in it. And what then could remain but an invisible evil being, himself already apostate and corrupt, hostile to God, and willing to draw man into a companionship in rebellion and in misery?

And if God permitted this temptation, where is the impeachment upon his goodness? Could the restraint be more gentle? Could it be more clearly expressed, than—*of the tree in the midst of the garden, thou shalt not eat?* Could the penalty be expressed in terms more alarming than—*if thou eatest thou shalt die?* And why should not our first parents be tempted? Are not *we*, (and we impeach not God's goodness),

goodness), are not we tempted? Have not angels undergone a probation? The truth is, without a trial there had been no virtue; nor could there, without an attack, have been a possibility of victory.

And now—man being thus created, honoured, instructed, clearly forewarned, and peremptorily threatened with death—*what could have been done more* (as the prophet speaks) *to this vineyard of the Lord, that the Lord had not done in it*—*for this vine which his own right hand had so eminently planted, and the branch that he made so strong for himself?* But *when he looked,* (when he might reasonably have expected), *that it should bring forth grapes, it brought forth wild grapes.* What wonder then, if *God look down from heaven, and behold, and visit this vine?* What wonder, if it *be burnt with fire, and cut down, and perish at the rebuke of his countenance?*

To enter minutely into this great transaction, falls not within the limits of this discourse; and I shall only subjoin the few following observations.

Adam fell from his innocence, and forfeited his immortality: but God in the midst of judgment remembring mercy, promised him a redeemer— one who should crush the powers of the devil, that enemy who had tempted him—one who was to raise Adam, with all his sinful and mortal posterity, to life after death, and recover for him everlasting happiness, which he had thus forfeited.

As

SERMON VIII.

As to *the tempter*, it was a serpent, that is an evil spirit actuating the organs of a serpent, seducing the woman by a denial of the penalty threatened by God, and by a promise that she should become wise as God her maker. *She eat, and gave also to her husband.* This is the history, and does not St. Paul affirm the same? *Eve being deceived was in the transgression, but Adam was not deceived,* that is, Eve was deceived first, and immediately, by the serpent; but Adam fell, partly by the arguments, and partly by the solicitations of her, with whom as he had shared in happiness, he resolved also to share in misery.

Should it be enquired — how could a spirit actuate the body of a serpent? I would answer, by asking, what connection is there between the power of thinking, and a piece of marble? What connection between the soul of man, and a body of clay? And if he own, that spirit and matter are joined in himself, without his knowing how his own body is acted upon by his own spirit, what is certain in his own case, let him acknowledge possible in the other.

Christ himself, in the parable of the tares, asserts the primitive innocence of man, and that evil was introduced into the world, by means of the devil. —*The field,* says he, *is the world,* in which *good seed was at first sown. But whence then hath it tares?* He answers—*An enemy hath done this*—and the

SERMON VIII.

enemy that hath done this is the devil. And here does Chrift alfo confirm the doctrine, that *death* was introduced by the *lying deception of the devil,* where he fays, *the devil was a* MURDERER *from the beginning,* and (in the fame verfe) *he is a liar, and the father of it.* If then the feducer was the devil (called elfewhere in fcripture *the old ferpent, that deceiveth the world,* and in the text *the enemy and the avenger*) no doubt, *he* was the being principally condemned, when God entering into judgment with the offenders, paffed upon the ferpent this fentence—*that the feed of the woman fhould bruife the ferpent's head*—words full of important meaning, as has been fince gradually difcovered to the world.

That our firft parents fhould enter into the compleat fenfe of this prophecy, we need not fuppofe. They were become finners, and therefore not entitled to fuch confolation. And yet as thefe finners, though become mortal, were to be the parents of mankind, and to live the monuments of divine mercy, fome comfort was neceffary to prevent defpair; and fome comfort they muft receive from this obfcure fentence on their deceiver.

That their deceiver was fomething more than a brute, they might infer from the nature of his affault—that he was of an evil nature, they knew from the malice of his temptation. And if, amongft other notices from their maker, they were previoufly acquainted with the apoftacy and punifhment

of

SERMON VIII.

of the fallen angels, (and certainly what might have been useful may not be improbable), they might then suppose one of those evil spirits the contriver of their misery.

From the sentence itself they might expect some kind of recovery, some redeemer to arise in that feed of the woman, which was to bruise the serpent's head, to heal their sorrows, and triumph over their destroyer. It is probable also, that they were soon acquainted with the manner of this redemption, so far as that it was to be effected by the redeemer's *death*. For if animal sacrifice was divinely appointed, to atone for sin, in virtue of its relation to the great sacrifice, then future, and to be offered in the fulness of time; and if this service was instituted, (as is generally allowed), soon after the great transgression of our first parents —doubtless the institution was accompanied with some discovery of its meaning and use, in order to make it *a reasonable service.*

But then in what age this Saviour was to arise, and with what circumstances his birth and death were to be attended, the first pair might not be informed. Possibly they expected him in the person of their *first son*, and it is probable, that had they been told, this happiness was to have been postponed for four or five thousand years, they would have sunk into despair—*they would have sat down in darkness and the shadow of death; because they had rebelled*

rebelled against the word of the Lord, and lightly regarded the counsel of the most Highest.

That they were not to die immediately, they found by their being doomed to labour and distress—that their enemy also was punished, they might infer from the visible change in the form of the serpent, and from that gracious promise, that *woman*, who had been first deceived, should bring forth a son who was to triumph over their deceiver.

How severe, how awful, must have been the sentence of misery and of death! Yet how mild, and mixed with mercy, in comparison with what Adam might have expected from his offended God!

Let us therefore conclude, in supposing Adam, with hands devoutly uplifted towards Heaven, to have broke forth into strains of gratitude like the following.

Praise the Lord, O my soul, and forget not all his benefits! The Lord is full of compassion and mercy! He hath not dealt with us after our sin, nor rewarded us according to our wickedness. For look how high the heaven is in comparison of the earth, so great is his mercy! Look how wide also the east is from the west; so far hath he set our sin from us! In the multitude of the sorrows that I had in my heart, thy comforts have refreshed my soul. The snares of hell overtook me; but the Lord is become my salvation. Through the greatness of thy power shall thine enemy be found a liar unto

unto thee! Who is he among the clouds, that shall be compared unto the Lord! The right hand of the Lord hath the preeminence! The Lord hath chastened and corrected me, but he hath not given me over unto (immediate) *death. As long therefore as I live will I magnify thee on this manner, and lift up my hands in thy name.*

Now to God, the Father, the Son, and the Holy Ghost, be ascribed all honour and glory by *us*, and all his creatures, now and for ever. Amen.

THE END.

www.ingramcontent.com/pod-product-compliance
Lightning Source LLC
Chambersburg PA
CBHW032001300426
44117CB00008B/861